The Connected City

This unique and innovative text provides advanced undergraduate and beginning graduate students with a clear introduction to the rapidly growing area of urban networks. It stands apart from other books by (1) providing a primer on network methodological issues that makes the substantive material accessible to newcomers; (2) including a range of interesting substantive urban issues including immigrant assimilation through networks, networks of urban infrastructure, and the emerging contours of a world city network, thereby appealing to a wide audience of students; (3) is organized around distinct levels of analysis in urban network inquiry (i.e., micro/individual, meso/institutional, and macro/global) to help students conduct their own research projects.

Zachary P. Neal is an Assistant Professor of Sociology and Global Urban Studies at Michigan State University, and serves as Associate Editor of *Global Networks* and on the Editorial Board of *City and Community*. His research on cities and networks has appeared in *Urban Studies*, *Global Networks*, *City and Community*, the *Journal of Urban Affairs*, and *Geographical Analysis*. He is also the co-editor of *Common Ground? Readings and Reflections on Public Space*.

The Metropolis and Modern Life
A Routledge Series
Edited by Anthony Orum, *Loyola University of Chicago*
Zachary P. Neal, *Michigan State University*

This series brings original perspectives on key topics in urban research to today's students in a series of short accessible texts, guided readers, and practical handbooks. Each volume examines how long-standing urban phenomena continue to be relevant in an increasingly urban and global world, and in doing so, connects the best new scholarship with the wider concerns of students seeking to understand life in the twenty-first century metropolis.

Books in the Series

Common Ground? Readings and Reflections on Public Space
edited by Anthony Orum and Zachary Neal

The Gentrification Debates edited by Japonica Brown-Saracino

The Power of Urban Ethnic Places by Jan Lin

Urban Tourism and Urban Change by Costas Spirou

The Connected City by Zachary Neal

The World's Major Cities edited by A. J. Jacobs

Exploring the City edited by Richard Ocejo

Also of Interest from Routledge

The Community Development Reader, Second Edition
edited by James DeFillipis and Susan Saegert

Housing Policy in the United States, Second Edition by Alex F. Schwartz

Neobohemia: China and Globalization, Third Edition by Doug Guthrie

Foodies: Democracy and Distinction in the Gourmet Foodscape
by Josée Johnston and Shyon Baumann

Branding New York: How a City in Crisis Was Sold to the World
by Miriam Greenberg

City Life from Jakarta to Dakar by AbdouMaliq Simone

The Connected City

How Networks are Shaping the Modern Metropolis

Zachary P. Neal
Michigan State University

Routledge
Taylor & Francis Group

NEW YORK AND LONDON

First published 2013
by Routledge
711 Third Avenue, New York, NY 10017

Simultaneously published in the UK
by Routledge
2 Park Square, Milton Park, Abingdon, Oxon OX14 4RN

Routledge is an imprint of the Taylor & Francis Group, an informa business

Library of Congress Cataloging in Publication Data
Neal, Zachary P.
  The connected city: how networks are shaping the modern metropolis/
  Zachary P. Neal.—1st ed.
  p. cm.—(Metropolis and modern life)
  1. Social networks.   2. Cities and towns—Social aspects.   3. Technological
  innovations—Social aspects.   4. Social groups.   I. Title.
  HM741.N43 2012
  303.48′3—dc23
  2012007170

ISBN: 978–0–415–88141–8 (hbk)
ISBN: 978–0–415–88142–5 (pbk)
ISBN: 978–0–203–10172–8 (ebk)

Typeset in Caslon
by Florence Production Ltd, Stoodleigh, Devon

CONTENTS

METHOD NOTES

FIGURES

FOREWORD

The Connected City by Zachary P. Neal joins the other fresh and original monographs that we have published in this series on cities. It shows in particular how social network analysis can furnish both a theory and a method for the study of cities. In a grand synthesis of many literatures on social networks, it reveals how networks operate within cities, as between residents, but also between and among cities, as important connections of people and economic trade. Social networks, as the highly popular social media such as Facebook and Linked-In reveal, represent an emerging tool for organizing and working in the world today. This book not only provides essential ideas for thinking about cities, but it also furnishes some of the essential intellectual apparatus that people will need to navigate their way through this world in the future. Its breadth will make it appeal to people in many different academic disciplines, from geography to political science. And its accessibility in terms of its writing and imagery will make it an important, even indispensable means for teaching students that range from beginning undergraduates to advanced graduates.

Anthony Orum
Co-Editor

1
INTRODUCTION
WHY CITIES? WHY NETWORKS?

This is, first and foremost, a book about cities. But, why write about cities? Because at least since the industrial revolution, people have been moving to cities in search of both opportunity and stimulation. The shift of the world's population into cities—*urbanization*—is clear from a few simple statistics. In 1800, only 3 percent of the world's population lived in cities, but by 1900 this number had increased to 14 percent, and passed 50 percent in 2008. This number is expected to continue climbing, to 70 percent by 2050. The rapid urbanization of the population has been even more dramatic and complete within the United States, where 6 percent lived in cities in 1800, nearly 40 percent in 1900, and now over 80 percent. Clearly, then, cities are worth studying because they are where the majority of people are today.

But, cities are not just dense clusters of people. They are also dense clusters of all sorts of human activity including research, commerce, tourism, and culture. Indeed, even in the past, when the majority of people lived in the rural countryside, cities were still vibrant centers of activity. Major cities of the classical age such as Athens and Rome served as centers for religion and government, where pilgrims and concerned citizens traveled to worship and be heard. During the medieval period, cities and towns served as bustling marketplaces where local farmers and worldly merchants came together to offer their products for sale. Later, large institutions such as universities but also small ones such as coffee houses sprung up in cities during the age of enlightenment, which helped bring together like-minded individuals seeking to break with rural superstition in the pursuit of science. Even today, those living in small towns frequently visit cities to take part in their recreational amenities, for example, museums and parks, and to patronize their diverse commercial establishments such as unique shops and ethnic restaurants. So, cities are not just where the people are today; cities are where the majority of human activity has always been.

In addition to being a book about cities, this is also a book about networks. But, again, why write about networks, especially in a book about cities? The goal of this book is to demonstrate the answer to this question. Scholars have long recognized that cities play an important role in society, and have been trying to understand how cities work for centuries. Using networks to understand cities can be helpful in several ways.[1] First, networks can bring greater precision to existing theoretical concepts. For example, Robert Park's classic description of the city as "a mosaic of little worlds which touch but do not interpenetrate" becomes more concrete when we think about how an urbanite's social network may include 'work friends' and 'school friends' who don't know one another.[2] More recently, a complex topic such as globalization is more manageable

1

if we think about it as simply the effect of distant places such as London and New York being connected to one another by networks of airline traffic or internet communication. Second, networks offer a different way of thinking about how the world is organized, and thus can help us consider new (and potentially better) answers to some old questions. For example, it is hard to understand what holds a neighborhood together if it is simply a group of people living in a particular area. But, thinking about a neighborhood as a set of people that regularly interact with one another sheds light on how neighborhood associations and block parties are possible. Finally, networks offer a way to bridge a major conceptual gap in the social sciences known as the *micro–macro problem*: how do little individual behaviors give rise to big urban phenomena. For example, while it is not immediately obvious how broad patterns of segregation throughout a city can arise from the behaviors of individual people, the linkage is easy to see when we consider the fact that each individual tends to form friendships with people who are similar to themselves. In examining a range of urban issues such as these from a network perspective, this book aims to explore and demonstrate how networks can be useful for making sense of cities.

What Are Networks?

The idea of networks has been around quite some time, and has been used in many different ways. In this book, networks are viewed as *specific and observable patterns of relationships that can be directly or indirectly examined*. Of course, these relationships might take many different forms, and they might connect people, or buildings, or cities. The key point is that, whatever the relationships are and whatever they connect, networks have a specific and observable content that can be studied. Focusing on this type of network represents a distinctive way of trying to understand the social world that directly focuses on these patterns or structures. Therefore, it is important to consider what it means to adopt a network-based approach to thinking about cities and urban life, and how it differs from other more traditional approaches.

Most social science research focuses on the attributes of the things being studied. In some cases these are objective characteristics such as a person's age or a city's population size. In other cases they are more subjective characteristics such as a person's attitudes toward other racial groups or a city's political climate. These individual characteristics are then used, perhaps with a methodology such as multiple regression or ANOVA, to explain some phenomenon. For example, a study on neighborhood diversity and openness might examine the ages and racial attitudes of a large sample of people in an attempt to understand why some communities are more welcoming of difference than others. Similarly, a study of urban unemployment might examine the sizes and political climates of U.S. cities to understand why some areas have fewer available jobs than other areas.

This traditional approach to studying the social world has become the standard for a number of reasons. The vast majority of existing data, such as that available from the U.S. Census Bureau, provides information about the characteristics of individual people, neighborhoods, or metropolitan areas. And, when existing data sources are insufficient, collecting additional data on the characteristics of individual people or places is relatively straightforward using surveys. Additionally, the methods used to analyze such individual-level data are commonly taught in introductory statistics courses, and are simplified using widely available software. But, this traditional approach suffers from two major shortcomings. First, it is categorical: it places things into predefined categories—a person's age or attitude, a city's size or political climate—and uses those categories to explain the world, even though we know the world is not so neatly organized into boxes. Second, it is individualistic: it treats each person or place as independent and isolated, even though we know that people and places are connected to one another through relationships such as friendship or political alliance.

Focusing on the networks or relationships that exist among people or places, rather than their individual characteristics, overcomes these challenges. Such a network-based approach, sometimes called *structuralism* because it examines the structure or pattern of relationships, does not depend on predefined categories and does not treat social creatures as independent. First, it is non-categorical: instead of grouping people and places into categories based on characteristics such as age or population size, adopting a network approach instead considers which people and which places interact with each other. Second, it is not individualistic but relational: instead of treating them as independent, a network approach recognizes that people and places influence one another through their relationships. To summarize, while traditional social science approaches concentrate on the individual characteristics of people or places to explain and understand the social world, a network-based approach concentrates instead on the complex patterns of relationships between these people or places.[3]

Although researchers have been thinking about and using networks for a long time—even longer than many of the more widely used approaches—they represent a significant departure from traditional social science.[4] As a result, there are many misconceptions about networks and structuralism. Some believe networks are simply a quantitative methodology for data analysis. While it is certainly true that 'social network analysis' is often a numbers-based method for examining data, many researchers examine networks in more qualitative ways through interviews and other methods, focusing on issues such as how people think about and manage their social networks. Similarly, networks and structuralism more generally are not simply a methodology for analyzing data, but also a way of thinking about the social world; they are equal parts methodological approach and theoretical perspective. Another widely held misconception about networks is that they are complicated and abstract. Again, while some network analyses may be very complex, the basic ideas are really quite simple: relationships are important, and different patterns of relationships have different consequences in the social world. This book aims to demystify networks and network analysis, and to demonstrate that understanding them need not be rocket science. A final common misconception is that a network-based approach ignores other important contextual factors such as culture. Quite to the contrary, the networks—the patterns of relationships among people, institutions, and whole cities—are the context! By looking carefully at how people or cities are related to one another, we can often gain a better understanding of where 'culture' comes from.

Not a Book about 'Networks'

While the previous section clarifies what networks are, it is also helpful to be clear what networks are not, at least as they are considered in this book. This book avoids viewing networks as a loosely defined, commonsense, or metaphorical notion that society is built up through connections between people who are related to one another as if linked in a network. The conception of networks as simply the idea that people are connected to one another, and that such connections are important, has been advanced by many scholars writing at different times and in different traditions. For example, German social philosopher Karl Marx (1818–1883) argued that "society is not merely an aggregate of individuals; it is the sum of the relations in which these individuals stand to one another."[5] Similarly, American sociologist Charles Cooley (1864–1929) suggested that "a man may be regarded as the point of intersection of an indefinite number of lines representing social groups."[6] Finally, English anthropologist A. R. Radcliffe-Brown (1881–1955) noted that "human beings are connected by a complex network of social relations."[7] While there is no question that such claims are true and are closely related to the topic of this book, they are also relatively obvious and are the basis of nearly all of the social sciences and humanities. As a result, they tell us very little about what networks are or how they work, frequently because they do not identify exactly who or what is connected, or how. To understand networks, it is important to observe, measure, and analyze them. This also requires recognizing that networks are not merely useful metaphors for how the social world is structured, but really are the way the social world is structured. Thus, this book adopts the stance that people and cities are not merely related to one another *as if* connected by a network, but are in fact connected to one another by real, measurable networks.

In addition to being used as a metaphor, the word 'network' is sometimes used to refer to things other than patterns of relationships. Often, a group or coalition calls itself a network, referring to the fact that its members are somehow connected to one another. For example, many organizations aimed at combating social problems, like those associated with globalization, have used the word 'network' in their name: Continental Direct Action Network, Third World Network, The Network of East–West Women. Similarly, groups of cities and city leaders that come together to solve common problems also frequently describe themselves as networks, including the Healthy City Network organized by the World Health Organization, the Creative Cities Network organized by UNESCO, and the Eurocities Network of major European cities. Although these people, organizations, and cities might be connected to one another by the patterns of relationships among them, simply calling something a network does not make it one.[8]

In other cases, the word 'network' is used as a verb to describe the act of 'networking,' or the deliberate formation of relationships to achieve a desired end. Often notions of networking appear in business settings, where individuals might attend networking events such as receptions and charity dinners to establish new business contacts and solicit potential clients. In other cases, politicians might be described as networking when they make public appearances and take an opportunity to shake constituents' hands. And, the act of networking has now expanded beyond the corporate and governmental arenas; nearly everyone engages in some form of networking, facilitated by social networking sites such as Facebook or Twitter. Such technology is used by people to form new relationships, to maintain existing relationships, and to rekindle past relationships, all in an effort to stay connected or to grow one's social network. While networking, whether in person or online, is certainly important today, it is only a tiny sliver of the formal study of networks as a social phenomenon. In this book, the focus is not so much on organizations that call themselves networks or on networking to make friends and find clients, but on how these institutions and behaviors influence cities and life in them.

Finally, this book does not directly address the theoretical perspective known as Actor–Network Theory (ANT). Although it includes the word 'network' in its name, it shares little in common with the network and structuralist perspectives that are the topic of this book. ANT emerged in the French post-structuralist tradition, and initially focused on analysis of technological systems, where relationships among social actors such as people are considered, but also the relationships among the ideas they create and the things they use.[9] The theory aims to explain how these people, concepts, and objects come to be related to one another, and how these relationships influence social interactions. Often the focus is on how things such as laws and other social conventions develop and acquire meaning through their relationships to people and other ideas. More recently, the ANT approach has been applied to the study of cities.[10] Although this has become an influential approach to understanding how cities develop, it is not directly considered here, except briefly at the end of Chapter Four, where the networks of urban politics are contrasted with the politics of urban networks.

To summarize, although the idea of networks has been used in a variety of ways, and has even found its place in everyday talk, the focus of this book is relatively specific and not overly complicated: how do networks, as observable patterns of relationships, influence cities and help us understand life within them?

Theory or Methodology?

One unique feature of networks—indeed, one that is a common source of confusion—is its simultaneous role as both a theory and a methodology. In the social sciences an idea is often thought of as either theoretical such as 'social class' or methodological such as 'multiple regression.' However, networks offer both a theoretical framework for understanding the world and a methodology for using this framework to collect data, test hypotheses, and draw conclusions.

A number of excellent books have been written about networks as a methodology.[11] While they serve as useful reference guides, the trouble with methodologically focused books is that they are often boring to read and offer only limited applications that illustrate how the techniques can be used to answer interesting questions. Similarly, a number of equally good books have been written that use network theories to examine cities and urban life.[12] These often tell interesting and engaging stories about cities, and use the idea of networks to understand old issues in new ways, but they rarely explain the nuts-and-bolts of network methods.

This book aims to combine discussions of networks as both theory and methodology.[13] The bulk of the text uses network theories to consider questions about how cities work and how urban life is organized. When a new methodological concept or technique is introduced, a separate 'method note' is included that provides a brief introduction to the practical issues of using networks in research. Just as with any complex methodology, each of these method notes builds on the others that precede it. However, they do not assume any prior experience with network analysis methodologies, or any particularly sophisticated mathematical background beyond addition and subtraction. Although networks are often perceived as mathematically complicated, this is a misconception. Anyone able to do basic math, and draw circles and lines, already has the ability to use network methods.

A number of software packages designed for examining networks are available. Two commonly used programs, UCINET and NETDRAW, are available to download at www.analytictech.com/ucinet. The former is used to conduct network analysis, while the latter is used to draw sociograms or graphical depictions of networks. The UCINET commands that correspond to the methodological concepts introduced in the text are indicated in the method notes. These programs include several example network datasets that can be used for experimenting with different analyses. Additional example network data is available from the UC-Irvine Network Data Repository at http://networkdata.ics.uci.edu. Such programs are useful for examining networks, but because they cannot tell the user which type of analysis to perform or how to interpret the results, they are not a substitute for understanding network analysis. That is, although they can produce results and draw sociograms with some random pointing and clicking, it is important to understand where these results come from and what they mean. The method notes throughout this book are designed to introduce some common network analysis techniques so that the software can be used as a tool rather than a magic wand.

With this layout of main text and method notes, it is possible to read this book in a number of ways. For the most complete introduction to the theory and method of networks in the urban context, reading both the main text and the occasional method notes from beginning to end is best. However, for the reader who is primarily interested in the relevance of networks for cities, but not in the methodological details, the main text is designed to be comprehensible and to flow smoothly even if the method notes are skipped. Similarly, for the reader who is primarily interested in learning how to use networks in research, the method notes can be read in order as a brief introduction to network methods.

Organization

In the 1960s, geographer Brian Berry argued that cities could be examined at multiple, nested levels of analysis, by viewing cities as systems within systems of cities.[14] This book adopts the same general idea, but extends it by recognizing first that cities and urban life can be examined as networks, and second that these urban networks can be examined at many different levels that build upon one another.[15] Thus, it focuses on the three types or levels of urban network depicted in Figure 1.1: micro-, meso-, and macro-urban networks. Each level requires a distinctive set of theoretical and methodological tools that make it possible to consider different types of questions. At one extreme, some researchers examine mainly the networks that exist within cities, such as the social relationships among neighbors that generate a sense of community and belonging. At the opposite extreme, others focus primarily on networks between cities, such as the web of nonstop airline flights that make face-to-face business meetings possible. What makes this book unique is that it aims to collect and synthesize the insights and tools of the multiple scales of urban networks. The chapters are grouped into three major sections by the level of analysis and scale of network they focus on: micro-, meso-, and macro-urban networks.

Micro-urban Networks. The smallest scale urban networks that might be examined are the personal social networks that link together the individuals living, working, and playing in cities. Legendary urbanist Jane Jacobs poignantly described such relationships, noting that

> Most of it is ostensibly utterly trivial but the sum is not trivial at all. The sum of such casual, public contact at a local level . . . is a feeling for the public identity of people, a web of public respect and trust, and a resource in time of personal or neighborhood need.[16]

While some of the personal social networks of urban dwellers are informal and casual, such as the sidewalk friendships Jacobs describes, others are more formalized, such as the relationships between a local politician and his or her constituents. But, whatever form they might take, the linkages among a city's people play an important role in city life. The chapters in the first part of the book explore how.

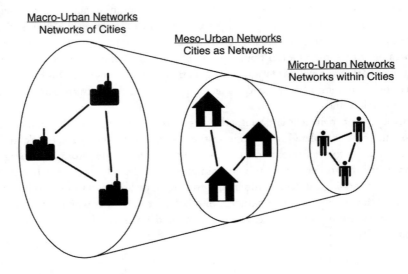

Figure 1.1 Nested Levels of Urban Networks.

Chapter Two asks what role community plays in modern city life? Some have argued that when people move to big cities, community and feelings of solidarity are lost and get replaced by isolation and feelings of loneliness. But, adopting a network-based approach, others have argued that community is alive and well in the numerous and varied relationships that city dwellers maintain. Chapter Three then considers how, in such busy and crowded places as modern cities, social groups such as subcultures and ethnic enclaves form. The formation of such tight-knit groups might seem impossible in the big city, but from a network point of view, having a close circle of friends and acquaintances who all know one another and belong to the same clubs and organizations helps create pockets of order in a sea of chaotic diversity. Finally, Chapter Four examines why some people are influential in running cities and controlling urban affairs, while others are relatively powerless. While political and social influence might seem to depend on individual characteristics such as one's leadership ability or wealth, a person's position in an urban social network can be even more significant.

Meso-urban Networks. Transitioning to a larger scale of network, rather than focusing on the networks within cities, the second part views the city itself as a kind of network. More specifically, the second part of the book conceptualizes the city as a collection of intersecting, interacting, and overlapping networks that bind the many different parts of the city into an organic whole like a living organism, giving it both form and function. Unlike the personal social networks within cities, the contents of these networks are not people, but spaces and institutions. Chapter Five concentrates on cities' physical layout—their form—to consider how different physical arrangements influence how we experience the city. More than just aesthetics and efficiency, a city's infrastructure networks—its streets, sidewalks, mass transit—guide us to use the city in specific ways. Then, Chapter Six focuses on how all the services, organizations, and agencies get coordinated to keep a complex city functioning, rather than dissolving into confusion. The delivery of the wide range of urban services such as trash collection, health care, education, and recreation are rarely the result of a single centralized plan. More often they are made possible by a complex network of interorganizational relationships that allow providers to join forces through collaboration, or to dominate through competition.

Macro-urban networks. The third part of the book shifts to a still broader level of analysis and larger scale of network, to focus on networks that link entire cities to one another. Scholars focusing on these networks of cities have argued that they can be considered within three geographic domains: regional, national, and global.[17] The chapters in this section are organized along these lines. First, Chapter Seven asks how a city becomes a metropolis by looking at how groups of cities in a particular region are linked together by networks of commuting workers, partnerships among business firms, and cooperation between local governments. These regional city networks can transform a single city with a single downtown area where all the activity is concentrated into a metropolitan area where activity is concentrated in multiple places. Then, Chapter Eight considers how cities are related to one another across longer distances and larger areas such as an entire country. Often intercity networks, when they occur on a national level, serve to establish a national urban system in which cities play specialized economic and social roles that require a level of urban interdependence. Finally, Chapter Nine turns to the global arena, asking what makes a handful of major 'world cities' such as New York, London, and Tokyo so important. Is their importance related to their giant population size, their prominent businesses, and their role in history, or is it due to their position in a world city network?

The concluding chapter explores some of the universal features that cut across networks at these different levels. For example, in a phenomenon frequently described as 'six degrees of separation,' it is common for people who do not know one another to have the same friends, or friends of friends. This often leads people, when they discover that they share mutual acquaintances, to remark: "Gee, it sure is a small world." But the ways that streets connect to one another, and that cities around the world maintain diplomatic ties with one another, tend to follow the same pattern. The big city is a small world indeed, but just how small? Similarly, although most of us have only a handful of friends in our social network, we usually know someone who seems to know everyone. But the same is true for city politicians and urban organizations; most have just a few connections to others, while a few have the lion's share. Why, and what are the risks and benefits of such inequality? These patterns can be seen not only at all levels of urban networks, but indeed in virtually every type of network ranging from the circulatory system of an animal to the World Wide Web.

Throughout each of these chapters, the focus is more on broad patterns than on facts and figures. That is, the purpose of this book is not to provide a detailed discussion of specific research findings. Because the field of urban networks is still rapidly developing, to do so would make it outdated as soon as it is published. Instead, this book aims to explore how a network perspective can be useful for making sense of cities and urban phenomena.

Acknowledgements

Not surprisingly given its topic, this book would not have been possible without a large network of people, institutions, and cities that provided invaluable support and inspiration. I first want to thank Steve Rutter and Anthony Orum for recognizing the importance of urban networks and the value of a book such as this one. But, I myself did not always realize the importance of, much less understand, network methodology or urban networks. For that, I owe thanks to Yoosik Youm, Pamela Popielarz, and Dennis Judd. In a book about cities, places matter too. Nearly a decade living in Chicago helped me appreciate the many levels of urban life, from the well-defined neighborhoods with their unique characters, to the elegance of Burnham's only partly realized plan, to the global reach of the city's cultural events. In contrast, the long winters in East Lansing proved a powerful motivator to stay indoors and focus on writing. At Michigan State University, my students in SOC931 (Spring 2011 and 2012) and SOC361 (Fall 2011) endured early versions of this book, and their reactions helped me think carefully about the messages I was trying to convey. In addition, MSU's Humanities and Arts Research Program (HARP) and Center for the Advanced Study of International Development (CASID) provided critical funding for this work. Finally, I must thank my loving wife Jenna, without whose reassurance I would never have bothered to finish even Chapter One.

PART ONE
MICRO-URBAN NETWORKS
NETWORKS WITHIN CITIES

2
COMMUNITY
LOST OR FOUND

We all have some common-sense notion of a community as a close group of friends and relatives that surround us in our daily lives. Idealized versions of communities are often depicted in the media. For example, the sitcom *Cheers* was set in a friendly, neighborhood bar where patrons formed a close community in which 'everybody knows your name.' Similarly, most of the action in *The Simpsons* plays out in the town of Springfield, where every town resident's name and story is known to every other . . . there are no strangers in Springfield. Such portrayals of tight-knit communities are even more common in earlier programs, set in times past, such as *Little House on the Prairie* and *Leave it to Beaver*. But, did this kind of community ever exist? Does it still exist today?

The issue of how communities have been affected by larger changes in the world has been called "The Community Question."[1] For over a century, people have offered a grim answer to this question, arguing that community has been lost. They claim that the good old days when neighbors really were neighborly have been replaced by a fast-paced, highly mobile urban lifestyle based on fleeting encounters with strangers. In 1887, German sociologist Ferdinand Tönnies, reacting to the changes brought about by the industrial revolution such as the growth of large cities, noted a shift in the way society was organized: away from strong bonds between family and friends, and toward temporary connections among strangers that dissolve as soon as they're no longer useful. This narrative of loss has continued to the present day, in bestselling works such as *Bowling Alone* that document Americans' decreasing participation in group activities and their tendency to engage in solitary, individual pastimes.[2]

However, a different answer to the community question is possible. If we adopt a network perspective and look at the large numbers of varied social relationships that people continue to have, communities appear to be thriving in modern cities.[3] Of course, this is not to say that they have not been affected by city life. For example, in the past, a person's community might have included mainly those living nearby, perhaps in the same neighborhood. But, with fast transportation and cheap text messaging, it is now possible to maintain close connections with a community of friends and relatives, even if they live far away. That is, today *communities are networks, not places*.

In this chapter, I explore how a network perspective sheds new light on old questions about the nature of community. I begin with the community question, and the traditional answer that community has been lost. I then consider how the idea of community can be cast in terms of networks, not as a place or population, but as a pattern of relationships. By viewing communities as networks, it becomes clear that communities are not lost, but in fact have been saved from the changes associated with life in modern cities, and even liberated from the geographic boundaries of cities altogether. As the foundation of communities, the chapter examines what the social networks of urban dwellers look like and how they form. Then, pushing this further, I ask whether the rediscovery of urban community in networks extends even to the cities' social edges, among its poor and minority residents, and to its spatial edges, in the suburbs. Finally, I conclude by exploring the many useful roles that communities and personal social networks play in daily urban life.

Community Lost

The industrial revolution brought about major changes in the way society was organized. For example, the development of mechanized farm equipment reduced the number of people who needed to work in the fields, while the rise of machine-based manufacturing created a new demand for labor in large factories. Together with other innovations that made transportation easier and cheaper, such as the steam locomotive, these technological changes made life in cities not only possible, but also necessary. The resulting movement of people from rural countrysides to large cities, or *urbanization*, radically changed their day-to-day living arrangements. Scholars of the time were keenly aware of these transformations, and were concerned with the impact they would have on other aspects of society. Of particular interest was the community question: how would the large-scale social and technological changes of the industrial revolution—especially life in big, crowded cities—affect small-scale communities of friends and relatives?

Ferdinand Tönnies (1855–1936) was among the first to directly address this question.[4] Born into a wealthy farming family, he witnessed first hand the transformation of rural, agricultural life in small villages into urban, industrial life in large cities. Thinking about pre-industrial village life, he used the term *gemeinschaft* to describe a society where social groups were based around strong and enduring bonds between family members and close friends. The members of these social groups played many different roles at once, as co-workers, business partners, confidants, and companions. In contrast, he used the term *gesellschaft* to describe life in cities, which he argued was based around weak, temporary, and instrumental relationships among strangers. Each interaction with another person was initiated for a specific purpose, such as that between a customer and shopkeeper, and lasted only as long as necessary. As a result, Tönnies argued that the residents of modern cities lacked community because they did not have the close, personal relationships that were common in small, rural villages.

Several decades later, Georg Simmel (1858–1918) offered a similar account of city life and its effects on personal relationships. Many of his claims rested on the observation that city life is fast-paced. Because all the sights and sounds of the city provide more sensory stimulation than rural towns, those living in cities must devote more of their attention to just navigating their day-to-day lives. To deal with all the complexities of urban life—crowded streets and busy schedules—he argued that "the metropolitan type of man . . . develops an organ protecting him . . . he reacts with his head instead of his heart."[5] As a result, the emotional and sentimental relationships that might have been possible between villagers get replaced in the city by an objective and calculating attitude that asks whether a friendship is 'worth it.' In fact, because city dwellers are forced to interact with so many other people during a typical day, and each time only for a specific reason or for a short period of time, they have few opportunities or reasons to develop close relationships. Rather than being outgoing and neighborly, urbanites tend to be reserved, leading to situations where "we frequently do not even know by sight those who have been our neighbors for years."[6]

While the 'community lost' ideology originated in Europe where the industrial revolution's effects were felt first, as urbanization took hold in America, similar ideas appeared there too. In his essay, "Urbanism as a Way of Life", which is often viewed as a definitive statement of urban sociology, Louis Wirth (1897–1952) examined how three key features of modern cities—their size, density, and heterogeneity—impacted life in them.[7] First, although residents of large cities likely know more people than residents of small villages, this represents just a tiny fraction of the total number of people they interact with daily. Thus, more time is spent in cities interacting with complete strangers, and less time is available for cultivating relationships and building community. Second, although dense cities bring people into closer and more frequent contact because they live and work in the same areas, this contact often does not result in the formation of community because these individuals are forced to compete with one another for resources such as housing or jobs. Finally, because cities are often very heterogeneous or diverse, both in terms of the people living in them and in the range of things to see and do, each urbanite can pursue his or her own individual interests. But, with each person 'doing their own thing,' relationships are less likely to develop than in small towns where all the children attend the same school or all the adults shop at the same grocery store.

The 'loss of community' argument has also not been restricted to the early days of urbanization when scholars focused on cities and city life as new phenomena. These ideas have continued to find supporters, who have shifted the focus of the community question to examine how other large-scale changes have impacted personal relationships.[8] With city life becoming the norm by the 1940s, but with many Americans still living in rural areas, some sought to compare these two groups, finding that relationships with others in the area are stronger and more frequent for those in small towns than big cities.[9] By the end of World War II, reasons for the loss of community shifted again, to concentrate on the changing shape of cities, and on one pattern in particular: *suburbanization*. Although they were once seen as a place to find real community and caring neighbors, some features of suburbs may reduce interactions among their residents and lead to a loss of community, including the larger distances between homes, the reliance on individual automobile transportation, and the use of gates and fences to mark property lines and keep others out.[10] Still more recently, the Internet and the media have been cited as the culprit responsible for declining relationships and community participation among city residents, replacing face-to-face interaction and allowing individuals to spend their leisure time enjoying individualized entertainment, alone.[11] Thus, a long history of both scholarly research and everyday experiences offer evidence that with each passing day, community is vanishing. But, is it?

Community as Place, Population, or Pattern

Evaluating the claim that community has been lost is actually quite challenging because the very idea of community itself is difficult to define. By the 1950s, long before the advent of new kinds of communities such as FaceBook or Twitter, researchers were using a hundred different definitions of community.[12] Despite this great variety, two conceptions of community have been particularly dominant: community as a place, and community as a population.

The community-as-place perspective views a community as a group of people who live or work within a bounded geographic area. Because they mark particular parts of the city, this perspective often equates urban communities with city neighborhoods. This geographic approach to defining community can be appealing because it provides an intuitive and common-sense way of locating and identifying people as members of a particular community. Similarly, the community-as-population perspective views community as a group of people who share social or demographic characteristics. For example, within a city there might be talk of 'the black community' or 'the professional community'. This approach can be appealing because it offers a shorthand way of referring to an entire group of people. But, these two perspectives on community are potentially problematic. In some neighborhoods, the residents may not know one another or may even dislike one another, while members of some demographic groups in a city, such as African Americans, may have nothing more in common with one another than the color of their skin. By defining community in terms of places and populations, there is a risk of calling a group of people a community even if they do not know one another or have little in common. Of course, communities *could* be located in particular places, and they *could* be composed of people with similar characteristics, but they do not need to be.

A potentially more useful approach is to think of community as a type of social pattern. The community-as-pattern perspective views community as a group of people engaged in repeated social interactions with one another, that is, as a network. From this point of view, community is not a characteristic of individuals, but instead a characteristic of their relationships with each other. These interactions and relationships might include family members who live together to help one another out, the members of a local book club who get together to talk about what they're reading, or neighbors who watch after one another's children in the street and shop in the same local stores. Unlike the one-time interactions among strangers that some have argued are increasingly common in cities, because these interactions take place again and again, over time they help to build up trust and feelings of cohesion or togetherness among the participants. Notably, these interactions could take place between people in the same neighborhood, or could take place between people who share a demographic characteristic, but they also could take place between people who live far apart and are very different. Thus, when investigating communities, it is more useful to focus on the social interactions among individuals than to focus on where they happen to live or who they happen to be.[13]

A group of American psychologists and sociologists who had developed a method for measuring social relationships that they called *sociometry* were the first to adopt a network perspective for investigating communities. The networks that early sociometry examined, and that modern network analysis uses today, are built from two basic components: *nodes* and *edges*. The nodes are the actors in the network, and can be people, organizations, or even entire cities. The edges are the relationships that connect actors to one another, and similarly can take multiple forms: friendship between children, cooperation between organizations, or airline traffic between cities. The pattern of edges connecting nodes can be represented in the mathematical form of a *matrix* and the graphical form of a *sociogram*.

Seeking to move beyond the individual-focused approach of Sigmund Freud and other psychologists of the time, Jacob Moreno (1889–1974) adopted sociometry as a way of highlighting that "the psychological situation of a community viewed as a whole has a discernible ordered pattern."[14] Much of his work aimed to understand how community emerges from patterns of relationships among individuals, or social networks, in different settings such as Public School 181 in Brooklyn, New York and the New York State Training School for Girls in Hudson, New York. By asking individuals to identify others with whom they interact, he produced numerous depictions of the structure of the community's social networks. For example, he frequently used sociograms to visualize how children in a classroom interacted, representing boys with triangles and girls with circles, connected by lines when they played together. Looking at the resulting images, perhaps not surprisingly he saw that the lines mostly connected triangles to other triangles, and circles to other circles; the boys played together, and the girls played together. Such an observation might seem obvious and trivial, but calls attention to the importance of examining actual interactions when investigating community. One might have assumed that a classroom, like a neighborhood, is a community. However, Moreno's sociogram illustrated that it was actually two different and quite distinct communities organized and separated by gender.

METHOD NOTE 1: THE MATRIX AND SOCIOGRAM

Networks are composed of two basic parts: *nodes* (the actors in the network) and *edges* (the relationships between the actors).[15] While nodes and edges can take many different forms—children connected by friendship, organizations connected by cooperation, or cities connected by airline traffic—they must be clearly and precisely defined. Thus, for any research involving networks, it should be relatively straightforward to answer two questions: What are the nodes and what are the edges?

Data that capture the nodes and edges in a social network can be represented in two ways. A *matrix* is a mathematical representation that allows networks to be analyzed using statistical techniques, but it can be difficult to interpret visually. A *sociogram* is a graphical representation that makes it possible to see the patterns of relationships, but it can be difficult to draw when there are many nodes or edges. A single network can be represented in both matrix and sociogram forms, and it is easy to convert one form into the other. Below is a hypothetical network among five neighbors, shown as both a matrix and a sociogram. In this case, the nodes are people and the edges represent the relationships 'talks to.'

Matrix —   Sociogram —

	Alan	Beth	Carl	Dana	Erin
Alan		1	0	1	1
Beth	1		1	0	1
Carl	0	1		1	0
Dana	1	0	1		0
Erin	1	1	0	0	

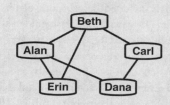

In the matrix, a cell contains a 1 if the people in the corresponding row and column talk to one another. For example, because Alan and Dana talk to one another, there is a 1 in Alan's row and Dana's column, and also a 1 in Dana's row and Alan's column. In the sociogram, this relationship is represented by a line connecting Alan and Dana.

If two neighbors do not talk to one another, this is represented by a 0 in the matrix, and by the absence of a line connecting them in the sociogram. For example, because Alan and Carl do not talk to one another, there is a 0 in Alan's row and Carl's column, and also a 0 in Carl's row and Alan's column. Similarly, in the sociogram, there is no line connecting Alan and Carl.

Notice the diagonal line of cells in the matrix that are empty. For example, the upper left cell, in Alan's row and Alan's column, does not contain a 1 or a 0. This indicates that Alan cannot talk to himself . . . or at least that he shouldn't.

Following its development by Moreno in the field of psychology, sociometry became a popular tool for studying communities in other fields. In some cases, it was applied as a method for solving social problems. In the 1930s a federal resettlement agency in the United States helped families struggling with poverty during the great depression by establishing new communities on the outskirts of urban areas where they could find affordable housing and employment opportunities.

To "promote more harmonious neighborhood structures," families were assigned to houses based on their existing friendships, for example, placing the highly religious families in one group of houses and the families led by men with the same occupation in another.[16] In other cases, sociometry was used to understand the structure of existing communities. Like Moreno's classroom above, these studies often found that villages and towns were not communities themselves, but rather were composed of multiple, distinct communities: groups of people that regularly interacted with others in their group, but not with those outside it.[17]

Nearly twenty years after the development of sociometry, a group of British anthropologists associated with the University of Manchester in England and the Rhodes–Livingston Institute in Africa adopted and further refined the social network approach to studying community.[18] Building on long-standing anthropological notions of webs of kinship, like those depicted in family trees, this group started using the term network systematically to refer to "a set of points some of which are connected by lines [where] the points of the image are people, or sometimes groups, and the lines indicate which people interact with each other."[19]

The anthropological approach to social networks differed in two important respects from the earlier sociometric approach. First, rather than collecting information about individuals' social interactions by asking them questions, it often involved direct observation of individuals' interactions with one another. For example, to learn about the social network of Chanda, a resident of the African town of Ndola, the researcher asked him to keep a detailed diary of his daily activities, which included descriptions of his encounters with other people.[20] Second, rather than examining a *complete network* that included the relationships among all members of a community, it typically concentrated on an *ego network* that included only the relationships among a single person of interest and his or her own contacts or *alters*.

Through such detailed and highly focused studies, it became clear that individuals' social networks had different characteristics, and that these different characteristics had real consequences for individuals' lives in their communities. Perhaps the simplest characteristic of a person's social network is its *size*, or the number of people one is connected to. Having a large social network has more benefits than simply the status or pride that comes with having many friends. A large social network provides a person with many potential sources of support when it is needed. For example, a person who needs a small loan will have a better chance finding one if he has many friends to ask rather than just a few. Similarly, a person seeking election to a local office will have a greater chance of success if she knows many of her neighbors, who can mobilize on her behalf, rather than only a small group.

But, sheer size is not the only important characteristic of a person's social network. *Density*, or what the anthropologists initially called knit, is also important, and describes the extent to which a person's alters know one another. A network is described as dense, tightly knit, or cohesive if many of its members interact with one another. In contrast, a network is described as sparse or loosely knit if its members interact with only a few others. Being part of a dense or cohesive network can have many different influences on a person's behavior in the community. On the one hand, having neighbors who all know one another can lead to a stronger sense of community and belonging than having several isolated friends. As a result, dense networks are often characterized by higher levels of trust and more exchanges of social support among their members. On the other hand, dense networks can also constrain a person's behavior. For example, urban couples tend to do things independently when they are part of a dense network, but do things together when they are part of a sparse network. The dense network provides both husband and wife a source of social support aside from one another, leaving them free to be more independent, while a sparse social network brings husbands and wives together as they seek social support from one another.[21] The constraining effects of dense networks can be seen elsewhere too. If all the neighbors in a

METHOD NOTE 2: COMPLETE NETWORKS AND EGO NETWORKS

Social networks can be examined at two different scales. At the larger scale, a *complete network* (sometimes also called a *whole* or *global network*) includes all the nodes within a given setting and all the relationships among them. At the smaller scale, an *ego network* focuses on a single node called 'ego' and only includes other nodes that are directly connected to ego.

Complete Network —

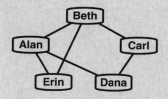

Alan's Ego Network —

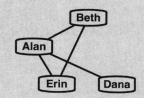

The network on the left is an example of a complete network. It includes all the relationships among all the neighbors in this hypothetical community. Complete networks are useful for examining the structure of the whole setting, but they can be difficult to measure for two reasons. First, they require that the researcher identify a boundary for the setting to decide what nodes should be included.[22] Second, it can be costly and time consuming to locate every node in the setting, and to determine whether it has a relationship with every other node in the setting.

One alternative is to focus on the network of just a single person, or an ego network. The sociogram above depicts Alan's ego network. It does not include Carl or any of Carl's relationships because Carl and Alan do not talk with one another. However, it does include all those neighbors that Alan does talk with—Beth, Dana, and Erin—as well as all the relationships among them. In an ego network, the focal node is called *ego*, while all others with whom the focal node has a relationship are called *alters*. Thus, in this case, Alan is the ego, while Beth, Dana, and Erin are his alters. Ego networks are useful for examining an individual's personal community. For example, it can indicate whether a person has many friends to call upon for help, or just a few. Measuring ego networks are much simpler because they only require obtaining information from one person, but they do not provide any information about the wider setting.

community know one another, as might be common in a small town, news (or gossip) is likely to spread quickly. Such a dense arrangement of relationships may lead community members to be very careful about what they say or do, because they know their actions will be known not only to those around at the time, but to the whole community.

A final network characteristic that anthropologists identified and documented was *reciprocity*, or the extent to which a relationship is 'a two way street.' Some types of relationships are reciprocal by definition. For example, if Alan lives next door to Beth, then Beth also lives next door to Alan; being someone's neighbor is a *reciprocal* or *symmetric* relationship. A network composed of entirely reciprocal relationships is described as *undirected* because the relationships have no particular direction. But, many types of relationships are not necessarily reciprocal; they can be asymmetric. For example, Alan might do a favor for Beth, but this does not necessarily mean that Beth will do a favor for Alan; exchanging favors between neighbors can be a *non-reciprocal* or *asymmetric* relationship. A network in which some or all of the relationships are non-reciprocal is described as *directed* because the direction of the relationships is important. Whether or not a relationship is reciprocal, the direction of non-reciprocal relationships can shape life in a community. Indeed, many scholars have sought to understand the entire social world as a complex system of reciprocal and non-reciprocal exchanges among people.[23] When a community is composed of many reciprocal relationships, its members are dependent upon one another (interdependent) and are bound

METHOD NOTE 3: SIZE AND DENSITY

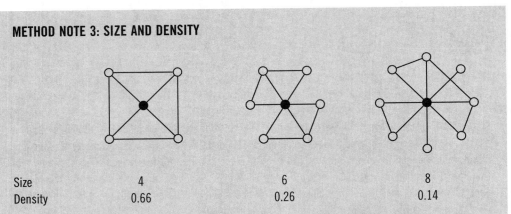

Size	4	6	8
Density	0.66	0.26	0.14

While it is obvious that these ego networks (ego is the shaded node in the center) are very different from one another, the structural characteristics of size and density help to describe exactly how they are different.

The *size* of an ego network is measured by counting the number of alters. In this example, the network on the left is the smallest with four alters, while the network on the right is the largest with eight alters.

The *density* of an ego network is measured as the proportion of possible relationships among alters that are actually present. A simple formula helps count how many relationships among alters are possible: $(N^2 - N) / 2$, where N is the number of alters. Thus, in the network on the left there are six possible relationships among the four alters because $(4^2 - 4) / 2 = 12 / 2 = 6$. Of these six possible relationships, only four of them actually exist. Thus, the density of this network is 0.66 because $4 / 6 = 0.66$, which means that 66 percent of the relationships that could exist actually do exist. As these examples illustrate, size and density are often inversely related; smaller networks tend to be denser, while larger networks tend to be sparser. In UCINET: Network → Ego Networks → Egonet basic measures.

These examples are all ego networks. However, the size and density of complete networks can also be examined and compared. The computations are the same, but because there is no specific ego in a complete network, all of the nodes are treated as alters. For example, if the network on the left is viewed as a complete network, then its size is 5 because there are five nodes. There are ten possible relationships among these five nodes because $(5^2 - 5) / 2 = 20 / 2 = 10$. Only eight of them are actually present, so its density is 0.8 because $8 / 10 = 0.8$, which means that 80 percent of the relationships that could exist actually do exist.

together by mutual obligations. Thus, they are more likely to help one another out in times of need, knowing that the favor will be returned in the future. In contrast, when a community includes asymmetric relationships, there are often winners and losers.

Those adopting both sociometric and anthropological approaches pioneered the definition and study of community from a social network perspective, which focuses on the importance of interaction, not just of members' geographic location or demographic characteristics. However, the social network-based study of community has continued to develop in many fields, with sociology leading the charge. Most of the recent research on the social networks among people living in cities has focused on ego networks, conceptualizing community as a personal phenomenon where each person's set of relations constitutes his or her community. However, other research has begun to examine the relationships among ego networks, considering how these combine into larger and larger complete networks. The other chapters in this section consider such progressively more complete networks and examine how they facilitate the formation of groups or of whole political systems, but this chapter focuses on individuals, their own networks, and their own personal communities. By focusing on individuals' personal networks as a way of thinking about community, it is possible to return to the community question—how has community been affected by major changes such as urbanization—and to reconsider whether community really has been lost.

Community Saved

Through the nineteenth and early twentieth centuries, most theorists argued that the massive social changes associated with the industrial revolution, including urbanization and the growth of large cities, would bring about a death of community. However, as sociologists and others began looking closely at the personal social networks of urban residents in the 1950s, it became increasingly clear that community was not lost, but in fact had been saved.[24] Numerous studies asked those living in cities how well they knew, and how often they interacted with, their neighbors. Across many different settings—a housing development near the university of Minnesota, the compact neighborhoods of San Francisco, the rapidly growing new city of Los Angeles, and the Latin American metropolis of Mexico City[25]—researchers consistently discovered that neighbors knew and interacted with one another, and that community was thriving even in the city. These urban personal communities included not only friends and neighbors, but also family members, and often were characterized by interactions that were even more intense than in rural areas.[26]

The North and West End neighborhoods in Boston provided much evidence for the notion that urbanites still had personal social networks. In the 1950s, both areas were crowded, inner-city neighborhoods, considered by city leaders and urban planners as the city's worst slums, and much in need of demolition. However, journalist and activist Jane Jacobs was struck by "the general street atmosphere of buoyancy [and] friendliness," in which residents chatted with one another on the sidewalk and children played in the street.[27] From Wirth's account of urban life, these close personal interactions were just the opposite of what one might have expected to find in such a place. She also wondered about the source of funding to maintain the neighborhood, since at the time no bank would provide loans to a 'slum,' much less one filled with Italian immigrants. She found, again contrary to expectations, that the neighborhood was maintained through networks of favors and helping hands that connected residents with each other, and more importantly with those who had the resources they needed. In his study of the West End, sociologist Herbert Gans found many of the same patterns: an immigrant slum neighborhood, but with dense social networks among the residents that formed the basis for a strong community life. As he described it, "the basis of adult West End life is peer group sociability . . . [which] for the West Ender, is a routinized gathering of a relatively unchanging peer group of family members and friends that takes place several times a week."[28] Put into social network terms, community in many of Boston's most urbanized neighborhoods was constituted by the overlapping ego networks of their residents.

All of these early findings challenged the widely held 'community lost' perspective. They also raised questions about whether the 'good old days' of strong communities in small, rural towns ever really existed, or whether community was ever really in danger of being lost. It seems unlikely. Indeed, as sociologist Barry Wellman has forcefully argued, although "at all times, most people have feared that communities had fallen apart around them . . . community has never been lost."[29]

So, if community has not been lost in the shuffle of the big city, but rather has been saved from it, then how can we learn more about the communities—the personal social networks—of people living in modern cities? The first step, and one that was overlooked by those alleging the loss of community, is to actually measure these networks, typically through *name generator* questions in surveys. The second step involves looking for patterns and trends in these networks. One common pattern of urban social networks involves their size: the networks of urbanites tend to be larger than those of their more rural counterparts, and to include a wider range of different people. Although "the breakdown of the family has long been a subplot of the decline of community drama," even in cities, one's family members are often an important part of one's community.[30] Indeed, nearly 80 percent of people report having at least one family member in their personal social network, and family members often make up at least 30 percent of one's most active relationships.[31]

Still, relationships with non-kin tend to be more common among city residents than relationships with family members. One reason non-kin relationships are more common, and may even replace relationships with family over time, is the vast range of non-kin one can interact with in large cities. For example, non-kin relationships can form among neighbors, but also among co-workers or fellow members of local organizations.[32] When examining the members of an individual's community, one important distinction to be made is between *multiplex* and *segmental* relationships. A multiplex relationship is one in which two people interact in multiple ways, for example as both

METHOD NOTE 4: COLLECTING SOCIAL NETWORK DATA USING NAME GENERATORS

Social network data are often collected through surveys. Some of the earliest network data in cities was gathered in the *Detroit Area Study*, while the ongoing national *General Social Survey* (GSS) continues to provide researchers with a source of data. Network data is also sometimes collected in more specialized surveys, such as the *National Longitudinal Study of Adolescent Health* (AddHealth).

In most cases, network data are collected in surveys through one or more *name generator* questions, so-called because they are designed to generate the names of the individuals who are in the respondent's personal social network.[33] A name generator question might ask the respondent to name those from whom they could ask to borrow money, or to name those whom they consider to be a close friend. In some cases, the number of names a respondent is allowed to provide might be limited. For example, a survey might ask a respondent to name his or her three best friends. However, because limiting responses in this way can create bias in the data, it is generally better to allow respondents to provide as many names as they wish.

Name generator questions are usually followed by additional questions designed to learn more about these relationships. For example, to learn about the structure of the ego network, it is important to also ask whether the people identified by the name generator question know one another.[34]

neighbors and as co-workers, while a segmental relationship involves only one type of interaction. Although Simmel and Wirth expected urban communities to be characterized by segmental relationships, it seems that most continue to include at least some multiplex relationships, with many urbanites having three or more different types of interactions with some of their contacts.[35]

Another common phenomenon observed in urban communities is the tendency for people to associate or interact with others that are similar to themselves. The idea that 'birds of a feather flock together' is known as *homophily* in the language of social networks.[36] Homophily is observed in the personal social networks of urbanites in many different ways.[37] People tend to have relationships primarily with others at the same stage in the life cycle. For example, the friends of a young, unmarried urban hipster are likely to be predominantly other young, unmarried individuals. Demographic characteristics such as race or ethnicity also frequently form the basis for homophily in one's networks. For example, whites tend to associate primarily with other whites, while African Americans tend to associate primarily with other African Americans. In other cases, homophily can occur around beliefs and attitudes, including religious or political affiliations, for example, with Republicans associating primarily with other Republicans. What is particularly striking is that personal social networks exhibit high levels of homophily even in very diverse cities where one might run into many different kinds of people.

This raises questions about the causes and consequences of homophily in urban areas. Although cities tend to have diverse populations, observing homophily in urbanites' personal social networks is not particularly surprising because even the strangers we encounter on a daily basis are already likely to be similar to us. For example, those living in the same neighborhood have similar incomes, those working in the same building have similar jobs, and those we meet at parties have similar groups of friends. These kinds of homophily can have a number of effects on urban life. On the one hand, it can allow groups of individuals to form a collective identity, which provides a sense of belonging and allows them to stand apart from the crowd. In fact, cities are often home to numerous subcultures, each held together by the relationships among people with similar interests.[38] On the other hand, it can also erect boundaries between different groups, which can lead to feelings of suspicion and animosity.[39] However, urbanites' relationships are not always with similar others. Residence in diverse neighborhoods, employment in diverse workplaces, and simply having many friends all appear to reduce the homophily of individuals' communities, pushing them to interact with a more diverse set of friends and acquaintances.[40]

A final important characteristic of urban communities is density, or the degree to which a person's contacts also interact with each other. Urban communities tend to be less dense, primarily because urban residents have opportunities to form relationships with many different people in many different roles, who have little reason to get to know one another. For example, in a large city, one may know the barista at the corner Starbucks, the person living in the apartment next door, and a co-worker who commutes in from the suburbs, but none of these people are likely to know one another. In contrast, in a small town where there are fewer people to interact with, and where people have lived together for a long time, it is more likely that 'everyone knows everyone else.' Because those in denser communities generally feel closer to their friends and interact with them more frequently, it may seem that the sparseness of urban communities is detrimental, and confirms the fears of the community lost perspective. But, membership in a sparse community is not without benefits. Sparse networks provide more sources for information (or gossip), compared to dense networks that simply recirculate the same information over and over. This can also mean that sparse networks promote more open-mindedness in the community, while dense communities are more likely to hold on to and reinforce existing ideas.[41]

Clearly, community is not lost, but can be found rooted in the personal social networks of urban residents. However, the realities of urban life may have transformed what communities look

METHOD NOTE 5: HOMOPHILY

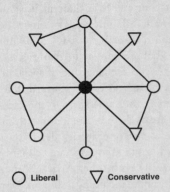

○ Liberal   ▽ Conservative

The example sociogram depicts an ego network in which circles represent people with liberal political views, and triangles represent people with conservative political views. In an ego network, the *observed homophily* is the proportion of alters that are similar to ego on a particular characteristic. In this example, the characteristic of interest is political ideology. Five of the eight alters are similar to ego, so ego's observed homophily is 62.5 percent because 5 / 8 = 0.625. This means that 62.5 percent of ego's contacts are like him or her.

$$\text{Observed Homophily} = \frac{\text{\# of alters similar to ego}}{\text{ego's total \# of alters}}$$

But, ego's level of observed homophily does not take into account ego's expected homophily, given his opportunities to form relationships with similar and dissimilar others. If there were many liberals in ego's neighborhood, then ego would be expected to have many liberal friends just because liberals are so common. In contrast, if ego's neighborhood were home to very few liberals, then ego would be expected to have only a few liberal friends because there just are not very many to pick from. In a given setting, the *expected homophily* is the proportion of the setting's whole population that is similar to ego. For example, if ego's neighborhood contains 100 people, and 25 of them are liberals, then ego's expected homophily is 25 percent because 25 / 100 = 0.25.

$$\text{Expected Homophily} = \frac{\text{\# of people similar to ego}}{\text{total population}}$$

Ego's observed and expected levels of homophily can be compared to arrive at an unbiased measure of homophily that takes into account opportunities to form relationships with similar or dissimilar others.

$$\text{Unbiased Homophily} = \frac{\text{Observed Homophily}}{\text{Expected Homophily}}$$

Using this revised measure, a couple of outcomes are possible. If it is *equal to 1*, it means that the level of homophily in ego's relationships is exactly what would be expected given his opportunities to form relationships. If it is *greater than 1*, it means that ego's relationships are *more* homophilous than expected at random. If it is *less than 1*, it means that ego's relationships are *less* homophilous than expected at random (this is called *heterophily*). In UCINET: Network → Ego Networks → Egonet Homophily.[42]

like. Compared to pre-industrial and rural life, the personal social networks of those living in cities tend to be larger and less dense, but continue to be characterized by a high level of homophily. With a sense of what urban communities look like from a network point of view, many researchers have turned their attention to understanding what features of the modern city influence their formation and organization. Although personal preference may play some role in the relationships urbanites form, for those adopting a social network perspective, structural "forces typically beyond the control of the individual are regarded as providing the determinative causal force."[43] Many of these structural characteristics are influential because they provide opportunities to form relationships, and as a result are often described as *opportunity structures*.

Perhaps the most obvious feature of urban life that provides an opportunity structure for forming networks and communities is physical proximity. Urbanites tend to interact most often with others located nearby, especially when this includes family members.[44] This is particularly important in diverse neighborhoods, where proximity can create opportunities for interaction between people with differing attitudes or lifestyles whose paths might otherwise never cross. Residential stability can also promote the formation of relationships among neighbors.[45] As individuals live among one another for longer periods, with few people moving in or out of the neighborhood, there are more opportunities for repeated interactions and enduring relationships. Indeed, even when neighborhoods start to change and old population groups are replaced by newer ones, small clusters of relationships among the remaining long-time residents may endure as they cling to their old ways of life. Indeed, because people tend to associate with others similar to themselves—homophily—the composition of the neighborhood provides another influential opportunity structure. When individuals are surrounded by others of the same race or income level, they are more likely to form relationships, and their relationships with similar others are likely to be stronger and denser.[46]

A range of sites, organizations, and roles in the neighborhood provide a final set of opportunity structures that influence how and when urban communities form. In some cases, relationships grow around locations such as local public schools, libraries, or parks that draw people together, offering a place to both see old friends and meet new ones.[47] In other cases, opportunities for interaction are provided by formal organizations such as churches and workplaces, as well as informal organizations such as book clubs and bowling leagues, which can be especially influential in linking people who live in different parts of the city or who are otherwise dissimilar.[48] Finally, the roles that people play—co-worker, classmate, or neighbor—shape what interactions are likely and how networks form. For example, relationships with some co-workers is likely to lead to new relationships with other co-workers, but not necessarily with classmates or neighbors, and vice versa.[49] Together, these types of opportunity structures inform the *limited liability* view of urban communities, which suggests that relationships do not form among neighbors simply because they are neighbors. Instead, they develop in more limited ways around the particular activities or interests of each individual, as people invest time and energy in only some aspects of the neighborhood.[50] Others, however, have questioned whether neighbors and the local neighborhood are the right place to look for community in modern cities.

Community Liberated

In seeking evidence that community is saved from the ravages of urbanization, communities are often equated with neighborhoods, based on an assumption that most of a person's social contacts are located in the immediate vicinity. In fact, for more than a century, urban planners and social reformers have worked to promote the development of community in neighborhoods. As Jacob Riis, a turn-of-the-century urban activist, explained, "I want to arouse neighborhood interest . . . to link neighbors to one spot that will hold them long enough to take root. Something of the kind must be done or we perish."[51] As a result, studies of community have often begun by identifying a geographic area of interest—a neighborhood, a housing subdivision, a city—and then examine the social interactions that occur among the people within it. Of course, there are cases where the most important interactions do occur within neighborhoods, and thus where neighborhoods really are communities: when neighbors have places in the neighborhood to meet, are motivated to do so, know few people outside the neighborhood, and depend on one another.[52] But, what about all the other cases; where is community then?

Perhaps assuming that individuals' social networks are concentrated in specific geographic locations is not a good place to start. After all, Herbert Gans noted that in the ethnic communities of Boston's West End "the neighborhood plays a minor role in people's lives and in their predispositions," while more recently cell phones and email allow people to interact with each other over long distances and form "community without propinquity."[53] Drawing on these ideas, many have suggested that communities do not necessarily have geographic boundaries, but are driven primarily by the interactions among people, wherever they might be. This new conception of community has led to a new answer to the community question: community certainly hasn't been lost to the forces of urbanization, and it hasn't merely been saved from them either. Community has been liberated from the boundaries of cities and neighborhoods altogether.

The liberated form of community was first investigated in the East York neighborhood of Toronto.[54] Consistent with the 'community saved' approach, the residents of East York continued to have strong social networks despite their highly urban environment, with nearly all having one close friend, and many having five or more. But, a number of differences emerged as well. First, only a few of the East Yorkers' friends actually lived in East York themselves, suggesting that East Yorkers' communities were not confined to the neighborhood. Of course, friends who lived far apart did not see one another often, but kept in touch by phone (or today, by Twitter and Facebook), and could still be called upon for help in an emergency. In addition, because an individual's friends often did not live nearby, contrary to expectations, moving from one neighborhood or city to another did not destroy his or her community or create a sense of isolation. In fact, individuals who have moved frequently and lived in many different places tend to have personal social networks that span larger geographic areas than those who have lived in the same place their entire lives.[55]

Second, East Yorkers' communities included densely connected family members, but also sparsely connected groups of friends and co-workers. As Figure 2.1 illustrates, this suggests that urbanites do not participate in a single community, but in fact are members of multiple, loosely connected communities that each play unique roles. Focusing just on the sparse relationships with a small group of friends might seem like evidence that community is lost, while focusing just on the dense set of relationships among kin might seem like evidence that community is saved. But, the whole picture of complex, overlapping relationships indicates that community is actually liberated, not only from the boundaries of space, but also from the boundaries of such simple categories as friend or family.

Since the mid 1970s, Americans' communities have increasingly come to resemble this model, as their social networks include fewer ties within their neighborhood and more outside it.[56] However, this general trend may mask a more subtle change in how communities are organized, as some urbanites' social networks and some entire urban areas are characterized by mostly local relationships, while others are composed of primarily non-local relationships. On the one hand, this may suggest that urban community is slowly evolving from saved to liberated, and currently is somewhere between the two. On the other hand, it may suggest that lost, saved, and liberated communities can exist simultaneously, with portions of an individual's social network including dense relations among local neighbors and family, but other portions including sparse relations among distant friends.[57]

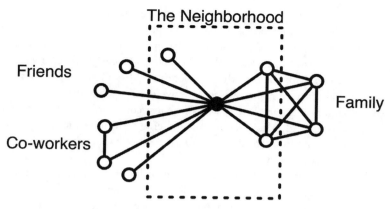

Figure 2.1 A 'Liberated' Community.

What urban forces might be responsible for these changes? One possibility is that in crowded urban areas, the search for privacy and personal space pushes urbanites apart, leading them to prefer relationships with those further away than next door. As Jane Jacobs put it, "cities are full of people with whom . . . a certain degree of contact is useful and enjoyable; but you do not want them in your hair."[58] Another possibility is that neighborhoods in large cities are surrounded by other neighborhoods, and further out by suburbs and smaller towns, which pull urbanites out of their local areas by offering competing social opportunities, or alternative opportunity structures.[59] Indeed, people today are more mobile than in the past, often living in or visiting many different places of their lifetime, making friends and acquaintances along the way. A final possibility is that faster and more convenient communication technologies (first the telephone, and later the cell phone and Internet) and transportation technologies (first the train, then the car, and later the airplane) have simply reduced the importance of distance for social relationships.

In fact, while the original community question asked how technological changes introduced by the industrial revolution have impacted community, more recently attention has shifted to the technological changes introduced by the Internet. Mirroring the community lost perspective that emerged in the nineteenth century, many have argued that as people spend more time alone on their computers rather than with one another, community is being lost. But again, the evidence suggests otherwise. The Internet has made possible the birth of online and virtual communities that are so completely liberated from geographic boundaries that individuals can form relationships without knowing where their online friends are located. Although these new kinds of communities have no 'place,' they are still communities because they are rooted in the repeated interactions of people. Many of these relationships focus on exchanging information, but they can also be an important source of social support, especially around sensitive topics where some level of anonymity is desirable.[60] Moreover, virtual interactions can facilitate face-to-face interactions and the formation of more traditional neighborhood-based communities. Email and phone interactions are just as common over short distances as long. Thus, neighbors with access to high-speed Internet or who participate in local online discussion boards are often likely to also interact face-to-face and to get involved in local activities and issues.[61]

Viewing urban communities and personal social networks as liberated from space also helps to make sense of some puzzles about city life. In 1964 Catherine 'Kitty' Genovese was murdered on the streets of New York as thirty-eight bystanders failed to provide any assistance. The sensationalized *New York Times* account, and many writers since, have suggested that this event illustrates the harsh and cruel reality of city life, and provides evidence for the argument that community has been lost. How, they asked, could she have become so estranged from her fellow neighbors? But, recognizing that urban communities and social networks are often not located within neighborhoods, psychologist Stanley Milgram (1933–1984) offered an alternative explanation: "There is no evidence that the city deprived Miss Genovese of human association, but the friends who might have rushed to her side were miles from the scene of her tragedy."[62] Thus, the liberated community can masquerade as the lost community, and can become a double-edged sword. On the one hand, Miss Genovese could enjoy a little privacy away from her friends and neighbors, despite living in a crowded city. On the other hand, when she needed help most, her closest friends were not nearby.

Looking back, the usefulness of adopting a social network perspective in the study of community is clear.[63] First, the language of social networks offers a narrower and more specific conception of community as the interactions that exist among people. Second, social networks make it possible to precisely describe and examine the characteristics and patterns of those interactions. And finally, they help to clarify the various answers that have been offered to the Community Question (see Figure 2.2). The *gemeinschaft* societies of the pre-industrial, rural past had been characterized by small, dense networks of interaction, primarily among kin-based groups located in villages. But, as large cities emerged, the nature of community changed. Some suggested that community was lost, leading individuals to be isolated from one another, having just a few weak and fleeting relationships. Others suggested that community has been saved from destruction, and that urban communities are composed of the large and dense relationships among friends and neighbors in the city. Finally, still others have argued that community has been liberated from the boundaries of space, with modern communities held together by the relationships among diverse groups of friends living both in the city and elsewhere.

Communities at the Edge

Each of these perspectives considers how personal social networks constitute modern urban communities, but they do not consider their members' positions in society or in the urban area. However, it is important to ask whether these ideas also apply to the communities of those pushed to the edges of society by the color of their skin or the size of their bank account, as well as those who reside at the edges of the city in suburbs and outlying areas.

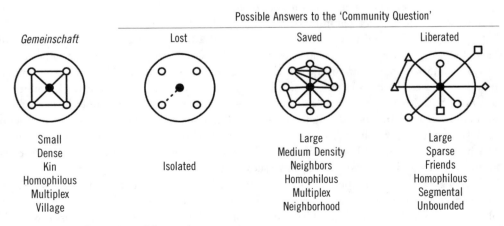

Figure 2.2 Network Conceptions of Community.

Predominantly African American neighborhoods have been described by some as disorganized or chaotic, where crime and poverty have fueled the loss of community.[64] But, there is little evidence to support this view. Indeed, focusing on the patterns of interactions among residents in these neighborhoods reveals complex social networks and the persistence of community. A range of historical and cultural forces has shaped the organization of these networks to retain *gemeinschaft*-like characteristics. First, the high levels of residential segregation in cities have forced networks in African American neighborhoods to be racially homophilous. Similarly, because this segregation has reduced opportunities for families to drift apart, these communities also tend to include many more family members than the communities of more privileged groups. Second, because local institutions such as churches play an important role in the community's identity and bring neighbors together in a common place, they lead to the formation of dense networks within neighborhood boundaries. All of these factors—homophily, kinship, density, spatial concentration—intersect to create feelings of obligation among community members, where day-to-day challenges are dealt with by sharing resources through reciprocal relationships.[65] Such dense and geographically bounded networks can give the community an identity and individuals a helping hand, but they can also have a downside. Because they have few connections to others outside the African American community, such networks make it difficult to bring resources and opportunities into the community, instead serving to simply recirculate disadvantage.[66]

Network-based communities also play an important role in the survival of the urban poor, not only in the United States, but globally. In fact, some have argued that for them "survival consists . . . of managing social ties to gain access to resources."[67] Unlike the social networks found in African American communities, because poverty is often either the cause or consequence of lost relationships with family members, the communities of the urban poor have few *gemeinschaft* characteristics. Instead, their networks are shaped by the uncertainty that accompanies life in poverty. Those with a place to live often hover between saved and lost communities. They develop strong relationships with neighbors who are in similar circumstances, forming small communities that are able to share what resources they have. But, when forced to locate to new housing elsewhere as urban neighborhoods gentrify or public housing is demolished, many of these supportive connections are lost. In contrast, the homeless urban poor often participate in the 'community of the streets,' which can have both saved and liberated characteristics. Some remain in a single location, building relationships with local others through community institutions such as shelters and soup kitchens, while others move from place to place, forming a vast network of connections that can span many cities.[68]

Location at the racial or economic edges of urban society can impact the organization of one's social network and community, but so too can location at the physical edges of the city. Just as Louis Wirth proposed that urbanism constituted a distinct way of life, characterized by the loss of community, some have asked whether suburbanism is also a way of life. The earliest studies of suburban life described high levels of interaction among neighbors who were very similar to one another—middle class, white families—and shared common interests, thus forming a dense network characteristic of a community saved.[69] However, many of the physical features of suburbs can actually reduce interactions among their residents, leading to the smaller and more isolated social networks characteristic of a community lost. First, those living in suburbs typically commute to work or school, often for an hour or more, which not only takes time away from interacting with local neighbors, but also leaves little time to socialize with co-workers and others in the city. Second, because suburban housing developments tend to be large and sprawling, most day-to-day errands require the use of a car, and result in more time spent alone. Finally, suburbs increasingly feature barriers like gates and walls that provide exclusivity and status to the residents inside, but also impose barriers to forming relationships with others outside the neighborhood.[70] Of course, these features do not turn suburbs into social wastelands with no traces of community. But, they can impact how relationships are formed and can lead suburban social networks to focus inward on one's own family and immediate neighbors, rather than expanding to include multiple groups of people in multiple parts of the city.

Putting Community Networks to Work

Different types of capital allow people to achieve goals and satisfy their wants and needs. For example, economic capital in the form of money allows individuals to buy things. Similarly, human capital in the form of skills that individuals acquire through formal education and life experiences provide the tools to solve problems and secure employment. The personal social networks that generate communities offer another important type of capital: *social capital*. Social capital, like financial or human capital, is a type of resource that can be used to achieve a goal, but instead of relying on the use of cash or skills, it relies on the use of relationships. Although the term social capital is used frequently, precisely what it is or where it comes from is left to the imagination. However, social capital is not mysterious or invisible, but comes from patterns of relationships such as those in Figure 2.3.[71]

One type of social capital is provided by weak and bridging networks. In this example, ego's personal social network includes *weak ties* to four people that she does not know well or does not interact with often. Because each of these four people have their own sets of friends, these weak ties are also *bridging ties* that indirectly connect ego to others she does not know at all. The social capital that this type of network provides can facilitate access to diverse groups of people, who can serve as sources for such things as information about job opportunities or resources such as tools for home repair. Thus, bridging ties are also sometimes called *brokering ties*, because they broker or facilitate interaction and exchanges of resources between groups. In addition, because such ties connect different groups, they can help to break down barriers such as those erected by race or class differences. However it can also have a downside. Because the relationships are weak and sparse, it may not promote feelings of belonging to a close and caring community.

The case of a neighborhood beautification project in New Haven, Connecticut offers one example of how bridging social capital can work in an urban community. The residents of an economically disadvantaged and predominantly African American area of the city wanted to improve the look of their neighborhood by creating a community garden. Unfortunately, the members of the community lacked the resources necessary to get started. However, by attending a meeting of the Good Government Committee, one member of the community had met a resident of a nearby and more affluent part of town, who happened to be familiar with a local program designed to support the construction of community gardens. This single relationship, although it was only a weak casual interaction, bridged two very different communities. As a result, the residents

Weak & Bridging   Strong & Bonding   Combined

Figure 2.3 Network Structure and Social Capital.

of one community gained access to new resources located elsewhere, in this case, the knowledge of funding for community gardens.[72]

In contrast, strong and bonding networks provide a different type of social capital. In this example, ego's network includes *strong ties* to four close friends and family members that he knows well and interacts with often. Because these four people all know and interact with each other, these strong ties are also *bonding ties* that link them all into a dense group.[73] Because the dense group has a clear boundary that keeps the community closed to outsiders, these types of ties are also sometimes described as producing *closure*. The social capital that this type of network provides can be beneficial in several ways, but again can have some drawbacks as well. The dense and close relationships among the members of such a network often foster a sense of mutual obligation, in which community members are expected to help one another out. Sometimes called 'support networks' or 'helping networks,' the assistance that is provided through them might take many forms, including a neighbor offering childcare in an emergency or a parent sending money to a child attending college. Thus, as philosopher Thomas Hobbes explained, "to have friends is power, for they are strengths united."[74] However, just as this type of network can be an important source of social support in times of need, membership in such a community can also be emotionally or financially draining when others routinely seek assistance without reciprocating.[75]

The social capital provided by strong and bonding networks can also be an effective tool for enforcing community norms and expectations. This might happen in a number of ways. First, in a community where 'everyone knows everyone else,' it can be difficult for a community member to do something without others knowing about it. To maintain their reputation, community members are likely to behave in accordance with others' expectations. Second, when an outsider enters such a tight-knit community, they can quickly be identified as a 'stranger' and closely monitored. This is the logic behind neighborhood watches as a deterrent to crime. Finally, the strong bonds between neighbors can facilitate trust among them, and the expectation that community members will watch out for one another. For example, parents in communities with this type of social capital often let their children play unsupervised in the neighborhood, knowing that, as Jane Jacobs put it, other trusted friends and neighbors have their "eyes on the street."[76] Although using community networks to monitor behavior in the neighborhood may prevent crime and provide residents a sense of personal safety, it can also suppress individuality and intolerance. For example, community members may feel unable to express unpopular opinions for fear of being ostracized, and newcomers may feel excluded until they find a place in the network.[77]

Finally, membership in a network of dense relationships can foster an emotional or sentimental attachment to the community and its residents. Indeed, this is frequently a two-way street: those who have strong relationships with their neighbors feel a connection with their community, while those who feel connected to their community are more likely to get to know their neighbors. Even highly mobile professionals whose jobs require that they travel around the world maintain strong relationships with neighbors, which at the end of a business trip, provides the stability of a place to call home. While such a feeling of connection and belonging can be good for individuals' mental well-being, it can also be beneficial for the entire community. Cohesive communities are able to function as a group, solving problems together and acting in the best interest of all the residents. But again, cohesion and attachment can also have downsides. If community members have only tight connections among one another, but few relationships outside the community, they are not likely to be exposed to new ideas.[78]

These various forms of social capital are created by distinct patterns of relationships in a community, but they are not mutually exclusive. It is also possible for a single social network to facilitate both types of social capital. The outward-reaching casual relationships bring resources in from elsewhere, while the inwardly focused close relationships focus and concentrate on friendships. The examples in Figure 2.3 illustrate that the functioning of community networks does not depend on who is in them. The nodes in these networks represent people, but they could be any people: friends, family, co-workers, or classmates. The functions of community networks depend not on who their members are, but on the patterns of relationships among their members: strong vs. weak, bridging vs. bonding. And while different patterns in these networks can create different kinds of social capital for their members, social capital is not universally good. In some cases it can bring useful new resources into a community, or can encourage neighbors to help one another out. But, in other cases, it can insulate community members from outside ideas and breed conformity among them.

Although the community members themselves can often use their community networks and the social capital they generate, these can also be strategically used by outsiders to achieve certain goals. One of the earliest uses of social networks in an urban setting was by government agencies in the United States, who in 1930 attempted to deliberately engineer networks among neighbors when new communities were built.[79] A similar attempt was made in the former East Germany, as the communist party sought to promote friendship between social classes.[80] Both experiments were met with limited success, partly because community networks are complex and many factors contribute to how they are organized and evolve over time. However, working with community networks that already exist, researchers have had much success helping communities implement solutions to local problems. For example, by recruiting the help of community members with bridging social networks, researchers can quickly spread information about new health or education programs. Similarly, those with bonding social networks can often help researchers convince other community members to take advantage of such new programs. Indeed, the role of community social networks has become a central element in national political agendas such as the 'Big Society' program, in which British Prime Minister David Cameron aims to empower communities by transferring power from national politicians to local community leaders.[81] Thus, social networks can work in a variety of ways, some beneficial, and some not.

*   *   *   *   *

Adopting a social network perspective that focuses on the interactions and relationships among people, rather than on their individual characteristics, has made it possible to think about urban communities in new ways. Communities in modern cities do not depend on living in a particular place, close to friends and family. Neither do they depend on membership in a particular group, based on race or social class or ideology. If they did, communities might be lost as cities continue to grow larger and more diverse. But, urban communities do continue to exist, even if they have changed a bit, in personal social networks. Of course, this chapter has just scratched the surface of how urban communities work. But, it provides the tools to think about communities from a social network perspective, which offers a unique approach to tackling other questions, such as: How do these communities and other social groups form in cities that are dizzyingly large and diverse?

Discussion Questions and Activities

1. Would you describe your personal social network as a community lost, a community saved, or a community liberated? Why does it have this pattern of relationships?
2. Did the community you grew up in have social capital? What kind? How was it helpful to you and the community, and how was it was harmful?
3. Draw a sociogram of a hypothetical ego network with 6 alters. Use circles to represent people who think like ego, and triangles to represent people who often disagree with ego. What would the matrix for this sociogram look like? What is the network's density and ideological homophily. What sort of person might have an ego network like this one?
4. Write a name generator question and survey five people you know to map their ego networks. Are their ego networks similar or different? Do any of their ego networks overlap?

3
SUBCULTURE
FINDING YOUR CROWD IN A CROWD

In 1915, Robert Park described the city as "a mosaic of little worlds" populated by groups of people with a common way of life.[1] These subcultural 'little worlds' within cities have been around for centuries, and despite all the diversity and social mixing, subcultures and other social groups can still be found in modern cities today. Some of the most visible are the ethnic enclaves. Nearly every large city in America has a Chinatown, but other groups are found in cities around the world, for example, in Koreatowns or Japantowns. Subcultural little worlds can also be found rooted in major institutions such as churches or schools, or focused on special interests such as body building at Muscle Beach in Venice, California, or breakdancing in the streets of New York. Other urban subcultures that depart more significantly from the cultural mainstream persist under the radar, often known only to their own members. For example, many cities are home to underground Goth and Rave scenes, while in some places a subculture is developing around the patronage of underground restaurants operated out of individuals' homes.[2]

Although the mere existence of urban subcultures and other social groups is obvious, it raises a number of tough questions. First, are subcultures simply groups of individuals with a common way of life, or is something more necessary to qualify as a subculture? Second, if subcultures are constituted by like-minded groups of people, how are they able to form in highly diverse cities where it can be hard to find 'your own crowd'? Third, do city dwellers simply scan the landscape of subcultures and join in those that seem appealing, or is the process of joining and leaving such groups more structured? Thinking about urban subcultures and other types of urban social groups from a network perspective helps to shed some light on these questions. Subcultures are not just groups of unconnected people with common interests, but are dense clusters of people that interact with one another. They can form in large and diverse cities because such places offer focal sites for the formation of social networks among potential members. And, entering a particular subculture or group is not simply a matter of personal preference, but a matter of who you know . . . and who they know.

In this chapter, I explore how networks can help us understand the phenomenon of urban subcultures and groups. I begin by considering what a subculture is, and how they are shaped by urban life. Then, I examine the possibility of thinking about urban subcultures and groups from a network point of view. The network perspective makes it clear that subcultures are made possible by individuals' membership in what Georg Simmel called 'intersecting social circles,' which form the basis for many different types of groups, including those focused on intellectual, religious, cultural, and criminal pursuits. I conclude by taking a closer look at one of the most visible and important subcultural groups in the modern city: the ethnic enclave. The networks among members of an ethnic enclave not only define the boundaries of the community, but also have far-reaching effects on their members' participation in the economy and their migration patterns.

The Foundations of Urban Subculture

The earliest discussions of subcultures described them as "highly organized . . . population segments grouped according to sex, age, class, occupation, region, religion, and ethnic group—all with somewhat differing norms and expectations of conduct."[3] Thus, subcultures were initially conceptualized as being grounded in individual characteristics, composed of groups of people that share similar social and demographic traits, and thus also share ways of life. This definition was later refined to reflect the notion that these social and demographic traits do not merely get added together, but instead combine and interact to produce unique subcultures. For example, a middle-class white individual is not the same as a middle-class African American except for their differing race. The influence of being middle class may be different for whites and African Americans, and thus lead to different subcultures. Similarly, there may be many subcultural variations even within a single population segment. As one early scholar described in an example that is no less relevant today:

> Football, to male adolescents of one subculture may mean a chance to hawk programs and peanuts and make some money, to those of another, enthusiastic attendance at the High School game on Saturday afternoon, and to those of still a third, inviting girls up to the campus for a house-party week-end.[4]

Of course, the subcultures that appear within different segments of the population might arise in small, rural communities, or might be spread across entire nations. But, modern cities play an important role in the process because they allow individuals to participate in *intersecting social circles*. Everyone is a member of many different social circles based on the roles they play in society and the interests they have. As Figure 3.1 illustrates, in pre-urban communities, an individual's social circles tended to be concentric. In this example, all adults in the society are also farmers, and all farmers are also village members. Because there is nothing to distinguish one adult from

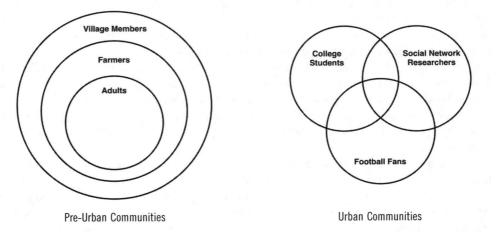

Pre-Urban Communities   Urban Communities

Figure 3.1 Social Circles.

another, it is unlikely that specific subcultures and groups would arise. In contrast, an individual's social circles tend to intersect in urban communities. In this example, not all college students are football fans or social network researchers. When the various social circles in a community intersect, they allow smaller and more narrowly focused subcultures and groups to form, for example, among college students who also follow football and are interested in social network research. By viewing cities as places where many unique combinations of roles and interests can emerge, it becomes clear why they are a prime setting for the development of subcultures.[5]

But, if subcultures are the result of clusters of people who move in similar social circles, then how are subcultures possible in cities, where the population tends to be highly diverse? Challenging Wirth's earlier claim that city characteristics lead to 'urbanism as a way of life,' the 'subcultural theory of urbanism' argued that large cities could actually lead to many different ways of life.[6] Although cities' heterogeneity might make it difficult to find others with similar interests, cities' size can serve to counteract this by providing a 'critical mass' of potential subculture members. For example, consider a person with an interest in brewing beer, a process with which only maybe one in 10,000 people are familiar. In a small town with a total population of 25,000, there is almost no chance of a homebrewing subculture forming because only two or three people share this interest. In contrast, in a large city with a total population of five million, despite the high levels of diversity one would expect to find in such a big place, there is still a critical mass of 500 homebrewing enthusiasts around whom a subculture might form. Thus, it seems likely that subcultures should be more common in larger cities. However, the evidence in favor of this perspective has been limited, which suggests that the development of urban subcultures depend on more than just the city's size.[7]

What other factors might be important? The previous chapter noted that community is not built simply upon individuals' physical location in a particular neighborhood, but on their interactions with one another. The same approach can also be taken toward understanding subculture. A subculture is not simply an aggregate of people with similar individual characteristics. For example, although young people share the common individual characteristics of age, height, and weight, this is not enough to assume that they are all members of a 'youth subculture.' Similarly, subculture is not the inevitable result of a critical mass of people with common interests. For example, the mere presence of 500 people in a city with an interest in homebrewing does not necessarily mean there is a homebrewing subculture; it could just mean there are 500 separate individuals each interested in brewing beer in their homes. Like communities, subcultures are built upon the patterns of interactions among their members. These interactions, which form a social network among individuals, serve as channels through which subcultural values and tastes are spread and reinforced. A young person may be drawn into the punk youth subculture by interacting with a friend who is already part of the subculture. Once drawn in, he is likely to meet and interact with still other members of the subculture, who draw him further into the group and the network. Thus, subcultures and other social groups are not simply collections of separate individuals who have similar characteristics, but are dense networks of interaction among their members.[8]

The Network *Is* the Subculture

Each of these insights about the nature of urban subculture moves closer to a network-based understanding of the concept. First, subcultures tend to form among groups of people with similar social and demographic characteristics, which is consistent with individuals' tendency toward homophily. Second, subcultures are more likely to form in larger urban settings. A large population not only offers a critical mass of potential subculture members, but also ensures that the network among urban residents will be sufficiently large and sparse to allow for small clusters of density. Finally, subcultures and groups do not simply float 'out there' in the world independently of the interactions and relationships among people. Instead, subcultures and social groups arise out of specific patterns of interactions and relationships.

Somewhat paradoxically, when studying groups such as subcultures from a social network perspective, the focus is not actually on groups and their boundaries, but rather on individuals and their relationships. Figure 3.2 illustrates the distinction between these two possible approaches. In the image on the left, four subcultures focused on their members' particular interests are clearly visible. The circles mark the boundaries of each subculture, and show which individuals are members of the subculture, and which are not. Thinking about subcultures in this way can be useful, but requires that we already know what subcultures exist, who their members are, and where their boundaries are located. In contrast, the image on the right shows only the interactions between people in a community. Although it does not show the boundaries of any particular subcultures, it is still easy to see that such subgroups exist. By focusing only on the relationships between individuals, it is possible to consider whether subcultures and groups exist without assuming in advance that they do.[9] How, then, do the social networks that constitute subcultures and groups form, and what features of these networks are most important?

When water is cooled, it does not all suddenly turn to ice when the temperature reaches 32 °F. Instead, as the temperature approaches this point, tiny ice crystals begin to form around impurities such as dissolved minerals in the water that give the water molecules something to freeze on. Once these initial ice crystals form, they provide a surface for still more ice crystals to form, and thus grow into larger and larger crystals, and eventually blocks of ice. Very pure water with no impurities can be cooled below 32 °F without freezing because there is no surface on which the first ice crystals can form. Thus, it is the impurities that allow water to undergo what physicists call a phase transition, in which the water shifts from a liquid to a solid state. The clustered social networks that give rise to social groups and subcultures develop in much the same way. Like the impurities in water that facilitate the formation of ice, places and events known as *foci* facilitate the formation of relationships. They make possible a social phase transition in which individuals shift from a disconnected and disorganized state to a clustered one organized around social circles and groups.[10] Although the most significant feature of foci is that they bring individuals together in a joint activity, they can take a wide range of forms. In some cases, an organization or group might be a focus. For example, a book club or a college course bring people together in a common activity, and provide a venue within which relationships among members might form.

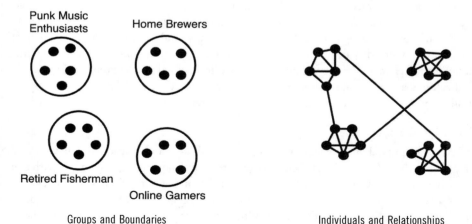

Groups and Boundaries   Individuals and Relationships

Figure 3.2 Two Views of Subculture.

In other cases, an event can be a focus; one often meets new friends at parties. In still other cases, a place can be a focus. For example, local schools and libraries are frequently places where parents and other community members meet and get to know one another. Even neighborhood sidewalks and parks can be important foci that lead to the formation of social networks, and ultimately to subcultures and cohesive social groups.

It may seem relatively obvious that such places and activities facilitate the formation of new relationships. But, why do these new relationships form the sort of dense clusters that are the basis of subcultures and social groups? Thinking about the process of relationship formation from a social network perspective helps to answer this question. Of critical importance is the fact that relationships tend to be *transitive*. In mathematics, the property of transitivity means that if A = B, and B = C, then A = C. In social networks, it works in much the same way. If a person interacts with two friends, it is likely that these two friends also interact with each other. The sociograms in Figure 3.3 show how such a tendency toward transitivity leads to the formation of social networks with dense clusters. Consider a small block watch group that starts with just two members; the group is a focus because it brings these two together in a common activity and encourages interaction between them. Later, one of the group's members recruits a neighbor to join the group; they know one another, but the new member does not know the other original group member. However, because the new member and the original group member now have both a focus and a friend in common, they are likely to spend time together and to interact with one another around the neighborhood watch activities. Thus, over time, a relationship is likely to form between the new and original group members, resulting in what is known as a *transitive triad*. As still other new members are recruited into the neighborhood watch group, the tendency for relationships to be transitive produces a dense cluster of relationships, which might now be identified as a social group or social circle with a distinctive subculture.

When social networks grow through the formation of transitive relationships, the structure of the network that results has a unique property known as *closure*. Closure describes a situation in which all or most of the relationships in a network are with other members of the same group, while few or none are with members of other groups. As Figure 3.4 illustrates, network closure is a matter of degree; some networks can be completely closed, but as the number of relationships between groups increases, they become more open. Thus, the more closure is present in a social network, the more social groups are literally closed off from one another. By thinking about closure as a key structural feature of the networks that hold social groups and subcultures together, it is possible to return to Robert Park's quote at the beginning of this chapter. While he described the city as "a mosaic of little worlds," he went on to explain that they "touch but do not interpenetrate." That is, there are many different social groups and subcultures in modern cities, and while they may influence one another, the closure of their members' networks ensure they do not all merge together into one.[11] Long before the development of formal social network methods, the role of relationships and closure for urban subculture was clear.

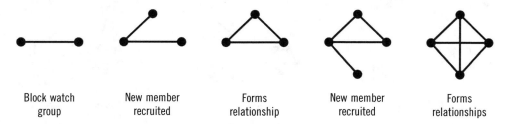

| Block watch group | New member recruited | Forms relationship | New member recruited | Forms relationships |

Figure 3.3 Transitivity and Group Formation.

Closure is important for social groups and the maintenance of a subculture for several reasons. First, the boundaries of a social group with a closed network are stronger than the boundaries of a social group with an open network. In the completely and relatively closed networks in Figure 3.4, it is easy to see who is a member of which social group, but in the relatively open network distinctions between member and non-member are harder to make. Such membership distinctions are critical because they allow members of social groups to develop a sense of cohesiveness and identity, and make it possible to view the group as a real entity rather than just a collection of loosely connected individuals.

Second, closure facilitates the enforcement of norms and expectations that define the group's subculture. In a closed network, an injustice to a fellow member is often perceived as an injustice to other members, and to the whole group. Similarly, punishments or sanctions for such an injustice can be imposed not just by the individual who was wronged, but also by the group as a collective. For example, in a close circle of friends, if one member insults another, the group may collectively decide to exclude the transgressor from an upcoming event. In contrast, in a more open network where circles of friends are more fluid, such a punishment would be difficult to impose. Thus, in closed networks, trust among members is facilitated because the group monitors every member's behavior. The wholesale diamond market in New York City offers one classic, and particularly dramatic, example. Entire bags of diamonds, often worth millions of dollars, are frequently exchanged between merchants wishing to inspect the stones and broker sales. The safe return of the stones is guaranteed not by a contract or insurance policy, but by a handshake. How is this level of trust possible? In New York City, the diamond market is primarily operated by Jews, whose networks tend to be closed for cultural reasons such as high rates of intermarriage, but also because they share foci such as Brooklyn neighborhoods and synagogues.[12]

Through a tendency to develop transitive relationships, foci such as groups, places, and events play a major role in the formation of closed social networks, which allow subcultures to flourish. However, some have suggested that there is another, complementary way of thinking about the relationship between people and foci. The discussion above focuses on the fact that two people are likely to have a relationship if they share membership in a common group, for example, if they both attend the same school. But, this idea can be reversed: two groups are likely to interact with one another if they have a common member. For example, if a single person both attends a particular school and lives in a particular neighborhood, then the school and neighborhood groups are likely to interact. Thus, there is a *duality of people and groups*: not only do people build relationships with each other through groups, but groups build relationships with each other through people. Or, put another way, what makes a group unique is its specific combination of members, while what makes a person unique is the specific combination of groups in which he is a member.[13]

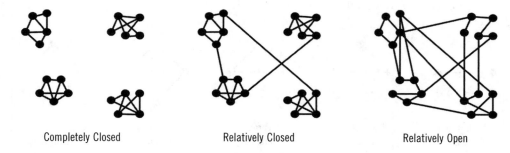

Completely Closed   Relatively Closed   Relatively Open

Figure 3.4 Degrees of Network Closure.

METHOD NOTE 6: TRANSITIVITY AND CLOSURE

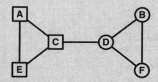

The *transitivity* of a network is measured as the number of *triads* that are transitive, divided by the total number of possible triads. A simple formula indicates how many triads are possible: N! / 6(N − 3)!, where N is the number of nodes. In the example network, there are 20 possible triads among the six nodes because 6! / 6(6 − 3!) = 720 / 36 = 20. Many of these possible triads are not transitive; they are intransitive. For example, the triad A-C-D is not transitive because A and D do not have a relationship. Similarly, the triad C-E-F is not transitive because there is no relationship between C and F, or between E and F. In fact, only two of the possible triads are transitive: A-C-E and B-D-F. Thus, the transitivity of this network is 10 percent, because 2 / 20 = 0.10. In UCINET: Network → Cohesion → Transitivity.

The degree of *closure* in a network can be measured using the E–I Index, which measures whether relationships are primarily Eternal or Internal to groups. The E–I Index is based on a simple formula:

$$\text{E–I Index} = \frac{\text{\# of external ties} - \text{\# of internal ties}}{\text{\# of external ties} + \text{\# of internal ties}}$$

The index ranges between +1 when the network is completely open and −1 when the network is completely closed. Using the E–I Index to compute network closure requires defining groups based on some characteristic of the nodes. Suppose that the square nodes (A, C, and E) are men, while the circle nodes (B, D, and F) are women. Of the seven total ties in the example network, six of them are internal to one of these gender-based groups; three are between only men, and three are between only women. Only one of the ties, the relationship between C and D, is external to the groups because it is between a man and a woman. Thus, the E–I Index in this network is −0.71 because (1 − 6) / (1 + 6) ≈ −0.71. This confirms what the sociogram above suggests visually: the network has a high degree of closure around gender. In UCINET: Network → Cohesion → E–I Index.[14]

Figure 3.5 illustrates this notion of duality, showing how it can help explain the formation of subcultural social networks and the ways that different subcultures or social groups can interact with one another. On the left is a person-to-group network that shows how people belong to groups that might serve as foci for the formation of social networks. For example, Alan is a member of the band, so these two nodes are connected. This type of network is called a *two-mode affiliation network* because it includes two different types of nodes—people and groups—and shows how one is affiliated with the other. From this information, it is possible to derive two different social networks. First, the person-to-person network in the upper right shows the relationships among people based on their shared foci. For example, one would expect that Alan and Beth interact because they are both members of the band. Similarly, one would expect that Carl and Erin interact frequently because they attend the same school *and* live on the same block. Second, the

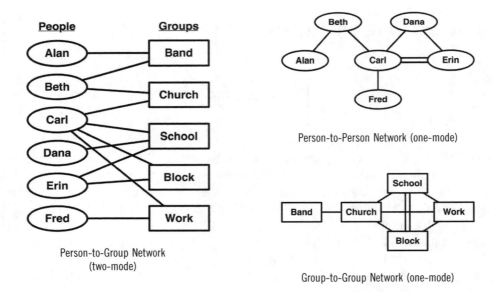

Figure 3.5 The Duality of People and Groups.[15]

group-to-group network in the lower right shows the relationships among groups based on their shared members. For example, one would expect that information will be exchanged between the band and church because Beth is a member of both groups. Similarly, one would expect that even more information would be shared between the school and the neighborhood block because these two groups are connected through both Carl and Erin. Both the person-to-person and group-to-group networks are examples of *one-mode* networks because, unlike the two-mode network from which they were derived, they each contain only one type of node.

This way of thinking about the relationship between people and groups can provide insight into the potential for social groups and subcultures to emerge. The person-to-person network is complex, but includes the transitive triad of Carl, Dana and Erin. These three are all likely to interact because they attend the same school, and moreover because Carl and Erin also live on the same block. As a result, they may come to view themselves as a cohesive social group, which could grow as existing members recruit others, such as Fred, whom Carl knows from work. The group-to-group network is similarly complex, but also includes a small dense cluster that includes the school, block, church, and work. The 'little social worlds' that form around these foci are likely to interact with and influence one another. For example, new church members could be recruited from the school, which are linked to one another by Carl's participation in both. The band's subculture, however, is unlikely to be influenced by the other groups because it is only weakly connected to them, sharing only a single member with any of the other foci.

Social Circles in the City

Using social networks to understand what subcultures are—how they are formed and maintained—can be applied widely. There are national subcultures, for example, among those who follow the work of a particular band or artist. With the rise of global media and technologies such as the Internet providing the ability to communicate with others across long distances, even international subcultures are possible. Enthusiasts of manga, Japanese comic books, form a subculture in which fans from around the world interact with one another at conferences and in online discussion

METHOD NOTE 7: TWO-MODE NETWORKS

Deriving a one-mode network from a two-mode network—a process known as *projection*—can be a useful method of obtaining social network data because two-mode data can be easier to collect than one-mode data. Collecting a one-mode network can be difficult for two reasons. First, it requires obtaining information about each node's relationship with every other node, but even in a small network of fifty people, there are more than 1,000 possible relationships! Second, information about the actual relationships between nodes, such as the number of phone calls between cities, may be difficult to obtain. In contrast, two-mode data is often available from common sources. For example, people's affiliations with clubs are recorded in membership lists.

For a small two-mode network, like the one shown in Figure 3.5, drawing a one-mode projection is possible by hand. But, for larger two-mode networks, one-mode projections can be created using *matrix multiplication*. The process begins with the two-mode data in the form of an actor-to-affiliation matrix: the rows are the actors, the columns are the affiliations they might have, and the cells in the matrix indicate which actors have which affiliations. Next, a second matrix called the *transpose* is created; the transpose simply swaps the rows and columns so that the rows are the affiliations and the columns are the actors. From these two matrices—the original and the transpose—there are two possibilities: (a) original × transpose = an actor-to-actor network, while (b) transpose × original = an affiliation-to-affiliation network. Notice that unlike ordinary multiplication, matrix multiplication is not commutative: $A \times B \neq B \times A$. Although multiplying matrices is mathematically simple—it only involves adding and multiplying numbers—it involves several steps. In UCINET: Data → Affiliations (2-mode to 1-mode).

Although one-mode projections can be a useful tool, they must be used with caution. First, a one-mode projection is only a realistic portrayal of a social network if it is true that when two actors share an affiliation, they are likely to interact. This might be the case for two people who play in the same band, but not for two people who attend the same large convention. Second, the process of creating one-mode projections tends to create dense and clustered networks. Therefore, it is difficult to draw conclusions about a network's actual density and other structural features when using this approach.[16]

groups. But, social circles and subcultures are particularly important for urban life. First, cities are where subcultures often form: they are sites of sufficient diversity and density for new subcultures to emerge as regular interactions among strangers with common interests form. Second, subcultures can be helpful for urbanites: social circles and the subcultural practices they support can appear as small pockets of order in an otherwise chaotic sea of urban diversity, giving city residents a sense of belonging and stability.

Urban social circles form among individuals brought into interaction by their common interests. Frequently the structure of such groups is informal, with their membership and boundaries remaining quite fuzzy. For example, in a large city, one may find a social circle of people interested in hydroponic gardening. They likely interact with one another on occasion, as they shop at the same gardening supply stores, or seek advice on new techniques. However, they may not participate in regularly scheduled meetings, and likely do not have formal criteria for membership that entitle them to carry such symbols as 'membership cards.' Instead, they are simply an amorphous group of individuals who, through their repeated interactions with others in the group, develop a common way of life, at least with respect to their gardening pastimes.

Such informal social circles can develop around a wide variety of interests and other individual characteristics. One of the earliest studies of social circles in urban life focused on a group of individuals living in New York City in the 1930s who participated in psychotherapy, either as patients or practitioners.[17] This group did not form a perfectly dense social network; each psychotherapy participant knew only a few others. But, two key features of this group permitted it to develop not simply as a collection of individuals with similar interests, but as a group with a distinctive subculture. First, members were more likely to interact with other members than with non-members; the network may not have been dense, but it exhibited closure. For example, when seeking a referral for a therapist or wanting to discuss a recent therapy session, one is likely to seek out interaction with another who also views psychotherapy in a positive light, rather than a friend or relative who might view it with suspicion. Second, those engaged in psychotherapy also tended to have other similar interests, especially in the arts; while the network was not dense, it was composed of people with intersecting social circles. Thus, even when they were not participating in a therapy session, or talking about one, members of this group often ran into one another at the same theaters, concerts, museums, and art galleries. Thus, from the vast diversity of New York City, the repeated interactions among a group of individuals formed a sparse, but closed and intersecting network that gave rise to a subculture of artistic patronage and psychological open-mindedness.

Of course, not all urban social circles are as elite as a group of socialite psychoanalysts. Informal groups can also emerge around more mundane or day-to-day activities as one's occupation or pastime. For example, in many larger cities, skilled construction workers who lack regular employment often form an occupational social circle as day laborers, with their own unique subculture. As a consistent group of workers meets at the same location each day to be hired by contractors, they socialize with one another and learn about job opportunities, but also form group norms around hiring order and other practical matters. Similarly, social circles can form around pastimes such as knitting, which has become a popular activity among young urbanites, because participants are more likely to interact with other participants than non-participants.[18] Like occupations and pastimes, religious affiliations can give rise to social circles as well. Indeed, because churches "have focused more on reinforcing within-group networks and, therefore have neglected or discouraged ties outside of the congregation," they are key institutions that generate the closed types of social networks that foster subcultures.[19]

Recalling the ideas of community explored in the previous chapter, even geographic locations can produce exclusive social circles with their own subcultures. For example, long established neighborhoods may be home to a group of old-timers who, through their dense and closed network of interactions that can span several decades, maintain a particular way of life in the area. Newcomers to the neighborhood, because they cannot gain access to this closed network, are often excluded from the local subculture, and may ultimately be forced to cultivate their own subculture as they form friendships with other newcomers.[20] Still others have suggested that geographically concentrated groups of people with specific individual characteristics can give rise to unique subcultures because their proximity to one another encourages patterns of repeated interaction. For example, some have argued that a 'culture of poverty' can emerge in economically disadvantaged urban neighborhoods where poor residents interact primarily with other poor residents. While on the one hand these interactions can yield a beneficial subculture of mutual aid in which members of the community help one another get by, it can also lead to a detrimental subculture of despair and hopelessness.[21] Similarly, race-based subcultures can emerge through residential interactions. If the networks among residents of predominantly minority neighborhoods are closed, that is, primarily among other residents of the same neighborhood, they can produce a strong subculture that promotes neighborhood pride and identity, but also prevents accessing the resources of other neighborhoods and subcultures. Subcultures of residential etiquette can also emerge from such race-based networks. For example, in racially segregated neighborhoods in Chicago and elsewhere, socializing with neighbors on the front porch is considered acceptable in African American neighborhoods, but not in predominantly white neighborhoods, where socializing is expected to take place inside the home, or out of view in the backyard.[22]

But not all urban social circles are as informal as a casual knitting group or a loose network of neighbors. Characterized by a somewhat more rigid structure, gangs are another type of social circle that produces a distinctive urban subculture. Early studies of 'slum' neighborhoods characterized them as the product of interactions among small, street corner-based gangs that, through the patterns of interactions among their members, sought to advance their particular agendas.[23] More recently, criminologists and other social scientists have turned to social networks to understand how urban gangs form and operate, viewing them as a special type of social circle. Although a member of one gang may occasionally interact with members of other gangs, the vast majority of their interactions are with other members of their own gangs. That is, gang networks tend to exhibit very high levels of closure, which is useful for understanding how urban gangs work in at least two ways. First, focusing on the patterns of individuals' interactions offers a direct and objective way of locating the membership boundaries of a gang. For example, one study examined the patterns of 'hanging' in a Mexican gang in Chicago's Taylor Street area. Although all the boys identified as members of 'The Erls,' it became clear that the gang was actually composed of two distinct, but partly overlapping, groups that traveled the neighborhood or fought together. This type of information can be useful for social workers seeking to help youth leave gangs, or for police seeking to monitor gang activity. Second, the gang subcultures that arise in such dense and closed networks can facilitate the recruitment and socialization of new gang members, which helps explain why networked criminal activities such as gangs can persist despite law enforcements' attempts to eradicate them.[24]

When, in the 1830s, Alexis de Tocqueville described the strength of American democracy as resting on the fact that America was a 'nation of joiners,' he likely did not have in mind that statesmen and community leaders were joining street gangs. Instead, he saw the role of still another type of social circle, the voluntary association, as critical.[25] Moreover, while Tocqueville focused on the importance of social clubs and civic associations for politics at the national level, Wirth recognized their importance for urban life, noting that "being reduced to a stage of virtual impotence as an individual, the urbanite is bound to exert himself by joining with others of similar interest into organized groups to obtain his ends."[26] Thus, many researchers have focused on understanding what types of organizations urbanites tend to join, and to what extent they tend to participate in the organizations' activities. Following a theory of mass society, participation in voluntary associations by urban dwellers has been viewed as providing an institutionalized buffer against the potential anonymity and isolation of living in a large city. That is, the range of religious, social, educational, recreational, and civic clubs urbanites might join made big city life more livable by creating little worlds, each run according to its own subculture and each providing its members with a sense of belonging. For this reason, some have raised the alarm that Americans are no longer a nation of joiners, and that urban community is once again at risk of being lost.[27]

At first glance, unlike informal social groups or even gangs, it may seem that voluntary organizations are not related to networks. After all, they often have official procedures for joining such as an application, an official meeting place and time, and possibly even elected officers and a formal system of governance. But, a closer look reveals that even the subcultural social circles of highly formalized voluntary associations are closely related to networks. First, voluntary associations can lead to the growth of personal networks by serving as foci like those discussed above. For example, one might join a club based on a special interest, but through membership

METHOD NOTE 8: THE ETHICS OF SOCIAL NETWORK RESEARCH

Networks can be used to investigate individuals' participation in urban street gangs, as well as other sensitive topics, including the spread of sexually transmitted diseases and the corrupt use of political influence. Thus, the use of social network analysis in research can raise important questions about ethics and privacy, and can present challenges for obtaining approval from Institutional Review Boards (IRBs).

First, it is generally important to assure study participants that they will remain anonymous, or at least that they will not be identifiable in the data. In traditional data formats, such as survey responses, this can usually be achieved by removing the participants' names or omitting certain variables. However, it can be more challenging to ensure anonymity in network data because the patterns of relationships—the network structure itself—can sometimes be used to identify specific individuals. For example, in a network capturing the order-giving relationships among employees in a company, it may be obvious which nodes represent workers and which represent managers. In a small company with only one or two managers, such a network could reveal the participants' identities, even if the network itself is not labeled with names.

Second, it is usually necessary to obtain informed consent from individuals before they participate in a study. This ensures that individuals are not forced or tricked into participating in a study when they do not want to participate. But, in social network research, the definition of 'participant' can sometimes be unclear. Collecting network data using a name generator question involves asking a participant to identify others with whom they interact. For example, collecting an individual's ego network may involve asking with whom they discuss important matters, to which a person might respond, "My father." This answer not only gives some information about ego, but also about his father. Thus, it raises the question: is the father also a study participant? Such individuals are often described as *secondary participants*, who do not directly participate in the study but nonetheless about whom some data are collected. It is typically not necessary to obtain informed consent from secondary participants—such a requirement would make collecting network data nearly impossible—but steps should still be taken to protect their privacy.[28]

in the club, form personal relationships with other members, and ultimately become enmeshed within a new social network. Second, personal networks can lead to the growth of voluntary associations, because personal networks serve as channels through which new members are recruited. For example, in most cases, one joins a new club or organization because a friend or acquaintance is already a member. Thus, individuals' networks grow by expanding within voluntary associations, while voluntary associations grow by expanding outward through their members' networks.[29]

The relationships between networks and organizations are brought together in a conceptual framework known as *Blau Space*, which was initially developed by researchers studying the networks and affiliation patterns of adults living in several Nebraska towns.[30] Figure 3.6 illustrates a hypothetical Blau Space, and shows how networks can create, and be created by, such urban groups as voluntary associations. In panel A, the individuals in a town are represented as dots, organized by their age and education like a scatterplot; some of them are younger and less educated and others are older and more educated. The network among these people is not likely to be random.

Following the principle of homophily, two people who are similar to one other are more likely to interact. Thus, the network among them likely resembles the one shown in panel B: the younger and less educated people interact with one another, while the older and more educated people interact with one another. The Blau Space framework is particularly useful because pairs of people who are similar, and thus who are more likely to have a network connection, are represented by dots that are close to one another. For example, the older well-educated residents are all in the upper right corner, and indeed, most of the relationships these individuals are part of are also located in the upper right corner. Similarly, the younger less educated residents are in the lower left corner, and the relationships they are part of are also located in this area. This calls attention to the fact that *social networks are localized in social space*.[31]

By thinking about networks as embedded in a social space, it is possible to examine the location of voluntary associations in relation to the networks and space. In panel C, two different associations are shown by dotted circles: a sports team and an organization of city leaders. The dotted circles represent the association's *niche*. Just as in biology where different species have different niches depending on the resources they need to survive, such as food or water, associations have niches depending on the type of members they need to survive. In this example, the town's sports team needs relatively young members, while the city leaders club needs older, well-educated members. Additionally, it is clear that within the groups, there is a network of interaction among their members. Indeed, because these groups play the role of foci, by bringing a set of individuals into regular contact with one another, they facilitate the formation of relationships and networks among members.

Over time, existing members may recruit new members into the association. However, new members are not simply recruited randomly from the whole town's population. Instead, new members are usually recruited from existing members' networks. In panel D, a member of the sports team has recruited two of his friends, and a member of the city leaders club has recruited

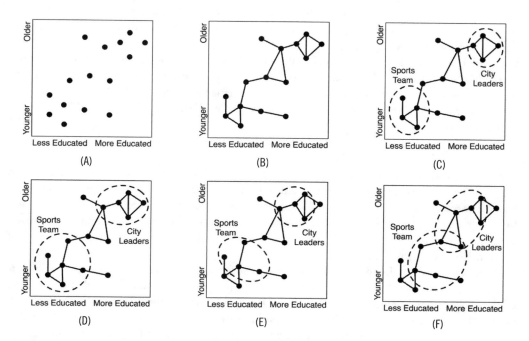

Figure 3.6 Networks and Voluntary Associations in Blau Space.

one of her contacts. As new members are recruited, the association's niche expands. Members may also leave an association, which can cause the association's niche to contract. In Panel E, two members leave the sports team and one member leaves the city leaders group. Through recruitments and departures, which are driven by the structure of members' networks, the character of a town's voluntary associations can change over time. These changes are expressed in the organizations' shifting niches. Comparing the niches in panels C and E, the sports team's niche has shifted as it focuses on slightly older members than before, while the city leaders group has shifted as it focuses on members with more moderate levels of education.[32]

In some cases, these changes may cause two or more associations' niches to overlap, as in panel F. In this example, the niches overlap and both include the two middle-aged people with average education in the center of the space. They are potential members to be recruited by both the sports team and the city leaders club. However, with only 24 hours in a day, they each have only a limited amount of time to spend participating in different groups and activities. They must decide whether to focus their energy on practicing with the sports team, or attending a local business meeting with the other city leaders. Just as two different species that need to eat the same food must compete with one another, these two associations must compete with each other for these members' time. And, just as the natural world evolves through the survival of the fittest species, the world of organizations also evolves through the survival of the fittest—the best as recruiting and retaining members through social networks—social group.

Using this approach has cast new light on how urban social circles may (or may not) serve as a buffer against the complications of big city life. On the one hand, membership in voluntary associations and other social circles does provide individuals with ready-made sets of relationships, and can facilitate the formation of new ones. On the other hand, because social circles grow and evolve along homophilous social networks, their members tend to be homogeneous. As a result, although voluntary associations may provide urban dwellers with opportunities to interact with others, they may not provide access to a diversity of information or experiences because those others tend to be just like them. For better or worse, social circles driven by social networks serve to insulate urbanites from the larger urban world. In addition to any effects on individual urbanites, however, this approach also highlights how a city's social circles and subcultures can evolve over time. Urban subcultures are not static, but they also do not change randomly. Instead, they evolve based on the structure of their members' social connections. In the example above, it is easy to imagine how the subculture of a sports team might change as it shifts to focus on older players, for example, by shifting from celebrating a win with a cooler of juice boxes to celebrating at a neighborhood bar.

The Ethnic Enclave

There are a wide range of social circles, social groups, and other subcultural entities in modern cities. Indeed, this chapter has briefly considered how networks are important for the formation and maintenance of subcultures in informal groups such as psychotherapy participants, quasi-formal groups such as street gangs, and formal groups such as voluntary associations. However, one type of subcultural social circle has played a particularly critical role in the development of modern cities: the ethnic enclave.

As a nation of immigrants, studies of ethnic and immigrant enclaves have been particularly common in American cities. In this work, a range of perspectives on defining and characterizing ethnic enclaves has emerged. In some cases, ethnic enclaves are defined in terms of employment, to describe geographic clusters of immigrant business owners and entrepreneurs.[33] In other cases, they have been defined in terms of residents, to describe geographic clusters of immigrant households or neighborhoods in which a particular ethnic group is overrepresented.[34] As a result, there has been much confusion about what an ethnic enclave is.[35] Adopting a network perspective in the study of ethnic enclaves can be useful because it places the focus on the structure of relationships within the enclave, and between ethnic enclave members and others, without making assumptions about where individuals may live or work. Moreover, by thinking about an ethnic enclave as special type of social circle, with a robust and well-defined subculture, the crucial roles of such network features as foci and closure are highlighted.[36]

Much like the community lost perspective discussed in the previous chapter, some research on ethnicity may appear to suggest a similar 'ethnicity lost' perspective. For example, there are numerous accounts of the cultural assimilation of ethnic groups over time, describing how ethnically specific behaviors and practices such as language or cuisine get replaced by the behaviors and practices of mainstream society. Similarly, the theory of ethnic succession describes how immigrant ethnic groups occupy the lowest social positions in cities, but that as one group achieves success and moves up the social ladder, newer immigrant groups take their place at the bottom.[37] However, despite the processes of assimilation and succession, much research suggests that ethnic groups and ethnic subcultures are not lost in cities, but in fact are reinforced and flourish in urban settings.

Homophily, although commonly observed in all social networks, is particularly important and strong in the social networks of urban ethnics. Members of urban ethnic populations share at least one characteristic in common, their ethnic background. But, they often share many other characteristics as well, including their language, education and social class, and cultural tastes. Their similarity on many different dimensions, combined with the availability of other fellow ethnics with whom to interact, means that homophily facilitates the development of especially strong and dense ethnic networks in cities with large populations of particular ethnic groups.[38] However, these ethnically based relationships are not necessarily also spatially based. The strength of relationships rooted in a common ethnic heritage allows them to be maintained over long distances, across different neighborhoods and municipal boundaries.[39] Thus, like communities in general, ethnic enclaves are not simply built around their members' ethnicity or place of residence, but are built around their ethnically based relationships. Moreover, like other kinds of communities, ethnic enclaves are not lost to assimilation, and are not merely saved by their members' common backgrounds, but represent a kind of liberated social group, albeit one that is able to maintain a distinctive subculture and identity.

But, how can ethnically based relationships give rise to a distinctive subculture and identity? As with the formation and maintenance of other types of subcultural social circles and groups, the role of foci are critical. In some cases, a specific neighborhood may serve as an important focus organizing ethnic relationships, especially when the members of the enclave all live in close proximity to one another. This might occur by choice or because newly arriving immigrants often live with immigrants who arrived earlier. But, location is perhaps most powerful as a focus when ethnic groups are spatially clustered through forced segregation, as in the case of the Jewish ghetto in Venice, Italy in the 1500s, or the many African American ghettos formed in American cities during the twentieth century through Jim Crow laws and restrictive lending practices. In other cases, employment in a particular industry or occupation may be important, especially when members of an ethnic population are pushed or pulled into particular types of jobs.

Although location and employment may serve as organizing foci, cutting across these and still more important as organizing foci are the various institutions that exist to serve the ethnic population. As with any segment of the population, particular institutions exist to serve particular ethnic groups. These might include restaurants and grocery stores that offer familiar dishes and ingredients, community and cultural centers that host such events as screenings of foreign films or recitals of traditional music, and religious institutions that reflect the theological traditions of the homeland. Indeed, even establishments offering routine goods and services such as car repair or cell phones can be ethnically specific institutions if they are operated by members of the community or cater to the community's language needs. Whatever the nature of the institutions that serve as ethnic groups, they serve as central foci that organize the relationships of their members. Relationships among fellow ethnics are formed and maintained through repeated chance encounters doing even the most mundane of errands because all the group's members are funneled into the same set of grocery stores, restaurants, churches, and cultural venues.

The extent to which such institutions serve as foci for a particular ethnic group depends on the group's *institutional completeness*. An ethnic group is described as institutionally incomplete if they can obtain some goods and services from institutions within the ethnic community, but must rely on mainstream institutions for other needs. While a member of an ethnic group may repeatedly encounter and form relationships with fellow ethnics in the handful of institutions that serve his own ethnic community, he is also likely to encounter and form relationships with members of the native population while patronizing institutions that serve the wider population. In contrast, an ethnic group is described as institutionally complete if its members can obtain all the goods and services needed on a daily basis from their own, ethnically specific institutions. In such cases, there are limited opportunities for ethnic group members to form relationships with non-group members because there is little need to leave the community. Thus, when ethnic groups are characterized by a high level of institutional completeness, the networks among their members are likely to exhibit a high level of closure.[40]

The social boundaries around an ethnic enclave that distinguish members from non-members are of critical importance in maintaining the subculture and identity of the enclave. After all, no social circle or group could exist without some form of boundary. The boundaries, or more specifically, the membership that such boundaries imply, play at least two important roles. First, they allow the enclave to claim specific individuals as their own, including influential individuals whose behaviors and status in the community are markers of its subculture. Second, they allow individuals to claim the enclave as their own, thus permitting individuals to draw on the group's cultural symbols and practices. But, an ethnic enclave's boundaries are not simply the result of individuals' ethnic background and do not simply exist out there in the world. Instead, these boundaries are built upon the closure of individuals' social networks. Of course, the persistence of an ethnic enclave with a subculture of its own does not require that its members be completely isolated from the larger urban society in which they are located. But, greater levels of closure, achieved through greater residential or economic segregation, or through greater institutional completeness, make an enclave's boundaries more recognizable and defensible. In contrast, as enclave members increasingly form relationships with non-members, reducing the level of closure, the enclave's boundaries become blurred, and may disappear entirely.[41]

Thus, from a network perspective, an ethnic enclave is not necessarily a place, nor is it even a group of people with a common ethnic background. Indeed, many cities have very large populations of specific ethnic groups, possibly even living in close proximity, but no ethnic enclaves. Instead, an ethnic enclave is a specific pattern of relationships among individuals, wherever they may live or work, characterized by high levels of density and ethnically based closure. Enclaves, like other social groups, can maintain distinctive subcultural practices, but also can significantly influence the migration and economic patterns of its members within the city. For most members of urban ethnic enclaves, the selection of a host city and of a job on arrival are guided by information obtained through relationships with earlier waves of migrants, a process known as *chain migration*. The dense and ethnically closed networks serve as channels for information about where to go, as well as channels through which jobs within the community are distributed. Ordinarily such dense and closed networks yield a bonding form of social capital that, while useful for the maintenance of subcultural practices, is the 'wrong' kind of network for obtaining new jobs or other useful resources. However, in the case of ethnic immigrants, these networks can provide more than simply bonding social capital. They provide membership in an enclave community, which as a recognizable group with an identity known even to non-members, becomes a resource in itself by making its members visible to potential employers.[42]

The academic literature is filled with examples of specific ethnic enclaves in cities around the world, but just a few help to illustrate that the role of networks is not merely theoretical.[43] In some cases, like that of the Hmong community in Minneapolis-St. Paul or depicted in the 2008 Clint Eastwood film *Gran Torino*, ethnic enclaves are held together through kinship networks. Networks based on descent and marriage place significant restrictions on membership in the community, thus ensuring its closure to outsiders, including other Hmong individuals lacking the necessary kinship ties. Moreover, because these restrictive networks also shape membership in economic and political networks, this network closure offers a way of preserving not only subcultural practices but also of keeping resources within the community.[44]

In other cases, kinship ties may play a significant role, but relationships based on other cultural similarities such as religion or occupation may be more important. Populations claiming Jewish heritage have long formed enclaves with clearly marked geographic and network boundaries, and thus have been a common focus for research on ethnic enclaves. Of particular interest have been the Hasidic Jewish enclave in New York city, focused around employment in garment and jewelry trades, and the densely networked groups of Israeli immigrants in Los Angeles, many of whose interactions are focused around their former participation in a kibbutz. Indeed, even the original Jewish enclave—the Venetian Ghetto of the sixteenth century—was occupationally focused around those involved in money lending. In each of these cases, the dense and closed networks permitted members of the enclaves to develop skills in, and near monopoly control over, particular economic activities in their respective cities, in turn highlighting the enclave's boundaries and giving it a subculture and identity of its own. Moreover, perhaps more than enclaves maintained by other ethnic groups, Jewish enclaves often maintain their closure through very high levels of institutional completeness: Kosher delis, Hebrew bookstores, and yeshivas devoted to the study of religious texts. Enclave members have few needs to venture outside the community, and thus few opportunities (or inclination) to form relationships with non-members.[45]

In still other cases, ethnic enclaves can find cohesion through network-based strategies for dealing with their members' shared challenges. For example, communities of poor Mexicans living at the edges of Mexico City, or having recently arrived in central Los Angeles, often form tight-knit communities that take on the characteristics of ethnic enclaves and allow their members, as a cohesive group, to confront the daily struggles of living in poverty. Illustrating the function of reciprocity, enclave members provide assistance for one another when they are able, with the expectation that others will provide assistance when it is needed. Indeed, reciprocity plays such a crucial role in these enclave communities that it has become an institutionalized element of their subculture known as *confianza*. This level of reciprocity is facilitated by yet another subcultural practice that is also rooted in networks of relationships. The practice of *compadrazgo*, or fictive kinship, allows for the formation of very strong network connections even between individuals who are not related to one another. Based on patterns of reciprocated interactions, unrelated individuals come to be viewed as if they were, in fact, members of one's own family. As these examples illustrate, ethnic enclaves are a network phenomenon that may arise from combinations of kinship relations, community institutions, and subcultural practices made possible by the networks themselves.[46]

Of course, ethnic enclaves are not walled-off islands in urban areas. Instead, they influence and are influenced by the other ethnic groups and the majority of groups that surround them, in the case of cities, often in very close physical proximity. But, how do enclaves, which by definition have boundaries based on their lack of interaction with non-members, come to engage the rest of the urban world? It can be useful to consider two kinds of openness and closure. First, an enclave may be either weak or robust, based on its level of institutional completeness. In weak enclaves such as the Polish immigrants in Chicago, members must go outside the community to obtain various goods and services, while in robust enclaves such as the Hasidic Jews in New York, members can remain inside the community for their entire lives. Second, an enclave may be permeable or impermeable, based on membership requirements and the ease of joining its network. In permeable enclaves such as the Cuban community in Miami, inter-ethnic marriages are common and provide access to outsiders, while in impermeable enclaves such as the Hmong in Minneapolis, access to the network is restricted to blood relatives. Thus, weak and permeable enclaves are more likely to interact with their host societies than robust and impermeable enclaves. But, other factors can also be important. For example, enclave members that participate in ethnic businesses are more likely to have closed networks, while those with more education, income, and time in the host society are more likely to have open networks. Most importantly, however, network closure and the bonding social capital that makes enclaves possible does not preclude network openness and the bridging social capital that makes integration possible. That is, because an individual's or a community's network can have both bridging and bonding characteristics, the goals of preserving ethnic subcultures and integrating newcomers into the mainstream culture are not necessarily in conflict. Indeed, as T. S. Eliot observed, "A people should be neither too united nor too divided if its culture is to flourish."[47]

*   *   *   *   *

Despite the great diversity and crowding in modern cities, urban dwellers nonetheless find themselves drawn into recognizable social groups and circles. Much of what makes those groups distinctive are their members' particular patterns of behavior, their subcultures. But, groups and subcultures do not simply float in urban areas waiting for people to join them. Adopting a network perspective to understanding urban subculture demonstrates that they arise from the patterns of relationships among people. In their simplest form, a social circle is simply a collection of individuals that interact more with one another than with those outside the circle. This type of network closure draws a boundary around the group, and allows its members to cultivate, maintain, and enforce their own subcultural practices. Of course, as this chapter has demonstrated, there is striking variety to the groups and subcultures that can be found in cities, ranging from informal social clubs, to organized criminal gangs, to formal voluntary associations, to ethnic enclaves. Even more striking, however, is that just below this great diversity are many of the same kinds of networks. Diversity, however, also calls attention to another fact of urban life: some people and groups are powerful and influential, while others are powerless and marginalized. Why?

Discussion Questions and Activities

1. What would happen to the social world if there were very few locations, events, or groups that could serve as foci around which social relationships and networks could form? Could this ever happen?

2. Make a list of the organizations that you and four friends are each affiliated with. From this information, create two different one-mode networks: a person-to-person network and an organization-to-organization network. Does the person-to-person network show the potential for one or more unique subcultures to develop? Does the organization-to-organization network show the potential for some organizations to influence others? Do these patterns match your expectations?

3. Think about a voluntary association (a team, club, organization) to which you belong. Has its niche changed over time? Why has it changed? Did these changes have an effect on the association's subculture?

4. From the perspective of social networks and social capital, is there a difference between an ethnic enclave and a ghetto? What accounts for the economic vibrancy of the former and the vicious circle of poverty in the latter?

5. How could the methods introduced in the first chapter be used to study the concepts introduced in this chapter? Similarly, how could the methods introduced in this chapter be used to study the concepts introduced in the first chapter?

4
POLITICS
WE DON'T WANT NOBODY NOBODY SENT

Communities and social circles play an important role organizing life in modern cities, and as the last two chapters have demonstrated, thinking about them from a network perspective helps to show how. But, within modern cities, their communities and social circles, some individuals and groups are more powerful and exercise more influence over urban life than others. In nineteenth-century New York, William "Boss" Tweed wielded enormous political power and influence behind the closed doors of Tammany Hall. From 1955 to 1976, Mayor Richard J. Daley controlled the political scene in Chicago from within the slightly more open city council chambers. And even more recently, individuals and groups across the political spectrum, including Barack Obama and the Tea Party, have turned to completely open new media outlets such as FaceBook and Twitter to cultivate support and broadcast their messages to cities across America. Locating these political insiders has long been of interest, especially to muckraking journalists seeking to expose corruption by asking "Say, kid, who is 'it' around here . . . What I mean is, who's running the shebang? Who knows what's what and—who decides?"[1]

But, simply knowing who is politically powerful in cities is only part of the story. A far more interesting question is, why are they powerful? Where does influence over urban affairs come from? Although the names and issues change from city to city, and from decade to decade, power and influence in urban politics have always been a matter of strategically built and maintained relationships, and thus of networks. But, what kind of networks? Abner Mikva's story about trying to break into mid-century Chicago politics gives some indication:

> The year I started law school, 1948, was the year that Douglas and Stevenston were heading up the Democratic ticket in Illinois. I was all fired up from the Students for Douglas and Stevenson and passed this storefront, the 8th Ward Regular Democratic Organization. I came in and said I wanted to help. Dead silence. "Who sent you?" the committeeman said. I said, "Nobody." He said, "We don't want nobody nobody sent." Then he said, "We ain't got no jobs." I said, "I don't want a job." He said, "We don't want nobody that don't want a job. Where are you from anyway?" I said, "University of Chicago." He said, "We don't want nobody from the University of Chicago in this organization."[2]

We frequently hear the claim that "it's not what you know, but who you know." Clearly this was true in Mikva's case. Simply being a well-educated individual, attending one of the most prestigious law schools in the country, was not enough. Because he didn't know anyone inside the Democratic Party—because no one had 'sent' him—he was not part of the political network and was treated as an outsider. But in many cases, it's also not just who you know, but who *they* know. Mikva may have known a few politically connected individuals from the student group, Students for Douglas and Stevenson, but unless they also had some political connections, who had some political connections, and so on, even these may have done him little good.

In this chapter, I explore how a network perspective can help make sense of two enduring questions of urban politics: who is influential, and why? I begin by considering a long-running debate between sociologists and political scientists about the nature of community power and how to measure it. Many of these questions can be resolved by considering a special type of network—an exchange network—in which individuals and groups are connected to one another and gain power and influence through their ability and willingness to exchange favors and resources. In many cases, individuals can gain still greater power through their position within exchange networks with the help of political organizations that concentrate network interactions and provide strength in numbers. But, acquiring and exercising political power through networks is not restricted just to elite movers and shakers. Even small-scale grassroots efforts toward urban social change and activism rely critically on managing networks of relationships among supporters and detractors. While most of this chapter focuses on the networks of politics, I conclude by considering something slightly different: the politics of networks. Not only are networks important for exercising political power, but political power is also important for building networks, like the roads and power lines and fiber optics that give modern cities their shape.[3]

The Community Power Debate

Although it is often clear that some people are more influential in urban politics than others, identifying who is influential and why in a systematic way can be quite challenging. As a result, much of the research on community power from the 1940s until the 1970s focused on a debate about the best way to identify who is influential. The earliest approach, known as the *positional approach*, assumed that the most influential and powerful members of a community are those that occupy the top official positions. For example, adopting the positional approach to understand how influence is used to guide the affairs of a city, one might study the behavior of the city's mayor or the president of a local bank. Because such individuals occupy positions that give them official powers and authority—the mayor to make laws or the bank president to approve or deny loan applications–they are viewed as the most able to influence the behavior of others. Additionally, occupying these important positions also suggests that these individuals have control over resources—the mayor over the city's tax revenue or the bank president over the bank's deposits—that can be used to influence others. This logic has its origins in the work of Marx, who argued that "the history of all hitherto existing societies is the history of class struggles," where the capitalist class or bourgeoisie exercised power over and influenced the behavior of the working class or proletariat through their control over resources and official authority.[4]

The positional approach has been used to identify those with influence in many different settings, ranging from small towns to entire nations. For example, in their study of Middletown, the Lynds discovered that the X family controlled many of the town's affairs. As one of the town's residents put it, "if I'm out of work I go to the X plant; if I need money I go to the X bank . . . my children go to the X college; when I get sick I go to the X hospital . . . "[5] In this instance, the X family was influential because they occupied key positions in each of the town's major institutions. Similarly, in his study of national politics, C. Wright Mills found that those occupying key military and corporate positions exercised the greatest influence over national affairs.[6] In many studies adopting the positional approach, once influential individuals are identified based on their position in the community, attention turns to locating individual characteristics that explain why they occupy these positions, and thus why they are influential. Early studies used detailed life histories or simple demographic characteristics such as occupation and education to explain the influence of, for example, political bosses in Philadelphia or school board officials in a small Midwestern town.[7] More recently, it has become common for studies in management and business to search for the personal traits of effective business and political leaders.[8]

Although it may seem intuitive to assume that those in a community's top ranking positions and those with the characteristics of strong leaders are the most influential, many were critical of the positional approach's focus on individual characteristics. Critics argued that, because influence and power are exercised over specific others, the search for influential individuals should focus on relationships between people. An alternative to the positional approach, the *reputational approach*, drew on Moreno's method of sociometry by asking community members to identify those whom they believed to be influential. Early studies adopting the reputational approach found that those with a reputation for being influential often did not occupy key positions. For example, one study found that the town newspaper's editor received only one nomination as an influential person, and the professors at the town's university were viewed as influential no more often than any of the town's other residents. These early findings suggested that while individual characteristics such as occupying an important position might contribute to being influential, they certainly do not make an individual influential.[9]

Building on these early studies, a vast body of research emerged that adopted the reputational approach and increasingly drew on network perspectives by focusing on relationships of influence between people. Guided by sociologist Floyd Hunter's study of Atlanta, which he called "Regional City," this work examined several different cities. Despite the differences between these cities, the reputational networks that researchers found consistently told a similar story about how relationships structure influence in urban politics. First, all community members tended to identify the same set of people as the most influential. For example, in the network that Hunter observed in Atlanta where lines (edges) connect people (nodes) who viewed one another as influential (see Figure 4.1), the study participants consistently viewed person 14 and person 27 as influential. Second, these highly influential people tended to view each other as influential. In Atlanta, person 14 and person 27 as well as those around them all viewed one another as influential.

Together, these findings suggested that urban political influence is concentrated in the hands of a relatively small *elite* group of individuals. Most community members' opinions about local issues were heavily influenced by the elite, while the opinions of the elite were primarily influenced by one another. In network terms, this elite had the properties of a *clique*: a group of densely connected individuals embedded within a larger network. Such an arrangement made it possible for the elite to wield a great deal of political power, not only because they were highly influential, but because they could operate as a single, monolithic entity: as THE elite. As with social capital, such a political network can have both positive and negative effects. For example, in a city with a cliquish political network among elites, decisions can often be made quickly, but only because those with alternative points of view have little opportunity to influence their outcomes.

By introducing a network perspective, the reputational approach brought research on urban politics closer to directly examining the structure of community power. However, it was criticized on two grounds. First, because researchers asked "Who is influential?" rather than "Is anyone influential?" when measuring the reputation network, they assumed in advance that some individuals were highly influential and thus that some elite group dominated the community. Second, the focus was on individuals' reputations for being influential, rather than on their actual influence over the outcomes of specific decisions.[10] Thus, critics suggested still another approach—the *decisional approach*—that also drew upon a network perspective, but concentrated on individuals' involvement in a range of political issues. One of the most influential studies adopting the decisional approach focused on the individuals who participated in making decisions about urban

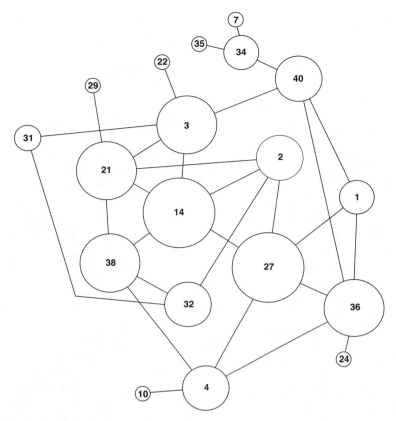

Figure 4.1 A Reputational Influence Network.[11]
Source: reprinted with permission from University of North Carolina Press.

redevelopment, public education, and political nominations in New Haven, Connecticut. Led by political scientist Robert Dahl, these researchers examined official documents and interviewed key informants to understand which citizens were influential in making decisions about each issue-area.

Although their focus was often on the specific details of each individual's involvement in the political process, viewing participation in decision making as a type of network helps to clarify some of their findings. The decisional approach focuses on which people participate in making decisions about which issues, which can then be represented as a two-mode network like the one on the left in Figure 4.2. In this example, person B participated in making decisions only about urban redevelopment, but person C participated in making decisions about both redevelopment and public education. This two-mode network can be transformed into a one-mode network, as shown in the right panel of Figure 4.2 (see Method Note 7), where two people are connected if they both participated in making a decision on the same issue. Because those participating in making a decision about the same issue are likely to try to influence one another, this network shows who influences whom.

The network in 4.2, and the findings of Dahl and others using the decisional approach, revealed the presence of cliques that exercised influence in certain issue areas. For example, the A-B-C clique exercises influence over issues of redevelopment, while the D-E-F clique exercises influence over issues of public education. However, unlike the reputational approach networks in Figure 4.1, none of the cliques is clearly more influential than another. In fact, while clique members focus

METHOD NOTE 9: CLIQUES

When examining a large network, there is often interest in locating smaller sub-structures embedded within it. A *clique* is a general term for a set of nodes in which the members of the clique are more connected to each other than to non-members. Cliques are important because they define the immediate environment for a node. These local environments can often influence behavior as much as, or more than the structure of the network as a whole.

There are many different ways to define and identify cliques. The simplest, but also most restrictive, definition of a clique is the *maximal complete subgraph*. A maximal complete subgraph is a set of nodes that are all connected to one another. In the example network above, there are three such groups: A-B-C, D-E-F and X-Y-Z. This definition of clique is very narrow; it requires that every member be directly connected to every other member. However, groups of people might be influential even if they do not meet this strict criterion. For example, democratic city council members may still work in unison as a political party, even if they do not all know one another.

To take this possibility into account, the maximal complete subgraph definition of a clique can be relaxed so that clique members do not need to be directly connected to one another. One possibility is a 2-clique: A node is a member of a 2-Clique if it is no more than two steps away from every other member. In this example, there are several different 2-Cliques. By relaxing the definition of a clique in this way, Q joins X-Y-Z because it is one step away from Z, and only two steps away from X and Y. Similarly, Q also joins D-E-F because it is one step away from E, and two steps away from F and D. Two even larger 2-cliques are also present: A-B-C-D-F and A-C-D-E-F.

The maximal complete subgraph definition can also be relaxed so that clique members do not need to be connected to every other member. One possibility is a 2-Core: A node is a member of a 2-Core if it is directly connected to at least two other members. In this example, there are two 2-Cores: A-B-C-D-E-F and X-Y-Z.

There are still more ways of defining a clique. For example, using the definitions above, it is possible to search for a 3-Clique or a 5-Core. There is no one 'right' way to define a clique; different definitions are appropriate in different research settings. But, in the sociogram above, the 2-Core definition seems to do the best job of identifying the two visually obvious substructures. In UCINET: Network → Subgroups → Cliques and Network → Regions → K-Core.[12]

on particular issue-areas, they also influence those in other cliques. For example, although the A-B-C clique is primarily influential over decisions about redevelopment, it also plays some role in decisions about education and nominations through person C. Such a pattern suggests that urban political influence is not concentrated in the hands of a small elite, but instead that decisions are made by a *plurality* of overlapping and interacting groups. Such pluralistic distributions of political influence tend to be especially common in larger cities, cities with diverse economies and populations, and cities with governments that encourage citizen participation. They more closely approximate the ideal of democracy by giving multiple groups a voice at the table. However, they

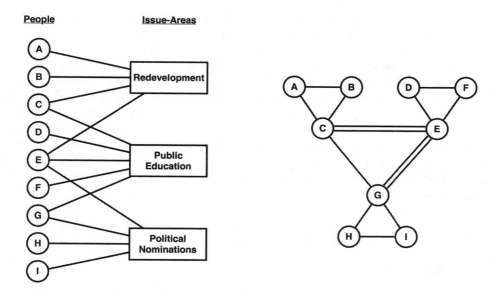

Figure 4.2 A Decisional Influence Network.

can also be inefficient and instigate political battles, especially when the multiple groups cannot find common ground.[13]

Some have called attention to a troubling pattern in this research: the type of political structure a city seems to have depends on what kinds of questions the researcher asks. Sociologists using the reputational approach tend to find that cities are governed by elites, but political scientists using the decisional approach tend to find that cities are governed by a plurality.[14] This highlights the importance of considering a city's political scene from multiple angles when trying to understand not only who is influential, but more generally to understand whether a city has a concentrated or diffuse power structure.[15] For example, one might use the positional approach to generate an initial list of potentially influential people, and then use networks of both reputation and decision making to add other influentials, or to remove those who are not influential.[16] Using such a multifaceted approach, different types of city leaders often emerge. The highly visible heads of a community's institutions often serve as 'institutional leaders' who have a reputation for being influential, even if they rarely participate in the actual making of decisions. In contrast, the 'effectors' and 'activists' may lack the visibility and reputation of institutional leaders, but are involved in the day-to-day decisions that guide a city's affairs.[17]

Drawing together these various ways of viewing the urban political landscape, it can be helpful to think about influential individuals as playing a series of metaphorical games, where each game has its own goals. For example, business people play the 'business game,' where the goal is to generate profit, while politicians play the 'political game,' where the goal is to remain in office. To succeed, players in one game often use players in another game to influence the outcome of a particular issue. For example, a business person seeking to encourage the passage of a pro-business law may draw a politician into the business game. This perspective, known as the *ecology of games*, shows how urban politics emerges from the linkages among different people, playing different games, who are brought together around specific issues of mutual interest. Each person may have a reputation for being influential, each game may have particularly powerful positions, and each issue requires a series of decisions.

The case of the debate surrounding the construction of Paul Brown Stadium in Cincinnati, Ohio illustrates how individuals' reputations, positions in games, and decisions about issues are linked by a network that guides community affairs. Through much of the 1990s, the political scene in Cincinnati was dominated by discussion about the pros and cons of building a new home for the Bengals to play football. The discussion involved several key actors, including Bengals owner Mike Brown, Cincinnati Reds owner Marge Schott, the city council, and the general public. Each of these actors were involved in different 'games,' such as business competition for the team owners and urban development for the city council. Finally, the larger debate involved several sub-issues, including whether the existing Riverfront Stadium could simply be renovated, and where a new stadium would be located. The outcomes in this case were not guided by an all-powerful elite like Hunter's reputational networks might suggest, nor by a democratic plurality as Dahl's decisional networks might suggest. Instead, they were driven by a more complex pattern of linkages among people, the games they were involved in, and the sub-issues that were most important. Only by paying attention to these multiple elements of urban political decisions, and how they are linked to one another, it is possible to understand who—or what—is running the show.[18]

Quid Pro Quo

Adopting a network perspective helps clarify who is influential in urban politics. Indeed, by combining several different network-based ways of thinking about political influence, the ecology of games approach can provide a holistic picture of the political landscape, telling a more complete story about individuals' influence over particular decisions and in particular settings. However, a deeper question remains: How do influential individuals actually exercise their influence? It is one thing to observe that certain people play key decision-making roles, but quite another to understand why they are able to do so.

Networks can also be helpful to understand how and why some individuals or groups are able to exercise more influence than others. Specifically, exchange networks and exchange theory are useful. Exchange theory argues that much of the social world can be understood as the result of exchanges of resources between individuals. The resources can be physical objects such as money or a gift, non-physical such as information, and even symbolic such as friendship. It is possible to view major systems such as capitalism as built up from a series of exchanges: workers and managers exchange labor and wages. But, even daily personal interactions are structured as a series of exchanges: friends exchange companionship and social support. An exchange network focuses on the patterns of these kinds of exchanges, asking who exchanges with whom.[19]

Figure 4.3 illustrates several different types of exchanges. The simplest type of exchange relationship occurs between two people, or a *dyad*. Dyadic exchanges can be symmetric, as when two neighbors do favors for one another: one may borrow a proverbial 'cup of sugar,' while the other later offers to help rake leaves. Communities' social relations are often organized around these types of exchanges, where informal and unspoken dyadic contracts allow individuals to expect that favors and other exchanges will be reciprocated. These informal contracts work because each member of the dyad gets something from the exchange and because violations of the contract can be punished: if the neighbor does not return the favor by offering to rake leaves, he cannot ask to borrow sugar in the future. However, dyadic exchanges can also be asymmetric, as when a local official can either grant or withhold a building permit for a homeowner. It is in asymmetric exchanges such as this where power and influence can arise. In this example, there is little the homeowner can do if he is dissatisfied with the official's decision; there is no give-and-take in this exchange.[20]

Dyadic exchanges can help explain the interaction between two people, but when many dyadic exchanges overlap, they can form larger political structures that help explain how influence is

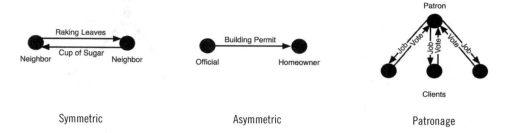

Figure 4.3 Types of Exchange Networks.

exercised in the wider community or city. One example of such a structure is a patronage system, where reciprocal exchange relationships form between an influential patron and several relatively less influential clients. The Sicilian Mafia is a classic example of such a patronage system. The local mafia boss, acting as a patron, offers a town's residents protection from the corrupt local government in exchange for their loyalty as clients. Similar systems can be found in other cultures, including small Mexican villages where an influential individual who distributes resources to others is described as a *cacique*.[21] Patronage systems are also found in modern American cities, with the Chicago Democratic machine offering the most visible example. During his time in office from 1955 to 1976, Mayor Richard J. Daley distributed jobs to the city's residents, especially new immigrants and members of white ethnic neighborhoods, in exchange for their loyalty at the poll.[22] Although such systems are functional—Daley secured the support of voters, and voters secured much needed jobs—they also undermine the basic ideas of democracy, and serve to perpetuate the patron's influence.[23]

Dyadic and patron–client exchanges are the building blocks of political influence in urban settings, but they often combine to form still more complex exchange networks. Individuals that participate in many different exchanges, and with many different partners, are more likely to be involved and influential in community affairs.[24] But, certain positions and roles in exchange networks can make some individuals especially powerful. In some cases, individuals can become powerful by playing the role of a *broker*. In an exchange network, a broker is an individual that facilitates an exchange between two others who are not connected. The example information exchange networks among three politicians in Figure 4.4 illustrate what a broker position looks like, and why a broker can be powerful. Suppose person C needs some information from person A about an upcoming vote in the city council. In the network on the left, where A and C are directly connected, they can exchange this information directly; there is no need to rely on a broker. In contrast, in the network on the right, where A and C are not directly connected, they cannot exchange this information on their own. Instead, they must rely on person B, who can act as a broker. In this case, B is powerful because she can demand something in exchange for her assistance, such as C's support in an upcoming election. For this reason, brokers are often described using the Latin phrase *tertius gaudens* or the 'third who benefits.'

Brokers, sometimes called power brokers, are often the most influential individuals in urban politics, even though they may not have a reputation for being powerful, or may not directly participate in making decisions. That is, the most powerful brokers often wield their influence 'behind the scenes.' For example, Robert Moses' near complete control over the development of New York City from the 1920s to the 1960s has been attributed to his ability to play the broker role between local and national groups. Moreover, brokers have been key players in urban politics for centuries. The Medici family ruled the Italian city of Florence from the late 1400s until the

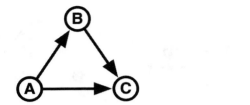
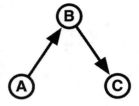

Figure 4.4 Brokerage in Exchange Networks.

early 1700s because, through a strategic network of marriage and business partnerships, they acted as a broker between the region's other noble families.[25]

While individuals can become powerful by acting as brokers in exchange networks, they can also achieve power through others' dependence upon them. Figure 4.5 shows two possible networks among a group of politicians who exchange political support for one another's projects. Suppose B needs one extra vote for a proposal he has introduced in the city council. In the network on the left, he could get this extra vote from A, but he could also get it from X, Y, or Z. As a result, he is not particularly dependent upon A for the vote he needs. In contrast, in the network on the right, A is the only person who can give B the extra vote he needs; B must depend on A. Because B is dependent upon A, A has some power over B. For example, A might be able to demand a political favor in exchange for her vote. This simple example illustrates the idea that 'it's not who you know, but who they know.' A knows B in both networks, but A is only powerful over B in the network on the right. Why? Because in the network on the right, B does not know anyone else who can give him the political support he needs, but in the network on the left B knows many others and can ignore any demands that A might make.

Thinking about power and influence as coming from dependence in exchanges helps make sense of something that Hunter found puzzling when he studied the elites in 1950s Atlanta. Looking at the sociogram that appears in figure 12, he noticed that "Number 14, George Delbert, ... might be considered the 'star' since he has the highest number of mutual choices. However, the study of [Atlanta] was convincing on the point that number 40, Charles Homer, was the more powerful man."[26] How could this be? Although Delbert knew many people, they also knew many people. Because the people connected to Delbert had many other contacts as well, they were not dependent upon him, and thus Delbert had relatively little power over them. In contrast, Homer knew just a few people, but of the people he did know, they did not know many others. Because the people connected to Homer had few other contacts, they were dependent upon him for access to Atlanta's political scene, and Homer had power over them.[27]

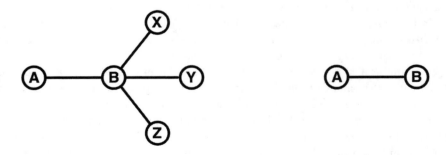

Figure 4.5 Dependence in Exchange Networks.

METHOD NOTE 10: POWER IN EXCHANGE NETWORKS

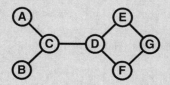

There are many different approaches to measuring how much *power* a node has in an exchange network. One simple approach defines a node's power as the sum of the reciprocal of each of its alter's number of connections. For example, in the network above, node D has three alters: C, E, and F. Node C has three connections (to A, B, and D), node E has two connections (to D and G), and node F has two connections (to D and G). To compute node D's power, take the reciprocal of each of these numbers, then add the reciprocals together: $1/3 + 1/2 + 1/2 = 1.33$.

Compare this to C's power in the network. Node C also has three alters: A, B, and D. Node A has one connection (to C), node B has one connection (to C), and node D has three connections (to C, E, and F). To compute node C's power, take the reciprocal of each of these numbers, then add the reciprocals together: $1/1 + 1/1 + 1/3 = 2.33$.

In this network, nodes C and D have the same number of connections. So, why is C more powerful than D? Power in an exchange network depends on more than just how many alters a node has ("who you know"), but also on how many alters your alters have ("who your friends know"). Node C is powerful because two of its alters—A and B—have no alters of their own except C. Thus, in an exchange between C and A, if C offers an unfair trade, A has nowhere else to turn; C can dominate and control A. Similarly, C can also dominate and control B. In contrast, node D is not particularly powerful because it cannot completely dominate and control any of its alters; each of its alters have alternatives if D tries to offer an unfair exchange. The 'centpow' command in the STATA statistical software can compute power scores for each node in a network.[28]

Strength in Numbers

Many studies of urban politics, whether they adopt a network perspective or not, attempt to identify and explain the behavior of the most powerful or influential individuals. However, power and influence in urban politics are not exercised by individuals alone, but also by coalitions of individuals that are linked to one another in a network. These coalitions often form to help their members achieve common political goals such as defeating an opponent or ensuring the passage of a new law. By operating as a single entity, such coalitions can draw on the influence of their individual members, and can exercise more power over political outcomes than any single politician or business leader working alone. As a result, urban leadership programs are often formed with the goal of bringing local leaders into contact with one another and forging coalitions that can more effectively address issues.[29]

Coalitions are not necessarily composed just of major politicians in large cities, but are often a natural way to confront conflict even in small villages and towns. Indeed, many early anthropologists who adopted a network approach were concerned with documenting the formation and operation of coalitions to exercise power. In one case, competing coalitions of ranch owners from neighboring villages in Sicily formed to defend their rights to their land, while in another, the relationships among the men in a Tunisian village changed following a conflict over land ownership as they 'took sides.'[30] But, in his description of liquor bootlegging and illegal gambling in one American city in the 1930s, sociologist William Foote Whyte (1914–2000) provided a particularly colorful account of how power and influence in the neighborhood shifted from a single individual managing relationships with others, to a carefully run coalition, or racket:

> Mario was powerfully built and, using fists or a gun, did his own fighting. T.S. fought when he had to, but he built up an organization which cut violence to a minimum. Mario was a pirate; T.S. is a businessman.[31]

Although less criminal in nature, similar kinds of coalitions can be found among city council members, who work and vote together to achieve their political goals. Such voting coalitions can overcome gridlock and endless debate, but, as has been the case in some cities such as Chicago, can also transform the city council into a rubber stamp that simply follows the orders of a powerful mayor.[32] Still larger political coalitions, known as regimes, extend beyond groups of politicians to include other community and business leaders. Urban political regimes form because local governments, to be successful, must cooperate with other local groups who control resources or are influential in the community. Thus, regimes are groups of individuals focused on a particular political agenda, and linked to one another through exchange relationships that allow them to trade information, resources, and political support. Although the individuals participating in a regime may change over time, regimes themselves can persist as others take their place in the network. As a result, regimes can span longer periods of time than an individual mayor's administration or an individual business leader's stint as CEO.[33]

In many cases, urban regimes are composed of individuals focused on an agenda of urban economic growth, and especially on downtown redevelopment. In fact, regimes with this focus are so common that they have a specific name: *growth machines*.[34] In growth machine regimes, networks of city and business leaders work together to encourage downtown investment and new construction, as well as to attract new businesses and residents, all with the goal of increasing the value of the land they own. However, regimes can also form around more targeted political agendas, and expand to include individuals outside political and business circles. For example, in the late 1980s, the pro-growth regime in Chicago drew together key figures from the area's corporations to pool support for hosting the 1992 World's Fair. Similarly, in cities seeking to make the downtown area more attractive to new businesses and residents by highlighting the arts, leaders from local non-profit and human service agencies are frequently drawn into the regime network.[35] But, regimes retain their power and influence over urban politics only as long as their members remain focused on a common goal. When the focus shifts, for example in Detroit from downtown development to education and more recently to managing population loss, or when the common focus disappears altogether as it has in Atlanta, the network connections that link regime members to one another weaken and the network begins to fall apart.[36]

Coalitions and regimes can serve to concentrate the political interests of individuals, pooling their power and influence. But, individuals can also act as brokers and liaisons that link different groups and organizations together, and allow them to share their power and resources.[37] Frequently, a single person will sit on the board of directors of multiple organizations, not only allowing the individual to reap the benefits of serving as a broker, but also allowing the organizations to influence one another and benefit from sharing information and resources. This practice, known as a 'board interlock' or an 'interlocking directorate,' was outlawed in 1914 between companies that are competitors, but remains common between companies that are not competitors, and especially between cultural organizations such as museums and theaters. The individuals that occupy these broker positions tend to be even more influential in urban politics than those who are top officials in just one organization. Similarly, the organizations that are well connected by these brokers also tend to exercise greater political power than organizations whose boards of directors are isolated. Not surprisingly, then, two types of organizations tend to be particularly important in cities: social clubs where political elites interact informally but nonetheless exert their influence over other elites, and banks that can channel loans and other resources to some causes and away from others.[38]

Everyday Action

Networks not only shape the political behavior of career politicians such as mayors or business leaders such as local bank presidents, but are also important for the more mundane and everyday political behaviors of urban dwellers and their communities. For example, the likelihood that 'regular folks' will participate in local politics by voting, or joining a protest, or volunteering to help a local candidate depends heavily on their personal social networks. Similarly, the likelihood that a whole neighborhood can act as a group to achieve a desired outcome, such as advocating for a change in the local zoning laws, depends on the structure of the network among the neighborhood's residents.

Participating in the political affairs of one's city or neighborhood can be both challenging and time consuming, but is also important for the democratic process. It is not surprising that those with more education or income, and those with a greater investment in the community such as homeowners and families with children, are more likely to get involved. However, moving beyond these simple individual characteristics, one's pattern of interactions with others in the area also plays an important role. Local networks provide pathways for the *diffusion* or spread of information about local issues and of behaviors such as the decision to vote. For example, those who frequently interact or discuss local issues with their neighbors are more likely to participate in local politics. Similarly, those who are around others who are participating in local politics are more likely to get involved themselves.[39]

The specific network characteristics that predict individuals' political participation, however, may differ depending on the circumstances. In cases where the goals are well defined, such as participation in a local political party, dense networks often yield more participation because each member can encourage the involvement of others. In contrast, when the goals are ambiguous or changing, such as the common but amorphous goal to 'improve the neighborhood,' encouraging local political action is more challenging. Those with strong, dense networks within the community are likely to know what the community needs, but may not be able to access necessary resources. Those with weak, diffuse networks primarily outside the community are likely to have access to key resources, but may not be able to cultivate support among their neighbors whom they do not know. Thus, in such cases, those most likely to participate politically in the community are those with a network that includes some interactions within the neighborhood that provide encouragement and some interactions outside the neighborhood that provide access to new information and resources.[40]

Just as the likelihood of individuals' political participation rests on their personal social networks, the likelihood of community-level collective action depends on the structure of the whole community's network. Neighborhoods characterized by high levels of network density—what might be viewed as traditional, close-knit, or strong communities—are highly effective at informally controlling behavior within the neighborhood. For example, in the face of rising crime, the residents of such neighborhoods can often band together to ensure the safety of the area by looking after one another. However, these 'strong' communities are much less effective at responding to issues that come from outside the neighborhood, or at representing the interests of their members. Here,

METHOD NOTE 11: DIFFUSION THROUGH COHESION AND STRUCTURAL EQUIVALENCE

It is often useful to understand how resources such as information and behaviors such as voting diffuse or spread through a network, passing from one node to another. There are two network mechanisms that shape diffusion: cohesion and structural equivalence.

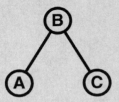

Resources such as information tend to diffuse through *cohesion*, which focuses on the direct connections between nodes. Resources diffuse from one node to the next, following a path of direct connections, much like the spread of the common cold or of a rumor. In the example network above, information is likely to spread from A to B because these two directly interact with one another.

In contrast, behaviors tend to diffuse through *structural equivalence*, which focuses on nodes that have similar patterns of connections. A's behavior is likely to diffuse to, or be adopted by, C because these two have the same pattern of connections: they are both connected to B, and to no one else. Imitation is one reason behaviors spread in this way: C imitates A's behavior because A is like him. There are many different ways to compute the degree of structural equivalence between two nodes. For example, the Jaccard Coefficient counts the proportion of times that two nodes both have a connection to the same alter. In UCINET: Tools → Similarities.

These two mechanisms often work together, in a two-step process. For example, in the context of political involvement, C is likely to learn about the candidates from B (cohesion). But, he is likely to decide to actually vote in the election by watching what A does (structural equivalence).[41]

neighborhoods characterized by sparse networks in which most residents' friends live outside the area or do not know one another—what might be viewed as a liberated community—are more effective. By drawing on the strengths of multiple residents with diverse network contacts, rather than on residents who simply know each other, these neighborhoods are more able to react to complicated outside forces.[42]

But, the ability of a neighborhood to pursue social change through collective action depends not simply on the density of the network. The case of Boston's West End offers an illustration. Researchers studying this Italian immigrant community found very dense, strong networks clustered around small groups of close family and friends. Neighbors knew one another, attended dinner parties together, and would help each other out. If any neighborhood could engage in collective action, the researchers thought, it would be this one. However, this community was unable to react to the city's 'urban renewal' program, which involved the demolition of large portions of the West End. Why? In addition to density, achieving neighborhood social change also depends on the presence of a specific type of connection within the network: bridging connections, or what Jane Jacobs intuitively called "hop-skip links."[43] Bridging connections link parts of a network that would otherwise be completely or mostly disconnected from one another (see the relatively closed network in Figure 3.4). They allow news about important neighborhood issues to spread, and for one group of close friends and neighbors to encourage other groups to join them in addressing these issues. The people at each end of the bridge, who make these important linkages possible by serving as liaisons, sometimes serve as community leaders, but other times may not even realize that they are glue that holds together otherwise disconnected groups of residents. The problem in the West End was the lack of such bridging connections; each dense cluster of family and friends was disconnected from the others (see the completely closed network in Figure 3.4). Thus, although each cluster might individually have been prepared to confront Boston's urban renewal program, they could not act together. In this instance, community collective action seemed easy from the researchers' up-close view that revealed dense networks, but stepping back to look at the community as a whole revealed a more fragmented network and helped explain why collective action never took hold.[44]

When the network among individuals generates the capacity for community collective action, this action can be applied to address a wide range of local issues. For example, small community-based groups have worked to bring sustainable transportation alternatives such as bicycling to their West London neighborhood. In other cases, community members work together to keep things such as landfills or power plants out of their neighborhood, rallying under the acronym NIMBY: Not in my backyard. Here, friendship networks lead to the expansion of collective action goals as one friend may enlist another to pursue her worthy cause, while linkages to outside political organizations can serve to keep community members narrowly focused on their cause. Such routine interactions among fellow cyclists or neighborhood friends can also pave the way for collective action on a much larger scale. The relationships that formed among residents of Paris's outer neighborhoods or *arrondissements* as they drank together in local taverns and wine shops became the foundation of the 1871 revolution and led to the creation of the Paris Commune, a short-lived but influential revolutionary government.[45]

The discussion of social capital in Chapter Two highlighted that it can come in two forms: bridging and bonding. But, this discussion of political participation and collective action highlights that it can also occur at two levels: individual and community (see Figure 4.6). Individual social capital, which can promote or facilitate individual political participation, depends on one's personal social network. In contrast, community social capital, which can promote or facilitate community

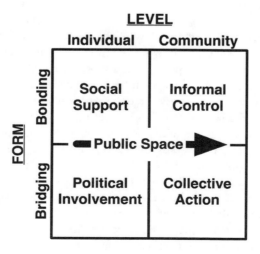

Figure 4.6 Forms and Levels of Social Capital.

collective action, depends on the structure of the community's network.[46] The question then remains, how might individual-level social capital and participation be transformed into community-level social capital and action? Some have suggested that the availability of public spaces in the city and neighborhood are critical. Public spaces such as parks, playgrounds, libraries, and community centers provide a place where neighborhood residents can interact with one another freely. Through these interactions, the bonding connections that give individuals a source for social support can become the bonding connections that allow whole communities to establish and enforce community norms. Similarly, they can transform the bridging network connections that encourage individuals to participate into the bridging connections that enable whole communities to band together for collective action.[47]

The Politics of Networks

This chapter has focused primarily on the networks of politics, that is, the patterns of interactions among people and groups in cities that give some more influence over urban affairs than others. While such networks of politics are important, it is also possible to think about the politics of networks. The next part of this book views the city as itself a type of network, and explores how various types of networks hold a city together, giving it both form and function. For example, the network of roads in a city gives its neighborhoods their distinctive shapes, and the network of cooperation among a city's agencies allows basic social services to be delivered to local residents. But, these kinds of networks do not simply appear fully formed; their structures are the result of much political maneuvering. Thus, while a focus on the networks of politics asks who is influential and why, a focus on the politics of networks asks why the roads go where they do.[48]

Questions about who controls the development of a city's infrastructure networks, or about what political forces influence the development of such networks, are certainly not new ones. In early nineteenth century American cities, police and fire response times were quite slow because citizens lacked methods of summoning their services. With the invention of the telegraph, networks of police and fire alarm boxes throughout the city offered a solution to this problem. However, networks of telegraph cables were installed initially only for fire services, but not for police. Why? At the same time that these network-based communication technologies became available, political forces aimed to reorganize the way fire protection services were provided, shifting from private and volunteer fire brigades to public and professional fire departments. The alarm networks provided a way for city officials to effectively control the operation of the new fire departments now under their authority. Similar reforms for police services were implemented only much later, and as a result, cities were much slower to build networks of police call boxes.[49]

This example illustrates the role of political regulation and control in shaping the development of urban networks of infrastructure. Throughout the twentieth century, many of the public services and utilities necessary in modern cities—water, electricity, roads, etc.—were provided or regulated by local governments. In the back-and-forth games of urban politics like those described earlier in this chapter, politicians and communities decided where these networks should go, and what services they should provide. However, by the 1970s, in search of greater efficiency and higher quality services, the provision of many services that rely on building and maintaining networks was privatized or deregulated. As services once provided by the local government were unbundled or splintered apart, many more groups began to play a role in building urban networks. For example, Internet service providers (ISPs) now decide where to route their networks of fiber optic cables based on demands from consumers, regulations from politicians, and a range of other influential actors. Thus, today the networks of infrastructure that snake through cities and make life in them possible are products of contentious political interactions.[50]

Some of the most intense political conflicts arise over networks that deliver basic human needs, including clean water. For cities in developing nations such as Buenos Aires and Delhi, but also for highly cosmopolitan places such as New York and Paris, maintaining a network that can sustainably provide water to the city's residents is a complex problem that involves many individuals and groups, some of whom are powerful but most who are powerless. For example, when the public water company responsible for providing water and sewer services to Buenos Aries residents was unable to meet the needs of the city, the private company *Aguas Argentinas* stepped in. This transition from public to private control over the city's water and sewer network led to a dramatic increase in the cost of water, and to the possibility that the city's poorer residents could loose their connection to the network (and their supply of clean water) completely.[51] Although not as essential as water, there are political tensions surrounding networks that meet other needs of modern urbanites as well, including access to the Internet. In cities such as San Francisco and Reykjavik, politically well-connected developers and corporations ensured the availability of access to the Internet by supporting the construction of the necessary network of cables. In contrast, these types of networks are underdeveloped in low income parts of many cities such as Lima, Peru, as well as in politically isolated cities such as the French island town of Saint Pierre et Miquelon, located nearly 3,000 miles west of Paris, off the coast of Newfoundland.[52]

Because they play such an integral role in urban life, the organization of transportation networks that allow movement within and between cities is also politically charged. The construction of a network of wide boulevards by Baron Haussmann in nineteenth century Paris was overtly motivated by a political aim: to make future rebellions and revolutions easier to control. In the twentieth century, decisions about when and where to build automobile-suitable highways has been significantly controlled, first by the political clout of automobile manufacturers, and more recently by that of environmental activists.[53] Like networks that carry private vehicles, the expansion of public transportation networks can be intensely political, as it has been in Bern and Paris. On the one hand, more extensive and efficient public transportation networks can reduce traffic congestion and pollution, leading to a more livable 'compact city.' But, on the other hand, the well-off businesses and residents that can afford offices and homes in prime urban locations near key nodes on these new networks stand to benefit more than poorer residents and small businesses, who can wind up even less connected than before if they are forced to move to cheaper areas of the city through a process known as gentrification.[54] Finally, even large-scale transportation networks such as the airline routes that link distant cities to one another are shaped by political forces. Before 1978, the government determined which American cities were connected by non-stop airline service, but today these routes are primarily determined by individual airlines. As a result, airline networks in the United States and elsewhere have a hub-and-spoke pattern that is cost effective for the airlines, but provides those living in a few 'hub' cities such as Chicago or Atlanta much greater transportation access than those living in poorly connected 'spoke' cities.[55]

*   *   *   *   *

Some individuals and groups are clearly more influential than others over how cities are run. Although these influential and powerful political actors may have some unique individual characteristics such as wealth or education, the network perspective calls attention to their position in patterns of interactions with others. Influence in urban political matters, as in other areas, often comes not from one's personal attributes, but from one's place in the network. In some cases, these networks of urban politics may concentrate influence in the hands of a small clique of elites, while in other cases, power may be divided up across a plurality of actors, each focused on particular issues. Moreover, networks are not only important for the politics of city hall and big business in major cities, but are also important for the everyday political actions of individual urbanites and their local communities. Indeed, by focusing on the network of interactions among regular folks, it is possible to understand why some people are politically active while others are not, and why some communities can respond to local issues through collective action while others cannot. Finally, networks are certainly important for urban politics, but urban politics are also important for building networks. The infrastructure networks of transportation, communication, and utilities that keep modern cities livable do not simply appear, and do not necessarily serve all of a city's residents equally; their creation and organization reflects the political interests of many different powerful groups. All of this, ultimately, highlights how the complex phenomena of urban politics both drive and are driven by networks.

Discussion Questions and Activities

1. Are you a member of a clique? How could you define the boundaries of your clique in network terms? What are the advantages and disadvantages of being part of a clique for you? For those who are not part of it?

2. Apply the definition of network power (see Method Note 10) to the network of neighbors in Method Note 1. Who is the most powerful? Who is the least powerful? How might this affect the way decisions are made in this neighborhood?

3. Suppose you lived in a neighborhood characterized primarily by individual-level, bonding social capital: each person is part of a small, densely connected group, but these groups are not connected to each other. What steps could be taken to encourage individuals to become more politically active? What steps could be taken to facilitate the community's ability to engage in collective actions?

4. Infrastructure networks are necessary to deliver basic needs such as water and electricity to a city's residents, but they can be costly to build and maintain. Who should be responsible for the costs of urban infrastructure networks? Who should decide, for example, whether a new Internet network is built first in downtown or in a low-income neighborhood?

5. How could the methods introduced in the previous chapters be used to study the concepts introduced in this chapter? Similarly, how could the methods introduced in this chapter be used to study the concepts introduced in the previous chapters?

PART TWO
MESO-URBAN NETWORKS
CITIES AS NETWORKS

5

FORM

GETTING FROM HERE TO THERE

As the last chapter demonstrated, urban political networks play an important role in determining which individuals and groups are influential over urban affairs. This can include determining who is influential over deciding how and where to build the infrastructure networks that help move people and other resources around the city. This chapter focuses on those infrastructure networks, and specifically on the structure of cities' street networks. But, why is the structure of a city's street network important?

For one answer, it's useful to consider a puzzle that confronted the residents of the village of Königsburg in the eighteenth century. In the center of the village, now known as Kaliningrad and located in present-day Russia, were two islands (see Figure 5.1). These islands were connected to the north and south banks and to each other by a series of seven bridges. After a few pints in the local tavern, the villagers enjoyed walking through town and over these bridges. However, despite their repeated attempts, none of them could find a path that allowed them to cross every bridge, using each one only once. Swiss mathematician Leonhard Euler (1707–1783) suggested that this problem could be understood by examining how the bridges connected different parts of the village like a network. Focusing only on the village's most important elements—the four land masses and the seven bridges that connect them—Euler drew a simpler map, which can be simplified even further as a sociogram that depicts the landmasses as nodes and the bridges as edges.

By examining Königsburg's bridge system as a network, Euler found that it is possible to visit each bridge exactly once only if either zero or two landmasses have an odd number of bridges. But, because all four landmasses have an odd number of bridges (one has five, the others each have three), taking such a path is not possible in Königsburg. No matter how hard they tried, the structure of the network made it impossible for the villagers to find the pleasant walking path they were looking for. That is, the structure of the network determined how the villager could (and could not) experience their urban surroundings.[1]

Of course, in addition to streets, there are many other kinds of infrastructure networks that link all the parts of a city together. And their structures also determine many features of the urban experience.[2] For example, the most basic of human needs—water—is delivered throughout cities by a network of pipes and pumping stations. The cost of water depends in part on the network's complexity, its purity depends on the network's quality, and its availability depends on the network's size. And once the water has been used, an equally complex network of sewers and waste treatment facilities carry it away and prevent the spread of disease. But, street networks are among the most

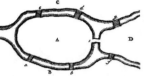

Euler's Drawing

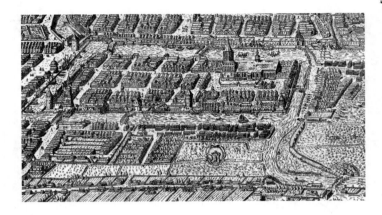

Sociogram

Figure 5.1 The Bridges of Königsburg.[3]

highly visible and frequently experienced infrastructure networks in everyday urban life. Common depictions of the modern metropolis often feature a tangled web of freeways and busy intersections, congested with both traffic jams and smog. Similarly, the classic portrait of a small town invariably includes 'Main Street,' with its quaint storefronts and churches. Street networks, perhaps more than any other kind of urban infrastructure network, shape how we experience daily life in the city. They define the boundaries of neighborhoods and districts, helping us know where we are. They channel our movements toward some places and away from others, making some parts of the city bustling centers of activity and other parts quiet and peaceful. In short, street networks not only help us get from here to there, but also tell us where 'here' and 'there' are, and researchers have been investigating how for over a century.[4]

Thus, in this chapter, I explore how the city itself can be viewed as a kind of network formed by the criss-crossing of major roads and small residential streets, asking: if the city is a network, how does it affect daily urban life? I begin by considering the various ways that urban residents, workers, and tourists perceive the city and its streets as a network, forming mental maps of the landscape that help them get where they are going. But, these mental maps are personal creations that do not necessarily reflect the real layout of a city. So, I then turn to consider the various ways that urban street networks can be carefully mapped and described using network methods. With these network mapping tools in hand, it is possible to ask what role the urban planner can or should play in designing cities' street networks, and how they can use these tools to solve problems such as traffic congestion. Finally, although street networks are made up of cold, hard pavement, I conclude by describing some of the ways that their structures can shape not just where we drive, but also our personal social lives, including who our friends are.

Seeing the City as a Network

A wide range of factors influences how individuals see and experience a city. The climate certainly plays an important role: cities with mild weather such as San Diego or Tampa can be experienced outdoors in parks and on sidewalks, while cities with harsh climates such as Minneapolis or Montreal are more often seen from inside the protection of buildings. The age of a city can also affect its 'feel,' as the historic architecture of older cities such as Rome or Athens produce a distinctly different experience from the modern buildings of much newer cities such as Phoenix or Dubai. Even natural features of the surrounding environment can impact the urban experience; for example, with mountains and rivers giving places such as Portland or Boulder an outdoorsy vibe.

However, a city's streets are one of the most significant features that influences how it is seen and experienced. The network of streets in a city determine where you can and can't go, how you can and can't get there, and what you will and won't see along the way. But, even more than simply determining how people get around cities, urban street networks give cities unique spatial forms that tell a city's story and project a distinctive urban image. Moreover, these street networks exist not only in the highly visible above-ground forms we are all familiar with, but also in more invisible below-ground forms such as the underground pedestrian networks found in cities with cold climates that allow people to walk throughout downtown without going outside.[5] As Figure 5.2 illustrates, many different types of street networks are possible and are replicated in cities around the world. Each pattern, although similar to cities elsewhere, results in a unique urban form that is seen and experienced in a particular way by its residents and visitors.[6]

The street networks in old cities such as London have an *organic* form that is the result of a gradual evolution over centuries. Major roads such as Cornhill follow ancient paths over natural features, while narrow alleys are built and redirected as needed by residents and businesses. As a result, London and other cities of similar age are often composed of a dense network of small streets that intersect at irregular angles. Such organic networks can easily disorient outsiders, but they also mark the boundaries of tiny districts that locals know like the back of their hand. Indeed, from just the small map fragment in the figure it is easy to see how a distinct neighborhood might form within the natural triangular boundaries of Cornhill, Lombard, and Church.[7]

In sharp contrast to the organic street network of London, other early cities followed rigidly planned designs that aimed to capture the *ideal* proportions of geometric shapes. The nine-pointed star design of the Italian fortress town of Palmanova can still be seen today, while only portions of the original ideal layout of Coevorden (Netherlands) remain as it has been transformed and surrounded by newer development. However, cities and neighborhoods with ideal street networks are still being constructed today. For example, the Palm Jumeirah housing development is an artificial island in Dubai shaped like a palm leaf. Designed for specific purposes, by planners and architects following specific rules, these networks are often a combination of art and science. As art, they often exhibit intricate patterns of symmetry, and may even form geometric or natural shapes when viewed from certain perspectives. As science, the street networks and overall urban form of ideal cities are engineered with specific aims in mind. The shape of Palmanova and Coevorden made them resistant to attacks from invading armies, while the shape of Palm Jumeirah ensures that each home offers expansive views of the Persian Gulf.

Arising through both natural growth and intentional planning, *radial* street networks often have characteristics of both organic and ideal networks. Their defining feature is the presence of cross-cutting streets that radiate out from major focal points such as landmarks. In early cities, when transportation on foot or by horse was relatively slow, radial streets were efficient because they connected important locations by the shortest possible path. Later, radial streets were frequently used in the rebuilding of old cities, or construction of new cities, for several reasons. In the rebuilding of Paris, Baron Haussmann incorporated a network of wide, radiating boulevards that would facilitate military action in the case of another revolution. In Washington, DC, Pierre L'Enfant used a radial street network to lend the new city a sense of history, and to draw attention to important state buildings. As the map in Figure 5.2 illustrates, most major streets in the American capital radiate outward from either the White House on the left or the U.S. Capitol in the center.

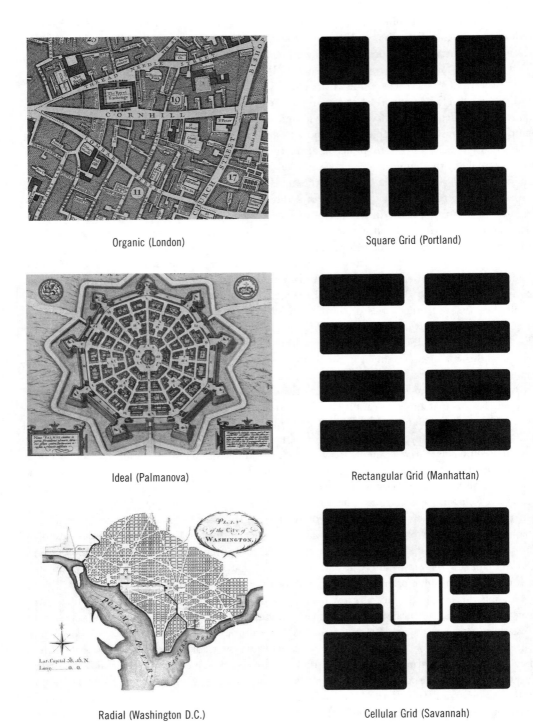

Organic (London)

Square Grid (Portland)

Ideal (Palmanova)

Rectangular Grid (Manhattan)

Radial (Washington D.C.)

Cellular Grid (Savannah)

Figure 5.2 Types of Street Network.[8]

While organic, ideal, and radial street networks remain in use throughout the world, the majority of modern cities feature *grid* street networks where intersections meet at perfect right angles. However, there are many variations on the basic gridiron design. The simplest relies on standardized *square* blocks, which can measure just 200 feet across in cities such as Portland or can span a full mile in cities such as Phoenix. The strict regularity of a square grid system provides few clues about where things are located, and unlike in London, it can be impossible to anticipate where neighborhoods may begin or end by just looking at a map. In Manhattan, city blocks are long and narrow, allowing for a *rectangular* grid system in which widely spaced avenues run the length of the island, while narrowly spaced streets run the island's width. This street network directly impacts the experience of walking in Manhattan: traveling from uptown to downtown can be slow but interesting because one crosses many intersections, while traveling from the Hudson to the East River is faster but provides less variety because one rarely needs to cross the street. Finally, the grid street network in Savannah combines both square and rectangular blocks into a *cellular* pattern that also incorporates parks and public squares. Because the streets are not continuous in this network, one must make frequent stops and turns around the central parks, mirroring the slower pace of Southern life.

These types of street networks, and the urban forms they generate, illustrate how the city can be seen as a network looking down from above. But, how do cities get seen as networks from the ground, by the people who actually live and work in them? Urban planner Kevin Lynch (1918–1984) argued that how cities are perceived by their occupants depends on their *legibility*. For cities, legibility describes "the ease with which its parts can be recognized and can be organized into a coherent pattern."[9] Legible cities are easy to navigate and live in because their layout makes it possible for residents and visitors to develop an accurate understanding of the city's overall shape and organization. The regularity of the streets and avenues in Manhattan's grid pattern make it highly legible; because higher numbered streets are further from downtown at the tip of the island, even newcomers can easily tell where they are. Similarly, although their street networks are less regular, London and Washington DC are legible because major roads connect prominent landmarks such as St. Paul's Cathedral or the Washington Monument. Illegible cities, in contrast, lack visual cues that would help people orient themselves.

If a city's legibility describes how easily the city can be 'read' like a book, then what are the 'words'? Lynch suggested that individuals' images of a city are composed of five key elements: paths, nodes, landmarks, edges, and districts.[10] Paths are, as the name implies, the actual routes that urban dwellers use (or know others use) to get from place to place. They may include streets or highways like those illustrated in Figure 5.2, but could also include more informal paths such as a shortcut one might take through a park while walking to work. Although different paths will be important to different people, some paths are more prominent than others, including streets that are especially wide or heavily used, and those that are close to major landmarks or that have their own identity. For example, in New Orleans' French Quarter, Bourbon Street is relatively narrow and is not particularly important as a transportation route, but it is a path known to both residents and visitors because it is the center of the New Orleans cultural scene.

Paths do not simply wind through a city indefinitely; they have starting and ending points, and they intersect with other paths along the way. These key points along a path—its beginning, end, and intersections—are nodes. Nodes are particularly important for how the city is experienced for several reasons. First, nodes are places where decisions must be made about which path to take, which can be straightforward if the city is legible, or quite confusing if there are many paths to chose from. Second, because nodes require slowing down and sometimes stopping altogether, they focus attention on the buildings and people located nearby, giving such places greater significance. Indeed, the corner store, like the corner office, is a far more visible and desirable location than a store located along a busy street. Whether making a decision or viewing the surrounding environment, landmarks serve as points of reference that aid in navigating a path from node to node. Landmarks are not always located at nodes, but when they are, both the landmark and the node become more significant. For example, Palmanova's public square, located in the node where all of Palmanova's main streets intersect, gives the whole city its distinctive shape and character.

The arrangement of paths and nodes often form edges within the city that mark the boundaries of specific areas, or districts. For children playing outdoors who are told not to cross the busy street, the busy street serves as an edge that defines their neighborhood. In many large cities, circular highways serve a similar purpose: Washington, DC's Capitol Beltway (I-495) in Washington, the London Orbital (M25), and the Shanghai Ring Expressway (G1501) are edges that enclose the greater metropolitan regions of these cities, distinguishing them from the suburbs. Edges and districts can powerfully influence the experiences and behaviors of a city's residents and visitors. For example, the 'bad' parts of town are often described as being 'on the wrong side of the tracks,' and in many cities some real barrier separates affluent from distressed neighborhoods. Similarly, what lies beyond an edge in another district can often be perceived as scary or foreign: downtown residents may view the suburbs beyond the highway as dull and boring, while suburbanites see the city inside the highway as dangerous and dirty. Such features of the urban landscape can even shape sports loyalties, as in the case of Chicago, where edges defined by the city's public transit system separate the pro-Cubs north side from the pro-White Sox south side.

Although Lynch and most city residents are not network researchers, these elements demonstrate that they implicitly view the city as a kind of network. That is, most people see the city as a complex pattern of connections (paths), intersecting at key points (nodes and landmarks), to form boundaries and neighborhoods (edges and districts). But, each individual sees the city in a slightly different way, paying more attention to some paths or nodes than others. By combining these different elements, and placing more emphasis on some than others, individuals construct their own *mental maps* of the city. To study how a person perceives a city's space, it can be useful to ask them to actually draw a picture of their mental map, not unlike sketching a map on a cocktail napkin to give someone directions. The features of the map they draw, including its accuracy and level of detail, can give insight into how they see the city. Some will draw a *sequential mental map* that focuses on the city's paths and nodes, and provides some details about how the street network is configured and where buildings are located within it. Others will draw a *spatial mental map* that focuses on edges and districts, indicating where various parts of the city are located in relation to one another. Although every individual's mental map is unique and there is no 'right' mental map, a city's own residents tend to see the city as a network of specific paths intersecting at nodes, while visitors tend to see it as composed of more general areas of interest such as the downtown entertainment district or the area around their hotel.[11]

Although most people have fairly detailed mental maps of the places they live and work, these maps are not necessarily complete or accurate. Several features of the city's real street network can be distorted in an individual's mental map. First, the map may not include, or may inaccurately depict, unfamiliar parts of the city. Second, areas that an individual perceives as more important— one's own house or neighborhood—are often drawn larger. Finally, there is a tendency for mental maps to create order and symmetry even when they do not exist. For example, a street that has several curves might be drawn as if it were straight, and two streets that intersect at an odd angle might be drawn as if they intersect at a right angle. Because the way we see urban networks can be very different from the way they actually are, designing livable cities requires understanding these differences and ensuring that their networks are not too confusing or disorienting.[12]

It Helps to Have a Map

Examining individuals' mental maps can provide insight into how they view a city's network of streets and neighborhoods. But, to understand how a city is actually organized as a network, and how those networks affect the lives of people living in them, a more formal map is necessary. Euler laid the foundations for mapping networks, or *graph theory* as it is called in mathematics, in the eighteenth century with his approach to solving the Königsburg bridge puzzle. Since then, two distinct approaches to mapping a city's streets as a network have emerged.[13] The first approach treats intersections as the network's nodes, and streets as the edges that link them together. A street network drawn using this approach, which is known as a *primal network* or *axial network*, tends to closely resemble the actual geographic layout of a city's streets and intersections. Figure 5.3 shows a street map of a hypothetical city and its primal network. The two images are very similar—the primal network is like an abstract representation of the more detailed street map— which makes primal street networks easy to read and interpret.

Primal networks are most useful when the focus is on specific city locations, such as intersections or landmarks. They can be examined to identify the various leisurely *walks* a city dweller might take, as well as the most direct *paths* between one location and another. Indeed, in most cases, travelers want to take the shortest route from their origin to their destination. Here, primal networks can be useful for finding the shortest route between two points, and the *geodesic distance* between them. For example, although there are many possible routes between the corner of Main and Midtown and the corner of Ring and Industry, the shortest route only requires traveling two

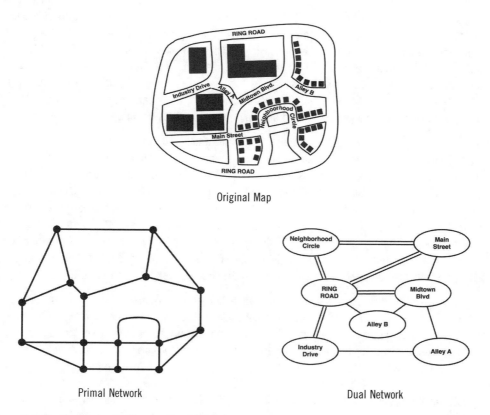

Original Map

Primal Network

Dual Network

Figure 5.3 Two Approaches to Mapping Street Networks.

blocks: first take Main Street to Ring Road, then take Ring Road to Industry Drive. The average geodesic distance in the primal network provides an indication of the city's *compactness*. In this network, the average geodesic distance is about 2.5, which means that every intersection in the city is on average only two or three blocks away from every other intersection.

Primal networks can also be used to identify places that are particularly important owing to their location or *centrality* in the city's street network. But, there are many different ways that a place might be described as having a central location. *Degree centrality* describes places that are important because they are located at the intersection of many different streets. These are places where travelers must stop for cross-traffic and decide which direction to go, and are often spots where people gather or where major stores are located. *Closeness centrality* describes places that

METHOD NOTE 12: WALKS, PATHS, DISTANCE, AND REACHABILITY

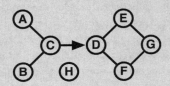

Although these terms are useful in everyday speech to describe how we get around cities, they have very specific definitions when applied to networks. A *walk* is a sequence of nodes that are connected to one another by edges. In the example above, a walk could include A → C → B or D → E → D → F; in fact, there are an infinite number of possible walks in any network. A *path* is a special type of walk in which each edge and each node are used no more than once. Although D → E → D → F is a walk that starts at D and ends at F, it is not a path because it includes node D twice. In contrast, D → E → G → F is another walk that starts at D and ends at F, but this one is also a path because each node and edge included in it is used only one time. In UCINET: Network → Paths.

Distance describes how far apart two nodes are from one another. But, distance often depends on the specific route used between the two nodes; some routes are shorter and others are longer. For example, the distance between nodes D and F is 3 using the path D → E → G → F because it requires three edges to get from D to F. But, the distance is only 1 using the more direct path D → F. Usually network researchers focus only on the shortest possible distance, or *geodesic distance*, between two nodes. A network's average geodesic distance, also sometimes called its *characteristic path length*, is a measure of the network's *compactness* because it indicates on average how far any two nodes are from one another. The characteristic path length of the example network is 1.87, indicating that on average two nodes are less than two steps from one another. In UCINET: Network → Cohesion → Distance.

In some cases, the distance between two nodes is undefined because one is not *reachable* from the other. This can happen when some nodes are not connected to the rest of the network. For example, because H is not connected to the rest of the network, it is not reachable from any of the other nodes; there are no walks or paths that include H. Certain nodes can also be unreachable in directed networks where some edges, such as one-way streets, allow movement in one direction but not the other. In this example, A, B, and C are not reachable from D, E, F, or G because the edge between C and D is directed and does not allow movement from D to C. In UCINET: Network → Cohesion → Reachability.

are important because they are only a few blocks away from many other places. As a result, they are conveniently located and easily accessible from many different locations. Finally, *betweenness centrality* describes places that are important because they are located in-between other parts of the city, and travelers must pass through these areas on the way to their destination. In this hypothetical city, the corner of Main Street and Midtown Blvd. is central in all of these senses. But, in other street networks, one place may be located at the intersection of many streets (degree central), while a different place is conveniently accessible from all other parts of the city (closeness central).[14]

While primal networks are useful when specific locations are the main focus, a different approach to mapping street networks is more useful when the streets themselves are the main focus. This second approach treats streets as the network's nodes, and treats their intersections with one another as the edges that link them together. A street network drawn using this approach, which is known as a *dual network*, generally looks quite different from the original street maps upon which they are based. Figure 5.3 also shows the dual network representation of the same hypothetical city, but it looks very different not only from the detailed street map, but also from the primal network. As a result, reading and interpreting dual street networks can be difficult initially. In this example, Ring Road and Midtown Blvd. are connected in the dual network because they intersect each other (in two places). In contrast, Ring Road and Alley A are not connected in the dual network because they never intersect one another.

Because dual street networks are different from primal street networks, examining them requires a different set of tools, known collectively as *space syntax*.[15] Three features are of particular interest when examining street networks from this perspective. First, *continuity* describes the number of blocks that compose a single, continuous street. More continuous streets, because they run for long distances, are more useful for getting from one place to another. For example, Ring Road has a high level of continuity because it is composed of nine blocks and can be used to get almost anywhere. In contrast, the two alleys have low levels of continuity; they are very short and are not very useful for traveling long distances. Second, *connectivity* describes the number of streets that a given street intersects. More connective streets, because they provide access to other parts of the network, are more useful. Ring Road is highly connective, and therefore useful, because it intersects with most other streets in the city; from Ring Road, one can get to nearly any other street.[16] Finally, *depth* describes how many intermediate streets are needed to get from one street to another. From a given starting point, shallow streets are more useful than deep ones because they are easier to get to. For example, for a person living on Neighborhood Circle, Ring Road is useful because it is only one block away. In contrast, Alley A is not useful because it requires at least two other streets to reach.

Although there are multiple approaches for mapping street networks, and multiple methods for examining these networks, some general patterns can be found in the street networks of small towns and large cities, ancient settlements and new suburbs. They tend to have network structures that make it possible to travel between any two points in the city by making only a few turns and using only a few streets. This happens when the nodes form dense clusters that are connected to each other by a few, very central hubs. Such a pattern is easy to see in the dual street network in Figure 5.5. First, there is an industrial cluster of streets that include Industrial Drive and Alley A, and a residential cluster of streets that include Main Street and Neighborhood Circle. Within these clusters, the streets all intersect, making travel fast and efficient. Second, two highly connected and central hubs—Ring Road and Midtown Blvd—make it possible to travel between the industrial and residential clusters. Although this is a very simple example, even large and complex cities with extensive street networks exhibit similar patterns. But, why?[17]

METHOD NOTE 13: CENTRALITY

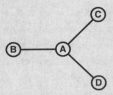

There are many different ways to think about a node's centrality in a network. Each conception of centrality is measured differently and focuses on a different aspect of a node's importance.

Degree centrality is the simplest measure of centrality. A node's degree centrality is measured by counting the total number of edges that are connected to it. In the example network, node A has a degree centrality of 3 because it has three edges: one connected to B, another to C, and still another to D. All the other nodes have a degree centrality of 1 because each of them has only one edge. In UCINET: Network → Centrality → Degree.

Closeness centrality focuses on how close a node is to every other node in the network. Computing a node's closeness centrality involves two steps. First, find the length of the shortest path (the geodesic distance) between the node and each other node in the network. Second, add each of these lengths together, and take its reciprocal. Focusing on node A: the geodesic distance between A and B is 1, between A and C is 1, and between A and D is 1. Thus, node A's closeness centrality is 0.33, because $1 / (1 + 1 + 1) = 0.33$. In contrast, focusing on node B: the geodesic distance between B and A is 1, between B and C is 2, and between B and D is 2. Thus, node B's closeness centrality is 0.2 because $1 / (1 + 2 + 2) = 0.2$. In UCINET: Network → Centrality → Closeness.

Betweenness centrality focuses on how necessary a node is to get from one part of the network to another. Computing a node's betweenness centrality first requires finding the shortest path between each pair of nodes in the network. Each time a node is located on one of these shortest paths, its betweenness centrality increases. The nodes with the most betweenness centrality are those located along many of the shortest paths. Node A is on the shortest path between B and C, between B and D, and between C and D, so its betweenness centrality is 3. The other nodes have a betweenness of 0 because they are not on the shortest path between any pair of nodes. In UCINET: Network → Centrality → Freeman Betweenness → Node Betweenness.[18]

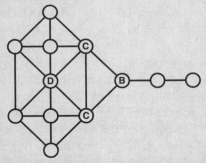

In the simple 4-node network above, node A is the most central no matter how centrality is defined: degree, closeness, or betweenness. But, this is not always the case. In this more complex network, node D has the highest degree centrality because several edges are connected to it. The two nodes labeled C have the highest closeness centrality because they are located equidistant between the dense part of the network on the left, and the sparse part on the right. Finally, node B has the highest betweenness centrality because it is necessary for getting between the left and right parts of the network.[19]

The Planner's Role

Understanding why even very different cities can have similar street networks requires asking where street networks come from. The most obvious answer is: urban planners. That is, with the approval of mayors and city councils, urban planners are typically responsible for identifying where new streets are needed, how they should be routed, which other streets they should intersect, and a range of other more technical issues such as the number of lanes and the type of pavement to be used.[20] But recently, some have offered a different and surprising answer: street networks grow and evolve on their own, in response to changes in their surrounding environments. This does not mean that urban planning is a waste of time, but rather that the role of planners in the creation of street networks may be secondary to some much broader forces.

Some have argued that urban form is a product of the specific technologies of the day. The earliest human settlements were shaped like circles because, at a time when threats from the environment including wild animals and unfriendly neighboring tribes were common, they provided the best view of the surrounding area and the best chance at survival. Thus, early cities often have radial street networks where streets radiate out from a central plaza or fortress. Radial street networks may also have developed as a solution to the relatively slow transportation options—traveling by horse or by foot—available in the past. Thus, the circles developed along major paths at about the distance one could travel in a single day, providing a place to stop and rest, and the opportunity to change paths and directions. Others have suggested that farming and building technologies shaped the pattern of road networks. Because fields and buildings tended to be square or rectangular, the spaces left over between these regular plots of land gave rise to grid street networks.[21]

Still another possibility is that cities are like living organisms and their street networks are like circulatory systems. Just as an organism's circulatory system delivers blood to cells, a city's streets deliver people to homes and businesses.[22] Indeed, this parallel is part of our everyday speech: the main roads that run through a city and allow for many cars traveling at relatively high speeds are often called arteries or arterial roads. Thus, asking why different cities' street networks look similar is much like asking why different animals' circulatory systems look similar. The goal of both circulatory systems and street networks is to deliver resources where they are needed as efficiently as possible. Over billions of years, the process of natural selection has favored animals with branching circulatory systems because they are very efficient. Similarly, billions of individual people each trying to get someplace quickly has favored the development of similarly structured branching street networks.[23] Notably, no single individual or group of individuals planned it this way. Instead, the common patterns observed in cities' street networks (and animals' circulatory systems) are simply the result of people (or blood cells) being in a hurry and doing what is necessary to get to their destination. Through a process known as *self-organization* or *endogenous evolution*, street networks grow on their own with such patterns or *emergent phenomena* arising naturally as a consequence of this growth process.[24]

But, even if planners play a secondary role in the development of a street network's overall structure, they still have an important role in making cities and their networks operate smoothly. By examining the organization of urban networks, urban planners are able to design solutions to problems that may seem relatively mundane, but that are quite important for building livable cities. The availability of GPS devices and smart phones with mapping capabilities have made it easier to navigate large and unfamiliar cities, but how do these gadgets know how to get us from point A to point B. By examining how urban street networks are structured and how people perceive this structure, urban planners together with computer scientists have developed methods for automatically locating routes through a city that are not only short, but are also easy to follow.[25]

Often, however, traffic jams or road closures may mean that the usual route is not always the best choice. Thus, others have focused on understanding how urban street networks can be structured to minimize traffic congestion, and to ensure that when some part of the network is unavailable, the whole system does not fall apart. For example, a street network in which each business or home could be reached using only one road would be problematic because even a minor road closure makes parts of the city unreachable. Thus, planners often seek to build redundant street networks, in which there are many different ways to reach each location.[26] And, when events that cause breakdowns in the street network do occur, such as traffic accidents, it is important to be able to locate them quickly. Using latitude and longitude coordinates is not especially helpful because traffic accidents and road closures cannot happen just anywhere; they happen on the network. Thus, urban planners increasingly use the language of networks, rather than the language of geography, to pinpoint specific urban locations.[27]

By thinking carefully about how the structure of urban networks influences how people use them, urban planners can also build cities that are more functional. Indeed, a number of general guidelines have been suggested for designing cities with livable network structures. First, it is important to build connections between nodes that are different but complementary, rather than between nodes that are the same. For example, it is far more useful to build a street between a neighborhood and a shopping mall than to build one between two shopping malls. Second, it is important to consider the scale of the network and the spacing of the nodes, because humans can only travel so far on foot. If the distance between intersections is long and there are few opportunities to rest or to change directions, people will be less inclined to walk places than if the city blocks are short and intersections are frequent. Third, because new streets or sidewalks are costly to build and maintain, only useful ones should be added to the network; useless and purely decorative paths should be avoided. Frequently in parks or on college campuses, although there are many sidewalks, there will be a few well-worn paths through the grass. These informal paths show where people really want to go, and where the paths should have been located in the first place. Combining these general guidelines, some have suggested that cities should be designed in a specific order to make them livable: first define the location of green spaces and pedestrian areas, then design the network of pedestrian paths, and finally arrange the buildings and streets. This has been the process for many older cities, but newer cities are often built in the opposite order, leading to networks that are good for cars, but bad for people.[28]

Although the efficiency and functionality of a city's networks are primary concerns for urban planners, equally important is designing city networks that are equitable. The most equitable networks have many points of access, and therefore allow many different people the opportunity to use them. For example, the airline network has very few points of access—one can only board a plane at an airport, but cannot switch planes mid-flight—and thus is inequitable because only those near an airport can benefit from the airline network. In contrast, a footpath through a park has infinite points of access—one can start at the beginning and stop at the end, but one can also start or stop at any point along the path—and thus is equitable because anyone in the park can benefit from the footpath. Increasingly, urban networks are becoming less equitable, providing only some people access to the network and its benefits, but not others. In some cases, urban networks are inequitable because they are built by private companies for use by paying customers, including many communication networks such as cable television and high-speed internet, but also distribution networks such as those that carry water or electricity to homes. In other cases, urban networks are inequitable because more influential residents are better able to advocate for network access. For example, as a public transit network is expanded, additional stops and faster service are more likely to be added in wealthy neighborhoods before poorer neighborhoods. These inequalities in access are important because urban networks provide access to many different important resources, and thus an individual's or community's lack of access to the network can exacerbate inequalities of health and wealth.[29]

Living in a Network

The previous sections have explored how urban networks in general, and urban street networks in particular, are structured. Apart from being useful for solving a range of urban planning problems, including finding short routes and dealing with traffic congestion, the structures of urban street networks also have significant implications for the everyday lives of urban residents. The organization of these networks shape how urbanites get around and how they form social networks with one another, but also where new businesses are likely to open and where crimes are likely to be committed. Indeed, very little of the urban experience is not directly affected by the pattern of streets that weave through the city.

Many street networks are designed to be well connected and compact, allowing a person to travel from one place to another using only a small number of streets. However, the street networks in some parts of modern cities—sprawling suburbs, in particular—often are not organized this way. What happens then? It is precisely this question, or more specifically, concern about the consequences of poorly connected neighborhoods, that motivates an influential perspective in urban planning: *New Urbanism*. Among other things, the New Urbanism movement aims to design cities and neighborhoods with high levels of *connectivity* because it reduces automobile traffic, improves access, facilitates walking and promotes the formation of social networks.[30]

Figure 5.4 shows two neighborhoods in Columbus, Ohio: an urban neighborhood located near downtown, and a suburban neighborhood located near the city's edge. The total number of streets in these two neighborhoods is similar, but they are clearly arranged very differently. The urban neighborhood's street network exhibits a high level of connectivity because each street is connected to many others, and there are multiple ways to get from one place to another. In contrast, the suburban neighborhood's street network exhibits a low level of connectivity; each cul-de-sac street is connected to only one other street, and there are only a few possible routes between different parts of the neighborhood. These differences in street network structure have a significant impact on life within them.

Perhaps most obviously, the street network structure affects automobile traffic. In the suburban neighborhood, traffic is likely to be heavy and congested along the few streets that provide access to the neighborhood from the main roads that surround it. And, this congestion may lead to higher levels of air pollution and more traffic accidents. In contrast, because there are many different routes between different places in the urban neighborhood, the traffic is more evenly distributed and congestion in any particular spot is unlikely. In addition to reducing traffic congestion, street connectivity also improves the accessibility of different areas of a city, which is

Urban Neighborhood   Suburban Neighborhood

Figure 5.4 Street Connectivity in Urban and Suburban Neighborhoods.[31]

particularly important in emergency situations. Suppose there is a fire at one of the suburban houses located on cul-de-sac B. To reach this house from a main road, the fire engine must pass through several intersections, and if either of them are blocked, the house could not be reached. In contrast, the houses in the urban area are accessible in many different ways, even if some intersections are blocked or some streets are closed.[32]

Street connectivity impacts not only automobile traffic, but also pedestrian traffic, by making cities and neighborhoods more or less walkable. First, in areas with low street connectivity, even places that are geographically nearby can be far away in the street network, and thus difficult to reach by walking. For example, in the suburban neighborhood, the houses on cul-de-sac A and B are located very close to one another. However, walking from one to the other requires traveling a long distance because there is no direct route. In contrast, there is a relatively direct route between A and B, and indeed between any pair of houses, in the urban neighborhood. Although communities that are walkable may offer greater convenience and more travel options, their residents also tend to be healthier because they have more opportunities to engage in physical activity.[33]

While greater street connectivity facilitates both automobile and pedestrian traffic, the New Urbanism movement also focuses on connectivity's social benefits.[34] Those in more highly connected communities are less dependent on their cars, and are more able and likely to walk to their destinations. As a result, they are more likely to encounter and interact with their neighbors. For example, those living in houses at A and B in the urban neighborhood are likely to run into and get to know one another. In contrast, poorly connected communities, where residents must use their cars to get around, offer only limited opportunities to get to know one another. Those living in houses on cul-de-sacs A and B in the suburban neighborhood, despite living very close to one another, will likely never cross paths or have an opportunity to get acquainted. Thus, not only does street connectivity facilitate movement, but it also facilitates the formation of social networks among a community's residents. Indeed for Jane Jacobs, whose work inspired many New Urbanist ideas, walkable streets that encourage casual contact among neighbors are the key to transforming neighborhoods into communities.

Although Jane Jacobs and later New Urbanists called attention to it, for nearly a century researchers have been exploring the processes through which street networks and other forms of spatial organization produce social networks. In his study of the Hudson School in the 1930s, Moreno examined how the arrangement of the girls' cottages into neighborhoods separated by roads and other buildings influenced the girls' interactions with one another. In the 1950s, others examined how the arrangement of homes in two neighborhoods—University Village near the University of Minnesota and Westgate Court near the Massachusetts Institute of Technology— shaped the relationships among their residents. Even historical studies have reached similar conclusions: the social relationships that fueled the 1871 revolution in Paris were shaped by the arrangement of the newly forming neighborhoods and street networks at the city's outer edges.[35] In each of these cases, relationships were common among those living nearby, but only when they could be reached without crossing a major street or going around a building; the social networks mirrored the walkable parts of the street network.

These early findings led researchers to focus on the relationship between physical distance and social network distance, asking whether are people who live or work near one another also connected to one another in a social network. Cities, and all geographic areas are, first and foremost, structured by distances: some people and places are closer than others. The 'community liberated' perspective discussed in Chapter 2 argued that faster transportation and communication has allowed those living in cities to maintain relationships with others located far away. However, distance is more important for some kinds of relationships than others. It is easy to stay in touch with family

METHOD NOTE 14: CONNECTIVITY

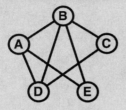

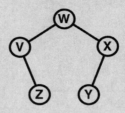

High Connectivity   Low Connectivity

Connectivity is not a single network feature, but rather describes a characteristic of networks that can be measured in a variety of ways:

Average degree centrality—This indicates the average number of connections each node has. In the high connectivity network, the average degree centrality is 2.8, while in the low connectivity network it is only 1.6. In UCINET: Network → Centrality → Degree.

Number of paths between nodes—In the high connectivity network, there are several different paths between each pair of nodes. For example, A and D are connected by four different paths: (1) A → D, (2) A → B → D, (3) A → B → C → D, and (4) A → E → B → C → D. But, in the low connectivity network, there is only one possible path between any pair of nodes. In UCINET: Network → Paths.

Cutpoint—A cutpoint is a node (or set of nodes) that, if removed, makes one node unreachable from another. In the high connectivity network, even if one or two nodes are removed, all the remaining nodes are still reachable from one another. But, in the low connectivity network, removing just one node makes some pairs unreachable. In UCINET: Network → Cohesion → Point Connectivity.[36]

members who live hundreds of miles away, but it can be difficult to make a new friend unless you both live or work relatively close to one another. A range of personal characteristics can also influence the geographic distance of one's social network: younger, better educated, and more mobile individuals tend to have networks that cover larger geographic areas. But, the evidence remains mixed about whether new urbanist-type communities, which aim to bring residents into more frequent contact, actually lead to stronger or denser social networks. Some studies of new urbanist communities have found that those living close to one another are more likely to have a relationship, while others have found that there are few differences in the neighborhood social networks seen in new urbanist communities and sprawling suburban communities.[37]

As these discrepancies highlight, trying to explain the formation of neighborhood social networks using geographic distance can often be misleading because it ignores the importance of street connectivity. In neighborhoods with low street connectivity, two houses can be very close to one another geographically, but still be far apart in the street network. Thus, the likelihood that two individuals in a neighborhood will encounter each other and possibly strike up a friendship does not depend on their distance from one another "as the crow flies," but more practically on their distance from one another in the street network. Moreover, although two houses may be nearby in the street network, they may still be practically far apart because they are separated by a busy intersection or freeway that pedestrians cannot cross. Thus, the likelihood of a social tie forming between two neighbors depends on their houses being connected by a walkable street network.

From this relationship between street networks and social networks, it is possible to predict where neighborhoods are likely to become real, cohesive communities in which the residents know one another. Figure 5.5 illustrates a part of a city's street network. The thick lines represent major roads, while the thin lines represent the smaller *tertiary streets* that run through neighborhoods. A tertiary or *T-community* is an area within which all of the locations are reachable using only tertiary streets. In this example, every location within T-Community A can be reached by walking along its tertiary streets, while every location within T-Community B can be reached via its tertiary streets. However, A and B are separate T-Communities; they are separated by a major road that neighbors walking through the neighborhood are unlikely to cross. Similarly, although B and C are enclosed by the same set of major roads, they are separate T-Communities; to get from one to the other would require a person to use one of the major roads.

Social networks among neighbors tend to form within T-communities like these, but not between them. For example, if the shapes represent the location of houses, the person living at the circle is more likely to know and interact with the person living at the triangle than the one living at the square. Although the circle and square are literally across the street from one another, because it is a very busy street, they are practically miles away. In contrast, although the circle and triangle are several blocks apart, they are linked by walkable tertiary streets that mitigate this distance. Thus, neighborhoods become communities based on the structure of the street networks within them.[38]

Looking at neighborhood street networks in this way not only illustrates how neighborhood social networks form, but also helps explain larger urban social processes, including residential segregation. Individuals often choose to buy homes or rent apartments in areas where their neighbors—the people with whom they are likely to interact on a regular basis—are like themselves. But, as the idea of T-Communities demonstrates, who one interacts with is not necessarily a matter of physical distance, but instead of distance in the tertiary street network. As a result, individuals acting on preferences to interact with similar others ultimately select their residence not simply based on its location in the city, but based on who is reachable by tertiary streets.

When large numbers of individuals act on these preferences, homogeneous T-Communities emerge. That is, the residents within a given T-Community tend to be similar to one another, while those in different T-Communities tend to be dissimilar. For example, although communities

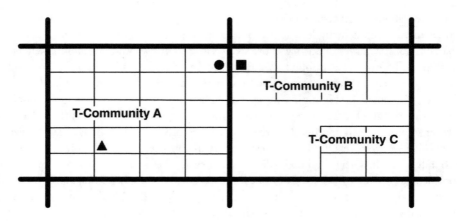

Figure 5.5 Tertiary Streets and T-Communities.

B and C are close to one another in Figure 5.5, it would not be surprising for one to be an entirely white neighborhood and the other to be entirely black. Despite being geographically close together, the fact that their tertiary streets do not connect effectively makes them separate social worlds. Although most research has focused on patterns of segregation by race, it is not the only form of residential segregation. Segregation by income is also common, where wealthy and poor households may be located very close to one another, but nonetheless kept separate by a busy street or other barrier that breaks up the tertiary street network. Indeed, 'bad' neighborhoods are often described as being 'on the wrong side of the tracks,' which calls attention to the important social role of barriers that interrupt networks. Although these forms of segregation can lead to conflict between groups—black vs. white, rich vs. poor—contact between them can lead to greater understanding and reduce prejudice. If well-connected tertiary street networks facilitate neighborly contact, and poorly connected networks produce segregation, then the careful planning of neighborhood streets may provide one approach to addressing problems of group conflict in cities.[39]

Of course, the demographic characteristics of one's neighbors are not the only factors that influences individuals' decisions about where to live. Crime and safety are also important, and these too are influenced by the structure of the street network. Criminals tend to commit crimes in parts of the city with which they are most familiar. Typically, the most familiar parts of the city are those most accessible or connected in the street network: cul-de-sacs are relatively inaccessible and thus only typically those who live on a cul-de-sac are familiar with its location, while major streets are easily accessible and thus city residents are often familiar with them. As a result, the majority of property crimes committed in the city occur along the most accessible parts of the street network, major roads not cul-de-sacs. Although reducing the connectivity of the street network may help to reduce criminal activity, as the discussion above illustrates, it would likely also have a number of undesirable outcomes including increased segregation and decreased physical activity. However, understanding how street networks impact the location of crimes can be useful for deciding where to increase police patrols or install surveillance cameras.[40]

Looking beyond the specific cases of residential segregation or crime, urban street networks shape the patterns of land use throughout a city. Figure 5.6 illustrates three different kinds of street networks, and the land-use patterns that they are likely to produce. In the earliest cities where highly centralized footpaths, or later train routes, brought people to a single central location, radial networks were common. Radial street networks, in which each part of the city is directly connected to the center, lead to a concentric circle pattern of land uses, in which the distance

Figure 5.6 Street Networks and Urban Land Use.

from the center determines how the land is used. In an early agricultural village, region A might be the site of the main marketplace, region B the location of the farmers' homes, and region C the location of the farmland. Similarly, in an industrial city, region A might be the downtown with high-rent office towers, region B may be a manufacturing or industrial zone, and region C may be the location of suburban neighborhoods. Many theories of urban land use adopt this concentric circle model; however, because modern cities' street networks tend to be more complex in reality, their patterns of land use also tend to be more complex.[41]

With the development of automobiles, later cities developed extensive grid street networks that allowed cars to reach any part of the city. Overlaid on this grid were a few major cross-cutting streets—cross-town freeways or major arterial roads—that radiate out from the center. In this type of street network, rather than organized as concentric circles, specific land uses tend to cluster along the main transportation routes. In the illustration, the downtown is still located in the center. However, the industrial and residential zones are now located along the major streets, forming specific sectors that each serve specific functions. This makes it possible to talk of 'the industrial side of town' or 'the run down side of town.' It also helps to explain why, in most cities, similar sets of businesses are clustered along a single major road. One nearly always finds Best Buy, Target, and other stores neatly lined up next to one another along the main road leading to the mall.[42]

Still more recently, a third type of street network and corresponding pattern of land use has emerged. Rather than having a regular grid, some newer cities have a street network that is clustered around a few dense cores. In such cases, the city's major functions and land uses are not regularly distributed, but instead form a patchwork over the urban landscape. This is particularly common in large metropolitan regions such as Los Angeles that have formed from the merging together of many smaller towns. The original city of Los Angeles itself has a grid street network, but as the region grew in population and size, its grid network started bumping into the grid networks of other nearby cities such as Anaheim and San Bernardino. Now, major roads and highways connect these previously separate clusters, where land in each is used differently. Land in Los Angeles is more costly and used for business and industry, while land in Anaheim tends to have more residential uses.[43] Although many variations are possible, the consequences are often the same: once a street network with a particular structure is built, it shapes city life for decades, and in some cases, centuries.

* * * * *

Many different types of infrastructure networks hold cities together, including the pipes that deliver clean water, the power lines that carry electricity, and fiber optic cables that carry digital information. But, perhaps the most highly visible urban infrastructure network is the system of streets that allow individuals to get from here to there. Urban street networks give cities their distinctive shapes, including the radial networks of ancient cities, the strict grids of modern cities, and the more organic networks that result from cities' evolution over time. Despite the apparent variety in street network structures, however, the majority of cities are actually quite similar when viewed as networks. Still, by formally mapping cities' street networks, urban planners are able to consider solutions to a number of seemingly mundane, but critical, urban problems such as traffic congestion. Moreover, beyond their usefulness for solving technical challenges, the organization of street networks shapes everyday life in cities. The New Urbanist movement has sought to promote street connectivity as a path to healthier and more livable cities, while others have explored how street network patterns play a major role in transforming neighborhoods into communities and determining how urban land is used. All of these observations reaffirm the importance of 'location, location, location,' and more specifically that what really matters is location in the street network.

But, it is also important to remember that the network is not static. As urban street networks change, so too do the experiences of the people living in them. In a 1944 allied bombing raid during World War II, nearly all the bridges in Königsburg were destroyed. Only some of them were eventually rebuilt, changing the structure of the city's bridge network that Euler originally examined in 1735. Modern-day Kaliningrad now has only five, not seven, bridges: two on each bank of the river, and three on each island. As a result, and following Euler's discovery using networks, it is now possible for the town's residents to take the walk they had always wanted to, crossing each bridge only once. This small change in the bridge network altered the way the residents could experience their town. But, it also raised a new problem: to take a walk crossing each bridge only once, one must begin on one island and end on the other. It's a good thing there are helicopters.

Discussion Questions and Activities

1. In the dual network shown in Figure 5.3, which node has the highest degree centrality? Find an example of a walk that is not a path. Find an example of a path. What is the average geodesic distance in this network? What is its diameter? Would you describe this as a compact network?

2. Go to www.walkscore.com and find the walkscore of (a) your current address and (b) the address where you grew up. What accounts for the similarity or difference of these scores? What are the advantages or disadvantages of living in a place with a high or low walkscore?

3. In Figure 5.5, suppose a trivial street was built that connected T-communities B and C. What consequences would this have for the demographic composition of these two areas? How would it change the social relations among their residents?

4. In figure 5.6, which street network has the highest connectivity, and which has the lowest? Why? What are the consequences of high or low connectivity? What changes would be necessary to make the low-connectivity street network better connected?

5. How could the methods introduced in the previous chapters be used to study the concepts introduced in this chapter? Similarly, how could the methods introduced in this chapter be used to study the concepts introduced in the previous chapters?

Sources for Street Network Data

U.S. Census Bureau and U.S. Geological Survey—The U.S. Census Bureau maintains the Topologically Integrated Geographic Encoding and Referencing System, or TIGER. This system provides map files that indicate the location of roads, and can be examined using Geographic Information System (GIS) software. These data are free and comprehensive, but do not provide details such as street names; see: www.census.gov/geo/www/tiger. Similarly, the U.S. Geological Survey provides high-resolution satellite images and detailed street maps that can be used to examine road network structures throughout the world; see: http://earthexplorer.usgs.gov

ArcGIS—The ArcGIS software package includes highly detailed street maps that allow not only the examination of street network structures, but also more complex analyses including locating the shortest route between two points. See: www.esri.com/products/index.html#data_panel

RAND—The RAND Center for Population Health and Health Disparities provides data on a wide range of factors influencing health outcomes, including neighborhood street connectivity. The data include measures of the number of streets and intersections, and the average block length and size, for several geographic areas in 1990 and 2000. See: www.rand.org/health/centers/pophealth/data.html

WalkScore—This website uses a variety of online data sources including Google Maps to compute a 'Walk Score' for a given address. The Walk Score considers aspects of street connectivity in the area, as well as the location of nearby amenities such as parks and grocery scores, to measure the area's walkability. To compute a Walk Score, see: www.walkscore.com

6
FUNCTION
WORKING TOGETHER

Complex, modern cities must have both form and function. A city may have a beautiful system of tree-lined boulevards or an easily navigable street grid, but these elements of form are useless if the city does not also have a way to perform such basic functions as keeping these streets clean or passing laws to regulate their use. The last chapter explored how the city can be viewed as a collection of infrastructure networks—streets, but also power lines, water pipes, and other conduits—that together give cities their distinctive physical forms. Complementing this perspective, this chapter examines how cities can also be viewed as a collection of networks among organizations—for example, city hall is linked to the county courts, or the high school is linked to the YMCA—that together allow cities to coordinate and perform practical functions.

It can be useful to think about a modern city like a machine with multiple, interconnected parts. If the parts are connected in just the right way, the machine runs smoothly. But just a couple missing or misdirected connections, and the machine doesn't work right or breaks down. In a city, when organizations and agencies are well coordinated, the public busses get people where they are going on time and the hospitals put sick people in touch with the right specialists. Of course, these various parts of the modern city are not always linked in ways that keep things running so smoothly. Think back to the last time you tried to get a question answered by a city agency. How many times was your call transferred to a different person, or to a different department entirely? Were you eventually able to get your question answered, and did it take more effort than it really should have? When dealing with city governments and other large organizations, we've all had the pleasure of 'cutting through red tape,' 'dealing with bureaucracy,' or 'getting the run-around.' These are all just euphemisms for broken or inefficient organizational networks. That is, they are cases where the person who picked up the phone was not the person with the answer, and worse yet, could not connect us to the person with the answer. This chapter is about how cities' various agencies and organizations are connected in a network, how they *should* be connected, and why it matters.

Thinking about how a city's organizations work is certainly not new. In the past, many sought to understand how urban organizations perform certain functions or exercise influence by studying the organizations themselves, focusing for example, on their size or age. However, this approach ignores the fact that organizations are not isolated and independent, but are linked to one another in networks of interaction that directly affect how they operate.[1] Others use the term 'network' metaphorically to refer to sets of organizations that perform similar functions, are located in a particular location, or are assumed to interact with one another.[2] This is also problematic because although such organizations *might* be linked to one another in a network, it is impossible to know how the network is structured, or even whether a network exists.[3] Viewing the city as a machine with multiple interconnected parts—as an interorganizational network—requires not simply studying individual organizations or sets of organizations, but examining the relationships that link them to one another.[4]

Thus, in this chapter, I explore how networks among the organizations in a city can be examined to gain an understanding of how key urban functions are coordinated and performed. I begin by asking why networks of urban organizations might form, what they might look like, and how they might be structured. Perhaps the most important way that organizations are linked to one another is through the exchange of resources, including money and members. Organizations' position within these resource exchange networks can be a source of their power, but can also assign organizations specific roles to play in the community. Of course, because cities contain many different kinds of organizations exchanging many different kinds of resources, urban interorganizational networks come in many different forms. After describing these building blocks of interorganizational networks, I turn to consider how governing a large and complex city is made possible through a process of collective governance, in which governmental agencies and other organizations that set public policy are linked by relationships of influence. These relationships are particularly important when the organizations' job is to keep a city's residents healthy. Thus, I conclude by examining how networks of social service agencies that coordinate the provision of health care and other services can be organized to maximize the community's well-being.[5]

A Network of Organizations

As Figure 6.1 illustrates, there are several different ways that the interactions between a city's organizations might be structured. A *market* structure describes situations when each organization interacts with other organizations only when it is necessary to achieve a particular goal. In the example, the restaurant might buy its cash registers from the office supply store, the bakery might buy ingredients from the supermarket, and in the most general sense, buyers buy things from sellers. Each of these interactions is independent: the restaurant buying a cash register from the office supply store has no effect on the bakery buying flour from the supermarket. Similarly, the restaurant may interact with the office supply store today, which has no effect on it interacting with the health department tomorrow. In such a system, each time two organizations interact, they alone negotiate the terms of their interaction and engage in what is sometimes described as an *arm's length exchange*. Interorganizational systems structured as pure markets are relatively rare; a stock exchange might be an example because each transaction between two brokers is independent from every other transaction. But, some have argued that neighborhood organizations are also structured in this way.[6]

At the opposite end of the spectrum, interactions can be structured as a *hierarchy* when organizations interact only with other organizations that are one rank higher or lower in status, following a rigid and often predefined pattern. In the example, the city's police headquarters sends orders to precincts that cover large parts of the city, which in turn send orders to police stations and beats in particular neighborhoods. In many cases, hierarchical structures of interorganizational interaction result from official or legal requirements: a city's laws may state that police organizations must interact in this way. In such a system, a single organization or office often has either direct or indirect control over those below it. Like markets, interorganizational systems structured as pure hierarchies are also relatively rare, appearing primarily in heavily regulated industries and in cities with centrally planned governments like those found in communist societies.

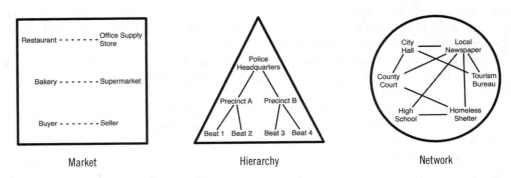

Figure 6.1 Forms of Interorganizational Interaction.

Market and hierarchy structures represent opposite ends of a spectrum that range from total independence to complete dependence on and control by a few key organizations. *Network* structures fall somewhere between these two extremes, and characterize the majority of interorganizational systems.[7] Interorganizational networks have two unique properties that are not found in markets or hierarchies: interdependence and embeddedness. *Interdependence* refers to the fact that each organization depends not only on those other organizations it interacts with directly, but also on the whole system of organizations. In the example, city hall depends on the county court to manage loitering in the local parks, which depends on the homeless shelter to provide the homeless a place to go, which depends on the local newspaper to advertise these services, which depends on city hall providing a business license to publish and sell newspapers. Similarly, *embeddedness* refers to the fact that organizations cannot simply do anything they wish; their behavior is constrained by the expectations of other organizations in the network. For example, if the local newspaper begins printing negative stories about city hall politics, then city hall may ask the tourism bureau to stop buying advertising space in the newspaper.[8]

The majority of research on interorganizational networks has focused on corporations and industries, examining how buyers and sellers around the world are linked to one another. However, attention has more recently turned to the networks among public organizations such as the governmental and social service agencies found in major cities, and more importantly, to the fact that public interorganizational networks are often different from their private counterparts.[9] Most significantly, unlike linkages between private companies, which tend to focus on managing competition in the marketplace, linkages between public organizations more often focus on developing cooperative or collaborative arrangements that are beneficial not only to the cooperating organizations but to the entire network. For example, the county court and local high schools may collaborate on a program for delinquent youth; the result could be disastrous, or at least much less beneficial, if the courts and schools instead tried to compete with one another on this goal.

In addition to their greater tendency toward collaboration, public organizations also face unique external pressures that affect the structure of the network among them. First, a wide range of public organizations commonly receive their funding from a limited set of state and federal sources. When two organizations receive their funding from the same source, they are not only likely to be connected to each other, but also likely to have similar patterns of connections to other organizations; in the language of networks, they tend to be *structurally equivalent*. Second, the priorities and staff of public organizations can change frequently and unexpectedly as new politicians and political parties advance new agendas after each election. As a result, public interorganizational networks are often constantly changing, with old relationships dissolving and new ones forming.

Finally, because they must be accountable to the taxpaying citizens, public organizations are often subject to strict regulatory requirements about how they interact. Although partnerships between companies in the business world can often be cemented by a handshake, partnerships between public organizations frequently require contracts and other formal arrangements.

The interorganizational networks that hold cities together, whether composed of public organizations, private organizations, or a combination of the two, can form in different ways. In some cases, certain organizations are required to interact with certain other organizations by an exogenous force, such as a legal or political mandate. For example, the high school is required to report to the school district, and the hospital is required to report to the health department. In other cases, interorganizational networks arise from an endogenous process. Organizations seek to form relationships with other organizations when cooperation could be mutually beneficial, but they must rely on their existing relationships to locate such opportunities. As new relationships form, additional information about collaboration opportunities becomes available, leading to the formation of still other new relationships: the evolution of the interorganizational network depends on its structure in the past.[10]

There are also multiple types of relationships that can link organizations into an interorganizational network. Organizations can be linked by formal or mandated relations, which typically have a hierarchical structure and are often represented in the form of an organizational chart. Nearly all major cities provide a copy of the organization chart that shows the linkages between city departments on their website. Organizations can also be linked by similarity in their characteristics, such as the types of functions they perform. Complementary organizations such as an elementary school and high school are linked because students progress from one organization to the next during their education, while organizations that serve unrelated or conflicting functions are not connected. But, perhaps the most commonly examined type of linkage between organizations in an interorganizational network is the exchange of resources. In some cases, organizations exchange information with one another, seeking new opportunities for funding or more efficient ways of doing things. In other cases, organizations exchange money and other material resources, such as when a school allows a local church to use its auditorium on Sundays. In still other cases, organizations can exchange moral or political support, advocating for one another. Notably, these different kinds of interorganizational networks often have very different structures, even for the same set of organizations. For example, although the police and fire departments may be linked to the city council but not to one another in the official organization chart, they likely exchange information and material resources more informally.[11]

Do interorganizational networks actually work? The diversity of types and forms of interorganizational networks in cities makes this a complex question to answer. At least three features of interorganizational networks are significant in determining how effective they are. First, the structure of the network plays an important but context-dependent role: a centralized network with a few leader organizations may be effective in one context, while in another context a decentralized network in which every organization contributes equally may be better. Second, the origin of the network can constrain its effectiveness: networks that form because they are mandated by law may be highly effective, but only for the narrow purposes they are designed to serve. Finally, the network's stage of development can influence its effectiveness: networks that are still evolving may not always be effective, but are often more flexible to adapt to new situations. Questions of interorganizational network effectiveness also require asking, effective for whom? Some features of the network may be beneficial only to individual organizations, while other features benefit the network as a whole. In the case of networks among social service agencies, the goal is often to identify features that will benefit not only individual organizations, or the network itself, but the entire city or community that the network and its constituent organizations serve. The rest of this chapter explores some of these features to understand how interorganizational networks make complex cities work.[12]

It's All About the Resources

Two closely related theories are often used to understand interorganizational networks: resource exchange and resource dependence. *Resource exchange* theories focus on how organizations obtain critical resources from one another. For example, nonprofit organizations obtain funding from federal agencies or corporate donors, social organizations recruit new members from other social organizations, and interest groups seek the support of political parties. Whatever the resource, these theories suggest that how organizations operate depends on their position within the networks through which these resources are exchanged. Similarly, *resource dependence* theories focus on organizations' sources for the resources they need. Some organizations can obtain the resources they need—money, members, and support—from many different sources, while others are highly dependent upon just a few sources. Those that are highly dependent often have more limited freedom to pursue their goals. For example, although a high school in a wealthy suburb may have all the resources it needs, it may be entirely dependent on a politically conservative school board for those resources. As a result, the school cannot take actions—for example, offering a seminar on safe sex—that conflict with the agenda of the school board. These two theories highlight that although different organizations' have different primary goals—schools educate students, hospitals treat patients, and stores serve customers—they all have two goals in common: maximize their flow of resources, and minimize their dependence on others for resources.[13]

A series of studies of the organizations operating in three mid-Western cities—DeKalb and Aurora, Illinois, and Indianapolis, Indiana—in the late 1970s first documented how the networks of interorganizational resource exchange impact the roles that organizations play in their communities.[14] In each case, the researchers asked representatives of the organizations with which other organizations they exchanged three different types of resources: money, information, and moral support. Their responses provided a picture of three different interorganizational networks: one that captured which organizations exchange money with one another, a second that captured which organizations exchange information, and a third that captured which organizations that offer one another moral support.

In such networks, the organizations that exchange resources with many others occupy highly central positions. However, exactly which organizations are central (or not) and the overall structure of the network, often depends on the type of resource being exchanged. In exchanges of money, the most central organizations tend to be major institutions such as universities, organizations with a wide audience such as local media outlets, and broad-based organizations such as the United Way. Although these central organizations exchange money with many others, most organizations exchange money with just a few others. Moreover, these exchanges tend to be clustered within either the private or public sector: public organizations exchange money mostly with other public organizations, while private organizations exchange money with other private organizations.

In contrast to this public–private divide in the money exchange network, exchanges of information and moral support are structured differently. In exchanges of information, organizations focused on general community issues such as the city council tend to be central, while less central organizations cluster their exchanges of information around more specialized issues such as business development or social services. Similarly, in exchanges of moral support, organizations focused on issues of collective importance such as health and education are often more central, while those focused on issues of individual interest occupy more peripheral positions. The existence of well-connected organizations in these resource exchange networks, highlights how some organizations play a bigger role than others in organizing the flow of resources in cities.

However, the differences between these networks also highlight that a single organization might be central to the flow of some resources, but not others.

Although describing the structure of resource exchange networks can illustrate how a city's organizations interact with one another, it is important to consider why some organizations are more central and why being central matters. Perhaps not surprisingly, wealthy organizations and large organizations with many members are generally the most central because they have more resources to exchange with other organizations. For example, when a neighborhood improvement association needs help building a new playground, it likely goes to the bank to obtain a loan or the United Way to recruit volunteers. Such patterns, when they are repeated, make organizations such as banks and the United Way more central in the community's resource exchange network. Central organizations like these are the ones that other organizations depend on for resources; their position of centrality means they can 'call the shots.' Thus, being central in resource exchange networks is important because more central organizations have more influence over other organizations and over the community generally.

Because organizations with resources tend to be central, and organizations that are central tend to be influential, it often appears that organizations with the most resources are the most influential. However, this ignores the critical importance of resource exchange networks. Organizations with resources are only more influential if that can transform their resources into centrality by participating in exchanges with other organizations. In the language of statistics: the relationship between an organization's resources and its influence is mediated by its position in the exchange network. Well-resourced but isolated organizations that keep their resources to themselves—a wealthy cult, or a bank that never makes loans—have little influence. In contrast, under-resourced organizations that reach out and interact with others—grassroots social movements such as Occupy Wall Street—can become quite powerful. This helps to explain how neighborhood associations even in underprivileged communities, when they form partnerships with other similar groups to share information and moral support, can take on major corporations that have few local connections.

Although centrality in exchange networks is important, it does not tell the whole story. The organizational world of a major city is complex, and frequently organizations specialize in the roles that they play, giving rise to an organizational division of labor. The particular role that an organization plays often depends on its position within these networks, and more specifically on whether an organization depends on others for resources, as well as whether other organizations depend on it. In the simplest case, there are four different kinds of roles:

Generators: Generator organizations are the initial source of resources in the community. Other organizations depend on generators for the resources they need, but generators do not depend on others. Organizations playing the role of generator often include businesses and government agencies that serve as sources of money, but can also include service clubs that serve as sources of volunteer manpower.

Consumers: Consumer organizations use resources obtained from other organizations to achieve their goals. They depend on other organizations, but other organizations do not depend on them. Many of a city's organizations, ranging from neighborhood associations to police stations, often play the role of consumers.

Transmitters: Transmitter organizations link generators and consumers, funneling resources where they are needed most. They depend on some organizations for resources, while other organizations depend on them. Banks and media organizations often act as transmitters by facilitating the flow of money and information between organizations.

Isolates: Isolate organizations are disconnected from the rest of the interorganizational network. They do not depend on other organizations for resources, and other organizations do not depend on them.

An organization's role, perhaps as much as its centrality, can determine its influence in the community. Clearly isolated organizations can have limited impact on urban affairs; they do not interact with other organizations, and thus have no opportunity to affect change. Consumer organizations may be somewhat more influential, but because they are totally dependent on other organizations, they too are limited. Although generator organizations are the source of the resources that keep a city's organizations running, even they are rarely the most influential. Instead, transmitter organizations tend to wield the greatest influence. As a critical bridge between generators and consumers, they can place demands on both in return for linking them with one another.

Organizational roles are rarely this clear cut. An organization may play the role of generator in some cases, and consumer in others; it may be central to the exchange of some resources, but peripheral for others. Consider, for example, the case of a single department within city government: waste management. Trash collection is an essential service in large cities, but one that is easy to ignore. Moreover, departments of waste management are embedded in complex exchange networks that not only ensure the trash gets collected, but also shape how other organizations relate to one another, and thus contribute to how the city functions. A city's waste management department plays the role of consumer when it interacts with local labor unions because it 'consumes' workers, but plays the role of generator when it interacts with a recycling company because it 'generates' or serves as a source for recyclable materials. Similarly, although the department may be peripheral in networks of monetary exchange, it is likely central in the exchange of information among government agencies concerned with such things as road conditions or environmental issues. Eliminating any one of these interorganizational linkages, or worse, eliminating the department from the network completely, would not only hinder trash collection, but could impact city functions ranging from union relations to road maintenance.

Why Mayors Aren't Monarchs

Over the past several decades, interorganizational networks have come to play an increasingly important role in how cities are governed. City governance has two broad functions: to provide services such as trash collection, and to create policies such as local building codes.[15] In the absence of a government to coordinate these functions, they would likely be carried out by a series of independent interactions organized like a market (see Figure 6.1). For example, each individual who wanted their trash collected would need to find someone to do it, and each individual who wanted to build a house would work out the details with the builder. Such an arrangement might be called *market governance*. Clearly, leaving the coordination of such important functions to a series of disconnected individuals and organizations could result in chaos: some trash might not get collected, and some houses may not be safe to live in.

As a result, city governance functions are often performed by a city government, which organizes the various departments and agencies that provide services and create policies into a strict hierarchy. For example, the mayor's office issues orders to the department of streets and sanitation, which in turn issues orders to the waste management division, which in turn collects the trash. Similarly, the mayor's office also issues orders to the department of housing and economic development, which in turn issues orders to the land-use planning division, which in turn drafts new zoning laws. Such an arrangement might be called *hierarchical governance*. In both cases, control over the services and policies ultimately rests with the organization or agency at the top of the hierarchy.

METHOD NOTE 15: ROLES AND BLOCK MODELING

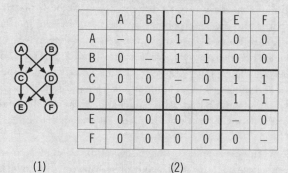

	A	B	C	D	E	F
A	–	0	1	1	0	0
B	0	–	1	1	0	0
C	0	0	–	0	1	1
D	0	0	0	–	1	1
E	0	0	0	0	–	0
F	0	0	0	0	0	–

	A/B	C/D	E/F
A/B	0	1	0
C/D	0	0	1
E/F	0	0	0

Generators A and B → Transmitters C and D → Consumers E and F

(1)   (2)   (3)   (4)

Frequently the roles that nodes play in their setting, whether they are people in a neighborhood or organizations in a city, depend on the positions they occupy in a network. *Block modeling* can often uncover patterns that indicate which nodes play different roles.

In the simple network in panel 1, nodes A and B send resources to nodes C and D, which in turn send resources to E and F. This network can be represented as the matrix shown in panel 2. Some patterns appear in this matrix: there are blocks of cells that all have the same value. For example, because A and B both send resources to C and D, the group of four cells in the top-center are all ones. Because nodes A and B both have the same pattern of connections to the same other nodes (C and D), they are described as being *structurally equivalent*. The dark lines in the matrix highlight the location of other blocks of structurally equivalent nodes.

When a set of nodes is structurally equivalent, they can often be treated as if they were a single node. Using this approach, it is possible to transform the matrix in panel 2 into the matrix in panel 3. The new matrix treats each pair of structurally equivalent nodes as a single node. For example, instead of including separate rows and columns for nodes A and B, these two nodes are treated as one (A/B). Similarly, nodes C and D are treated as one (C/D), as well as nodes E and F (E/F). The new matrix is called an *image matrix* because it provides a simplified image of the larger, more complete matrix.

From the image matrix, a new sociogram like the one in panel 4 can be drawn. This network does not include nodes for each of the individual actors (A–F), but only for sets of structurally equivalent nodes. By examining the pattern of connections within and between the structurally equivalent sets of nodes, it is often possible to interpret these as roles. In this case, nodes A and B both play the role of resource generators, nodes C and D both play the role of resource transmitters, and nodes E and F both play the role of resource consumers. In UCINET: Network → Roles & Positions.[16]

Such an organization might appear to make mayors into monarchs, giving them almost complete control over city government.

However, in reality mayors usually aren't like monarchs; their control is much more limited and dispersed owing to several important changes in government not only at the city level, but also at the state and national levels. Governments have increasingly stepped back from their past role as service provider by relying instead on private subcontractors to collect trash, teach students, or provide public housing. Similarly, public policies are no longer simply handed down from an all-powerful office at the top of a hierarchy, but are the result of negotiations between many different governmental departments and private organizations. These changes have given rise to what some have called the *hollow state*, in which the city government does not perform city governance functions such as providing services and creating policies by itself, but in conjunction with a whole system of public and private organizations. For example, the mayor's office may issue orders to the zoning board, but the zoning board may also receive pressure from an investment company that wants to develop land in the city. The policy outcome depends neither on a one-time arrangement between the zoning board and the investment company as it might under market governance, nor solely on the mayor's office as it might under hierarchical governance. Instead, under *network governance*, the policy outcome depends on the pattern of interactions among all these groups.[17]

The networks that lie at the heart of network governance can have several different structures, which each influence how governance activities are actually carried out. The top row of networks in Figure 6.2 illustrates some of the ways that organizations with distinct agendas might interact to create public policy. For example, in a discussion about how to use a neighborhood's vacant lot, suppose A, B, and C are local community groups, while X, Y, and Z are corporations. In some cases, all of the organizations interact with one another to collectively arrive at policies that arise out of consensus. This could yield a decision to build offices on the vacant lot, but to require the corporations to also pay for the construction of a playground for neighborhood children. At the opposite extreme, organizations' distinct agendas can polarize them into disconnected components, within which organizations pursue conflicting policies. The corporations may insist on an office building, while the community groups insist on a playground.

As a midpoint between collective and polarized policy networks, a bargaining network relies on a few organizations to bridge the gap through negotiation, seeking policies that may not enjoy complete consensus, but at least indirectly involve all the concerned organizations. Still another possibility is a polycentric network, in which some organizations with very different agendas work together, while others with similar goals do not. In these cases, new policies may form in clusters of the network—for example, with A, X, and Y collaborating—and spread outward to others. The

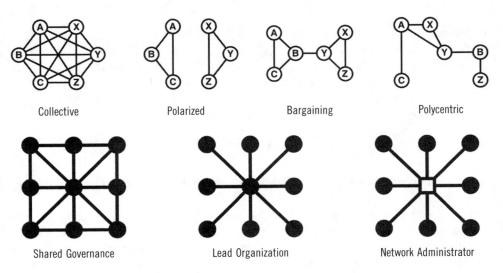

Collective   Polarized   Bargaining   Polycentric

Shared Governance   Lead Organization   Network Administrator

Figure 6.2 Structures of Network Governance.

former two structures—collective and polarized—are relatively rare: collective networks eventually form cracks as organizations' goals diverge, while organizations in polarized networks inevitably seek common ground in order to make progress. As collective networks become polycentric, or bargaining emerges in polarized networks, organizations' positions in these networks becomes more important: for example, organizations B and Y play a more significant role in developing policies in the network with a bargaining structure than they do in those with collective or polarized structures.[18]

A second way of thinking about the structure of governance networks involves focusing on *centralization*. Centralization describes the extent to which just one organization coordinates the activities of other organizations. The bottom row of networks in Figure 6.2 illustrates how governance may be more or less centralized. In a highly decentralized network, the activities of governance are shared by all organizations, and no single organization is in charge. For example, the local store owners on a town's main street may all work together to keep the street clean and safe, helping one another sweep the sidewalk or watch for criminal activity. Although no single organization is in charge of coordinating the street's maintenance, it still gets done. This form of network governance can be highly effective when there are just a few organizations and they agree on their common goals.

However, when there are many organizations or they may not all agree on the goals, a more centralized governance network is necessary. One possibility is for a single organization to take the lead in coordinating activities. The largest business on Main Street may coordinate the street-beautifying efforts of all the local businesses, for example, by posting a sign-up sheet for specific days or by delegating specific tasks such as sweeping and planting flowers. Notably, although the governance is still performed by a network of organizations, in a centralized governance network, the central organization plays a unique role and also has greater control over affairs. In still more complex settings, such as maintaining a major business district in a large city, the businesses themselves may not have the time or expertise to serve as a lead organization. In such cases, a separate network administrator organization may step in to coordinate governance. For example, the Grand Central Partnership in New York City is not itself a business, but instead is an organization that coordinates the activities of businesses near Grand Central Station. Indeed, it is just one example of an increasingly common form of network governance in major cities known as Business Improvement Districts, in which a range of local services including publicity and beautification are coordinated by an outside organization that links together local businesses.[19]

These possible governance network structures are ideal types that help to understand in general terms how such networks can be organized. However, because in practice they are more complex, understanding how governance networks actually function in urban settings requires considering some specific examples. In contrast to British cities, where public policy has been tightly controlled by a highly centralized national government, local urban policies in French cities are more often the result of decentralized governance networks. Such decentralized networks can often lead to large city budgets and excessive spending because there is little coordination and oversight; no one is 'in charge.' As a result, by 1989 the local government's cultural spending on museums, festivals, and performance venues in Rennes was out of control, and led to a local financial crisis. In response, a much more centralized policy network emerged. At its center, the Ministry of Culture provided expertise, the Rennes City Council provided funding, and a few local cultural elites provided legitimacy. Although these central organizations maintained contact with a large network of cultural institutions requesting money and support, the governance network's more centralized structure made it possible to better prioritize cultural spending.[20]

Although in the Rennes case, the governance network evolved from decentralized to centralized, other structural changes are also possible. Partnerships focused on urban regeneration or

METHOD NOTE 16: CENTRALIZATION

Centralized

Decentralized

Moderately Decentralized

Centralization refers to the extent to which a single node is highly central, while all the other nodes are non-central. The network on the left is highly centralized because one node has many connections, while the other nodes have very few. The network in the middle is minimally centralized (or, decentralized) because each of the nodes has the same number of connections.

In the case of degree centrality, a network's centralization is computed using:

$$\frac{\sum C_{max} - C_i}{(N-1)(N-2)}$$

Consider the 'moderately centralized' network on the right. To find the numerator of this formula, first determine the centrality of the most central node (C_{max}). In this case, $C_{max} = 3$ because node A is the most central node with three edges. Second, subtract the centrality of each of the other nodes from C_{max}: node B has a centrality of one ($3 - 1 = 2$), node C has a centrality of two ($3 - 2 = 1$), and node D has a centrality of two ($3 - 2 = 1$). Finally, add these values together ($2 + 1 + 1 = 4$).

The denominator for the centralization formula is comparatively easy to find because it is simply based on the total number of nodes in the network (N). In a network with four nodes, the denominator is 6 because $(4 - 1) \times (4 - 2) = 3 \times 2 = 6$. The final step in computing a network's centrality is to divide the numerator by the denominator. For the moderately centralized network above, its centralization is 0.66 because $4 / 6 = 0.66$. This indicates that the network on the right is 66 percent as centralized as a maximally centralized network of the same size. The UCINET software automatically computes a whole network's centralization any time it computes individual nodes' centrality.[21]

revitalization in British cities in the past two decades have followed a different trajectory. These partnerships often begin as loose and informal networks among organizations that may have overlapping goals or members. Although such decentralized networks may not provide the structure necessary to make urban regeneration happen, they can facilitate an interorganizational exchange of information that is necessary in the planning stages. As the partnerships solidify, they often shift from a network to a hierarchical form of organization, with one dominant organization emerging to shape the partnership's goals and procedures. In fact, some of the national funding programs in the U.K., including the Single Regeneration Budget program, required that requests came from a leader organization. However, once funding is obtained and the partnerships' individual organizations began to engage in regeneration activities—for example, providing funding or services to local communities—they tended to do so independently, shifting this time from a hierarchical to a market form of organization. Finally, when funding and regeneration activities concluded, the interactions among those organizations still interested in maintaining the partnership returned to the form of a loose and informal network.[22]

These examples, while different in many respects, both featured the emergence of key organizations that organize the structure of the governance network. But, how do some organizations become central in the network, and how do they justify occupying such a position and the greater power it affords them? Such questions are especially important for highly contentious urban issues such as environmental sustainability. However, studies examining interorganizational networks focused on environmental issues in Stockholm, Tampere, and San Francisco have found some common themes. First, central organizations can often acquire and justify their prominent positions in governance networks on the grounds that they offer expertise. For example, the environmental department in Tampere has occupied a key position in the governance network on environmental policy because it has technical expertise in such matters, much like the Ministry of Culture in Rennes has in matters of culture. Second, organizations can justify their network role because they provide democratic representation of local viewpoints. For example, more locally based environmental organizations in San Francisco have been more likely to collaborate with other organizations and to become embedded in the environmental policy network, in part because they are the key channels for local residents' views to be represented. Finally, still other organizations justify their centrality on the grounds that they are promoting a common good. For example, in Stockholm a centralized network of ecological management agencies monitoring several different areas of the city, rather than a decentralized network in which different agencies monitor different areas, could better protect the common environmental good.[23]

However, despite the potential benefits of network governance, others have argued that it may also have several downsides. In their ideal form, governance networks distribute power more evenly across multiple organizations and agencies in the city, ranging from corporations to small community groups. But, it is equally possible that informal and unofficial governance networks can concentrate power in the hands of a few powerful organizations behind the scenes. Although representative democracy rests on the notion that unpopular policy makers can be voted out of office, when policy decisions are made in decentralized networks in which the policy makers are invisible and cannot be 'removed from office,' urban policies run the risk of being less representative and less democratic. Similarly, in its ideal form, network governance is assumed to be more flexible than hierarchical governance because organizations and agencies can collaborate in ways that are not possible in a strict and rigid hierarchy. However, because no one is 'in charge' when basic city services are provided by a network of public and private subcontractors, if those collaborative linkages deteriorate, the entire system can rapidly crumble. Thus, it remains an open question whether network governance offers greater equality in urban policy and more efficiency in urban services, or simply a new and subtler way for the powerful to dominate.[24]

United We Stand . . . Sometimes

Although interorganizational networks are critical for the governance of modern cities, these networks are also important for organizing collective action in communities. Independent organizations often form partnerships or coalitions that allow them to pool their resources and influence to pursue collective goals. As the previous section illustrated, in some cases those collective goals can include influencing public policy and affecting how the city is governed. However, in other cases, coalitions among urban organizations can form to pursue very different collective goals, as when street gangs form alliances to more effectively control their territory.[25] Whatever the specific goals may be, one challenging question remains: how can independent organizations form coalitions that allow them to engage in collective actions as if they are one large organization?

Many researchers have sought an answer to this question, attempting to identify what is necessary to transform a disconnected set of organizations each pursuing their own goals into a coalition of collaborating organizations working together to achieve common goals. Some have argued that organizations' capacity to form effective coalitions depends on the attitudes of their members and leaders, the availability of resources, or the focus and realism of their goals.[26] All of these may play an important role in whether organizations can form coalitions, but they all focus on things inside the individual organizations: their own members, their own resources, and their own goals. Even more important than any of these is the wider environment, or *community field*, within which the organizations operate.[27] Beginning initially in rural communities, scholars have increasingly recognized that the potential for coalitions to form among organizations depends not on the characteristics of the individual organizations themselves, but rather on the characteristics of the entire set of organizations in the area. Coalitions, after all, are built upon the interactions between organizations, and thus are a type of interorganizational network.

There are several different ways that organizations in a given community might interact, and thus different ways they might be linked in a network. Organizations with potentially opposing goals, such as a city's churches and bars, may have relations of conflict, while organizations with complementary goals, such as a city's elementary schools and public libraries, are more likely to develop cooperative relations. Cooperative relations may take different forms as well. Organizations with very similar goals may be linked by strong social bonds, forged by friendships among their members or by the fact that the same individuals are members of both organizations. Organizational linkages based on friendship and overlapping membership often foster a sense of shared identity and purpose, bringing together similar organizations in dense network clusters. In contrast, organizations with different but complementary goals may be linked by more instrumental transactions in which they share information or collaborate on a one-time project. These more temporary and special-purpose interactions can act as bridges between organizations in different parts of the network that facilitate otherwise unlikely collaborations. For a coalition to be effective, both types of ties are important: strong social bonds that support a collective identity, and weaker ones that allow key resources to be shared.[28]

In addition to finding a balance between strong and weak ties, coalitions must also balance their cohesion and inclusiveness. A coalition characterized by a dense and cohesive network among its member organizations can develop a more narrowly focused plan of action, but may also exclude some organizations that are less directly connected to its goals, which in turn may form competing coalitions. In contrast, a coalition characterized by a sparse and diffuse network can cultivate broad-based support among a large number of member organizations, but may have difficulty in achieving consensus about how to pursue goals. This type of tension has been particularly relevant for one coalition aimed at school reform in Oakland, California. After years of mismanagement, the state took control of the Oakland school district from the local school board, which created an opportunity for a coalition of reform organizations to advance its agenda of smaller, more autonomous schools. Because its member organizations all shared a common vision and were closely connected to one another, the reform coalition was able to act quickly and decisively. However, at the same time, because it lacked connections to more traditional organizations including the teachers' union and state board of education, it was unable to cultivate broad-based support. Thus, in addition to balancing their weak and strong ties, effective coalitions must also balance having a core of deeply committed organizations with reaching out to a wide range of potential supporters.[29]

Indeed, given the many pressures that coalitions of urban organizations must balance, sustaining them is notoriously difficult. However, some have argued that the real challenge for coalition building is the fact that coalitions' network structures are poorly understood or taken for granted. That is, it is one thing to describe a coalition as a network among organizations working together, but an entirely different thing to actually understand which organizations are connected (or not) to which other organizations. Whether on their own or with the assistance of researchers, adopting a formal network perspective can help community coalitions enhance their effectiveness. For example, examining which organizations occupy central positions in the coalition network may reveal that some particularly critical organizations are in peripheral positions and should be more fully integrated into the network. Similarly, identifying dense clusters or cliques of organizations within the coalition network may point toward the need to establish new bridging ties to facilitate the movement of information and other resources among all organizations.[30]

Keeping the City Healthy

Perhaps the most important function that interorganizational networks perform in cities today is the coordination and delivery of human services that promote individuals' well-being. This role might be traced initially to the Community Mental Health Centers Act of 1963 that, through a process known as deinstitutionalization, prompted the closure of state-run mental hospitals and the subsequent release of their former patients into mainstream society. These individuals needed a range of different social and psychological services, which came to be provided in communities by networks of specialized organizations: some provided psychiatric care, while others provided help finding a job or home. Since this time, many different human services have come to be provided not by single comprehensive institutions, but by networks that link specialized organizations to one another. However, the effectiveness of these sets of specialized organizations in promoting well-being depends in large part on how the network among them is structured.

Figure 6.3 illustrates three different possibilities. In these examples, the nodes are organizations providing social services and the edges connect pairs of organizations that coordinate their services by referring clients to one another. For example, a homeless shelter may refer its clients to an employment agency, thus coordinating the services both provide—temporary housing and employment—to help individuals get back on their feet. What type of network structure is best for coordinating the delivery of social services?

It may seem reasonable to assume that more linkages are better than fewer linkages, and thus that a dense service delivery network is best. After all, if every organization can refer its clients to any other organization, then all their services can be coordinated; no one would 'fall through the cracks.' Indeed, this is the approach adopted by many communities seeking to improve the delivery of social services and the well-being of their residents. However, simply creating more linkages between organizations and increasing the density of the network is not necessarily effective, and actually can be quite detrimental. In a very dense network, where every organization is connected to every (or at least, most) other organizations, the people who are supposed to focus on delivering services ultimately spend much of their time simply maintaining the network. For example, while a hospital is supposed to deliver health care to sick patients, if it is responsible for coordinating

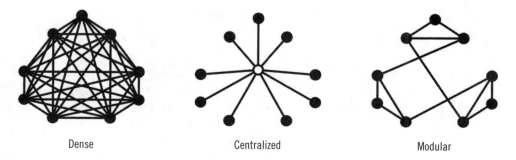

Dense   Centralized   Modular

Figure 6.3 Service Delivery Networks.

its services with every other organization in the city, the doctors and nurses will spend most of their time on the phone or filling out paperwork. Thus, while more linkages might seem better, the sheer weight of a dense network can become a burden for the organizations involved.

One solution to this problem involves centralizing the coordination of services, for example, in a city-wide call center or other organization that brokers or facilitates connections. This is a solution that many cities have implemented. In Chicago, dialing 3-1-1 connects residents to the city's central call center, where they can then be connected to the police to report vandalism, to streets and sanitation to find out why their street hasn't been plowed yet, or to the health department to complain about the fly in their soup. Centralizing the service delivery network around a call center or other lead organization is more efficient than a dense network because it relieves organizations of the burden of needing to coordinate services themselves. Such an arrangement can also make it easier for a city's residents to get in touch with the right organization; no matter what one needs help with, the first step is always the same: call the call center. However, despite its great efficiency, a centralized service delivery network hides one significant risk. If the centralized node is a call center, what happens when the phones aren't working? Or, more generally, what if the centralized node is missing from the network? Coordination of services becomes not only difficult but impossible because, without the central node, the whole network becomes completely disconnected.[31]

METHOD NOTE 17: MISSING DATA

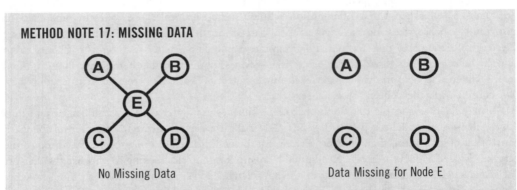

No Missing Data   Data Missing for Node E

In other types of data such as that collected by surveys, missing data can be problematic because it can create biases in the results. This is even truer in network analysis, where even small amounts of missing data can dramatically alter the conclusions. The example networks above illustrate why.

Suppose the network on the left is complete; it is not missing any data. This network is highly centralized, with node E playing a particularly important role linking all the other nodes to one another. If the nodes were social service organizations, then we might conclude that all the organizations are able to coordinate their services with one another through the assistance of broker organization E.

But, what if, while surveying organizations about their relationships with one another, organization E was not asked to participate or declined to participate? Now the network has a completely different structure: the network is completely disconnected and fragmented. This might lead to a completely different conclusion in the context of service delivery: we might conclude that the organizations are unable to coordinate their services with one another and that a humanitarian disaster is imminent. Thankfully, we would be wrong, but this highlights how missing data on even a single node can so radically alter a network's structure that it can lead to opposite and incorrect conclusions. Therefore, even more than in other types of research, it is important to minimize the amount of missing data in network research and to be cautious of analyzing networks that contain missing data.[32]

This is indeed a risk, but given the efficiency of centralization, maybe it is one worth taking. Perhaps not. In practice, centralized service delivery networks may not be terribly efficient either. One study examining the provision of services to those living with HIV/AIDS in Baltimore found that organizations more often collaborated directly with one another than with the assistance of a central coordinating organization.[33] In fact, whether addressing adolescent problem behaviors in rural Pennsylvania communities or substance abuse prevention in cities, service delivery tends to be most effective when the network among organizations or their leaders is neither dense nor centralized. A sparse network ensures that organizations can spend the majority of their time and energy on actually serving clients, rather than on simply maintaining their relationships with other organizations. And, a decentralized network ensures that collaborative arrangements are spread across many different organizations, rather than dependent on just one central organization.[34]

But, this may seem somewhat paradoxical. How can decentralized and sparse networks, in which there is no organizing center and few connections, possibly be effective at coordinating services in large cities? The answer lies in the efficiency of *modular* networks in which clusters of similar organizations are working together. In service delivery networks, organizations that provide similar services often form clusters. For example, organizations providing services for children including childcare centers and pediatric clinics tend to interact frequently with each other. Similarly, those providing services to the unemployed including employment agencies and professional schools are likely to collaborate. However, there are likely to be only a few, infrequent interactions between organizations in different clusters: there may be little need for pediatric clinics and employment agencies to work together.

A modular network, characterized by frequent interaction within clusters and infrequent interaction between clusters, offers two major benefits for service delivery. First, the frequent within-cluster interaction allows similar organizations to share information and resources that are useful for the entire cluster. For example, within a child services cluster, the childcare center can quickly alert pediatric clinics about a flu outbreak, while a professional school can direct graduates to the employment agency. Second, the infrequent between-cluster interaction allows organizations to focus on the services they specialize in, while still allowing them to connect clients to other clusters when necessary. For example, organizations focused on child services may not collaborate regularly with those focused on unemployment services, but a single linkage between just one or two organizations in these clusters allows an employment agency to link a newly employed individual with childcare services if the need arises. Thus, although the linkages between clusters may be used only infrequently, they are important because they hold the service delivery network together.[35]

Whether through organizations in brokering positions, or through a clustered structure, interorganizational networks play a key role in delivering services to urban residents. This has called into question the role of other factors formerly considered influential. First, organizations with many resources are usually assumed to be more effective at delivering services. For example, it may seem likely that a local health department with a large budget and staff will be more effective at delivering flu vaccines to the local population. While this may be the case, it is not the resources themselves—the money and people—that make the organization effective. Instead, having these resources allows the health department to form collaborative relationships with other organizations, and it is these relationships that make it effective. Therefore, an organization with resources is not necessarily more effective: a well-resourced organization, if it does not use those resources to build relationships with other organizations, will be ineffective. Second, residents in poor neighborhoods are usually assumed to have limited access to services owing to the isolating effects of poverty and segregation. For example, they may have difficulty obtaining a flu vaccine because the clinic is not located nearby and they do not know where to go. However, the social service organizations serving poor communities tend to be well connected because the needs of their community force them to forge collaborative relationships, and thus they are often able to link poor residents to the services they need. Therefore, living in a poor community does not necessarily put services out of reach: even poor organizations in poor neighborhoods, if they are well connected, can effectively deliver necessary human services to their constituents.[36]

Given the importance of these service delivery networks, many have raised concerns about the potential for 'cracks' to form in the structure that can limit their ability to deliver services effectively. There are at least three different ways that the effectiveness of service delivery could be hampered by network structure. First, if there are no links between clusters of different organizations, then different types of services cannot be coordinated. For example, child service organizations may collaborate and thus effectively provide services to clients, and similarly victim service organizations may collaborate and provide services effectively as well. But, if none of the organizations in these two clusters interact, it becomes impossible to coordinate services for some vulnerable individuals, such as mothers who experience domestic violence. Second, if there are some links between clusters, but they are between the wrong clusters, then services cannot be coordinated in meaningful ways. For example, in poor communities, the delivery of services that are needed the most may depend more on linkages between organizations in child services and victim services clusters, and less on linkages between child services organizations and local corporations. Finally, although there may be a sufficient number of linkages between similar organizations to form clusters, and between different organizations to bridge clusters, the linkages may not be strong enough. The relationship between organizations may be weak because they interact only infrequently, because their interaction is 'all talk' but little actual collaboration, or owing to a conflict in the two organizations' goals or procedures. But, in each case, such weak interorganizational ties limit the ability for organizations to coordinate their activities with one another.[37]

How, then, might the organizations in a community be able to confront such problems? One answer lies in the ways that interorganizational networks evolve and adapt to changing environmental conditions, such as a change in the needs of local residents or a change in support from state or local governments. Service delivery networks rarely form on their own, simply because a city's residents are not receiving adequate services. However, external funding such as a grant from a local foundation or a federal agency can often serve as a catalyst to encourage organizations to collaborate and coordinate their services with one another. As these networks begin to form, interorganizational relationships typically take the form of information exchanges first. Although such ties may be relatively weak, they set the stage for stronger ties to develop that involve not simply the exchange of information, but also the sharing of resources or the collaborative pursuit of a common goal.[38]

                              *   *   *   *   *

Similar to living creatures, modern cities are enormously complex organisms that require the careful coordination of many interdependent parts to operate smoothly. Keeping a city's residents healthy is not simply a matter of having a good hospital nearby, but rather of having community groups working with doctors to confront youth engaging in high-risk behaviors, or of traffic engineers working with ambulance companies to ensure quick response times. Similarly, city governance is not simply a matter of an all-powerful mayor issuing commands, but rather of various agencies and departments collaborating with some and conflicting with others to, in perhaps a messy way, get things done. Much of the operation of modern cities, from governance to collective action to service provision, can be understood by thinking about the interorganizational networks that link these interdependent parts. It is the structural features of these networks that largely determine whether a city is able to effectively handle a variety of tasks, ranging from the mundane collection of trash to the critical control of a spreading disease. Rigid hierarchies can provide much control over a city's organizations, while the free market maximizes organizations' flexibility to pursue their own goals. Lying somewhere between these two extremes, although they are not without their potential problems, interorganizational networks aim to balance control and flexibility to make life in modern cities possible.

Discussion Questions and Activities

1. Locate your city's organizational chart. What type of relationship is depicted by the lines that connect the various departments and agencies? How would the network look different if the lines represented information exchange? Sharing of resources such as staff or funding? How could data on these other types of relationships be collected?

2. Is one form of governance—market, hierarchy, or network—better than the others? Does the ideal form of governance depend on the context? What factors might influence this?

3. Find the centralization of each of the four networks in the top row of Figure 6.2: Collective, Polarized, Bargaining, and Polycentric. Which network is most centralized? Which network is least centralized? If the goal of a policy network is to develop public policies that will benefit the largest number of a city's residents, is a centralized or decentralized network likely to be more effective?

4. Think about the organizations in your city that are involved in public education. Which organizations likely occupy the four roles commonly found in resource exchange networks: Generator, Consumer, Transmitter, and Isolate. Which organization(s) are likely to be most central in the resource exchange network? Are they the most influential?

5. How could the methods introduced in the previous chapters be used to study the concepts introduced in this chapter? Similarly, how could the methods introduced in this chapter be used to study the concepts introduced in the previous chapters?

Sources for Interorganizational Network Data

Organization Charts—Formal organization charts are often readily available on websites and in official publications, and they clearly show the structure of relationships between organizations or departments within a larger setting. For example, the organizational or 'org' charts for Austin, Texas and Los Angeles, California are available at: www.ci.austin.tx.us/help/orgchart.htm and www.ci.la.ca.us/cao. However, these charts only show formal or official relationships, which frequently do not mirror the actual day-to-day interactions between organizations.

Member Interlock—One of the most important ways that organizations communicate is through their members. If a person is a member of two different organizations, then it is likely that information and other resources are exchanged between those organizations. Thus, it is possible to define an interorganizational network in which organizations are linked if they have overlapping members, that is, if some people are members of both organizations. This is a useful data collection strategy because it only requires the researcher to collect membership rosters from each organization. Using the techniques described in Method Note 7 and illustrated in Figure 3.5, these membership rosters can be transformed into an interorganizational network.

Behavior Trace—Closely related to the member interlock approach, behavior trace methods rely on organizational records that trace the organization's past behaviors to reconstruct interorganizational networks. For example, meeting minutes typically indicate who was present at an organization's meeting, including representatives from other organizations. Using such records, an interorganizational network could be defined in which organizations are linked if they attend one another's meetings. Similarly, corporations often release summaries of their charitable donations, which could be used to construct a network that reflects the exchange of material resources between private and nonprofit organizations.

Survey—Just as personal social networks can be collected from individuals using a survey, this procedure can be adapted to collect data on interorganizational networks. Typically, a representative of each organization is asked to complete the survey, which includes one or more name generator questions, such as "Which organizations has your organization collaborated with in the past year?" Although this method can allow the researcher to learn about types of interorganizational linkages that may not appear in organizational charts or organizational records, the accuracy of the data depends on the knowledge of the individual respondent. If the organization is small, a single representative may be able to answer the questions accurately, but for large organizations, it is unlikely that a single representative will be aware of all the organization's interactions with other organizations. One alternative involves administering the survey to multiple representatives in each organization and combining their responses.[39]

PART THREE
MACRO-URBAN NETWORKS
NETWORKS OF CITIES

7
REGIONAL
FROM CITY TO METROPOLIS

While networks surely exist within cities (Chapters 2–4), and cities themselves can be viewed as networks (Chapters 5 and 6), there are also networks that exist *between* cities. Moreover, as Figure 7.1 illustrates, these macro-urban networks exist at multiple geographic scales: regional, national, and global.[1] Chicago, for example, is part of a regional network of Midwestern industrial cities including Waukegan and Gary, but is also part of a national network of cities that includes New York and Los Angeles. Similarly, New York is part of this national network of cities, but is also linked to London and Shanghai in a global urban network. Just as one behaves differently when hanging out with friends or visiting family members, cities play different roles in each of these networks.

Regional urban networks have shaped human activity since the first farmer, looking for customers and an opportunity to make a living, brought his crops into the city to sell at market. In the agricultural past, regional networks connected tiny farming villages to large cities, establishing a symbiotic relationship in which city dwellers got food from the land, and rural farmers got

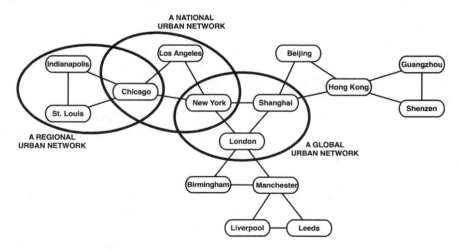

Figure 7.1 Geographically Nested Macro-urban Networks.

machinery from the factories. More recently, these same networks connect suburbs to downtowns, resulting in a very similar symbiosis: corporations hire workers from the suburbs, while suburbanites take home a paycheck. As these simple examples illustrate, cities are not self-contained, self-sustaining systems. Instead, give-and-take relationships such as those between a city and its suburbs link the various parts of a region into a network of interdependence in which each part relies on the others to perform key functions. It is through these regional networks that nearby cities are brought together and transformed into a metropolitan area. Thus, understanding what regional urban networks look like, where they come from, and how they function is essential to understanding not only cities but also the metropolitan areas they form.

Up to this point, this book has assumed that cities and their metropolitan areas are easy to recognize and define. But, on further reflection, explaining exactly what a metropolis is turns out to be fairly challenging. In this chapter, I begin by exploring how regional networks can offer one kind of definition. But, simply being able to identify a metropolitan area is only part of the picture; it is equally important to understand how its component parts—individual cities—fit together. Thus, I then explore some of the theories that geographers, economists and others have proposed over the past hundred years to explain the relationships between cities in a region, and how these relationships make some cities more important than others. I show how viewing these theories from a network perspective helps to simplify their basic arguments and to highlight the similarities and differences in how they conceptualize cities and their regions. Unfortunately, many of these theories are based on the outdated assumption that a metropolitan area is anchored by just one big city with one bustling downtown. Because a visit to any sprawling metropolitan area confirms they often have multiple centers of activity, network-based theories are beginning to emerge to make sense of these new multi-centered, or polycentric, urban regions. Ultimately, however, urban regions and their multiple centers do not create themselves. Recognizing this, I conclude by considering how, although cities are the nodes in regional urban networks, lurking just below the surface and responsible for creating the network are collaborating governments, competing firms, and commuters just trying to get home.

What is a Metropolis?

In the 1964 case of *Jacobellis v. Ohio*, U.S. Supreme Court Justice Potter Stewart famously remarked that pornography is impossible to define, but that "I know it when I see it."[2] A metropolis is similarly hard to define, although we usually know when we are in one. Cities, in contrast, are relatively easy to define. A city is simply a type of political entity that has been given the right to exercise specific powers within a geographic area, such as the power to govern itself through locally elected officials. The boundaries of a city's jurisdiction, and the powers it can exercise within them, are often defined by an act of state or national government.[3] For example, the City of Chicago was created in 1837 by an act of incorporation passed by the Illinois state legislature, which allowed the people of Chicago to elect a mayor, collect taxes, and regulate local businesses. This formal, legal definition describes what is known as the *city proper*, and is particularly important for understanding urban politics because it highlights, for example, that a city's elected officials have power over what happens inside their city's borders, but much less power over what happens just outside of them.

However, a metropolis is not a city proper. Such a legal definition is not useful for understanding how the metropolis is actually experienced because the invisible political boundaries between cities proper are rarely noticed as people go about their everyday activities in metropolitan areas. For example, a commuter driving to work in the greater Phoenix area might leave from a home in the City of Peoria and drive to an office in the City of Tempe, watching a continuous stretch of homes and businesses pass by, as he crosses through the City of Glendale, the City of Phoenix, and the City of Scottsdale. Unless he is issued a speeding ticket along the way by one of these cities' independent police departments, he is unlikely to know which of these cities he is technically in at any given moment. Although the greater Phoenix area is a mosaic of legally independent cities, everyday social and economic activities proceed as if taking place in one single metropolis, known locally as the Valley of the Sun.

One alternative to the legal approach involves defining the metropolis spatially by focusing on population size and density.[4] Together, these characteristics pick out the type of places one usually has in mind when thinking of a city: a large number of people concentrated in a relatively small area. For example, in 2010 the Chicago metropolitan area contained over nine million people in less than 10,000 square miles. Although this area is criss-crossed by the official political boundaries of numerous cities proper in several states—for example, Chicago in Illinois, Kenosha in Wisconsin, and Gary in Indiana—it functions as a single socially and economically integrated metropolis known locally as Chicagoland. But, is the Chicagoland area's large population size and high density what give it the character of a single, integrated region? That is, would the land along the Southern shore of Lake Michigan still function as a single metropolitan area if, to borrow a tourism slogan, what happened in Kenosha stayed in Kenosha, and what happened in Gary stayed in Gary? Probably not.

These examples highlight that a metropolis is not a legal or spatial phenomenon, but a functional one, and thus requires a functional definition that focuses on how it actually works. They also point to the key ingredient in such a functional definition: relationships with the surrounding environment. As sociologist Roderick McKenzie (1885–1940) noted nearly a century ago:

> . . . the city is more than an aggregation of people or an agglomeration of buildings. It is an organization of activities, an economic and social organism. The metropolitan region thus . . . is primarily a functional entity. Generalizing, it may be said that the economic [and social] unity of the metropolitan region is based on a pattern of economic [and social] relations.[5]

Thus, what makes the Valley of the Sun or Chicagoland function as a single metropolis cannot be reduced to any single political entity such as the City of Phoenix or the City of Chicago, nor to the sheer size and density of these regions. Instead, their metropolitan character comes from the fact that the independent parts of these regions—cities, suburbs, towns—are really not independent at all, but are closely linked to one another in a wide variety of ways. A person who lives in Peoria may go to work in Tempe, go to church in Glendale, and go out with friends in Scottsdale. Similarly, a company headquartered in Chicago may do its manufacturing in Gary, but have its payroll checks processed in Kenosha.

Figure 7.2 illustrates three different functional conceptions of the metropolis that highlight different types of relationships in the surrounding environment. The city and hinterland model was initially proposed by German economist Johann Heinrich von Thünen (1783–1850) to describe agricultural areas in which a city proper was surrounded by fertile land used for farming.[6] The city and its agriculturally productive hinterland were dependent upon one another: the hinterland provided food and other raw materials consumed in the city, and the city provided a market for farmers to sell their crops. Las Vegas offers a more recent example, with the majority of its resort casinos located on Las Vegas Boulevard South, or 'The Strip,' which lies outside the official boundaries of the City of Las Vegas. Although not agricultural in nature, there is a close relationship between the hinterland and city: the former provides jobs and tourism revenue for the area, while the latter provides workers and key services such as banking. This model calls attention to the fact that the metropolis—whether an agricultural region or a tourist mecca—includes both the

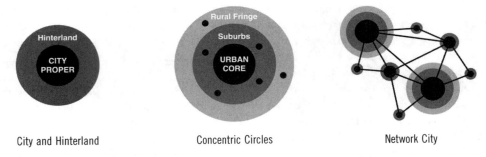

City and Hinterland   Concentric Circles   Network City

Figure 7.2 Functional Conceptions of Metropolis.

city proper and the surrounding territory. These two components serve different functions and are functionally linked by their dependence on one another.

The concentric circle model proposed by sociologist Ernest Burgess (1886–1966) and later by economist William Alonso (1933–1999) extends the simple city–hinterland model by recognizing that the area surrounding an urban core may be divided into several different zones each of which plays a unique role in the region and has particular relationships with the others.[7] In an agricultural setting, the urban core is home to the central market, while just outside its boundaries farmers grow crops that are difficult to transport such as tomatoes, and still further away they grow crops that are easy to transport and require more land such as corn or wheat. In a more industrialized setting, the urban core is the site of high-rise office towers and downtown apartments, surrounded by a ring of suburbs, and still further out by smaller towns in the rural fringe. The concentric ring pattern is driven by transportation cost and land value: land that is further from the urban core is less expensive because it is more costly to travel to the core, and thus is put to less costly uses. The city at the center of this formation and each of the suburbs and towns surrounding it are independent cities proper with their own boundaries, laws, and elected officials. But functionally, all of these elements depend on each other and collectively operate as a metropolis.

Both the city–hinterland and concentric circle models view the metropolis as including an urban center and its surrounding territory. However, a third functional conception of the metropolis— the network city—recognizes that a metropolis does not necessarily have only one urban center surrounded by continuously developed territory. Instead, a metropolis can include multiple large and small cities that each have their own hinterlands, and that are separated by areas of undeveloped land, but which are connected to one another by commuting workers, cooperating governments, or competing firms. The Randstad or 'rim city,' a metropolitan area in the Netherlands, is a clear example of this. It is anchored by four large cities—Amsterdam, Rotterdam, The Hague, and Utrecht—separated by a less urbanized area known as the 'Green Heart,' but still closely linked by their dependence on one another. For example, despite having their own local suburbs and despite being separated by 40 miles of thinly populated wetlands, people and businesses in Amsterdam and Rotterdam routinely interact with one another. Thus, the network city model focuses not on the density of the area's population, but instead on the density of the network of interactions within it.[8]

Notably, none of these functional conceptions of the metropolis rely on a city proper's political boundaries, nor do they rely on the population size or density of the region. Instead, they concentrate on patterns of relationships in a region, including those between a city and its hinterland, and those between entire cities separated by otherwise undeveloped land. Thus, they view the metropolis as a kind of network. How, then, can this functional and network-based definition of the metropolis be used to identify actual metropolitan areas? Since the 1950s, the U.S. Office of Management and Budget has officially defined metropolitan areas. Although these definitions and the names of the entities they describe have been revised numerous times, in each case they aim to identify sets of counties that together formed a functionally unified metropolitan area. The most recent definition of such an area—now called a Core Based Statistical Area or CBSA—explicitly incorporates the notion that patterns of interaction are the defining characteristic of a metropolis. A CBSA begins with one or more 'central' counties that contain a large urban population, to which additional 'outlying' counties are added when at least 25 percent of their residents work in the central counties or vice versa. Based on this definition, in 2009 there were 374 metropolitan areas in the United States, with updated lists and boundaries released annually.[9]

Many of these metropolitan areas are composed of just one or two counties, but others are quite large: the New York metropolitan area is composed of twenty-three counties spread across three states. This raises questions about how large a metropolis can be, and still remain recognizable as a metropolis. Just as interactions among cities and counties give rise to metropolitan areas, similarly, interactions among metropolitan areas can give rise to what has been called a megalopolis or mega-urban region. One of the most frequently noted mega-urban regions is BosWash, which stretches more than 400 miles along the East Coast from Boston to Washington, DC, and including New York, Philadelphia, and Baltimore along the way. This region, although certainly larger than any traditional conception of a city or metropolis, does have a certain functional unity as the financial and governmental center of the nation. In an even more striking example, some have argued that the entire nation of Switzerland can be viewed as a single metropolitan area because its cities are so highly dependent on one another.[10]

The appearance of such large urban regions and metropolitan areas, however, should not be surprising. The metropolis arises from patterns of interaction, and the communication and transportation technologies that make such interactions possible are continually advancing. As these large metropolitan areas and urban regions replace cities and suburbs as the setting for the urban experience, successful urban planning and governance must go beyond the mere political boundaries of cities proper; it must be regional. But, planning and governing entire metropolitan areas and urban regions requires more than simply recognizing that they arise out of a network of interactions in the region. It also requires understanding the structure of those regional networks.

From Regional Theories to Regional Networks

It is one thing to argue that cities in a metropolitan area or urban region are interdependent, but quite another to say how. That is, while it is useful to define the metropolis as a kind of network among cities, the structure of that network is important and makes a big difference in the roles that cities play within the region. Over the past century, several different theories have been developed to explain the patterns of interactions among cities within a region, and more specifically, to explain how those patterns can make some cities dominant and others subordinate within a region. Although the details of theories about urban regions can be quite complex, their main ideas can often be expressed by the structure of relatively simple networks and by different conceptions of cities' centrality within those networks.[11]

One perspective on the patterning of relationships within urban regions, *economic base theory*, begins with the observation that cities are not self-sustaining and rarely produce everything their residents need. Instead, through a territorial division of labor, different cities specialize in producing different goods and services. Each city meets the needs of its local population by exporting the surplus goods and services it produces, and importing goods and services that other cities produce. Thus, within a region, each city depends on others to meet its needs. For example, because Detroit produces more cars but fewer financial services than its residents demand, it can export cars to other cities but must rely on other cities to meet its citizens' banking needs. These patterns of import and export among cities are significant because they can make some cities more influential or dominant in a region. The more a city exports, the more influential it is within the region because other cities depend on it. In contrast, cities that primarily import are less influential because they must depend on other cities to meet their populations' basic needs.

Although not originally proposed as one, economic base theory can be viewed as a kind of network-based theory of urban regional economics. Cities are linked to one another in a network formed by the import and export of goods and services they specialize in producing. The left panel of Figure 7.3 illustrates one such regional network in which the shaded city specializes in producing a resource that it exports to six other cities. Economic base theory predicts that cities will have more influence in the region when they are net exporters, while cities that are primarily importers will be more subordinate. However, by viewing the region as connected by an import–export network, it is also possible to identify dominant and subordinate cities based on their network centrality. But, what kind of centrality? Among the multiple conceptions of network centrality discussed in Chapter Five—degree, betweenness, and closeness—only one matches the way economic base theory explains urban regions: degree centrality, and more specifically, out-degree centrality. Out-degree centrality measures the number of edges that are directed away from a node, and thus in the context of an import–export network it measures the number of places to which a city exports. The shaded city has the high out-degree centrality and is expected to be most dominant, while the unshaded cities have low out-degree centrality and are expected to be more subordinate. Although in practice the actual network of imports and exports between cities can be difficult to measure, thinking about economic base theory from a network perspective highlights that what really matters is not the network's overall structure, but each cities' degree centrality within it. Without directly measuring the network, *location quotients* that are computed using employment data can be a useful way to estimate whether a city has a high out-degree centrality and thus is primarily an exporter, or a low out-degree centrality and thus is primarily an importer.[12]

Location theory offers another perspective on the pattern of regional urban interactions that builds upon economic base theory by recognizing that goods and services are not simply produced in one city and consumed in another. Instead, the production and delivery of goods and services frequently involves multiple stages spanning multiple cities, and therefore depends on transporting those goods and services between cities. For example, as Upton Sinclair colorfully described in *The Jungle*, livestock raised in small Midwestern farming towns was first brought to Chicago for large-scale processing and to be loaded onto trains for distribution to cities throughout the region. Location theory calls attention to the critical role and regional dominance of cities such as Chicago, which serve as gateways linking different parts of a region, and different parts of the process of producing and delivering goods. First, because these gateways minimize the transportation costs

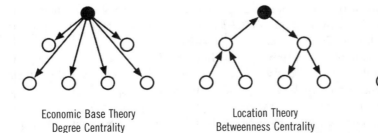

| Economic Base Theory | Location Theory | Central Place Theory |
| Degree Centrality | Betweenness Centrality | Closeness Centrality |

Figure 7.3 Centrality in Urban Regions.

METHOD NOTE 18: LOCATION QUOTIENTS

The *location quotient* estimates whether a city produces more or less of a given resource than its local population needs, and thus whether it imports or exports the resource. It is based on employment, and is computed as:

$$\text{Location Quotient} = \frac{\text{Percent of a city's workers who are employed in an industry}}{\text{Percent of the nation's workers who are employed in that industry}}$$

Consider the case of the motor vehicle manufacturing industry, which is industry 3,361 in the North American Industrial Classification System (NAICS). In 2010, 1.78 percent of the workers in Detroit were employed in this industry, compared with only 0.14 percent of the workers nationwide. Thus, for this industry, Detroit has a location quotient of 12.71 because 1.78 / 0.14 = 12.71. This can be contrasted with the finance industry (NAICS 52), which employed 4.36 percent of Detroit workers, but 5.17 percent of all workers nationwide. Thus, for the finance industry, Detroit has a location quotient of 0.84 because 4.36 / 5.17 = 0.84.

Location quotient values can range between 0 and infinity, and are centered around 1. A location quotient of exactly 1 indicates that a city that produces exactly the number of resources that its local population needs; it neither imports nor exports. A location quotient less than 1 indicates that a city must import resources because it does not produce enough on its own to satisfy the needs of its residents. In the example above, the financial industry location quotient of 0.84 suggests that Detroit must rely on other cities for financial services. A location quotient greater than 1 indicates that a city exports resources because it produces more than its own residents can consume. Again, in the example above, the motor vehicle manufacturing industry location quotient of 12.71 suggests that Detroit exports cars and that other cities rely on it to perform this function. The U.S. Bureau Of Labor Statistics offers an online tool to automatically compute location quotients for a range of industries in each county and metropolitan area in the United States at: http://data.bls.gov/location_quotient.[13]

involved in moving goods from producers to consumers, they help businesses maximize their profits. Second, because the activities involved in serving as a gateway require not only laborers to load trains, but also lawyers to oversee contracts, bankers to handle the exchange of money, and a range of other professionals, such places often become the site of sophisticated metropolitan economies.[14]

As with economic base theory, location theory can also be viewed as a network theory of urban regions. In this case, the transportation network through which goods and services flow as they transform from raw materials to finished products links cities to one another. The middle panel of Figure 7.3 illustrates one such regional network in which the shaded city helps to move goods from the cities on the left where they are produced to the cities on the right where they are consumed. While location theory contends that cities become regionally dominant when they play a critical role in the transportation of goods, the most dominant cities can also be identified by their centrality in the transportation network. However, once again, selecting the right conception of centrality is crucial. Although out-degree centrality captures what makes cities dominant from the perspective of economic base theory, it is not useful in the context of location theory; it would identify the wrong city as most dominant. Instead, betweenness centrality more closely matches how location theory explains urban regions by measuring the extent to which one node helps connect two otherwise disconnected nodes. In this example, the shaded city has the highest betweenness centrality, and is expected to be most dominant because it is necessary to transport goods from any city on the left to any city on the right. In contrast, the unshaded cities at the bottom of the network have the least betweenness centrality and are expected to be the most subordinate because they play no role in the movement of goods from place to place.

A third approach to regional structure—*central place theory*—adopts a somewhat different approach by focusing on the size of the population necessary to support businesses offering different types of goods and services. Businesses such as grocery stores and gas stations that cater to routine needs can survive even in small towns because everyone needs to buy food for their homes and gas for their cars. However, businesses such as art galleries and art-house cinemas that cater to more specialized and uncommon desires require much larger populations to thrive because only a small percentage of people may want to purchase fine art or watch foreign cinema. Such businesses depend not only on those who live in the cities where they are located to be potential consumers, but also on those who live throughout the region. Therefore, they tend to appear in cities that are centrally located and easily accessible to the wider region's population. Central place theory predicts that these cities, known as central places, have the most diverse economies and are the most dominant in the region because they can draw people in from outlying towns and cities to support their businesses.[15]

As with the other two regional theories, central place theory can also be viewed in network terms. The network of consumers' movements as they travel to obtain goods and services links cities to one another. The right panel of Figure 7.3 illustrates one such network, in which consumers in the cities at the bottom may travel to cities in the middle, and then to the shaded city at the top, in search of the goods and services they desire. In this hypothetical region, central place theory predicts that the shaded city will have the most diverse economy and be dominant because it draws consumers in from all the other cities in the region to support its economy. As the name of the theory implies, centrality is important for this outcome, but what kind of centrality? Closeness centrality parallels central place theory's argument by measuring the extent to which one node is close to the other nodes in the network, or in the context of urban regions, the extent to which one city is accessible to the others. The shaded city's dominance stems from the fact that it is located only one or two steps away from every other city in the regional network, thus allowing its businesses to benefit from the largest possible pool of consumers. In contrast, the unshaded cities are less dominant and have less diverse economies because they are less close to other cities in the network, and their businesses must rely on smaller pools of consumers.[16]

Each of these regional theories—economic base, location, and central place—is far more complex than these brief summaries would suggest. However, they serve to illustrate several important points. First, networks lie at the heart of many different theoretical perspectives, and even theories that are not obviously about networks can often be expressed in network terms. Second, although centrality is commonly used to describe positions within networks, it is not a one-size-fits-all concept. There are several different ways of thinking about centrality and each one is appropriate only in particular situations. For example, although betweenness centrality does a good job identifying cities that location theory would predict are regionally dominant, closeness centrality is more appropriate when considering the predictions of central place theory. Finally, the regional role of a city depends more on its relationships with other cities in the region than on its individual attributes, such as its population size. Indeed, none of these theories suggest that large cities are necessarily more dominant than small cities, but instead focus only on their position within the network. Thus, making sense of the roles cities play in their regions does not require measuring how large they are or how much their businesses produce, but instead requires understanding the pattern of interactions they have with one another.[17]

Two Downtowns Are Better than One

Despite the differences in the networks described by economic base, location, or central place theories and illustrated in Figure 7.3, they share two characteristics: they are monocentric and hierarchical. First, they contend that urban regions are monocentric, or centered around a single city—in these examples, the shaded one—that is particularly dominant and influential within the region. Of course, as the discussion above demonstrated, each theory has a different explanation for why a given city is dominant and a different conception of centrality, but all of them ultimately focus on just one dominant and central city. Second, they contend that the relationships between cities in an urban region are hierarchical, running in one direction and linking cities that play different roles in the system. For example, economic base theory views urban regions as resting on the movement of goods from exporting cities to importing cities, but not the other direction and not between importing cities or between exporting cities. Similarly, central place theory views consumers in small towns traveling to larger cities to buy specialized goods, but not consumers in large cities traveling to small towns and not consumers traveling between two small towns or two large cities.

Assuming that urban regions are monocentric and hierarchical may have been quite reasonable in the past when large cities and the urban regions around them were just beginning to take shape. For example, in an industrial age when economies depended on giant factories employing thousands of men who must commute by slow, steam-powered trains, concentrating the region's economic activities in a single, centralized location was efficient. But, many things have changed since the rise of the industrial city. The primary economic activity in cities is no longer the production of goods by large factories, but the delivery of services by small businesses. Commuters are no longer restricted to trains that channel everyone into downtown, but can rely on extensive road systems and private cars that make it possible to work not only downtown, but anywhere in the region. And, it is no longer only the male head-of-household who commutes to work; households now include multiple wage earners who often work in different places and at different times. With these changes, the activities of an urban region no longer need to be, and indeed cannot be, so highly centralized. Thus, modern urban regions are increasingly characterized by multiple, dominant centers and by more complex patterns of relationships among them; they are becoming polycentric and non-hierarchical.

An emerging theory of *polycentricity* aims to make sense of such polycentric urban regions.[18] However, describing it is complicated by the fact that there are at least three different conceptions of polycentricity, illustrated in Figure 7.4: morphological, normative, and functional. The morphological conception focuses primarily on the sizes and locations of cities in an urban region. A region is described as morphologically polycentric when it contains multiple large cities that are located close to one another, but separated by more rural land. For example, the Randstad region in the Netherlands is morphologically polycentric because its four primary cities all contain between 300,000 and 700,000 people, and because they are close to one another, but still separated by the more rural 'Green Heart' area. In contrast, a region is described as morphologically monocentric when one of its cities is much larger than the others, or when all the cities blur together into a single, continuous expanse of urbanization. For example, the Chicago metropolitan area is morphologically monocentric because one of its primary cities, Chicago, is much larger than the others, Gary and Waukegan, and because these cities have no rural land separating them. The morphological conception of polycentricity has become popular because it is easy to measure and study cities' sizes and locations, but it is of limited use for understanding how polycentric urban regions actually work because it does not take into account whether their cities are linked in a network of interactions with one another. For example, although there is little interaction

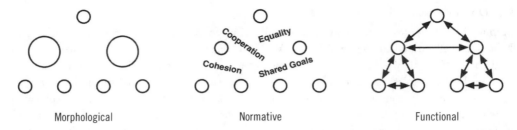

Figure 7.4 Three Conceptions of Polycentricity.

between Glasgow and Edinburgh and thus no regional urban network, central Scotland can still be described as a morphologically polycentric urban region simply because these two cities are nearby, separated by some open space, and similar in size.[19]

The normative conception of polycentricity is less an attempt to define polycentric urban regions than it is a loose set of ideas and values that together form a political ideology and urban planning agenda. It emerged initially in Europe where centuries of unplanned urban development had led to fragmented urban regions in which individual cities' governments enacted conflicting or redundant policies and their economies were locked in competition with one another. To address these issues, in 1999 the European Commission adopted the position that social equality and sustainable economic growth could be achieved though the development of polycentric urban regions in which cohesive groups of cities formed networks of cooperation to achieve shared goals. Although the commission's report highlighted the benefits of polycentricity and networks, neither of these concepts was clearly defined.[20] Nonetheless, government officials and business leaders in urban regions throughout Europe, as well as in North America and Australia, have sought to "build their regions' networks," to "work together," and to "become more competitive through cooperation."[21] Despite its widespread adoption, the normative conception of polycentricity has been criticized, both for being an ambiguous concept that is not sufficiently defined to provide clear policy directions, and for lacking evidence that cohesive urban regions are more egalitarian or economically competitive.[22]

Unlike morphological and normative conceptions of polycentricity, which merely imply that cities within a polycentric urban region interact with one another, a functional conception defines polycentricity in terms of specific patterns of interactions, and thus in terms of a regional urban network. The network of a polycentric region, like that illustrated in the right panel of Figure 7.4, resembles the monocentric and hierarchical networks of earlier regional theories illustrated in Figure 7.3, but is different in at least two important ways. First, the linkages between cities are reciprocal, making cities not simply either dominant or subordinate, but interdependent. For example, goods and services do not simply move from an exporting city to an importing city, but rather each city in a region imports some things and exports others. The cities are interdependent because they depend on some cities for imports, and are depended on by others for exports. Second, in addition to vertical linkages that connect cities playing different roles, polycentric urban regions also have horizontal linkages that connect cities playing similar roles. For example, commuters not only drive from the suburbs into the city, but also from one suburb to another. Thus, a functionally polycentric region is defined by a large number of interactions spread evenly among the region's cities, or in network terms, by a network that is dense and decentralized.

Functionally polycentric urban regions can form in different ways, as the development of Southern California and the Randstad regions illustrate. Beginning in the 1950s, as large numbers

METHOD NOTE 19: FUNCTIONAL POLYCENTRICITY

A network is functionally polycentric when it contains a large number of edges (it is dense), and when these edges are evenly spread among the nodes (it is not centralized). A network's functional polycentricity ranges between 0 and 1, and is measured using both its density and centralization as:

$$\text{Functional Polycentricity} = \text{Density} \times (1 - \text{Centralization})$$

	(A)	(B)	(C)	(D)
Density	0.50	0.50	0.70	0.70
Decentralization	0.83	0.42	0.50	0.08
Functional Polycentricity	0.09	0.29	0.35	0.64

Network A is not functionally polycentric because it contains relatively few edges, and the edges it does contain are centralized around just one node. These two characteristics are reflected in the network's low density and high centralization scores, which combine to give it a low functional polycentricity score of 0.09 because $0.50 \times (1 - 0.83) = 0.09$. When expressed as a percentage, this score indicates that network A is only 9 percent as functionally polycentric as possible; it is functionally monocentric.

Networks B and C are moderately functionally polycentric because they both have one characteristic of functional polycentricity, but not the other. Network B is not dense or centralized, while in contrast, network C is both dense and centralized.

Finally, network D is the most functionally polycentric among these examples. It has a relatively high density because it contains many edges. Additionally, it is not centralized because these edges are not focused on any single node, but are spread across the network. These two characteristics—its high density and low centralization—combine to yield a high functional polycentricity score, which indicates that this network is 64 percent as functionally polycentric as possible.[23]

of people flocked to Southern California, outlying suburbs in areas such as the San Fernando Valley and Orange County developed. This suburbanization created a functionally monocentric urban region in which all of the region's suburbs were dependent upon Los Angeles; individuals living in suburbs such as Glendale or Burbank or Anaheim would all commute to work in the city. As a regional urban network, the linkages were all vertical, between suburbs and a dominant city. However, as these suburbs grew, they began to interact not only with Los Angeles, but also with one another; increasingly one might live in Glendale but work in Burbank, bypassing the city of Los Angeles altogether. The formation of such horizontal linkages between suburbs shifted some of the activity away from Los Angeles and into newly emerging suburban centers, creating a more polycentric region.

The Randstad region illustrates a different trajectory. For centuries, its key cities—Amsterdam, Rotterdam, The Hague, and Utrecht—were similarly sized, but relatively independent both socially and economically. For example, workers lived in the same city where they worked, and products were consumed in the same city where they were produced; there was limited commuting or commerce between cities in the region. Thus, the region was only morphologically polycentric, containing multiple larger cities, but without a network of interactions among them. However, as these cities continued to grow and as transportation and communication technologies developed, interactions between them became more practical and common. For example, motorways and high-speed rail in the region made commuting from one city to another possible, while telephones and later email simplified business partnerships across the region. These interactions transformed the region from simply a collection of isolated cities into a dense regional network. Thus, functionally polycentric urban regions can develop when functionally monocentric regions such as mid-century Southern California become more polycentric through the growth of new urban centers. But, they can also develop when morphologically polycentric regions such as the early Randstad become more functionally integrated through the growth of linkages between historically independent cities.[24]

The emergence of polycentric urban regions raises an important question: are these new kinds of urban regions better than more traditional regional structures? Some of the potential advantages for small and medium-sized cities are obvious. In monocentric regions, such as those described by location or central place theories, the majority of resources and economic activity are concentrated in a single large city that dominates the region and overshadows other cities. However, polycentricity provides opportunities for multiple cities within a region, rather than just one, to become major economic centers because productivity and prosperity are more evenly distributed. Polycentricity can also be beneficial for the entire region because it allows cities specializing in different, but complementary, activities to work together and achieve more than they could individually. For example, consider a region in which one city is home to a major university and specializes in research, another is home to major banks and specializes in funding new business ventures, and a third is home to small manufacturers and specialized in making electronic equipment. Individually, each of these cities could be economically competitive, producing cutting-edge research, investing in global markets, or making high-tech devices. But, if linked together through a network of cooperation and partnership, they could be something more: the center of the computer industry. To be effective, however, functionally polycentric regions must rest on multiple types of networks, including both the 'soft' or informal social networks of people who exchange good business ideas, and the 'hard' or formal economic networks of businesses who engage in strategic partnerships and governments who encourage and make such cooperation possible.[25]

The Real Actors

The very notion of urban regional networks, whether they are monocentric or polycentric, implies that cities within a region somehow interact with one another. However, cities are not like people; because they do not have brains, or hearts, or limbs, cities cannot act or interact. To say that cities interact with one another is actually just a convenient shorthand way of saying that actors in different cities are interacting with one another. Thus, although urban regional networks can be conceptualized at the level of entire cities, it is also important to consider exactly who the actors are that forge these networks. Although there are many possibilities, three broad types of actors account for cities' apparent ability to engage in network interactions themselves: governments, firms, and commuters.

Urban regions are composed of multiple, politically independent cities and towns whose own governments—whether in the form of a mayor, city council, or city manager—exercise power only within the boundaries of their own jurisdictions. Although this arrangement gives cities and their residents the freedom of self-government, because the political boundaries of cities rarely match the functional boundaries of urban regions, it can also result in numerous problems. First, it can be difficult to coordinate the basic maintenance tasks necessary to keep an urban region running. For example, because major roads often pass through multiple cities that are each responsible for maintaining only the portion within their city's boundaries, some sections may be pristine while others are riddled with potholes. Second, the laws in each of a region's cities may be slightly different, which can complicate business transactions. For example, if each city within a region enacted its own building codes, then a contractor licensed to work in one city may not be qualified to work in neighboring cities. Finally, it can be costly and inefficient for each city to perform many of the same services within their own boundaries. For example, maintaining a regional fleet of garbage trucks is more cost effective than each city maintaining its own garbage truck. Seeking to overcome these challenges, the independent governments of cities and towns in an urban region often interact with one another, forming regional networks of cooperation.[26]

One common form of government cooperation is the *interlocal agreement*, through which two or more nearby political entities arrange to work together to provide a service or coordinate a function. These arrangements can be formalized through laws and contracts, such as a small town that subcontracts its police protection to the county sheriff, but can also be more informal agreements, such as when neighboring towns pool their fire departments to assist battling an especially large fire. They can also cross both state and national borders, more closely mirroring the functional rather than political boundaries of a region: interlocal agreements in the Kansas City metropolitan area exist among cities in both Kansas and Missouri, while in the Transmanche Metropole they exist among cities on both the British (Southampton, Portsmouth, Bournemouth, Poole) and French (Caen, Le Havre, Rouen) sides of the English channel. Whatever their particular purpose or location, however, interlocal agreements create an urban network in which cities within the region are linked when they agree to cooperate with one another.[27] Such agreements and the regional networks of cooperation they create can also be an initial step toward regional governance, or governance that takes place at the level of the entire urban region rather than separately within each of its independent cities and towns. However, despite the potential advantages of linking all the cities within a region into a single, dense network of interlocal agreements, local political leaders are often reluctant to trade autonomy for efficiency.[28]

Regional networks among cities can arise from the relationships that exist among governments, but they can also be rooted in the relationships that exist among firms operating in the region's cities. When a firm operating in one city interacts with a firm operating in another city, this interaction links not only the two firms, but also the cities where they are located because it involves the exchange of information, or money, or workers between the two places. These firm interactions can be driven by several different factors, including proximity, complementarity, and synergy.[29] Economist Alfred Marshall (1842–1924) observed that small firms tend to cluster together in close proximity, or agglomerate, to form industrial districts. The firms within such Marshallian industrial districts interact not necessarily because they intend to, but because their close proximity forces them to share resources. They must hire from the same regional pool of workers, sell to the same customers, buy supplies from the same suppliers, and strategize based on the same rumors. When these industrial districts span multiple cities in a region, the interactions between firms in different cities can forge a regional urban network. The Tuscany region in Italy is an example of a regional urban network held together by the proximity of firms in an industrial district. The cities and small towns in the Tuscan countryside are linked together in a regional urban network by the interactions among the many small manufacturing firms—some focused on leather and shoes, others on textiles and clothing—located within them.[30]

Regional urban networks can also develop when the firms located in different cities throughout the region interact because their activities complement one another. Two firms may be complementary because one supplies products or services needed by another, such as a logging company supplying lumber to a furniture manufacturer. Alternatively, they may be complementary because they focus on different aspects of a single activity, such as a restaurant and a hotel that are both focused on tourism. Metropolitan Detroit illustrates one regional urban network that is held together by the complementarity of the firms located in its cities. For example, the Jervis Webb Company in Farmington Hills manufactures conveyor belt systems, while General Motors in Detroit manufactures cars. Although these two firms are engaged in very different activities, they nonetheless interact because they are complementary: Webb supplies GM with the conveyor belts that move cars along the assembly line. This supplier–client interaction not only links these two firms, but also links the cities of Farmington Hills and Detroit. Moreover, hundreds of similar supplier–client relationships between other firms link other cities in the region together, thus forming a regional urban network. Similar regional urban networks driven by complementary firms can be observed in other industries and places as well, including electronics in Madrid, aerospace in Seattle, and film in Los Angeles, and wine in Napa.[31]

Finally, regional clusters of firms can be driven to interact by the potential for synergy. In contrast to complementarity networks that link firms focused on different but complementary activities, synergy networks form among firms engaged in the same activities. Although such firms ordinarily compete with one another, in some cases they collaborate on projects that are too large or complex for either of them to tackle individually. These types of collaborative relations are especially common among firms that are too small or highly specialized to be competitive, and thus are driven to cooperate with one another. For example, the cities in the urban region surrounding Toledo, Ohio are home to several small greenhouse manufacturers. Because there is little advantage for dozens of small greenhouse manufacturers to compete with one another, these firms have formed partnerships with one another that have created a regional urban network in Northern Ohio. Synergy networks are also common among high-tech firms where collaboration is useful for developing new technologies. Here, Silicon Valley offers a dramatic example. The cities in this region are home to dozens of small electronics firms: Apple in Cupertino, Google in Mountain View, and Facebook in Menlo Park. Collaborations among these firms lead not only to the development of new technologies, but also to the formation of a regional urban network that links Silicon Valley cities into a functional metropolis.[32]

Ultimately, both governments and firms depend on workers, who must travel from home to work. Thus, commuters are still another type of actor that links cities together in regional urban

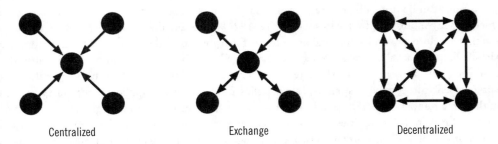

Centralized   Exchange   Decentralized

Figure 7.5 Commuting Networks.[33]

networks. As Figure 7.5 illustrates, regional commuting networks can have several different structures. A centralized commuting network is often observed in cities with a traditional city-suburb pattern of development, including those in the American Midwest and the English Midlands, in which individuals live in many different cities in the region, but all commute to the same place. The exchange network is similar, but incorporates commuting flows that are bi-directional: some live in the suburbs and commute to the city, but others have a so-called reverse commute because they live in the city and commute to the suburbs. This pattern has become increasingly common as a result of urban gentrification, in which individuals move to inner cities seeking real estate values or the excitement of downtown living. Finally, the decentralized commuting network most closely describes polycentric urban regions such as Southern California or the Randstad where commuters travel between many different pairs of cities, or in large cities such as London where commuters travel between many different districts and boroughs. As with other networks, different commuting networks offer both advantages and disadvantages to urban regions. Commuting times and distances tend to be shortest when the region has a centralized structure; however, economic growth tends to be strongest in regions with exchange or decentralized structures.[34]

* * * * *

As the world's population increasingly shifts to cities and urbanized areas, metropolitan areas and urban regions are a common part of daily life for many people. However, they remain very difficult to define. Because they are not simply political or geographic entities, but functional entities with many interacting parts, networks help to understand both what they are and how they work. From a network perspective, an urban region can be defined as the entire set of cities, suburbs, and towns that are linked because they depend on one another. Theories designed to explain how urban regions operate are reflected in the specific pattern of those linkages. The earliest theories hypothesized monocentric urban regions in which much of the activity was focused on a single, dominant city, while more recent theories have focused on the emergence of polycentric urban regions where the activity is distributed across many different cities. In all cases, however, viewing these theories as networks confirms that the most important feature of an urban region is not the sizes, or locations, or other characteristics of their cities, but rather the structure of the network that links them together. Moreover, not only can urban regional networks have different structures, but they are also grounded in the actions of different actors. Governments and other political entities can link a region's cities through cooperative interlocal agreements, firms through their complementary roles, and commuters just by driving to work.

Discussion Questions and Activities

1. What are the similarities between a neighborhood as a network of nearby people and an urban region as a network of nearby cities? What are the differences?
2. Use the Bureau of Labor Statistics' location quotient calculator at http://data.bls.gov/location_quotient to compute your metropolitan area's location quotient in three different industries. Based on the results, is the area likely to be an importer or an exporter in those industries? How would this look in a network? Is the area central in the network and dominant in the region?
3. Use the interactive map at http://hairycow.name/commute_map/map.html to look up the commuting flows for the zip codes in your area. What type of commuting network structure does the area have?
4. Of the different types of actors that forge linkages between cities in a regional urban network—governments, firms, and commuters—which one is the most important? Are there other types of actors that also forge linkages between cities?

5. How could the methods introduced in the previous chapters be used to study the concepts introduced in this chapter? Similarly, how could the methods introduced in this chapter be used to study the concepts introduced in the previous chapters?

Sources for Regional Urban Network Data

Political—Interlocal agreements are a type of political relationship that link cities and other political jurisdictions such as counties or school districts to one another. They can be used to define an urban regional network in which two political jurisdictions are connected if they have entered into an interlocal agreement with one another. In most states, interlocal agreements must be filed with the secretary of state or county clerk before they take effect. In some cases, cities and counties list their current interlocal agreements on their website. For example, Spokane, Washington lists its more than 150 interlocal agreements at: www.spokanecity.org/government/interlocal.

Economic—A firm's relationships with suppliers, clients, and subsidiaries elsewhere in the region are a type of economic relationship that links cities to one another. They can be used to define an urban regional network in which two cities are connected to the extent that firms in one have relationships with firms in the other. At the regional scale, such relationships can be identified via surveys that ask a firm's representative to identify his or her firms' regional suppliers and clients.

Transportation—Cities within a region are often linked by multiple modes of transportation. Information about a region's network of physical transportation infrastructures is typically available from organizations such as Chicago's Regional Transportation Authority (RTA) or New York's Metropolitan Transportation Authority (MTA), or from maps such as those produced by the U.S. Census Bureau/TIGER or ArcGIS. Information about the number of people actually utilizing that infrastructure, and thus flowing through the network, is available from a variety of sources. The Census Transportation Planning Package provides information about the number of commuters traveling between several different types of geographic areas in the United States including counties, cities, and census tracts at: www.transtats.bts.gov/DatabaseInfo.asp?DB_ID=630. An interactive map that uses this data to examine commutes to and from zip codes is available at: http://hairycow.name/commute_map/map.html. Similar data is available for commuting flows in the Netherlands from the Central Bureau of Statistics' National Travel Survey, and in the United Kingdom by using the Office for National Statistics' CommuterView software.

8
NATIONAL
THE ACTION IS IN *CITIES,*
BUT ALSO BETWEEN *THEM*

As the last chapter illustrated, regional urban networks link nearby cities into a functional metropolis. This chapter takes a geographically wider view to examine how national urban networks link entire metropolitan areas together to form national urban systems. For example, the Los Angeles metropolitan area is linked to the Chicago and New York metropolitan areas, which together form the backbone of the U.S. urban system. National urban networks can link metropolitan areas to one another in a variety of ways: transportation and communication linkages such as airline traffic and telephone calls keep people and information moving around the country, while finance and trade linkages facilitate the flow of investments and goods. These networks of exchanges between cities are important because they provide a structure for the activities of whole nations. Even small changes to national urban networks can radically alter the trajectory of a country, its cities, and their residents.

The United States urban system offers a particularly dramatic example because it was completely reorganized in the mid nineteenth century by the addition of just a few new linkages in the national urban network. From the 1770s and throughout the first half of the nineteenth century, St. Louis was America's premier western city. Its role as a major commercial center was driven by its central location on a natural transportation network formed by the Mississippi, Missouri, and Illinois rivers. The Mississippi river facilitated trade with New Orleans, and because New Orleans was a major ocean port, with the rest of the world, while the Missouri and Illinois rivers facilitated trade with the rapidly expanding frontier. As a result, nearly all the goods flowing in and out of the new American interior passed through St. Louis. However, this all changed in 1848 with the opening of the Illinois–Michigan Canal, which connected the river network with another natural transportation network—the Great Lakes—near the small town of Chicago (pop. about 25,000). This small addition to the national network was significant for Chicago for two reasons. First, by providing farmers and pioneers an alternative point of access, Chicago could compete with St. Louis for trade along the Mississippi river. Second, by creating a way to move goods from northern manufacturing cities along the great lakes to southern agricultural cities along the Mississippi river, Chicago became a key location along a new trade route. Chicago's advantage was further sealed in 1852 by the completion of the Chicago–Alton–St. Louis railroad, which provided an even faster and more direct linkage between the river and lake networks through Chicago. With its new-found central position in the national transportation and trade network, Chicago's population and economy grew rapidly, eclipsing the formerly dominant St. Louis to become America's 'second city.' The rest, as they say, is history.[1]

This chapter is about 'the rest.' I begin by exploring the concept of a national urban system, which can be viewed as a network of interactions among a nation's cities. Thus, it is useful to consider when and where such interactions emerge, and what types of patterns they produce. For example, are nearby cities more likely to interact than distant ones, and will these interactions lead to networks that are dense or sparse? Whatever their characteristics, such national urban networks do not simply appear fully formed, but are the product of initially independent urban areas gradually becoming interdependent over time. Focusing on different types of interdependence—communication, trade, finance, and transportation—I trace four historical narratives that try to explain this process. Among these different ways that cities can interact over long distances, perhaps the most visible is the movement of people via transportation networks. While rivers, railroads, and highways have all played a role, I focus on the airline network, which has become one of the most critical and widely used channels though which people and firms in distant cities interact. Of course, with globalization expanding the geographic scope of interaction and reducing the significance of national borders, it may seem reasonable to assume that national urban networks are giving way to global ones. Thus, I conclude by considering whether urban networks at the national level still matter for the flow of information and investment, and how they serve as the foundation of emerging global urban networks.

National Urban Systems as Networks

The notion of a national urban system often simply refers to a set of cities within a country's borders. For example, all the cities in the United States are sometimes described collectively as the U.S. urban system. Used in this way, studies of national urban systems typically aim to identify and describe national patterns in the cities' characteristics, such as their population sizes. One of the most well known of these patterns is the rank-size rule, which states that within a county, the population sizes and ranks of the cities follow a regular pattern: the second largest city has about one-half the population of the largest, the third largest city has about one-third the population, and so on.[2] Although such patterns are interesting, however, they tell us little about what actually makes an urban system a system. Systems are more than just sets of objects; they are sets of objects in which each is an interdependent part of a larger whole. For example, a clock is a system composed of gears that affect each other's movement, while an organism is a system composed of cells that affect each other's biological functions.[3] Similarly, the cities within a nation form a national urban system when their economic and social activities influence one another. The interactions that link cities (or gears or cells) into a system and give rise to their interdependence can be conceptualized as a network.[4]

There are many different factors that may influence which cities are likely to interact with which other cities, but the three factors known as *Ullman's triad* after American geographer Edward Ullman (1912–1976) are particularly useful: transferability, complementarity, intervening opportunity.[5] The first factor, *transferability*, views the potential for interaction between two cities as depending on the ease of transferring resources between them. This rests on the answers to two questions: how many resources do they have to transfer, and how far must they be transferred? Larger cities are more likely to transfer resources between one another simply because they have more resources to transfer. For example, the number of people traveling between two large cities such as New York and Los Angeles is likely to be higher than the number of people traveling between two smaller cities such as Providence and Sacramento. The former pair has more resources—people—that they could potentially transfer than the latter pair. However, the sheer number of resources available for transfer is not the only important consideration; the distance of

METHOD NOTE 20: GRAVITY MODEL

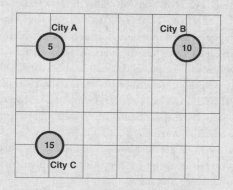
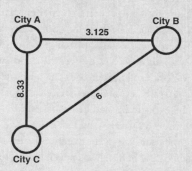

A gravity model is one approach to estimating the intensity of interaction between points in space. The interaction between two nodes, A and B, depends on their population sizes and on the distance between them, and is computed as:

$$(Size_a \times Size_b)/Distance_{ab}^2.$$

From the map on the left, city A has a size of 5, city B has a size of 10, and they are separated by four units of distance. Thus, a gravity model estimates that the intensity of interaction between city A and city B is 3.125 because $(5 \times 10) / 4^2 = 50 / 16 = 3.125$. The intensity of interaction between these two cities is low both because they are relatively small and relatively far apart. In contrast, a gravity model estimates that the intensity of interaction between city A and city C is 8.33 because $(5 \times 15) / 3^2 = 75 / 9 = 8.33$. This interaction is more intense because one of the cities is relatively large, and they are relatively close together.

The values produced by a gravity model cannot be interpreted as actual numbers of interactions such as the number of airline passengers or emails. Instead, they indicate a pair of cities' relative intensity of interaction. For example, there may or may not be exactly six emails sent between city B and city C per day. However, it is likely that there are roughly twice as many emails between B and C than between A and C, because 6 is about twice as much as 3.125.

If the actual network of interactions among a set of cities is unknown, a gravity model can be used to create an estimated network such as the one on the right based on the cities' sizes and locations. If the actual network is known, a gravity model can be used to examine whether cities' sizes and locations are useful for explaining the interactions between them.[6]

the transfer matters as well. Nearby cities are more likely to transfer resources because the transportation cost or time is lower. Thus, there is likely more interaction between New York and Chicago than between New York and Los Angeles, because the former are closer together. This approach to understanding the potential for interaction between two cities is commonly known as a *gravity model* because it closely resembles the way that Isaac Newton computed the gravitational pull between two objects.

Because St. Louis and Tampa are similar in size (about 2.8 million people) and distance from New York (about 1,000 miles), based on a gravity model one might expect that New York would have similar levels of interaction with each of these cities. However, in reality tourist traffic from New York to Tampa is much higher than tourist traffic from New York to St. Louis. A second factor, *complementarity*, helps to explain why. It suggests that interaction is greater between two cities when there is a supply of resources in one and a demand for them in another. In this case, there is a supply of sunny weather and sandy beaches in Tampa, and a demand for such things in New York, which increases the amount of tourism-based interactions between these two places. More generally, complementarity can push the level of interaction between two places above what might be expected based on transferability and the gravity model alone. Thus, in another example, despite their relatively small sizes and the large distance between them, a high volume of business communication exists between Silicon Valley in California and Route 128 in Massachusetts, because both urban regions specialize in high-tech manufacturing. Indeed, when complementarity is strong, it can generate intense interactions even between smaller or more distant cities.

Exerting an opposite effect, *intervening opportunity*, the final factor, serves to reduce the interaction between two cities when there are other cities with which they can interact instead. A significant amount of banking and investment activity occurs between New York and San Francisco, in part because they are both home to many investment companies and bank offices. However, the level of financial interaction between these two cities would likely be even stronger if Chicago, an intervening opportunity, did not exist. Also home to many financial firms, Chicago offers New York investors and bankers a closer alternative to San Francisco. In a sense, the presence of Chicago erodes the potential for more intense interaction between New York and San Francisco. Like intervening opportunities, intervening barriers can also reduce the interaction between two cities below what a simple gravity model might predict. For example, the Sonoran desert that lies between Phoenix and Los Angeles and the Cascade mountains between Seattle and Spokane serve to make interactions between these pairs more difficult and less likely. While barriers can be natural, such as deserts and mountains, they can also be political, such as national borders. For example, Amtrak passenger rail networks bring passengers to key crossing-points along the U.S.–Canada border, but they do not connect U.S. cities to Canadian cities; the national border serves to contain each nation's national urban networks and reduces interactions between each nation's cities.[7] Thus, drawing the three components of Ullman's triad together, transferability and the gravity model establish a baseline expectation for the interactions among cities, while complementarity can intensify these interactions and intervening opportunities can reduce them.

When examining the interactions of individual cities, it can also be important to consider its degree of external orientation: are its interactions primarily with other cities nearby, or are they primarily with more distant cities? In the Pacific Northwest, Portland and Seattle offer two contrasting cases. Portland, although a vibrant cultural and economic center, focuses much of its interactions with other cities in the Northwestern region of the United States. In contrast, Seattle serves as a major shipping port and railroad terminus, and is home to several major corporations including Amazon.com, Starbucks, and Microsoft. As a result, Seattle's interactions span significantly greater distances, linking it not only to other cities in the Northwest, but also to those in the Midwest and Northeast. A city's degree of external orientation indicates its integration into the wider national urban system and thus the system's dependence upon it. As a result, a natural disaster such as an earthquake in Portland could be devastating for the entire Northwestern United States, but a similar disaster in Seattle could have effects that reverberate across the nation.[8]

Also important for an individual city's role in the national urban system are the related notions of hierarchy and dominance. The interdependent relationships between cities that comprise a national urban system are similar to a food chain in the animal world; just as big fish eat small

METHOD NOTE 21: SINGLE LINKAGE ANALYSIS

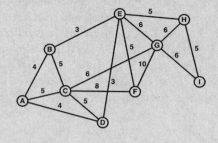

Original Network

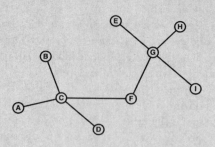

Reduced Network

In the original network on the right, numbers indicate the strength of the linkages between pairs of nodes. For example, the strength of the linkage between F and G is relatively strong, while the linkage between B and E is relatively weak. This network contains a wealth of information, but is so complex that it is difficult to see the underlying structure. *Single linkage analysis* is a method for simplifying the network, and can be useful for examining underlying structures, including identifying dominant and subordinate nodes within a hierarchy.

Single linkage analysis involves the construction of a new, reduced network. In the reduced network, only each node's strongest linkage is included; all other linkages are omitted. For example, node F's strongest linkage is with node G (a strength of 10), so this linkage appears in the reduced network. Similarly, node C's strongest linkage is with node F (a strength of 8), so it appears in the reduced network. This process, identifying a node's strongest linkage, is repeated for each node in the network. The reduced network is much simpler, and a hierarchical structure is now readily observable. Node F is the most dominant, followed by nodes C and G; the remaining nodes are subordinate.

Single linkage analysis can introduce some bias because it focuses only on each node's one strongest linkage, even if its next strongest linkage is also very strong. For example, node H's strongest linkage is with node G (strength of 6), so it is included. However, its two other linkages, with nodes E and I, are nearly as strong (strengths of 5), but are omitted. More sophisticated methods, such as multiple linkage analysis, aim to overcome this problem, but do not always reveal such clear structural patterns.[9]

fish, the most central cities in the national urban network exercise control over the more peripheral cities. In the same way that a hierarchy can be observed in the animal kingdom by examining species' positions in the food chain, an urban hierarchy can often be seen by examining cities' positions in the national urban network using tools such as *single linkage analysis*. National urban hierarchies are composed of several different levels, with cities at each level performing specific functions in the system. In the United States, New York is nearly always viewed as occupying the top position in the urban hierarchy. It orchestrates the economic activities of the entire national urban system through its stock exchanges and banks, and links the U.S. urban system to the rest of the world. Just below New York, at the second level of the hierarchy, are cities such as Chicago or Los Angeles, which focus their interactions in large regions of the nation, organizing the activities of cities in the Midwest or West. Below these, at the third level, are more regionally focused cities such as Minneapolis or Denver, which exercise dominance over cities within still narrower territories.[10]

Individual cities can vary in their levels of external orientation or dominance within a hierarchy depending on their position within a national urban network. However, several features of the network as a whole are also important. The strength and density of cities' interactions reflect the cohesion of the national urban system. An urban system in which the cities are engaged in intense interactions with many other cities is more cohesive—more systemic—than one in which the cities interact infrequently or with just one or two other cities. Such cohesive urban systems are more common in highly industrialized nations and facilitate the development of advanced economies that require the close coordination of multiple cities each playing different roles. The symmetry or reciprocity of cities' interactions is also significant because it indicates whether the urban system is characterized by simple dependence relationships or by more complex relationships of interdependence. For example, if all the cities with business ties to New York send their profits to the banks there, but never receive resources in return, they are merely dependent on New York. In contrast, if New York also sends strategic business information, then a relationship of interdependence is established that is more stable and mutually beneficial because each partner in the interaction is necessary. Finally, the centralization of interactions in a national urban network highlight the extent to which the urban system hinges on just one or a small number of cities. As the next section will illustrate, urban systems tend to be highly centralized early in their development, but become more decentralized over time.[11]

These characteristics of national urban networks and systems derive from the interactions between cities. But, there are many different ways that cities can interact, and each form of interaction can produce a unique network with distinctive structural properties. Communication, or more generally the exchange of information, is one of the most common ways that cities interact over long distances, and can include complex activities such as research collaborations that involve universities in multiple cities, but also more routine activities such as long-distance phone calls. Communication interactions frequently follow the predictions of gravity models because larger cities have more people with information (or gossip) to share and because these people tend to share it with others living nearby.[12] Trade interactions between cities, which involve the exchange of goods, are also common, especially as consumers demand products that are not available locally: seafood in Phoenix or oil in Chicago. Thus, trade interactions are driven primarily by economic forces of supply and demand.[13]

Finance networks, through which money is exchange between cities, take multiple forms including loans or other transfers of funds between banks in different cities, and the investment of funds by individuals or firms in companies located in another city. Because the largest banks and companies are headquartered in just a few cities around the world, financial interactions are frequently highly centralized around the one or two cities in a country that specialize in banking and investment.[14] Finally, cities can interact by exchanging people through transportation networks. Whatever the specific mode of transportation—water, rail, road, and air—the structure of cities' transportation interactions depend heavily on who is traveling and why. For example, networks of tourist travel are centralized on popular destinations such as Las Vegas or Orlando, while networks of business travel are more decentralized and link complementary pairs of cities that can benefit from business partnerships.

The Growth of a Networked Nation

Interactions driven by communication, trade, finance, and transportation can all serve to link cities into a national urban network. However, the formation of these networks is a gradual process through which a collection of independent and disconnected cities becomes an interdependent and cohesive national urban system. By the early 1800s, the United States already contained several major metropolitan areas, including New York, Philadelphia, Boston, and Charleston. At this early stage in the development of the U.S. urban system, each colonial metropolis was relatively independent: New York banks served New York businesses, while Boston newspapers informed Boston residents. As these urban centers grew in size and complexity, they began to—really, were forced to—interact with one another. A Bostonian may pick up a copy of the *New York Times* to read about the market, and a New York-based business may deposit money in a Boston bank to expand its economic reach. The growth of still newer metropolitan areas prompted the development of still more extensive networks of interactions. Today, thousands of people make the six-hour, 2,500-mile journey between New York and Los Angeles every day, highlighting the highly connected and interdependent nature of the present U.S. urban system. How does this process unfold? The multiple types of interactions that occur between cities suggest four related narratives that explain the emergence of national urban systems.

Cities cannot begin to interact with one another through trade or other more complex activities if they cannot first communicate with one another. Indeed, the hallmark of any system is the ability of the parts to 'talk to each other.' In the formation of the U.S. urban system, however, intercity communication was challenged by the limited communication technologies of the eighteenth century. Nonetheless, a national urban communications network did evolve, with information carried first by newspapers, and later by mail and telegraph. The circulation of information initially proceeded through a network of newspapers: a New York newspaper would publish a story, which was reprinted a few days later by newspapers in nearby towns such as Albany and New Haven, which was in turn reprinted by newspapers in still more distant cities such as Philadelphia and Boston. By relying on one another as sources of information that could be reprinted, early urban newspapers formed a network through which information could be transmitted, albeit slowly, across the nation.

This newspaper-based network facilitated the movement of public information, but it was relatively useless for private communication. Thus, by the early nineteenth century, formalized postal routes began to emerge, linking cities together and facilitating the regular exchange of not only public information through newspapers, but also private information through letters. In 1804 the postal routes covered the majority of East Coast cities from Boston to Savannah, while by 1834 they had extended as far west as St. Louis and New Orleans. The network of postal routes, however, was quickly replaced by still another national communication network: the telegraph. The first intercity link in this network, between Washington and Baltimore, was completed in 1844. By 1861 the network spanned the entire nation, linking New York and Sacramento and allowing information to be transmitted almost instantaneously between cities on the East and West Coasts. As these cases illustrate, the communication narrative views the development of a national urban network in the United States as the product of a succession of technologies. Each new technology offered a faster, cheaper, and more reliable method of allowing cities—that is, their residents, businesses, and governments—to communicate with one another, and demand for such a service fueled the continual expansion of the network.[15]

The exchange of goods and services between cities is closely related to the exchange of information. For example, information exchange can stimulate intercity trade, as when individuals begin demanding a new product after hearing about it from others. But, intercity trade can also stimulate the exchange of information, as when merchants in different cities share details about the prices and availability of their products. Thus, while communication technology is important in the creation of national urban networks, the role of trade offers a somewhat different, but related, narrative. The earliest intercity trade in the United States occurred between coastal cities in the Northeast and South, and experienced explosive growth between 1820 and 1840.[16]

Figure 8.1 shows the number of vessels traveling between eight major port cities during this period. These figures highlight a number of important patterns in the development of a national urban network of trade. First, trading relationships were (and, indeed, continue to be) both *valued* because some cities trade more than others, and *directed* because some cities export more than they import. Second, the most intense trading—the densest part of the network in the upper left of the matrices—took place among a few key Northeastern cities, around which a wider national urban network could grow. The early trading network was highly centralized around these few industrial port cities, upon which the Southern cities were dependent. Finally, changes in the trading volumes between 1820 and 1840 highlight the formation of a national hierarchy of cities in just twenty years that persists today. In 1820 trading volumes were relatively dispersed among these cities, while by 1840 New York and New Orleans dominated the economies of the Northeast and South.

These figures tell a story about the growth of a national urban network of trade among a few coastal port cities, but perhaps even more important than the volume of trade between specific cities is the evolving structure of the entire intercity trade network. The previous chapter introduced central place theory, which argues that cities organize trade within regional networks. In an urban system organized around central places, large cities trade with medium-sized cities located a medium-distance away, while in turn medium-sized cities trade with small cities located a short distance away. Following these predictions, the national urban trade network came to resemble the series of branching trees shown in the left panel of Figure 8.2. Here, there are clear patterns of hierarchy that mirror cities' sizes: the biggest cities are the most dominant, while smaller cities are less influential. Trade among U.S. cities was organized in this way for centuries, at a time

In 1820	New York	Philadelphia	Boston	Baltimore	New Orleans	Charleston	Savannah	Norfolk
New York	—	68	91	38	40	98	86	111
Philadelphia	100	—	43	13	12	38	22	29
Boston	101	72	—	56	19	46	41	17
Baltimore	54	12	72	—	10	27	14	2
New Orleans	81	41	44	21	—	17	4	3
Charleston	103	29	29	12	10	—	6	10
Savannah	125	20	15	11	1	10	—	7
Norfolk	79	26	11	1	1	5	1	—

In 1840	New York	Philadelphia	Boston	Baltimore	New Orleans	Charleston	Savannah	Norfolk
New York	—	233	245	144	189	198	125	105
Philadelphia	210	—	191	4	20	19	35	2
Boston	335	90	—	67	137	44	78	36
Baltimore	175	5	107	—	7	25	22	10
New Orleans	270	39	168	60	—	24	16	8
Charleston	125	4	37	26	16	—	10	9
Savannah	101	13	29	20	10	8	—	5
Norfolk	122	4	37	0	2	2	3	—

Figure 8.1 Trade Between Major Ports in 1820 and 1840, in Number of Vessels.[17]

METHOD NOTE 22: VALUED AND DIRECTED NETWORKS

Edges are either present or absent in *binary* networks, but in *valued* networks they can be stronger or weaker. A matrix representing a valued network can contain 1s and 0s, but also other values. For example, a 7 might indicate that two close friends speak to one another every day of the week, while a 1 indicates that more casual acquaintances speak only once a week. A valued network can also be represented as a sociogram in which stronger connections are shown as thicker lines.[18]

The relationship from A to B is the same as the relationship from B to A in an *undirected* or *symmetric* network, but in a *directed* or *asymmetric* network these two relationships may be different. For example, it is possible that Alan likes Beth, but Beth does not like Alan. In a matrix representing a directed network, the nodes in the rows are 'senders' and the nodes in the columns are 'receivers.' Thus, in 1840 (see Figure 8.1), 210 ships sailed *from* Philadelphia *to* New York, but 233 ships sailed *from* New York *to* Philadelphia. A directed network can be represented as a sociogram by using arrowheads to indicate the direction of the relationships.

Valued and directed networks contain more information than binary and undirected networks, and thus are more complex to analyze. In fact, many common network analysis techniques can only be applied to binary and undirected networks. Therefore, it is sometimes useful to transform a valued network into a binary network, or a directed network into an undirected network, to make it simpler. Creating a binary network from a valued one is known as *binarizing* or *dichotomizing*. The researcher selects a threshold, and counts an edge as present only if it is stronger than the threshold. Creating an undirected network from a directed one is known as *symmetrizing*, and can be done in more than one way. In some cases, A and B are considered connected only if *both* A → B and B → A, but in other cases they might be considered connected if *either* A → B or B → A. In UCINET: Transform → Dichotomize and Transform → Symmetrize.

Signed networks are a special type of valued network in which the relationships are positive or negative. A person's relationship with a friend is positive and is indicated in the matrix by a +1, while a person's relationship with an enemy is negative and is indicated in the matrix by a –1. Signed networks are usually analyzed using *balance theory*, which makes a series of propositions about patterns of positive and negative ties that are likely among *triads*, or sets of three nodes. For example: A friend of a friend is a friend, but a friend of an enemy is an enemy. In UCINET: Network → Balance Counter.[19]

when sheer population size was enough to dominate the regional economy and technological barriers hampered long-distance interactions. This configuration reached its peak influence over the U.S. urban system near the beginning of the twentieth century, when it was formalized by the selection of twelve Federal Reserve cities, which would officially anchor the economic activities of their respective regions.[20]

However, a range of changes—in communication and transportation technologies, in the diversity of the U.S. economy, in consumer tastes and demands—slowly caused this structure to shift away from one rooted in cities' location and sizes. The changes in the national urban network are illustrated in the right panel of Figure 8.2. First, while cities had formerly focused their trading activity primarily within the geographic boundaries of their regions, trading patterns expanded to cross regional boundaries. Thus, for example, Chicago may have retained strong trading

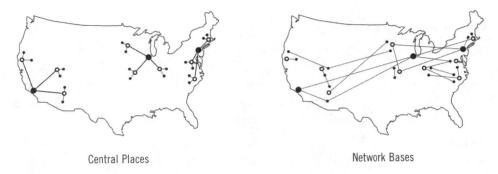

Central Places   Network Bases

Figure 8.2 Development of a National Urban Trade Network.

relationships with Midwestern, but also developed new trading relationships with cities in other regions. Second, while trading patterns had been organized by city size, they came to be organized by position in the network instead. Because smaller cities were increasingly forging new trading relationships of their own, the largest cities in the system were no longer necessarily the most central or most dominant. This transition in the structure of national trade—from central places to network bases—created three distinct types of cities. The primate cities such as New York and Chicago had dominated the early trading network by their large size, but continued to be dominant in the newer trading network by forging relationships outside their regions. A second type—the offline metropolis—includes cities such as Detroit and Cleveland that had been large and regionally influential in the past, but more recently have declined because they have failed to secure a spot in the emerging national network. Finally, wired towns such as Miami or Raleigh-Durham were small and regionally subordinate places in the past, but have seen their economic influence dramatically rise as they have come to occupy central positions in a new urban trade network. These changes highlight that in the national urban network of trade, while size may have mattered in the past, connectivity in the network has become more important.[21]

To make intercity trade possible, individuals and businesses need access to money and banking services. Thus, a national urban network of finance developed, as illustrated in Figure 8.3, in parallel with the network of trade. In the early nineteenth century, before the development of a national urban system, banks in each city handled its own residents' and businesses' financial needs: checks written in New York were cleared by a local New York bank, while checks written in Chicago were cleared by a local Chicago bank. However, as the population grew and the economy expanded, local banks were unable to handle the new volume or to provide for all the needs of the local population. The correspondent banking system emerged as a solution: a small local bank would deposit a sum of money in a larger bank, and in return the larger bank would provide specialized services such as check clearing and loan underwriting. A series of early laws, passed first in the state of New York in 1840 but later in other states, required banks to maintain a correspondent relationship with a bank in New York City. As a result, the earliest national urban financial network was a highly centralized one in which all cities interacted with New York, and indeed were entirely dependent on it for their financial needs.

The decentralization of the urban network began with the 1863 National Bank Act, which established eight reserve cities where banks would also be permitted to maintain correspondent accounts. This law was intended to relieve some of the burden from New York banks, and indeed some of the intercity financial transactions were diverted to Chicago, but the network remained heavily centralized. By the 1870s, Chicago had cemented its role as a key city in the urban financial network, and other cities also started to challenge New York's dominance. Thus, what had been a fully centralized network evolved to become a multilevel hierarchy, still with New York at the top, but with cities such as Chicago and Boston in the second tier, and emerging frontier cities such as Kansas City and San Francisco in the third. In a final wave of development, toward the end of the nineteenth century, large city banks forged relationships not only with small local banks in their regions, but also with large banks in other cities. These new horizontal ties transformed an urban system in which urban banks were dependent on still larger banks in other cities into an urban system in which urban banks and the cities they served were interdependent. In 1914, this network was radically altered by the establishment of the federal reserve system, and now correspondent banking relationships are no longer necessary for banks to provide services. However, this illustrates how the development of a national urban network—in this case, one focused on finances—progresses through multiple stages, each with a distinctive structure, on the path to a mature urban system.[22]

A final narrative that aims to explain the development of national urban networks focuses on transportation. The U.S. urban system has been strongly influenced by transportation, proceeding through roughly three historical periods that correspond to the mode of travel: ships and wagons until the 1830s, trains until the 1920s, and thereafter cars and planes. Despite the differences in these different periods and their dominant transportation technologies, the structure of the national transportation network has paralleled the development of cities and of a national urban system. This is clear in the story at the beginning of this chapter: Chicago owes much of its national prominence to its key position along a series of transportation networks, including the water-based network of the Mississippi River and Great Lakes, and later the land-based network of railroads. Moreover, this was not an isolated event. In the East, the completion of the Erie Canal in 1825 connected New York to the Great Lakes and assured its dominance over Philadelphia. Similarly, the completion of the Pennsylvania Railroad in 1854 connected Philadelphia to the territory west of the Allegheny Mountains and assured its dominance over Baltimore. In the West, the 1880s decision to route the Santa Fe Railroad to Los Angeles rather than to the, then larger, cities of

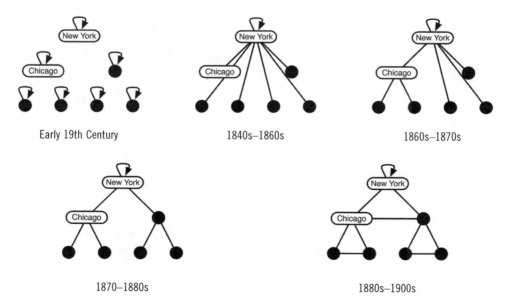

Figure 8.3 Development of a National Urban Finance Network.

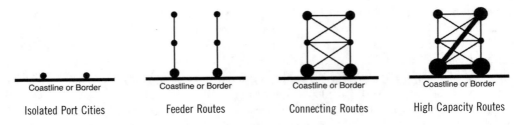

Isolated Port Cities   Feeder Routes   Connecting Routes   High Capacity Routes

Figure 8.4 Development of a National Urban Transportation Network.[23]

San Francisco or San Diego was responsible for the former's rapid growth and ultimate significance in the national urban system. Indeed, reaching further into history, the first-century network of Roman roads centered on London and the accessibility of Moscow along medieval river networks contributed to the rise of these cities over others. Throughout history, the structure of transportation networks has been responsible for the rise (and fall) of major cities.[24]

The development of such national transportation networks are subject to a range of political forces and geographic barriers, but the structure of these networks nonetheless tends to evolve through a set of common stages illustrated in Figure 8.4. Initially, isolated port cities form along national coastlines or other borders, but are not connected to one another or to other cities via transportation routes. As the nation's population expands outward from the border and frontier towns are settled, these isolated port cities become important both as key sources of supplies and as places for settlers to sell their crops and other products. Thus, feeder routes are established between port cities and the interior cities they serve, allowing people and goods to flow more efficiently. Further growth of these cities and their economies encourages additional communication and trade, not only between a port city and nearby interior cities, but also between major ports or between new but rapidly growing interior cities. This leads to the formation of connecting routes that, rather than simply allowing people and goods to be fed in and out of the nation, allow movement across regions. In the final stage, certain routes are expanded because they connect pairs of cities with larger volumes of traffic. At each of these stages, a similar process is responsible for the formation of new linkages in the networks: a need for interaction between two cities spurs the creation of a route between them, which in turn stimulates their growth, and ultimately leads to the need for still more interaction with other cities and the creation of still more and higher capacity routes.[25]

Going the Distance

Beyond its role in the historical evolution of urban systems, national urban networks of transportation continue to be among the most important and highly visible. Indeed, nearly everyone relies on an intercity transportation network at least a few times a year, perhaps at the holidays or during a vacation, while frequent business travelers rely on it daily. Just as there are several different modes of travel—train, car, airplane—there are several different national transportation networks. Figure 8.5 illustrates three major networks for passenger transportation between U.S. cities: Delta Air Lines, Amtrak trains, and the interstate highway system. It is clear that each of these networks has a distinctive structure. For example, the interstate highway network is evenly spread across the nation, while the train and airline networks are highly centralized. These patterns can have important implications for the cities that lie along the transportation routes. Cities with many connections are more easily accessible than those with just a few, and as a result may attract more businesses or tourists. Thus, by examining where cities are located within these networks,

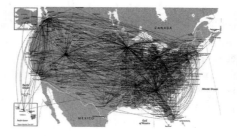

Delta Air Lines

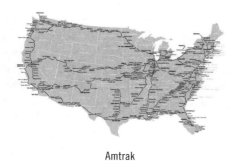

Amtrak

Interstate Highway

Figure 8.5 Planes, Trains, and Automobiles.[26]
Source: reprinted with permission from Delta Air Lines.

and how people and goods flow through them, it is possible to understand why some cities thrive while others struggle.[27]

There are many different ways to conceptualize the edges in a transportation network, even for a single mode of travel. That is, when two cities are viewed as linked in a transportation network, what does this linkage represent? Thus, before considering the effects of these networks, it is useful to think about how to define them. The first important distinction is between edges defined in terms of infrastructure, capacity, and flow. Two cities are connected in an *infrastructure network* when some form of transportation infrastructure exists that makes it possible to travel between them. In the case of automobile transportation, an infrastructure network simply identifies pairs of cities connected by a road or highway. Each of the networks shown in Figure 8.5 is an example of an infrastructure network because they simply indicate pairs of cities between which travel is possible. A *capacity network* can be more informative because the connection between two cities is based not simply on whether or not travel is possible, but on how much travel is possible. Thus, the linkages in a highway capacity network might be defined in terms of the number of lanes on the highway between a pair of cities. Finally, a *flow network* most closely captures urban interactions because the connection between two cities is based on how many objects—people, cars, goods, etc.—are actually moving between them. Here, the actual number of people driving between each pair of cities defines the structure of a highway flow network. These three ways of defining the edges in a transportation network are important because they can lead to very different urban networks. For example, two cities may be connected in an infrastructure network but not in a flow network if there is a road between them, but no one actually uses it.

Flow networks can further be divided into route networks and origin-destination networks. A *route network* tracks the actual route taken when traveling from one city to another. In this type of network, each leg of the route is treated as a separate linkage between two cities. For example, consider a businessperson flying from New York to Los Angeles with a layover in Chicago. A route network depicting this trip includes two separate linkages: New York is connected to Chicago, and Chicago is connected to Los Angeles. Route networks can be useful for understanding how people or goods actually get where they are going, or how things such as the flu can spread from place to place. For example, the New York passenger could spread flu germs first to others in Chicago, and later to others in Los Angeles. In contrast to a route network, linkages in an *origin-destination network* only appear between the initial origin and final destination cities. Thus, an origin-destination network depicting the same example trip includes only one linkage: New York is connected to Los Angeles. Origin-destination networks leave out intermediate or layover cities, such as Chicago in this case. This can be useful when the actual route taken is irrelevant to the purpose of the trip. For example, if the passenger is traveling to negotiate a contract with a client, the trip represents an economic linkage between New York (where the passenger works) and Los Angeles (where the client works), no matter where the passenger's layover happened to be.

A final important consideration when examining transportation networks is content. That is, what is actually traveling through the network? Broadly, people and goods move between cities through transportation networks, but different types of people and goods have distinct travel patterns. Consider the difference between business and leisure travelers. Because businesses are scattered in cities across the country, business trips may begin or end virtually anywhere. Some business people may travel long distances from New York to Los Angeles, while others travel short distances from Chicago to Detroit, and still others may travel to undesirable locations such as Phoenix in the summer or Fargo in the winter. As a result, the network of business travel in the United States is dense because at least some business people can be found traveling between every pair of cities, and is decentralized because business people travel to and from many different cities. In contrast, although leisure trips may begin anywhere, the vast majority end in just a small number of popular locations, including Orlando, Las Vegas, and Honolulu. Thus, the network of leisure travel in the United States is sparse because few tourists travel between most pairs of cities, and is centralized because most tourists travel to just a few destinations.[28]

With these characteristics in mind, it is possible to consider the transportation networks forged by different modes of transportation. Three major surface modes—water, rail, and road—define *planar networks*, so-called because the movement through these networks takes place on a single plane: the earth's surface. Ships and barges are among the earliest modes of surface transportation, and while they are now rarely used for passenger transportation, they continue to be used for long-distance shipping. In addition to ocean routes that allow global shipping, inland waterways provide low-cost shipping channels within national borders. The inland waterway network of the United States includes four major components: the Mississippi River system, the Ohio River system, the Intracoastal Waterway, and the Columbia River system. These networks are a complex combination of natural rivers, strategically linked by man-made canals. For example, the construction of a series of locks and canals extend the Columbia River network over 450 miles inland, reaching as far as Lewiston, Idaho. Together, these water-based transportation networks carry nearly one-sixth of all intercity cargo, including coal, petroleum, and agricultural products.[29]

Like water-based transportation networks, rail networks in the United States are used almost exclusively for shipping. Rather than a single network, the U.S. rail network is actually a series of eight overlapping but independent networks, each owned and operated by a different railroad company. Nearly all of these eight separate networks, although they serve different cities via different routes, converge on Chicago, which thus occupies a highly central position visible in Figure 8.5. Passenger rail service in the U.S. is provided by Amtrak, which does not operate its own infrastructure network but primarily uses tracks owned by other railroad companies. Although Amtrak serves cities in most states, the majority of traffic on this network is restricted to cities along the Northeast Corridor, stretching from Washington to Boston. In contrast, countries throughout Europe and Asia are dependent on rail networks for intercity passenger transportation. In both the U.S. and elsewhere, much of the development of modern rail networks focuses on improving accessibility by expanding the infrastructure network to include more cities, or on improving efficiency by expanding the capacity of the network to handle larger and higher speed trains.[30]

Even more commonly used for both cargo and passenger travel is the highway network. The majority of countries maintain high-speed freeway networks that link cities to one another, with the German autobahn system begun in the 1930s and the American interstate highway system begun in 1956 among the earliest. Although these networks were often originally designed to serve national defense purposes, they have become one of the principle transportation networks that allow people and goods to flow between cities. But, these networks have also introduced a network-based form of inequality because they have made some cities more readily accessible than others. For example, Atlanta is served by three different interstate freeways visible in Figure 8.5 as the six links radiating out from the city: I-85 linking it to Montgomery and Charlotte, I-20 linking it to Birmingham and Augusta, and I-75 linking it to Chattanooga and Macon. In contrast, until the 1970s Miami was served by only one interstate, I-95, which linked it to Jacksonville and can also been seen in Figure 8.5 as the sole network connection that descends to Florida's southern tip. Similarly, the majority of cities throughout Western Europe can be reached by highway from Luxembourg in eight hours, while only a few cities in Italy and Austria can be reached in the same time from Rome. In such cases, the more accessible cities often enjoy significant economic benefits from their network position, which make them a more attractive stop for travelers and location for businesses.[31]

Among the multiple modes of transportation that facilitate movement between cities, the most dominant method for long-distance high-speed travel is by air. Air travel has become particularly important as the speed of economic transactions and the pace of life generally has increased, with air transportation networks playing the greatest role in large countries such as the United States where cities are often separated by large distances. Since the development of commercial aviation, the structure of the air transportation network in the U.S. has undergone a series of changes, illustrated in Figure 8.6. Until 1978, the network of airline routes between cities was regulated by the federal government, which created a point-to-point network in which service was provided only between specific pairs of cities where a route was deemed necessary. This network structure was ideal for those living along major routes, but made travel difficult for others: in the example, three separate planes are required to travel from city A to city B.

In 1978, the Airline Deregulation Act allowed individual airlines to design their own route network structures. Almost overnight, the major airlines adopted a hub-and-spoke design, which was cost effective because it allowed them to serve the most cities with the fewest routes, and was functional because it increased most cities' accessibility. As demand for air travel grew, airlines often expanded their infrastructure networks in two ways. First, they added additional hubs to reduce the burden on individual airports, and to reduce service interruptions when one hub was experiencing inclement weather or traffic congestion. While Figure 8.6 depicts only a simple multiple hub structure, a more complex multiple hub structure can be seen in Figure 8.5: Delta Air Lines maintains hubs in Atlanta, Detroit, Minneapolis, Memphis, and Salt Lake City. Second, to serve pairs of cities with especially high demand for air travel, some airlines added point-to-point service that bypassed their hubs entirely. Today, the majority of airlines link cities together in a multiple hub or hybrid network, but the networks of some low cost carriers such as Southwest have a point-to-point structure.[32]

METHOD NOTE 23: PLANAR NETWORKS

  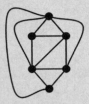

A planar network is a special type of network in which the edges cannot cross one another, or alternatively, in which a new node is created wherever two edges do cross. Each of the networks above is an example of a maximally connected planar network. Adding an additional edge to any of these networks would make them non-planar.

Many transportation networks are planar networks because when two transportation paths cross, a new node is formed. For example, when two roads cross, an intersection is created. Some transportation networks, and many other types of networks including social networks and interorganizational networks, are non-planar. For example, although the paths of two airplanes may cross, no new node is created at that crossing point.

The maximum number of edges in a planar network is smaller than in a non-planar network. A non-planar network can contain a maximum of $(N^2 - N) / 2$ edges, but a planar network can only contain a maximum of $3 \times (N - 2)$ edges. This is important for considering the density of planar networks. Consider a country with ten cities that are connected by twelve non-stop airline flights and twelve highways. Although the two networks both contain ten nodes and twelve edges, their densities differ. In the non-planar airline network there are forty-five possible edges because $(10^2 - 10) / 2 = 45$, thus its density is 26 percent because $12 / 45 = 0.26$. In contrast, in the planar highway network there are only twenty-four possible edges because $3 \times (10 - 2) = 24$, thus its density is 50 percent because $12 / 24 = 0.5$.

Both before and since the deregulation of airline route networks, accessibility and its implications have been a primary concern for travelers and businesses. Hierarchies of network accessibility often emerge within national urban systems. At the top of the hierarchy are the hubs, which are the most highly accessible because they offer direct airline transportation to all (or most) other cities in the system. At the bottom of the hierarchy are more peripheral places that are relatively inaccessible because they have direct airline service only to a hub, but not to any other cities in the system. For example, within the Midwest and Northeast region, Chicago is the most accessible city by air, followed by several second-tier cities including Milwaukee and Indianapolis, which in turn are followed by still less accessible cities such as Springfield and Lansing. In hub-and-spoke airline networks, the overall accessibility of the entire urban system rests on just a few key routes that carry passengers from major cities in a region to the region's airline hub city, or between two hub cities. Just as betweenness centrality identifies nodes in a network that take on special significance because they lie between other pairs of nodes, similarly *edge betweenness* identifies edges that are particularly important because they lie between other nodes. These highly 'between' airline routes often have the highest capacity with many non-stop flights daily, and the largest flow with many passengers using them.[33]

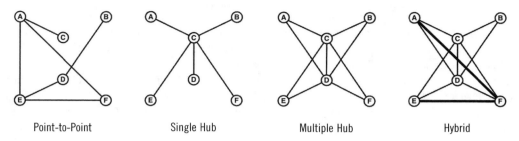

Point-to-Point   Single Hub   Multiple Hub   Hybrid

Figure 8.6 Types of Airline Route Networks.

Examining the structure of airlines' infrastructure networks—where and when they operate scheduled flights—can be useful for understanding the role of the airlines in linking cities, and for considering cities' accessibility to one another. However, these infrastructure networks capture only where passengers could fly, but not necessarily where they actually do fly. Thus, it is also useful to examine the flow networks of airline traffic between cities, which raise two broad questions: what factors are responsible for the amount of traffic between different cities, and what are the consequences of cities' positions within these traffic patterns? Following Ullman's triad, three factors seem to be particularly influential over the structure of the airline flow network. First, as a gravity model would predict, the heaviest traffic occurs between pairs of large cities because they have the largest numbers of people and businesses that may wish to interact with one another. Second, opposite of gravity model predictions, distant pairs of cities have more airline traffic than nearby

METHOD NOTE 24: EDGE BETWEENNESS

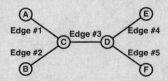

Edge betweenness focuses on how necessary an edge is to get from one part of the network to another. Computing an edge's betweenness first requires finding the shortest, or geodesic, path between each pair of nodes in the network. Each time an edge is located on one of these geodesic paths, its betweenness increases. As a result, the edges with the most betweenness are those commonly found on geodesic paths.

In the example above, edge number 3 has an edge betweenness of 9 because it is necessary to get between nine different pairs of nodes: AD, AE, AF, BD, BE, BF, CD, CE, and CF. All other edges in this example network have an edge betweenness of 5 because they are necessary to get between five different pairs of nodes. For example, edge number 1 is necessary to link the following pairs: AB, AC, AD, AE, and AF.

Identifying edges with high betweenness can be important because they are likely to carry the greatest volume, require the greatest capacity, be most at risk of congestion, and most reduce network accessibility if removed. In UCINET: Network → Centrality → Freeman Betweenness → Edge (line) Betweenness.[34]

pairs because air travel is used only for long-distance trips, while shorter distance trips may rely on rail or road networks. Finally, traffic is heaviest between cities that contain businesses engaged in complementary activities, and which therefore have a reason to interact with one another. Although these factors—population, distance, and economy—help explain the numbers of people that fly between pairs of cities, it is also important to consider who is flying and why because these characteristics may affect where they fly. For example, business passenger traffic may be influenced by cities' economic complementarity, while leisure passenger traffic may be influenced by cities' climate differences: people who live in cold places tend to vacation in warm places, and vice versa.[35]

These patterns of passenger flow between cities have a number of effects on cities, including their economic growth and the health of the people within them. First, cities with more central positions in the airline network—those that have large numbers of people passing through them—tend to experience greater job growth. This raises the question: which comes first? That is, do some cities have busy airports because employment opportunities are expanding, or are new jobs created in certain cities because people are traveling to and from them? While it may seem like common sense that the creation of new jobs would attract people to the area and explain the additional traffic, the evidence suggests otherwise: network position comes first and job creation follows. Cities that occupy central positions in the airline and other national urban networks enjoy certain advantages that stimulate economic growth. For example, as new people continually arrive from other cities, they bring with them a continuous flow of new ideas and new money to spend, which creates a friendly environment for entrepreneurship. Similarly, the businesses in such central cities have greater access to information, and to potential partners, which can facilitate their survival and growth through the ups and downs of the market.[36]

Second, the flow of airline passengers through the network guides the spread of many different things from city to city, including people but also information, money ... and germs. Thus, although cities that occupy highly central positions in such flow networks may enjoy greater job growth, they can also experience greater rates of infection for illnesses that spread easily, such as the cold and flu. Indeed, projections about the timing and severity of the flu season in cities now take into account their position within several different types of flow networks. When examining entire national urban systems, or cities with very large volumes of airline passengers, position in the airline flow network plays an important role in the spread of disease. In contrast, within urban regions and for cities that are less accessible by air and have fewer airline passengers, the spread of disease depends more on position within the highway flow network. This highlights a critical issue when considering the effect of national urban networks: different networks affect cities in different ways. While a communication network may impact which cities learn about the latest fashions first, a transportation network impacts which cities get sick first. And even more narrowly, while the airline transportation network affects the spread of disease at the national scale, the highway transportation network affects its spread at the regional scale.[37]

National Networks in a Global World

In the background, one question about the importance of national urban networks remains: do they really matter in an increasingly globalized world? That is, when such innovations as the Internet make interaction across national borders easy, do the urban networks within a nation's borders remain significant? To be sure, attention has recently turned to thinking about global city networks; indeed, this is the focus of the next chapter. However, national urban networks continue to play an important role in organizing national urban systems, and thus remain a key focus of national public policy. Indeed, in the face of globalization, even regional urban networks continue to play an important role in organizing metropolitan areas and remain the focus of regional economic development.[38] For example, concerns about the environmental and economic costs of transportation have generated interest in developing more efficient methods of traveling between cities. In response, the American Recovery and Reinvestment Act of 2009 allocated several billion dollars to the development of intercity high-speed rail service, while the Federal Railroad Administration has identified ten segments of the existing rail network as proposed high-speed corridors. These projects are focused on building regional and national, not global, urban networks.

Despite the increasing ease of global travel, because individuals' and businesses' need to travel between cities within national borders is not likely to disappear anytime soon, national networks of intercity transportation are likely to remain important. In nations with significant domestic tourism, the movement of tourists between cities mirrors the movement of money, which can represent substantial sources of revenue or loss for some places. In Spain, for example, most domestic tourists travel to Madrid, while very few travel from Madrid or between other cities. As a result, the circulation of money made possible by tourists traveling and spending patterns serves to enrich Madrid at the expense of most other Spanish cities.[39] Similarly, for nations still in the early stages of forging global relationships, these networks are shaping which cities will link their countries to the rest of the world. For example, changes in patterns of airline traffic within China suggest that this role has recently shifted from Beijing to Shanghai.[40]

However, other types of national urban networks remain important in the face of globalization as well. The linkages between corporations in one city, and their stockholders in other cities, are an example of one particularly critical intercity finance network. Modern corporations are financed through the sale of stock and their primary stockholders, often large investment firms and banks, exercise a great deal of control over how they are run. Thus, if much of a Los Angeles-based corporation's stock is owned by investment banks in New York, then a financing relationship exists between these two cities. Because the Los Angeles corporation depends on New York banks for financing, then New York (or at least its banks) has some level of control over the Los Angeles economy. At the center of such a network are key national financial centers that control and organize the national corporate landscape, including New York, Chicago, and Boston. In contrast, at the periphery are cities that may be home to corporations themselves but which do not exercise control over corporations in other cities, including Salt Lake City, Cincinnati, and New Orleans.[41]

In addition to finance relations between cities, two additional types of networks shape the economic influence of cities and their corporations: interlocking directorates and headquarter–subsidiary linkages. Briefly mentioned in Chapter Four because it can also play a role in the political influence networks within cities, an interlocking directorate occurs when a single individual sits on the board of directors of multiple corporations. When these corporations are located in different cities, the cities are linked to one another by this individual, who serves as a channel through which information can flow and influence can be exercised.[42] Similarly, when a corporation headquartered in one city maintains subsidiaries such as branch offices in other cities, a linkage exists between the headquarter city and each subsidiary city through which commands are sent from the former to the latter about what to do and when. For example, a large bank headquartered in New York might instruct each of its branches in cities across the country to increase loan interest rates. Through both interlocking directorate and headquarter–subsidiary networks, the actions of businesses in one city can affect businesses in other cities. Thus, cities that occupy central positions in these networks—those that have many connections to other cities—are key sites of corporate decision-making power because their businesses have the ability to influence businesses elsewhere. Frequently these national networks are highly centralized, with decision-making power concentrated in a single city: New York in the United States, Toronto in Canada, and São Paulo in Brazil.[43]

However, the national economic linkages that connect cities are not exclusively focused on controlling corporations. Cities are also linked by interdependent trading relationships. Moreover, although cities certainly engage in trade with global partners, trade with regional and national partners remains common and forms a national trade network with a number of complex patterns. Within a national urban network of trade, most cities interact primarily with cities at least as large as themselves. Thus, large cities such as Los Angeles and Chicago trade primarily with other large cities, while medium-sized cities such as Milwaukee and Indianapolis trade with both medium and large cities. As a result, smaller cities tend to be linked to a more diverse range of other cities in the trade network. Distance also plays an important role, but only for smaller cities. That is, large cities maintain trade linkages with other cities throughout the nation regardless of their distance, while smaller cities tend to have more regionally focused trade linkages. For example, firms in Los Angeles trade with firms on the West coast, but also those in the Midwest and East, while firms in Indianapolis trade mainly with firms located in other Indiana cities.[44]

Perhaps even more significant than the purely economic networks of finance and trade between cities is the exchange of information, which is vital for economic growth but also for cultural and social activities. As with other types of networks, although information can now move between international pairs of cities easily, information flows between domestic pairs of cities continue to grow. In some cases, these information flows are carried through communication networks that resemble those of the past, albeit much faster. For example, because business and legal correspondence often requires sending original hard-copy documents, high-speed mail services such as Federal Express facilitate intercity information flow. In these networks, some cities generate more information flows than others. Specifically, the largest cities tend to send and receive the most information, and do so over the longest distances, while other cities are involved in fewer information exchanges over shorter distances.[45]

More recently, however, information is increasingly exchanged between cities electronically, for example via the Internet, which requires an infrastructure network of fiber optic cables linking cities to one another. Major telecommunications companies operate overlapping Internet backbone networks within countries or multi-country regions that carry Internet traffic between cities, where it is then routed to individual homes and businesses. The structure of these national Internet backbone networks is important because it determines which cities have better or faster access. This has led many to conclude that while high-speed communication and transportation networks may have eliminated the impact of distance, they have not eliminated the impact of location, because some cities are better connected than others.[46] While the majority of U.S. cities are now served by at least one Internet backbone, constant upgrades to these networks keep access unequal. For example, Verizon announced in 2011 that it would expand the capacity of its backbone network to allow speeds of 100 gigabits per second, but initially only along selected portions of the network: Chicago-to-New York, Sacramento-to-Los Angeles and Minneapolis-to-Kansas City. Such modifications to the intercity communication network may give businesses in these cities at least a temporary advantage over businesses located elsewhere.[47]

The continued development of faster national transportation and communication networks, and the continued importance of national finance and trade networks, suggest that urban networks continue to matter even within national borders. However, it is also important to remember that national urban networks are nested within larger global urban networks. For example, the Internet backbone network being upgraded by Verizon is connected to a similar backbone network in Europe via an underwater transatlantic cable between New York and London. Similarly, Delta's airline network serves cities throughout the United States, but also extends to Europe where Amsterdam and Paris serve as hubs, and to Asia where it maintains a hub in Tokyo. Thus, beyond examining the structure of national urban networks within nations, it is important to consider how national urban networks connect to one another. Although most U.S. cities' strongest linkages in the airline flow network are with other U.S. cities, many also maintain strong linkages to foreign cities—New York exchanges many passengers with London, Miami with Caracas, and Seattle with Tokyo—which connect the U.S. national urban network to national urban networks in other countries. Still, despite these international connections, American cities' networks remain more nationally oriented while European cities tend to be more globally oriented.[48]

*   *   *   *   *

As the primary locations of social and economic activity, cities are the building blocks of modern nations. And, when they link to one another through networks of exchange and interdependence, drawn into interaction by forces that resemble a gravitational pull, together they form national urban systems. But, such national urban networks and systems do not simply appear. Instead, they are the result of a gradual evolution from an initial set of disconnected settlements into a cohesive whole. Four broad and overlapping narratives tell the story of this evolution: transportation and communication networks emerge from a need to circulate people and information, while trade and finance networks are born from a desire to exchange money and goods. Among these multiple types, transportation networks are among the most visible and regularly used, and can be conceptualized in different ways including as the physical infrastructures that help move people from city to city, and the actual routes passengers take along the way. Cities' positions within these networks—especially their accessibility and centrality—can have dramatic implications for urban life, providing quick access to the latest news but also to the latest disease. Thus, although intercity networks are expanding outward to connect cities across national borders, understanding national urban networks remains critical to building healthy and well-informed cities.

However, well-connected national urban networks are not always advantageous. In the 1850s, connecting the Mississippi River and Great Lakes networks certainly proved beneficial for Chicago. It was this small change to the nation's water transportation network, or more specifically its economic and social consequences, that led Sinatra to declare Chicago, not St. Louis, "My Kind of Town." But, more recently the tiny link between two networks that made Chicago into a major metropolis has also been responsible for a potential ecological disaster. The Asian Carp is an invasive, foreign species of fish found throughout the Mississippi River. Because they can out-compete native species for food and space, they can dramatically alter the delicate balance of aquatic ecosystems. There is now concern that the Asian Carp may migrate from the Mississippi River into the Great Lakes, via the modern Chicago Sanitary and Ship Canal, and disrupt the Great Lakes ecosystem. Indeed, the concern is so great that in 2002 the U.S. Army Corp of Engineers installed an electric fish barrier in the canal, and a bill—the Close All Routes and Prevent Asian Carp Today (CARPACT)—has been introduced in Congress to continue this effort. Thus, the same network modification that led to Chicago's rapid growth may also be responsible for the region's environmental problems. Still, this issue raises one obvious question: What kind of network let the Asian Carp get from Asia to the U.S. in the first place?

Discussion Questions and Activities

1. Use a gravity model to estimate the relative amount of interaction between five U.S. cities. Current city populations can be found using the 'population finder' at www.census.gov/popfinder, while distances between cities can be found using http://maps.google.com. Do the estimates from the model seem reasonable? What factors might cause two cities to interact more or less than the gravity model estimates?
2. Use single linkage analysis to create a reduced network from the data in Figure 8.1. Is there a clear national urban hierarchy? How did the network change from 1820 to 1840? How might this network look today?

3. There are several different ways to think about the linkages in a transportation network: infrastructure, capacity, route flow, and origin–destination flow. Think of a situation where each approach would be useful to examine. How might you collect the data that would be necessary to create each network?

4. Use a travel website such as www.expedia.com to create a capacity network among six different U.S. cities. For each pair of cities, record how many non-stop flights are available on a given day. Which city is the most accessible? Which is the least accessible? What implications might this network have for these cities?

5. How could the methods introduced in the previous chapters be used to study the concepts introduced in this chapter? Similarly, how could the methods introduced in this chapter be used to study the concepts introduced in the previous chapters?

Sources for National Urban Network Data

Communication—Communications providers often publish maps of their infrastructure networks, showing which cities are directly connected by high-speed or high-bandwidth cables. For example, the network map for Level 3 Communications, an internet service provider, is available at: www.level3.com/Resource-Library/Maps/Level-3-Network-Map.aspx. The Cooperative Association for Internet Data Analysis (CAIDA) also maintains an archive of internet-related network data; see: www.caida.org/data. Measuring the actual volume of communication between cities—whether telephone calls, FedEx packages, or emails—is difficult because these forms of communication are private and data is typically not publicly released. However, it is not impossible if access to such data private can be obtained: the New York Talk Exchange project examined all AT&T telephone traffic in and out of New York City, while another project tracked a large sample of FedEx packages sent in the United States.[49]

Trade—The Commodity Flow Survey, conducted every five years, tracks the movement of freight shipments between U.S. states and metropolitan areas; see: www.bts.gov/publications/commodity_flow_survey.

Transportation—The American Travel Survey, collected in 1995, documents the long-distance trips taken by a sample of 80,000 households; see: www.transtats.bts.gov/DatabaseInfo.asp?DB_ID=505. The Airline Origin and Destination Survey is collected every three months and provides details on a random 10 percent of all airline trips taken in the United States; see: www.transtats.bts.gov/DatabaseInfo.asp?DB_ID=125. Data on highway travel is typically collected by individual states. For example, California provides data on the number of vehicles traveling on each segment of highway in the state at http://traffic-counts.dot.ca.gov.

9
GLOBAL
NYLON HOLDS THE WORLD TOGETHER

Admittedly, nylon is an amazing material. This synthetic fiber, developed by DuPont in the 1930s, can be woven into fabrics that will not rip (good for parachutes) or puncture (good for luggage). However, despite nylon's durability, what really holds the world together from the perspective of global urban networks is NY–LON: the intense economic and social linkage between New York and London. As the twin centers of the business world, CEOs and other executives commute between them on over twenty-five daily nonstop flights. As home to the world's largest financial markets—the New York and London stock exchanges—billions of dollars change hands within and between them, eventually filtering down to other cities around the world. As capitals of culture, they exchange details about the latest developments in music and fashion to keep trendsetters on both sides of the Atlantic informed. This linkage, under development since 1664, is today the primary connection between 'old world' Europe and 'new world' North America. By facilitating— or in some cases, blocking—interaction between other cities throughout these continents, it plays a pivotal role in how business gets done and trends get set.

But, the linkage between New York and London is only a small part of a much larger global urban network. These two cities also have important economic ties to Tokyo, together forming a circuit through which investment and capital circles the northern hemisphere. As key administrative and governmental centers, Washington and Brussels regularly exchange diplomatic personnel and collaborate on matters of international policy. Similarly, as the primary connection between North and South America, immigrants and cultural resources continually flow between Miami and cities such as Caracas, Rio de Janeiro, and Buenos Aires. Still more mundane, but no less important, interactions also link less glamorous global locales. For example, weekly telephone calls and wages sent via financial networks such as Western Union keep migrants in Texas border towns connected to their families living in cities throughout Mexico. At the same time, cotton harvested in those Texas towns is sent to Colombo, Sri Lanka for processing, before the finished garments are ultimately sent to boutiques in New York and London. Together, these various linkages knit the world's cities into a complex economic and social system in which cities depend on one another, but where some cities have more privileged positions in the network than others.[1]

In this chapter, I focus on macro-urban networks at the widest geographic scale: global urban networks. Although talk of globalization is relatively recent, and of global urban networks even more recent, these phenomena have actually been unfolding and evolving for several millennia. Thus, I begin by tracing the development of global urban networks, and the process of globalization they make possible, from the early trade networks of the ancient world to the international networks of high finance and advanced telecommunications of today. Understanding these networks requires appreciating the diversity of the linkages from which they arise. For example, people can move through these networks as migrants, business travelers, tourists, and refugees, while exchanges of money and information can also take multiple forms. To consider these diverse possibilities, I explore how different types of networks can be measured, whether they overlap with one another, and to what extent they create a level playing field in which all cities are well connected. I then examine how the rapid expansion of global connections between cities has given rise to a new breed of cities—so-called world cities—that today occupy central and powerful positions within the network, and thus play a particularly dominant role in shaping the global economy. However, despite the heavy emphasis placed on economics, money is not everything: for global urban networks, culture and the arts matter too.

A Long Time in the Making

Globalization refers broadly to the increasing level of interaction among people and firms in distant places around the world, made possible largely through the growth of global urban networks of trade, transportation, and communication. Since the mid 1980s, scholars and activists alike have commented on the wide-reaching economic, political, and cultural consequences of these networks. However, global urban networks and their globalizing effects have a much longer history that predates recent innovations such as the multinational corporation or the Internet by several thousand years. Among the earliest global urban networks, illustrated in Figure 9.1, are the trade routes that linked cities in the ancient world. The overland Silk Road connected silk-producing cities in Asia with trading centers in the Mediterranean, while the maritime Spice Route carried valuable spices between cities in India and Europe. A few key cities occupied particularly important positions within these ancient networks, which facilitated their economic growth and dominance. For example, all roads really did lead to Rome, which served as the destination for many of the goods, while other cities such as Constantinople (note: it's now Istanbul) gained significance not as destinations but as gateways between the East and West.[2]

These early networks laid the foundation for the continued development of land and sea-based trade routes throughout Europe during the medieval period. In the south, they were highly centralized networks focused around two powerful Italian trading centers—Venice and Genoa— that controlled much of the flow of commodities for several centuries. In contrast, the northern trade routes formed a more decentralized trading network connecting a set of allied cities— London, Amsterdam, and Stockholm, among others—known collectively as the Hanseatic League. By linking ancient and medieval cities together, these trade networks served to shrink the economic and cultural distances between them and unite them into an interdependent global urban system.[3]

The development of electronically mediated communication set in motion another wave of global urban networking that brought distant cities even closer together. In 1858, upon the completion of a submarine telegraph cable between North America and Europe, messages were exchanged between Queen Victoria in London and President James Buchanan in Washington in a matter of minutes rather than days. This success prompted the installation of still more submarine cables, which by 1903 spanned the globe and linked cities on every continent except Antarctica. Moreover, as the map in Figure 9.1 illustrates by the sheer number of cables between them, NY-LON was already emerging as a key linkage in the global urban network by the early twentieth century.[4] The year 1927 marked still another leap forward, with the inauguration of transatlantic telephone service between New York and London and the first solo transatlantic flight between New York and Paris, leading sociologist Roderick McKenzie to observe that "the world is fast becoming a closed region . . . in which centers and routes are gaining precedence over boundaries

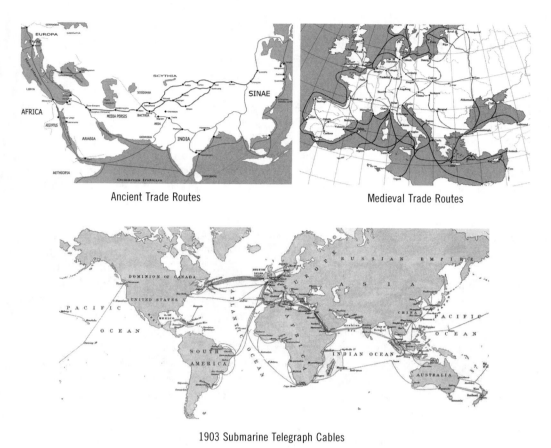

Ancient Trade Routes

Medieval Trade Routes

1903 Submarine Telegraph Cables

Figure 9.1 Early Global Urban Networks.[6]

and political areas." This comment highlighted a major transition that had been a long time in the making: the world is increasingly organized by the networks between places rather than by the places themselves.[5]

But, what sorts of 'places' are most significant in this emerging world system; what are the nodes in this global network? One possible answer is the nation-state, because it is between nation-states that wars are fought, treaties are signed, trade relationships develop, and immigrants travel. Thus, using what is known as *world-systems theory*, scholars have sought to understand how entire nations are diplomatically and economically linked to one another, and how this inter-national network organizes the global order. The nations with the most central and advantageous positions in this network—the United States, Japan, Australia and much of Western Europe, known as core nations—are the most economically advanced and hold the greatest influence over world affairs. In contrast, peripheral nations including the majority of Africa and much of Asia and South America have few connections in this network and through their dependence on core nations are economically underdeveloped and politically marginalized.[7] As useful as this approach is for understanding patterns of development in the world system, however, its focus on nations does not quite match reality. A corporation's headquarters does not cover an entire nation, but is located in a specific city, while trade and immigration do not occur between entire nations, but between specific pairs of cities within them. For example, the export of new cars by General Motors is an example of an economic flow emanating not from the United States as a whole, but specifically from Detroit. Thus, many scholars increasingly view cities, not nation-states, as the key places in the modern world system and as the nodes in a contemporary global network.[8]

Two different perspectives help to explain the role that cities play in globalization and global networks (see Figure 9.2). The first focuses on multinational corporations, large companies that have employees and facilities around the world, which first appeared in the early 1600s with the founding of the Dutch East India Company but rapidly multiplied in the 1950s and 1960s. In a typical multinational corporation, there is a division of labor among three groups of interdependent employees: front-line workers perform production tasks, middle managers coordinate them, and executives make strategic decisions. In addition, these different tasks are divided among three sets of interdependent cities: production factories are located in cities around the world wherever labor costs are low, coordinating regional offices are located in larger cities near the factories, and corporate headquarters are located in just a few key cities such as New York or London. This arrangement has created a *new international division of labor* in which different cities, just like different types of employees, play different roles in multinational corporations. Moreover, just as front-line workers are controlled by middle managers who are controlled by executives, production cities are controlled by coordinating cities that are controlled by decision-making cities. Cities in the new international division of labor are connected to one another by the corporate commands that come from above. For example, commands are issued by executives at the headquarters in one city and received by managers in another city. Thus, from this perspective, the few cities that are home to corporate headquarters and executives are the real centers of power.[9]

A second perspective focuses not on the multinational corporations themselves, but on the intermediaries that help these corporations to do business with one another. Conducting business across national borders is no simple matter because it involves multiple legal jurisdictions, languages, currencies, and cultures. To overcome these barriers, multinational corporations often rely on outside firms known as *advanced producer service firms* to help. For example, a multinational corporation might outsource the drafting of international contracts to a law firm, outsource its currency exchanges to a major bank, and outsource training its employees in foreign languages and cultures to a management consultant. These types of firms help multinational corporations in different cities throughout the world to 'speak the same language' and make it possible for them to interact with one another. It is the advanced producer service firms, not the multinational corporations themselves, that link cities in a global urban network because they make cross-border transactions

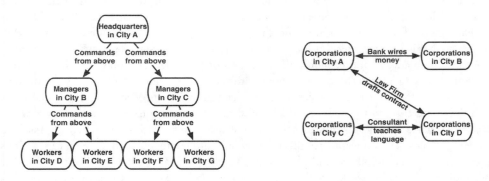

New International Division of Labor   Advanced Producer Service Firms

Figure 9.2 Two Perspectives on Cities in Global Networks.

possible. Thus, from this perspective, the most powerful cities in the global urban network are not necessarily the locations of corporate headquarters, but the homes of advanced producer service firms.[10]

With such a long history, it is difficult to precisely define the contemporary global urban network. However, much of the most recent thinking about global urban networks traces to one influential statement known as the world city hypothesis: "Key cities throughout the world are used by global capital as 'basing points' in the spatial organization . . . of markets. The resulting linkages made it possible to arrange world cities into a complex spatial hierarchy."[11] This statement made it possible to start *visualizing* what a contemporary global urban network might look like. But, it also makes several claims about the nature of a global urban network that are worth investigating further. First, while it is clear that a global urban network links cities to one another, what kinds of linkages are possible and how do different linkages produce different networks? Second, while some cities are likely to be more important than others based on their position in the network, which cities are at the top (or bottom) of this hierarchy? Finally, while global urban networks from ancient times to the present have been forged by economic forces, are they really only significant for movements of global capital? The rest of the chapter aims to answer these questions.

The Ties that Bind

Given the complexity of modern cities and the diversity of activities that take place within them, there are many different ways they can be connected to one another in a global urban network. These different types of connections often involve the exchange of resources in one of three forms—human, material, or information—which serve one of four broad purposes: economic, political, cultural, or social. Figure 9.3 illustrates how the two dimensions of form and function define a typology of types of global urban linkages.

The majority of research on global urban networks focuses on intercity linkages that serve economic functions. Economic linkages that take human form include the exchange of migrant workers, who have become a critical source of labor in many cities around the world. For example, in the rapidly growing city of Dubai, over 80 percent of the population are immigrants, many of whom have come from cities in Asia, Europe, and North America to find work. Cities such as Dubai rely on workers from cities elsewhere to fuel their economies because their native-born populations are too small, demand higher wages, or lack the necessary skills. Business travelers also represent a type of human economic linkage, one that is essential because face-to-face interactions between executives are often necessary when negotiating major contracts or establishing new partnerships. But, economic linkages between cities do not always involve the exchange of people; they also frequently take the form of information exchange. In some cases, information exchanges may involve people, as when business meetings are conducted via teleconference. In other cases, information can be exchanged 'behind the scenes' as part of a continual and automated flow of business data between international cities. For example, when stock is purchased on the New York Stock Exchange, this information is nearly instantly transmitted to London and dozens of other cities where stock prices are updated.

While the movements of people and information between cities power the global economy, these ultimately depend on economic linkages that take material form. The exchange of commodities—both raw materials and finished products—give migrant workers something to work on and investors something to buy and sell. The movement of commodities from city to city defines a specific type of network—a *commodity chain*—which traces the process through which raw materials are transformed into finished products. For example, selling a new cell phone in New York involves several steps spread across many different cities: the phone is designed in a Silicon Valley city, to include a display screen manufactured in a South Asian city, from glass

METHOD NOTE 25: VISUALIZATION

Networks lend themselves to visualization as sociograms. However, for any given network, there are many different ways to lay out the nodes in a sociogram. Consider the example of a global urban network, where the nodes are cities.

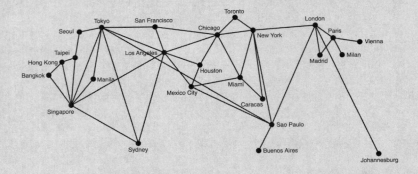

The nodes can be laid out based on their geographic locations. In this example, the distance between each node represents the spatial distance between each pair of cities. For example, the Chicago and Toronto nodes are close together because they are only about 450 miles apart, while the London and Johannesburg nodes are far apart because they are over 5,500 miles apart. In a social network among neighbors, a similar layout might use the distance between individuals' houses. A geographic layout can be helpful for identifying spatial patterns in networks. In this example, it is clear that most linkages are within regions—Asia, North America, or Europe—while relatively few edges are between regions. In NETDRAW: Layout → Attribs as coordinates.[12]

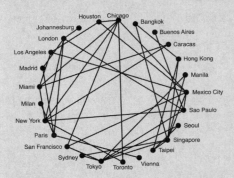

Nodes can also be laid out in a circular pattern, based on some attribute. In this example, cities located in core countries are arranged alphabetically on the left from Chicago to Vienna, while those in peripheral countries are arranged on the right from Bangkok to Taipei. A social network might divide nodes by gender or race, while an interorganizational network might divide nodes by sector. A circle layout can be helpful for examining whether nodes with different attributes are connected. Because there are many edges that cross through the middle of the circle, this example illustrates that there are many linkages between core and peripheral cities. In NETDRAW: Layout → Circle.

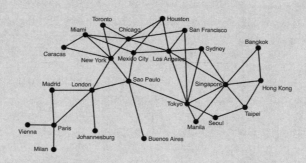

Spring embedding lays out nodes based on their geodesic distances. Nodes that are connected by short geodesic distances are close together, while nodes that are separated by long geodesic distances are far apart. For example, because Caracas is directly connected to New York—a geodesic distance of one—these two nodes are close to one another. In contrast, the geodesic distance between Caracas and Buenos Aires is three, so these two nodes are much further apart. A spring embedding layout is helpful for identifying cliques of nodes because it places nodes together if they are directly connected or indirectly connected by a short path. It is the most common layout because it is based on the structure of the network itself, rather than the characteristics of the nodes. This example highlights a cluster of European cities on the left and a cluster of Asian cities on the right, but also highlights that these two clusters are separated from one another in the network. In NETDRAW: Layout → Graph-Theoretic layout → Spring embedding.

When thinking about network visualization, two points are important to remember. First, there is no 'right' way to graphically depict a network. Each of these three examples depicts the same network with the same structure. Second, network visualization is not the same as network analysis, just as drawing a scatterplot is not the same as conducting a regression or ANOVA. Sociogram visualizations can be useful for spotting patterns or communicating results, but network analysis is based on examination of the network matrix and other values computed from it such as density or centralization.

		Form	
Function	*Human*	*Information*	*Material*
Economic	Labor Migration	Teleconference	Commodity
Political	Official Visit	Policy Collaboration	Mutual Aid
Cultural	Student Exchange	Music	Artwork
Social	Vacation	Phone Call	Care Package

Figure 9.3 A Typology of Global Urban Linkages.[13]

produced in still another city, with silicon dioxide (sand) processed elsewhere. At each step in the process, activities in these cities add value as sand is transformed into cell phones. Commodity chains can be difficult to map completely because they are very complex, even for relatively simple products. Nonetheless, they are an important way that cities are connected to one another globally, and cities' economic fates often rest on their positions within these chains. Exclusion from a commodity chain can decimate a city's economy, while a location at the intersection of several commodity chains can make a city invaluable to corporations.[14]

Although linkages that serve economic functions are among the most studied, linkages serving other functions are also possible. Cities often engage in political and governmental interactions with international partners. Such interactions can take human form when city officials meet with one another to discuss solutions to their common problems. For example, the C40 summit has brought together the mayors of the world's forty largest cities each year since 2005 to discuss climate change, while on a smaller scale mayors in specific pairs of cities engage in similar issues: Chicago's Richard M. Daley and Curitiba, Brazil's Luciano Ducca, for instance, met multiple times to explore the possibilities for sustainable urban transportation. Political interactions can also take the form of information exchanges when cities share policy documents or collaborate on the drafting of new policy, or material exchanges when cities pledge mutual aid to other cities in need following natural disasters. Social and cultural exchanges often follow as a result of strong economic and political linkages. For example, a human economic exchange such as labor migration between two cities may prompt a social information linkage such as phone calls to keep separated families in contact. Similarly, a political information linkage such as two city governments collaborating on downtown redevelopment policy may prompt a material cultural exchange such as the loan of a public sculpture to beautify the streets.

A few common characteristics cut across the different types of linkages that constitute global urban networks. First, nearly all exchanges between cities, no matter what function they serve or what form they take, also involve the exchange of money or capital. For example, labor migration is primarily a human exchange. However, it also frequently involves a monetary exchange in the form of wages sent back to family known as remittances. Similarly, although a loan of artwork is primarily a cultural exchange, it also likely involves some form of direct or indirect compensation. Second, it is not the cities themselves that forge these linkages, but rather a wide range of other actors. For example, commodities or artwork may be exchanged between cities, but it is actually specific corporations or museums that initiate these exchanges. Similarly, although two cities may collaborate on the development of new public policy, these policies are ultimately constrained by the laws of their respective nations. Finally, although the primary focus of global urban networks is the connections between cities, these connections depend in part on connections within the cities, that is, on micro- and meso-urban networks. Business leaders and corporations that are well connected to others within their own city are often more effective at establishing linkages to those in other cities.[15]

Despite the variety of global urban linkages, actually measuring the connections between cities at this scale can be quite challenging. National censuses and other common sources of information provide a wealth of details about individual cities, but rarely provide much insight into the relationships between cities that constitute urban networks. For example, the U.S. census can be used to track the population of New York and the U.K. census can be used to track the population of London, but neither of these can be used to examine the relationship between New York and London. Compounding this problem, much of the information available on cities is collected and provided by national governments, with each one asking different questions and using different tools. As a result, data collected by the U.S. about New York's economy may not be comparable to data collected by the U.K. about London's economy. These challenges have led researchers to look for more creative ways to think about, and to measure, global urban networks. Thus, a number of approaches have emerged that aim to combine a theory of global urban networks with a method for measuring them.[16]

The *corporate relations* approach draws on the notion of an international division of labor, and attempts to map the exchange of commands between corporations. Large parent companies own subsidiaries located in cities throughout the world, and while these subsidiaries may remain relatively independent on a day-to-day basis, they are still under the control of the parent companies that own them. For example, the St. Louis, Missouri-based Budweiser brewer Anheuser-Busch is a wholly owned subsidiary of Leuven, Belgium-based InBev. While Anheuser-Busch employees in St. Louis are responsible for actually brewing Budweiser every day, corporate commands about such operational issues as how much to brew come from Leuven. The corporate relations approach uses the patterns of parent companies' control over their subsidiaries to examine a global urban network of corporate command and control. This approach tends to highlight the role of cities that are home to large multinational corporations, not only in such obvious places as New York and London, but also in smaller places such as Peoria, Illinois (pop. 115,000; home to Caterpillar Inc.) and Wolfsburg, Germany (pop. 121,000; home to Volkswagen).[17] Closely related to the corporate relations approach, cities can also be viewed as linked through interlocking corporate directorates. When a single person sits on the board of directors of two multinational corporations that are headquartered in different cities, he or she forges a linkage between these two cities through which information and the power to control corporation actions flows.[18]

In contrast, the *interlocking branches* approach draws on the critical role of advanced producer service firms, and focuses on how these firms' branch office locations in different cities create a network of service provision. Advanced producer service firms maintain branch offices in many different cities, and these branch offices allow them to provide seamless service to clients throughout the world. For example, the accounting firm PricewaterhouseCoopers (PwC) is headquartered in London, but also has a major office in New York, which makes it possible for PwC's clients to easily conduct business between these two cities. In an interlocking branch network, two cities are connected when they both contain a branch of the same firm. Because London and New York both contain branches of PwC, they are connected in the interlocking branch network. The exchanges that occur between PwC's London and New York offices are, at least indirectly, exchanges between London and New York themselves. In some cases, a pair of cities may only be weakly connected because only one or two firms maintain offices in both of them, while in other cases such as that of London and New York, they may be strongly connected because several hundred firms maintain offices in both places.[19]

Figure 9.4 illustrates the subtle, but important, difference between global urban networks conceptualized using the corporate relations and interlocking branch approaches. Both approaches view cities A and C as linked, but for different reasons. In the corporate relations approach, cities A and C are linked because InBev headquartered in A owns and controls Anheuser-Busch located in city C. In contrast, in the interlocking branch approach, cities A and C are linked because they both contain branch offices of the advanced producer service firm, PricewaterhouseCoopers, which work together to serve clients in these two cities.[20]

Transportation represents a third approach to conceptualizing and measuring global urban networks. However, unlike urban networks at the regional or national scale where road and rail networks are important, at the global scale only air and water-based transport are viable. The network of global air transportation between cities is important for at least three different reasons. First, despite the availability of technologies such as email and teleconferencing that make long-distance interaction possible, in-person interactions remain useful for negotiating business contracts and are essential for sightseeing while on vacation. Second, in those cases where an email

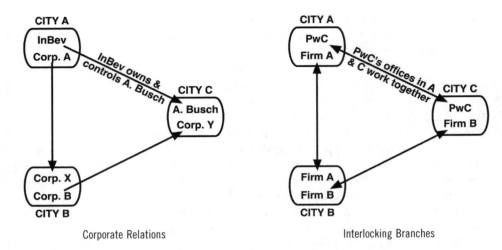

Figure 9.4 Economic Approaches to Measuring Global Urban Networks.

attachment is insufficient, air transport remains the ideal method for moving high-value but low-bulk materials such as original legal documents or high-tech equipment. Finally, apart from the functional utility of air travel, intercity linkages in a global air transport network have symbolic value. Press conferences are held and photographs of mayors are taken when a city announces a new non-stop service to New York, or London, or another seemingly prestigious destination. The creation of such linkages marks a city's movement from the periphery of the network to a more connected and central location.[21]

In contrast to air transport, which connects cities primarily by carrying people, water transport connects them by carrying goods. As a method that has been in use for thousands of years, at first glance moving goods by water may seem somewhat obsolete in a modern global economy. However, the shipping industry was revolutionized by containerization, or the practice of shipping goods in large standardized containers rather than loading and unloading each item individually. Container shipping is among the most cost-effective methods for moving high-bulk goods around the world, accounting for around 90 percent of all world trade. Thus, the network of container ship routes between port cities has become one of the most economically significant global urban networks. Two economic realities of transportation shape the global networks of both air and water traffic between cities. First, because traveling longer distances is more costly, these networks closely mirror geographic patterns with the heaviest traffic passing through cities located at the coastal extremities of the continents. Second, because airports and seaports are costly to build and maintain, these networks are highly centralized with the majority of people and goods relying on just a few critical hub and port cities.[22]

Finally, in addition to approaches that focus on companies and transportation, the global urban network has come to be viewed as a massive communications network as well. But, it is useful to distinguish two different types of global urban communications networks: a *physical link network* and a *hyperlink network*. The physical link network is composed of the actual physical cables and other infrastructures that facilitate communication between cities. This network is relatively easy to observe and is important because it determines cities' communication accessibility to one another, that is, which cities can efficiently exchange information. For example, in 2001 the global internet backbone network was structured so that data leaving Boston could reach São Paulo in about 500 milliseconds, but could reach Tokyo in just 180 milliseconds even though it was 1,900 miles further away. While such time differences have since narrowed and may seem trivially small, they make a big difference when it comes to fulfilling stock purchases in a rapidly fluctuating market. In contrast to the physical link network, the hyperlink network is composed of the click-able links that connect websites hosted on servers located in cities throughout the world. For example, my own website at www.msu.edu/~zpneal is hosted on a server in East Lansing, Michigan, but is linked to the Globalization and World Cities website at www.lboro.ac.uk/gawc, which is hosted on a server in the English city of Loughborough, thus forging a virtual linkage between East Lansing and Loughborough. This network does not capture how information physically moves from city to city, but rather how one might navigate from one city's virtual online presence to another's.[23]

Each of these approaches to measuring the linkages between cities yields a different view of the global urban network. For example, a global urban network based on the locations of accounting firm branch offices will highlight cities involved in corporate services, while a network based on maritime shipping routes will highlight cities involved in manufacturing and shipping. This raises questions about how many distinct global urban networks there are. Comparisons have shown that there is only a limited overlap among the corporate, air, water, and Internet components of the global urban network. That is, there is not simply a single global urban network that organizes the modern global urban system, but many different ones. The cities that are most closely linked to one another through corporate relations are not necessarily also closely linked by air traffic, or by data flowing through the Internet. However, the presence of some overlap suggests that there are commonalities cutting across these networks as well. The economics of efficiency, to reduce the distance people and goods and information must travel, demand that these networks be routed through just a few key cities. For example, New York is home to many parent companies that send commands to their global subsidiaries, to JFK and LaGuardia international airports, to a major container shipping port, and to one end of dozens of transatlantic fiber optic cables. But, what is so special about New York, or London, or Tokyo?[24]

METHOD NOTE 26: MANTEL TEST AND QUADRATIC ASSIGNMENT PROCEDURE

Normally, examining the statistical significance of a correlation coefficient is enough to determine whether two variables are related to one another. However, this approach cannot be used when comparing two networks. Tests of statistical significance assume that each observation in the sample is independent, that is, that the value for one observation does not affect the value for another observation. But, this is usually not the case for networks.

In networks, the observations are the relationships between dyads (pairs of nodes), and the presence of a relationship between one dyad often affects the presence of a relationship between others. For example, when A is friends with both B and C, it is very likely that B and C are friends as well (this is transitivity). These three dyadic observations—A–B, A–C, and B–C—are not independent because the existence of a friendship between B and C partly depends on the existence of a friendship between A and B, and between A and C.

The Mantel Test, also known as the Quadratic Assignment Procedure, provides an alternative to traditional tests of statistical significance, and thus offers a way of determining whether two networks are related despite the fact that the individual observations are not independent. In UCINET: Tools → Testing Hypotheses → Dyadic (QAP) → QAP Correlation.[25]

Cities of the World or World Cities

The world's economic and social activities have long been concentrated in just a few key cities, and the locations of those cities have shifted over time: Athens and later Rome in the ancient world, Paris and later London through the Middle Ages and Enlightenment, and most recently places such as New York and Shanghai. But, actually identifying and defining such places—*world cities*—has been the subject of much debate. The term 'world city' was first used to describe the English city of Liverpool in 1886:

> Liverpool, thanks to modern science and commercial enterprise, to the spirit and intelligence of the townsmen, and to the administration of the Mersey Docks and Harbour Road, has become a wonder of the world. It is the New York of Europe, a world-city rather than merely a British provincial.[26]

It appeared again in 1915, when Scottish biologist-turned-urban planner Patrick Geddes (1854–1932) used it to describe the recent emergence of major urban regions throughout the world that were much larger than any cities before.

However, the concept of a world city remained merely an abstract idea until British urbanist Sir Peter Hall offered a more concrete definition: world cities are those "great cities, in which a quite disproportionate part of the world's most important business is conducted."[27] Moreover, he went one step further by identifying the seven places he considered to be world cities at the middle of the twentieth century: London, Paris, Moscow, New York, Tokyo, the Randstad region surrounding Amsterdam, and the Rhine–Ruhr region surrounding Cologne. Such cities are not necessarily the largest or wealthiest—some South American capitals such as Mexico City are larger, and some oil-producing Middle Eastern cities such as Abu Dhabi are wealthier—but they are the centers of the world's economic and social activity. Although other rosters of world cities have been compiled and other terms for these places have been suggested, most notably the very similar-sounding term 'global city,' it is this definition and early roster of places that informed the world city hypothesis and the modern notion of a global urban network.[28]

Understanding which cities are world cities and how membership in this elite club changes over time requires knowing precisely what makes a place a world city. Many scholars have focused on particular attributes of the city, in part because they can be useful reflections of where social and economic activity is concentrated, and in part because they are easy to measure. For example, cities with large and diverse populations drawn from around the world are likely to have a worldly, cosmopolitan character. Similarly, cities that are home to large numbers of corporate headquarters, or stock exchanges, or international banks are likely major centers of economic activity. Even examining the host cities of major cultural spectacles such as the Olympics or, as one team of researchers suggested, the 1995 Rolling Stones world tour might be useful for locating the world's cultural centers.[29] The trouble with these attribute-based approaches is that they focus on cities individually rather than as a set of interdependent sites linked together in a network. A city that contains many corporate headquarters may be noteworthy, but what if its corporations only conduct business within the city and not with partners throughout the world? Can an isolated, independent city be a world city?

World cities are not merely concentrated sites of social and economic activity, but sites of activity that interact with and thus affect other places around the world. Therefore, finding world cities requires thinking about them not as independent places, but as nodes in a global urban network. But, what kind of node, or more specifically, what kind of position in a global urban network do world cities occupy? There are at least two possible answers. First, occupying a position of centrality in the global urban network may elevate a place to world city status. A city with a central position in a global communication network can send and receive information faster, while centrality in a global transportation network facilitates the easy movement of people and goods to their destinations. In both cases, centrality affords the city—its people and businesses—the ability to interact with others throughout the world. Second, world city status may come from occupying a position of power within the global urban network. A position of power in a network of financial exchanges can allow a city's banks to control how, when, and where investments move around the world, while a similar position in a network of corporate relations can give a city's business leaders significant influence over subsidiaries located elsewhere.[30]

However, centrality and power are not the same. They have different benefits for cities, and as Figure 9.5 illustrates, they come from occupying different positions in the global urban network. In the network on the top, the black city in the middle is central, but not particularly powerful: it can send and receive resources to and from many other cities, but it cannot control its partners— the gray cities—because they each have alternative partners of their own. In contrast, in the network on the bottom, the black city in the middle is powerful, but not particularly central: it can send and receive resources to and from only a few other cities, but it can directly control these cities because they have nowhere else to turn for interaction. Combining these two possibilities, the scatterplot shows how cities can have differing levels of centrality and power based on their positions within a global communication network. London and New York are *quintessential world cities* that are both central and powerful; they are the focal point of the world urban system because they simultaneously interact with and exercise control over large numbers of other cities.

But, other types of world cities are possible as well. Cities that are central but not powerful function as *hub world cities* that, although they may lack the ability to control the activities in other cities, are nonetheless critical because they are central points of convergence for different types of interaction. For example, many flights throughout Europe pass through Paris's Charles de Gaulle airport, global maritime shipments depend on the ports of Amsterdam and nearby Rotterdam, and international diplomats descend on Washington's embassies and the headquarters of the European Union and NATO in Brussels. In contrast, cities that are powerful but not central

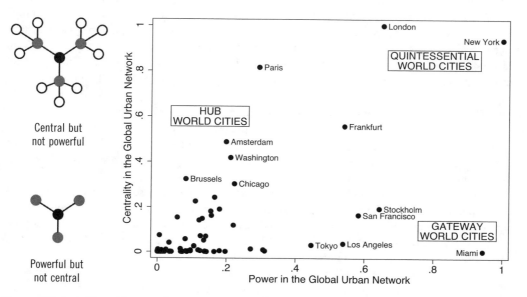

Figure 9.5 Centrality and Power in Global Urban Networks.[31]

can function as *gateway world cities* that, despite interacting with just a few other cities, serve as essential linkages between otherwise disconnected parts of the world. Miami is the principal gateway to North America for immigration and investment from the Southern hemisphere, while Tokyo and Los Angeles connect the East and West. These cities are particularly important because, as gateways, they can also function as gatekeepers that either facilitate or block global urban interactions.[32]

But, the very notion of world cities calls into question one common narrative about the effects of globalization, namely, that it is leveling the playing field. Some, like New York Times columnist Thomas Friedman, have argued that technological advances have allowed such a rapid expansion of global urban networks that today all cities are connected to all other cities. After all, Skype allows people anywhere to talk with one another and businesses can interact through e-commerce and electronic banking no matter where they are. Thus, according to the 'world is flat' perspective, world cities are obsolete; one no longer needs to be in New York or London to be connected to the world. Has the global urban network really become so dense and decentralized that every city is equal? No. In fact, just the opposite has occurred: rather than becoming flatter, the world has become much more uneven . . . or as some have noted, spiky. The newest linkages in the global urban network have not served to better integrate formerly peripheral cities in the developing world, but have instead simply made cities such as New York and London even better connected than before. Thus, the social and economic activity that has historically been concentrated in world cities is, today, even more concentrated in these places. Being located in a major city continues to be essential for businesses, but also for individuals who want access to a convenient non-stop flight, or the latest technology, or the most up-to-date fashions. Moreover, the uneven structure of the global urban network has made some cities not just slightly better, but dramatically better locations than others.[33]

Therefore, understanding the roles that modern cities play in the world requires not just knowing they are linked to one another in a global urban network, but knowing what positions they occupy in that network. As the title of this chapter suggests, New York and London occupy prominent positions within the global urban network, but what about other cities? Below this top tier, the picture becomes more complicated. In global urban networks forged by relationships among firms, a series of second-tier world cities can be found in Europe, the United States, and Asia. In Europe, Paris is London's closest competitor for a position of centrality and power, and plays a significant role in structuring economic exchanges between cities in the non-English speaking Western world. However, close behind it are several other cities that also occupy key positions, including a band of German cities stretching from Düsseldorf to Frankfurt to Munich, and the traditional banking capital of Zurich. Similarly in the United States, New York is followed by at least two secondary but still prominent world cities: Chicago and not Los Angeles, but San Francisco. In Asia, a still larger number of cities participate in the global urban network but lie in Tokyo's shadow, including Osaka, Singapore, Hong Kong, and Seoul. Although different scholars examining different data may highlight other cities, these examples point to a broader pattern: a place's world city status and position in the global urban network is not secure; there is competition.[34]

Cities' positions within global transportation networks take on a somewhat different but no less important meaning. Because the global airline network and many other global transportation networks have hub-and-spoke structures, whether a city occupies a hub or a spoke position has dramatic implications for its accessibility. Although only a small number of cities serve as transportation hubs, there are different ways to think about what makes a city a hub. In absolute terms, Atlanta might be viewed as a hub because more passengers used it to catch connecting flights than any other city: nearly 9.5 million in 2001. But, Charlotte might be viewed as a hub in relative terms because a large proportion of its passengers—over 58 percent—use the airport to make a connection. And, Chicago might also be called a hub because it offers the most connecting flights.[35] While it is striking that in all three senses—absolute, relative, and connecting flights—the most prominent hub cities in the world are all in the United States, non-U.S. hubs such as London and Tokyo play an important role as well. A location near one of these hub cities is essential for international travel because these places' high level of connectivity in the global urban network keeps times and costs low. For example, one can travel from any hub in the world to London in an average of about nine hours and for less than $700. Business located in cities elsewhere can easily interact with businesses there; the structure of the network makes London accessible and thus an ideal site for global firms. In sharp contrast, the trip from a hub to the African city of Bissau will take more than forty-seven hours and cost over $5,500; the structure of the network makes Bissau virtually unreachable and thus an impossible site for global business.[36]

But, cities' positions in the global urban network, whether well connected and advantageous or peripheral and marginalized, are not fixed in stone; the global urban network is constantly shifting. Although different global urban networks may change for different reasons—a corporate network due to mergers, a transportation network due to technological innovations—several broad patterns are clear in their evolution. Global urban networks of all types continue to grow in both their geographic scope and their connectivity, expanding to include previously disconnected places and strengthening linkages among cities that were already part of the network. This is relatively unsurprising, obvious in the increasing availability of international flights, the reduced cost of international phone calls, and the relative ease of international investing. Yet, throughout this growth and expansion, the positions of the most central cities have been remarkably stable. Cities such as London and New York have been deeply entrenched as the global urban network's core for centuries, and show few signs of losing their status as primary world cities.

However, despite this stability at the top of the hierarchy, patterns of change are evident in the positions of other cities. Many cities in the U.S. and Europe that have been viewed as occupying key positions in the global urban network—places such as Los Angeles, Miami, Frankfurt, and Cologne—have declined in their centrality. These losses have been driven in part by the high costs of doing business in these cities, but more importantly by the expansion of the network, which has made other previously peripheral cities more attractive locations. In particular, newly capitalist cities in the East have recently acquired more prominent positions in the global network, and thus also in the global economy. The opening of markets and loosening of restrictions on media and other forms of information exchange in China and Russia have allowed cities such as Shanghai, Beijing, and Moscow to expand their linkages to other places, thus paving the way for multinational corporations in these countries and facilitating explosive economic growth. Transformation of the network in the southern hemisphere, where cities have historically been economically underdeveloped, has been more mixed: cities in South Asia, the Middle East, and Africa have become more integrated in the global network, while those in South America remain largely isolated from the rest of the world. Collectively, these patterns of change have reinforced many of the old global inequalities, including the concentration of power in just a few key northern cities, but have also revealed the emerging importance of formerly peripheral regions in Asia.[37]

These recent changes in the global urban network highlight an important aspect of its structure: although it is global in scope, it is still organized around major world regions. That is, despite the ease of social and economic interactions between distant cities, linkages do not form between just any pair of cities, but instead tend to form within regions, creating regional clusters or cliques. For example, although a major city such as Seoul may interact with many other cities throughout the world, the majority of its interactions are with other Asian cities. Key activities in the global economy are often concentrated within these regional cliques: finance and shipping in Asia, international law in Europe, and consulting and accounting in the United States. In addition to geographically bounded cliques, similar politically bounded clusters can also be seen in the network. Most notably, cities that were once part of the British Empire—Toronto, Sydney, and Mumbai (formerly, Bombay), among others—despite being scattered around the world, are closely connected to one another socially and economically. These regional and political cliques and clusters are connected to one another by a set of cities that, metaphorically, keep one foot in their region and another in the global arena. For example, New York and London play the important role of bridging the gap between U.S.-based and Europe-based cliques (see Figure 7.1).[38]

Because the global urban network is organized partly around world regions, understanding its structure requires looking not just at the long-distance linkages between regions, but also at how cities are connected to one another within them. Indeed, each world region, despite comprising part of the same global urban network, has a unique internal structure. Within Asia, interactions occur primarily within two separate groups of cities: a powerful northern group that includes the more developed cities of Tokyo, Taipei, and Hong Kong, and a southern group that includes the rapidly developing cities of Beijing, Bangkok, and Singapore. In contrast, there is no clearly dominant world city in Central America, where cities are only weakly connected to one another. Instead, cities throughout this region rely on Miami to link them into a cohesive regional clique, leading some to argue that from a global urban network perspective, Miami is as much a part of Central America as it is the United States. The Middle East offers another example of regional uniqueness in the global urban network. Although financial relationships connect cities throughout the world, Islamic religious beliefs that prohibit earning interest or engaging in speculative investing require specialized financial institutions that comply with Shari'a law. As a result, a unique financial network has developed in this area, centered on the Bahrainian city of Manama and secondarily on Tehran and Dubai, which is connected to the wider global urban network through banks in London.[39]

It's Not Just the Economy, Stupid

A few key world cities occupy particularly central and powerful positions in the global urban network, while dozens more play equally important roles within their regions. However, some major cities and even entire world regions seem to be black holes in the global urban network, with virtually no linkages to other cities and thus seemingly no role to play in global affairs. For example, the city of Dhaka in Bangladesh and the Congolese city of Kinshasa both contain more than ten million people, but they are home to few headquarters of multinational corporations or banks, and do not feature major air or seaports. Without these institutions, these cities appear to lack connections to other places, and thus rarely enter into discussions of world cities or global urban networks. But, are they really so isolated?

The vast majority of research on global urban networks has focused on intercity linkages of an economic nature: companies exchanging information and investment, or planes and ships carrying executives and commodities. This narrow focus has resulted in a similarly narrow conception of the global urban network that leaves out many of the world's largest cities and a substantial portion of the world's population. However, by adopting a wider view of the ways that cities may be linked to one another globally, it becomes clear that although a particular city may lack connections in the world of corporate finance or international travel, it may nonetheless be a major node in another network. The Zambian city of Lusaka, for example, is certainly not a major banking center in the global flow of capital, but it is well connected to other parts of the world through humanitarian aid agencies and through its role as a center for trade in second-hand clothing. Moreover, the enormous diversity among cities such as Lusaka that participate in alternative global urban networks, but do so under the economic radar, means they cannot simply be regarded as "poor nodes"; they warrant as much attention as New York or London. Thus, understanding the structure of the entire global urban network, rather than just the economically oriented sliver focused on NY–LON, requires thinking broadly about the types of relationships that connect cities.[40]

The movements of people that link cities to one another include not only jet-set executives and middle-class tourists, but also struggling immigrants and temporary migrant workers. Indeed, there has been a broad tendency under the most recent wave of globalization for individuals to migrate from cities in poor countries, to cities in wealthy countries. This movement has been driven in part by immigrants' search for opportunity, and in part by wealthy cities' demand for low-paid service workers who can meet the needs of their well-off citizens. As a result, it is not surprising that large proportions of world cities' populations are immigrants: 27 percent in London, 34 percent in New York, and over 80 percent in Dubai. However, it is important to remember that these immigrants did not simply appear in these cities; they came from somewhere. New York's immigrant population is drawn from cities in Panama, Bangladesh, Russia, and at least thirty other countries. Thus, although New York's linkage to London is strong and important, its connection to places such as Dhaka are also necessary because they are a primary source of not only inexpensive labor, but also the city's social and cultural diversity. That is, New York owes part of its status as a world city and part of its position in the global urban network to these peripheral cities.[41]

These seemingly economically insignificant places can also have an impact on the wider world system as sources of disease. The spread of highly communicable diseases such as seasonal influenza (H1N1), bird flu (H5N1), and severe acute respiratory syndrome (SARS) does not simply follow the pattern of corporate or financial linkages among key world cities. Instead, these illnesses can spread from one city to another through a single traveler or foreign shipment. Thus, despite the strength of the NY–LON linkage, London is not New York's only or biggest threat as a source of disease. The role of global urban networks in the spread of disease takes on particular significance when major cities prepare for such mega-events as the Olympics or the World Cup. For example, preparation for the 2010 Olympic Winter Games in Vancouver involved examining the potential for influenza to be imported from a range of cities. In this instance, the primary concern was not with Vancouver's major economic partners such as New York or Tokyo, but rather with places that were common sources of influenza despite Vancouver's limited interactions with them: Jakarta, Hanoi, Cairo, and Mumbai. Thus, although some cities may appear to be disconnected from an economically focused global urban network, nearly all the worlds' cities are connected directly or indirectly by the exchange of germs.[42]

A large number of international organizations have emerged to monitor and assist cities in the developing world with common challenges, including the poverty that drives migrants to leave and the public health practices that facilitate the spread of disease. The presence of such organizations in cities throughout the developing world is still another way that these places are linked to one another. For example, Accra, Ghana and Quito, Ecuador are linked to each other and to the other eighty-eight cities that receive and share resources through the United Nations Children's Fund (UNICEF). The scope of a global urban network forged by these diplomatic and humanitarian institutions is quite extensive, with the United Nations alone maintaining seventy-eight different agencies with locations in over 400 cities. Thus, although not focused on business or transportation, these networks have become vital channels for the exchange of information and resources. More informally, information and resources are also shared between cities in the developed and developing world through technical visits in which delegates learn about local solutions that can be implemented in their own regions. For example, in 2002 Seattle hosted over 700 visitors, primarily from Asian cities, to share experiences and policy solutions on topics ranging from education to public utilities.[43]

Clearly, as sources of migration and as the key nodes in humanitarian networks, cities in the developing world are as much a part of the global urban network as any others. However, looking beyond economics can also reveal new patterns in the networks that exist even among economically powerful world cities. In addition to financial products such as stocks and bonds, or commodities such as cars and computers, these cities are also involved in the production of cultural products ranging from musical masterpieces to architectural ones. Because such products require many different services to produce—for example, mixing and marketing for music, interior design and construction management for buildings—their production often depends not on a single city, but rather on a network of media and design cities. Thus, while Paris and Los Angeles are secondary world cities when it comes to financial exchanges, they are virtual centers of the universe in the urban network through which music and movies are made. Similarly, the most central cities in a network of architectural design services highlight the places experiencing the most explosive building growth: Shanghai, Dubai, and Beijing.[44]

Scientific research is another product that requires global networks of cities, or more specifically, global networks of researchers in cities. To solve complex problems, researchers in different cities interact by working collaboratively and co-authoring research papers or by building on and citing one another's work. Indeed, even the ideas in this paragraph offer an example of the global urban network of research: As I write this sentence in East Lansing, I am building on the work of Christian Matthiessen in Copenhagen, who in turn was building on the work of Ron Boschma in Utrecht, and so on. Until recently, the most central cities in the global urban research network—those where researchers interact with others elsewhere—included Western cities that either focused on specific areas of research or were home to major research institutions: San Francisco on technology, Geneva on physics, and Oxford and Cambridge as home to the eponymous universities. However, increasingly they are being replaced by Eastern European cities such as Budapest and Asian cities such as Shanghai. Thus, because some cities offer more extensive collaboration opportunities, researchers' abilities to make cutting-edge discoveries may depend not only on their intellect, but also on where they are working.[45]

Still other non-economic intercity relationships are drawn together in the form of what are known as *sister cities* in North America and *town twinning* in Europe and elsewhere. These relationships were initially used to promote cultural understanding by linking pairs of European and American cities following World War Two. Now, sister city relationships exist between pairs of cities throughout the world and serve a variety of purposes. Many of these relationships focus on cultural exchange: Chicago, for example, has formed twenty new sister city partnerships since 1990 that have yielded opportunities for student exchanges to other world cities such as Paris and Milan, and are the focus of regular festivals and cultural events. However, they have also increasingly become an avenue for mutual aid: Denver has assisted its sister city of Axum, Nigeria with the construction of a school and municipal water system, while Urbana, Illinois is working to address local health and sanitation issues in Zomba, Malawi. Unlike many other types of global urban networks, in which the linkages are forged by powerful external forces such as multinational corporations or airline routes, the global network of sister cities is unique because the linkages are forged by the cities themselves. Thus, while many large world cities such as Chicago participate in this network, so do very small places—in 2005 a sister city relationship was formed between Gilbert, Arkansas (pop. 33) and Bride, United Kingdom (pop. 418)—that might not otherwise be on the global urban radar.[46]

*   *   *   *   *

Global urban networks capture how patterns of relationships impact the metropolis at the widest possible scale by focusing on the linkages between cities around the world. Despite the recent attention that the Internet and other technologies have received as forces of globalization, these networks have been evolving for millennia. The global urban networks of the past were forged by the routes of trading caravans and submarine telegraph cables, while in a strikingly parallel way they arise now from the business transactions of multinational corporations and submarine fiber optic cables. Indeed, there is no single network linking the world's cities, but rather multiple overlapping networks that serve different functions—economic, political, social, and cultural—by facilitating exchanges that take the form of people, material, and information. The rapid expansion of these networks to places around the world, however, has not leveled the playing field, but instead has created an even more unequal world of cities in which some places are far more central and powerful than others. By occupying strategic positions within the global urban network, these central and powerful places—the world cities—play a major role in organizing and controlling the global economy. New York and London, with the strength of the centuries-long economic linkage between them implicit in the NY–LON label, lie at the top of the hierarchy of world cities for now, but competing Asian cities such as Shanghai are closing in as they become more integrated in the network. Still, it is important to remember that major economic centers such as these are not the only participants in the global urban network; cities in the developing world and small towns maintain global linkages in their own way. The movements of migrant workers and political refugees, the exchange of humanitarian aid, and the cultural sharing between sister cities all serve to illustrate that global urban networks are not restricted to just a handful of prominent cities, but extend to an increasingly diverse range of places.

Discussion Questions and Activities

1. What are the differences and similarities between the global urban networks of the past and those of today? What influence have early global urban networks had on modern cities and urban networks?
2. Thinking about the typology in Figure 9.3, what kinds of global urban linkages have you participated in? What effect did the linkage have for the two cities, or for the businesses or people in them?
3. Is the city you live in a world city? What kind of position does it occupy in the global urban network, and how does this impact the role it plays in the world? Is its position or role changing?
4. Are economically focused global urban networks more important than non-economic ones? How might these different types of networks influence one another?
5. How could the methods introduced in the previous chapters be used to study the concepts introduced in this chapter? Similarly, how could the methods introduced in this chapter be used to study the concepts introduced in the previous chapters?

Sources for Global Urban Network Data

Interlocking Networks—The Globalization and World Cities (GaWC) research network maintains a collection of data that can be used to construct interlocking global urban networks at www.lboro.ac.uk/gawc/data.html. This data archive includes information about the branch office locations of specialized service firms such as law and accounting firms, which are commonly used to measure economically focused urban networks. But, it also includes information about the office locations of other types of entities, including United Nations agencies and architectural firms, which can be used to measure political or cultural urban networks as well.

Multinational Corporations—The LexisNexis Directory of Corporate Affiliations provides information about the linkages between parent companies and their subsidiaries; see: www.corporate affiliations.com. The Fortune Global 500, an annually updated list of the 500 largest multinational corporations, is often used as a starting point for global urban networks based on parent–subsidiary linkages.

Transportation—There are two primary sources for global airline data. First, online booking sites such as Expedia and Travelocity provide up-to-date details about flights available between cities. For a small network, this data can be entered manually, while for larger networks, webcrawler software can be used to automate the downloading and entry process. These data indicate where passengers could fly, but not necessarily where they actually do. Second, the International Civil Aviation Organization's (ICAO) On-Flight Origin and Destination data contain the number of people and tons of freight moved between each international pair of cities in the previous quarter; see: www.icaodata.com. These data indicate where passengers actually did fly. However, it is available only for pairs of cities located in different countries; for example, for New York–London but not for New York–Chicago. Data on maritime shipping routes are available from Lloyd's, which insures the majority of the global shipping fleet; see: www.lloydslistintelligence.com.

Creative Solutions—The general lack of global urban network data sometimes requires locating creative solutions. One study examined information linkages between cities by counting the number of times cities were mentioned in the business sections of one another's major newspapers. For example, if Shanghai is mentioned in the business section of the *Chicago Tribune*, this may indicate a flow of business information from Shanghai to Chicago.[47] Sister city relationships are another type of international urban interaction that is readily observable, but remains understudied. Most sister city relationships that involve a U.S. city are cataloged in the directory at www.sister-cities.org. Sister city relationships involving non-U.S. cities are often reported on the participating cities' websites.

10
CONCLUSION
THE NEW SCIENCE OF URBAN NETWORKS

This book has explored how networks are shaping the modern metropolis in a range of ways and at a variety of different levels. Within the city, micro-urban networks define what communities are, how subcultures and subgroups form, and who has the power to influence them. Viewing the city as a whole, meso-urban networks of roads and other infrastructure give cities their distinctive spatial forms, while networks of collaboration and coordination among organizations and agencies make large and complex cities manageable. Finally, the macro-urban networks that link entire cities to one another at regional, national, and global scales give structure to sprawling metropolitan areas and fuel the transformation of the world's urban landscape through globalization. Each chapter has tackled a specific urban issue, within a specific geographic scope, using specific network perspectives and techniques. After all, the social networks among immigrants within a tiny ethnic enclave and the economic networks among multinational corporations spread across massive world cities are very different from one another. But, are they? Are the patterns of friendships among neighbors really so different from the pattern of roads in a bustling metropolis, or from the pattern of fiber optic cables linking cities around the globe?

Although it is not obvious at first, there are striking similarities between these seemingly different types of urban networks. Moreover, there are similarities even between urban networks and other, completely unrelated types of networks including the network of synapses in a mammal's brain or the network of protein reactions involved in metabolism. The investigation of universal properties of networks found in the natural world—whether in cities, or animals, or molecules—is the topic of what has been called the 'new' science of networks. This new area of study—really only about fifteen years old—has been dominated by physicists and mathematicians, and is grounded in two deceptively simple observations. First, a network's structure is not random, but follows predictable patterns. For example, Chapter Three explored how the formation of groups of friends is shaped by a tendency toward transitivity (see Figure 3.3). Second, these predictable patterns can be found in many different kinds of networks, no matter what their nodes or edges happen to be. For example, the same transitivity that can be seen in a network where the nodes are people and the edges are the friendships among them can also be seen in a network where the nodes are organizations and the edges are collaborations, or even where the nodes are proteins and the edges are chemical reactions. The insights of the new science of networks show not only that the different types of urban networks are all related to one another, but also that nearly all types of networks are related to one another. To understand cities, but also virtually everything else, requires adopting a network perspective.[1]

In this chapter I explore how some of the patterns uncovered by the new science of networks manifest themselves in urban networks, and thus how the apparently different types of urban networks discussed throughout this book are actually quite similar. The first pattern—indeed, the one that started it all—is one with which most readers are likely already familiar: six degrees of separation. When it comes to personal relationships, nearly everyone is connected to everyone else by just a few friends. In fact, you likely know someone, who knows someone, who knows someone, who knows me. But, this same phenomenon can also be seen, for example, among city streets: the street where a person lives connects to a street, which connects to a street, which connects to a street, which is connected to the street where they work. A second pattern makes this possible: most nodes have very few connections, while a few have a large number of connections. Although only a few people are power brokers on the urban political scene, deals can still be made, and although only a few cities around the world are banking centers, international investments still circulate. These few, highly connected nodes—whether they are people, or cities, or something else—keep the rest of the nodes connected to one another. When the nodes are connected into relatively dense clusters, this can give rise to still a third pattern: communities. Of course, this book has already explored communities, in chapter two. But, thinking about communities as a type of network pattern highlights that communities do not exist only among people at the micro-urban level; there can be communities of organizations, communities of streets, and even communities of cities.[2]

Big City, Small World

It is not uncommon for a person to meet a stranger and, after talking for a while, discover that they share a mutual acquaintance. Upon making such a discovery, one of them often remarks that 'it's a small world.' But, how is it possible in such a large and complex world that a social network of mutual acquaintances connects two complete strangers to one another? And, just how small a world is it?

Psychologist Stanley Milgram set out to investigate these questions—what he called the *small world problem*—in the 1960s with a relatively simple experiment. He asked several people living in Omaha to each send a letter to a complete stranger, a stockbroker working in Boston. Rather than simply send the letter directly, they were asked to send the letter to a personal acquaintance who might know the stockbroker personally. These letters were tracked as they were sent from one person to the next, with each sender hoping to get it closer to the intended recipient. In some cases, the Omaha resident and the Boston stockbroker were connected by a single mutual acquaintance—the original sender knew a person who knew the stockbroker—and the letter arrived quickly via a fairly direct route. In other cases, these two people were connected by a long chain of mutual acquaintances and the letter arrived through a friend of a friend of a friend, etc. But, on average, only six intermediaries were needed to link the two strangers in Omaha and Boston. That is, Milgram found that two complete strangers, living in very different cities and coming from very different walks of life were actually quite close to one another, with only six degrees of separation between them.[3]

Following this experiment, social networks in which just a few intermediaries or mutual acquaintances connect every person to every other person have become known as *small world networks*. Such networks have since been discovered in many different settings. In a Hollywood network where co-stars are connected to one another, early film stars such as Charlie Chaplin are connected to more recent celebrities such as Justin Bieber by just a few co-stars: Chaplin co-starred with Marjorie Bennett in Monsieur Verdoux (1947), who co-starred with Fred Willard in Harrad

Summer (1974), who co-starred with Justin Bieber in School Gyrls (2009). Similarly, in a baseball network where teammates are linked, greats from the past and present are linked by just a few teammates: Babe Ruth played with Waite Hoyt on the 1921 Yankees, who played with Bert Hass on the 1938 Dodgers, who played with Minnie Minoso on the 1951 White Sox, who played with Jim Morrison on the 1980 White Sox, who played with Barry Bonds on the 1986 Pirates.[4]

However, the existence of small world networks such as these is surprising because they are seemingly impossible due to another common feature of most social networks: clustering. In most real social networks, people tend to form dense clusters or groups around foci such as the places, events, or shared interests discussed in Chapter Three. Within these groups, everyone may be connected to everyone else. However, when the groups are characterized by a high degree of closure, there is little contact between members of different groups. In such cases, it can be difficult and perhaps even impossible for those in one group to reach those in another group through a series of intermediaries. For example, it is likely that people living in Omaha in the 1960s knew primarily other people living in Omaha. How, then, did the letters in Milgram's experiment ever get out of Omaha and find their way to Boston? Similarly, it is likely that comedy actors co-star primarily with other comedy actors. How, then, are comedy actors connected to Shakespearian actors by just a few intermediate co-stars?

The key to small world networks lies in the role of bridges that link otherwise disconnected groups. In the Milgram experiment, this bridging role might be played by a person who recently moved from Boston to Omaha, while in Hollywood it is played by actors such as Kevin Bacon who frequently appear in films with large ensemble casts. The importance of bridging ties has already appeared several times in the preceding chapters, but research on small world networks has shed new light on their role. A completely clustered network, in which dense groups never interact with one another, can transform into a small world network, in which every person is connected to every other person through just a few network connections, with the addition of a very small number of bridges. For example, only one person who has acquaintances in both Omaha and Boston is necessary to ensure that a letter can get from one place to another, and only one actor who has appeared in both a comedy and a drama, are necessary to ensure that even very different actors are connected to one another by co-stars. Thus, it is possible for a social network to remain densely clustered, while still allowing all its members to reach all other members easily.

These small world characteristics—simultaneous clustering and connectivity—have routinely been found in social networks, including the micro-urban social networks that connect people within cities. Such networks can offer many advantages to their members. For example, consider first the case of a small world social network among the residents of a poor neighborhood. The dense clustering of relationships within the neighborhood can provide these residents with a sense of belonging and can allow neighbors to depend on one another in times of need. Simultaneously, the ability of residents in this poor neighborhood to reach residents of other, wealthier neighborhoods through just a few mutual acquaintances can provide them access to information about job opportunities and other valuable resources. However, small world networks can also have drawbacks in urban settings. For example, consider the case of a disease spreading through a city in which relationships among the residents are structured as a small world network. The dense clustering of relationships within neighborhoods will ensure that the disease spreads rapidly among neighbors, while the presence of bridges will allow it to also spread to other neighborhoods. When networks with small world structures are observed in social settings like these, their advantages and disadvantages are often referred to by another name: social capital. Recall from Chapter Two and Figure 2.3, bonding social capital is the effect of the clustering found in small worlds, while bridging social capital is the effect of small worlds' connectivity.[5]

METHOD NOTE 27: SMALL WORLD NETWORKS

Structure	Regular	Small World	Random
Characteristic Path Length	2.4	2.033	1.942
Clustering Coefficient	0.5	0.419	0.205

Small world networks can be identified by two characteristics: the *characteristic path length* and the *clustering coefficient*.

The characteristic path length is the average of the geodesic distances between every pair of nodes within the network. It indicates the average number of steps needed to connect any two nodes. Characteristic path lengths are longer in regular networks and shorter in random networks. For example, the characteristic path length of the regular network above is 2.4; between two and three steps are required to connect any two nodes in this network. In contrast, the characteristic path length of the random network above is 1.942; only one or two steps are required to connect any two nodes in this network. In UCINET: Network → Cohesion → Distance.

The clustering coefficient is the average density of each node's ego network. It ranges between 1, which indicates complete clustering, and 0, which indicates no clustering. Clustering coefficients are higher in regular networks and lower in random networks. The clustering coefficient of the regular network is 0.5, while it is only 0.205 in the random network. In UCINET: Network → Cohesion → Clustering Coefficient.

Small world networks are networks that have a short characteristic path length like a random network, but also have a high clustering coefficient like a regular network. The small world network above has a characteristic path length of 2.033, which is close to the value seen in the random network. But, it has a clustering coefficient of 0.419, which is close to the value seen in the regular network. Notably, only a small number of the ties in the regular network need to be 'rewired' to transform the regular network into a small world network.[6]

However, although it is natural to think about small world networks among people, they have also been discovered in many of the meso- and macro-urban networks discussed in earlier chapters. In the street networks of cities throughout the United States and Europe, tertiary streets tend to form dense clusters within neighborhoods and subdivisions, which are connected to one another by a few major roads. It is because street networks are small world networks that it is possible to travel between any two points in a city using only a few streets.[7] At the scale of national urban networks, the airline and rail networks that link cities in the U.S., China, and India display similar patterns.[8] Indeed, even global urban networks including worldwide airline and maritime shipping networks have small world characteristics.[9] Moreover, small world networks are not limited to the urban context, but have been found in some unlikely places. For example, the network of power cables and transformers that delivers electricity to the Western United States, and the network of synapses and neurons in the nervous system of the microscope nematode *C. elegans*, both have small world characteristics.[10]

The discovery of small world networks in nearly all settings, ranging from the social to the economic to the biological, both in cities and elsewhere, has been relatively recent. The specific reasons that this type of network structure is so common remains unknown, but it is unlikely to be the result of mere coincidence. Instead, the ubiquity of networks structured as small worlds suggests that urban networks at the micro, meso, and macro scales share much in common with one another, and indeed even with networks as seemingly unrelated as nematode nervous systems. One possibility is that all of these networks have evolved to have their current structures by following the same set of rules. That is, the social rules that shape when one person will become acquainted with another in a city's neighborhood may be the same as the biological rules that shape when one neuron will connect to another in an animal's brain. Much of the most recent research on networks, both urban and otherwise, has now turned to asking what these rules are and where they come from.

The Power of Urban Networks

The small world phenomenon, where nodes are clustered in dense groups but can still reach one another through just a few intermediate linkages, is just one common pattern found in many different types of networks. But it, and more specifically the bridging ties that make it possible, point to a second common pattern. Consider all the friends in your own social network. Each of your friends has several of their own friends, but one or two of them seem to know everyone; in network terms, a couple of your friends are far more central than the rest. Similarly, consider all the airports in the United States. From most of these airports one can fly nonstop to a dozen or so cities, but from a few airports—major hubs such as Chicago's O'Hare or Atlanta's Hartsfield Jackson—one can fly nonstop to over a hundred cities. Again, in network terms, a few airports are dramatically more central than all the rest. These particularly central nodes, whether they are especially outgoing people or especially busy airports, make the small world phenomenon possible because they link dense clusters of nodes to one another. For example, a friend who seems to know everyone serves as a bridge between two social circles that might otherwise never interact, while an airport with nonstop flights to everywhere serves as a bridge between cities in different parts of the country.

These examples highlight a pattern found in many different kinds of networks: a few nodes have many connections, and many nodes have a few connections. It can be seen not only in social networks among friends and airline networks between cities, but also in the neural networks of mammals and networks of rivers throughout the world.[11] Networks that exhibit this pattern are called *scale free networks*, and can be contrasted with *random networks* in which each node has roughly the same number of connections. Figure 10.1 shows two networks that each contains sixteen nodes linked by twenty-one edges, but one has a random structure while the other has a scale free structure. Each node is labeled with its number of connections, that is, its degree centrality. In the random network on the left, each node has about the same number of connections, between two and three. In contrast, in the scale-free network on the right, one node has six connections, while the majority have only two. The highly central node is important because it connects three different clusters to one another.[12]

Urban networks with both random and scale-free structures have already appeared several times in the preceding chapters. Chapter Five explored how the street network in a city can be conceptualized in two different ways: a primal network in which streets are edges and intersections are nodes, and a dual network in which intersections are edges and streets are nodes. Returning

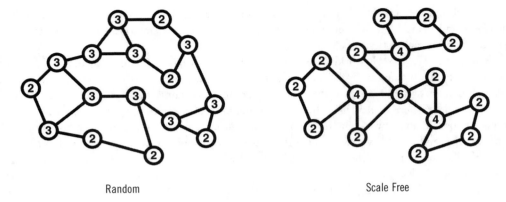

Random   Scale Free

Figure 10.1 Random and Scale-Free Networks.

METHOD NOTE 28: SCALE-FREE NETWORKS

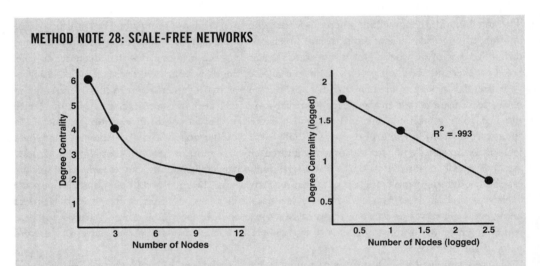

Scale-free networks can be identified by examining their *degree distribution*, that is, the distribution of degree centralities among their nodes. The graph on the left shows the degree distribution for the scale-free network in Figure 10.1. Each dot in this graph indicates the number of nodes with a given amount of degree centrality. In this case, there is one node with a degree centrality of 6, three nodes with a degree centrality of 4, and twelve nodes with a degree centrality of 2.

The degree distribution of a scale-free network follows a specific curve that has a high peak on the left, a rapid decline, and a long tail on the right. This type of curve describes a mathematical relationship between two variables—in this case, the number of nodes and the degree centrality—known as a *power law*. There are many sophisticated ways to determine whether the degree distribution of a network follows a power law and thus is a scale-free network. One simple approach involves redrawing the graph using the natural logarithm of the two variables, like the graph on the right. In this new graph, if the network's degree distribution follows a power law and the network is scale free, the points will be arranged in a straight line and the two logged variables will be highly correlated.

to Figure 5.3, the primal network of the hypothetical city's street system has a random structure, with each node having roughly the same number of connections. Indeed, this pattern is quite intuitive because nearly all street intersections have around three or four roads leading from them. In contrast, the dual network has a scale-free structure: Ring Road is connected to nearly all other streets and is highly central, while most of the other streets have only a few intersections. Ring Road, in this example, is important because it links different parts of the city together. In another example, Chapter Eight explored the different national transportation networks, with Figure 8.5 providing views of the interstate highway and Delta airline networks. Here, the interstate highway network has a random structure because each city is served by roughly the same number of interstates, usually two and almost never more than three. In contrast, the airline network has a scale-free structure: many cities offer nonstop flights only to Delta's hub cities, but the hub cities offer nonstop flights throughout the country and around the world. In addition to these two cases, nearly any urban network designed to distribute resources—favors to politicians, cars to houses, money to multinational corporations—has a scale-free structure.[13]

Unlike small world networks whose origin remains a subject of debate, there is some agreement about how scale-free networks form. Networks do not simply appear, but grow and evolve as new nodes and edges are added. For example, the street network of a sprawling metropolis grows as new housing developments are built and streets are constructed to connect them with older parts of the city. In most real world networks, when a new node is added, it does not simply connect to other existing nodes randomly. Instead, new nodes tend to be connected to existing nodes that already have a large number of connections themselves. Consider a family moving into a new neighborhood. They do not form friendships with the new neighbors at random, but are more likely to first meet the most outgoing person on the block who seems to know everyone. This process of network growth is known as *preferential attachment* because when new nodes appear, whether they are people or housing subdivisions or corporations, they appear to 'prefer' being attached to existing nodes that are already well connected. Preferential attachment leads to scale-free networks because, in the most colloquial sense, the 'rich get richer.' That is, the nodes that are well connected in earlier stages tend to become even better connected over time with the addition of new nodes. This helps to explain why New York and London are so central in the global urban network. Both cities started with a large number of connections to other places: New York as an early Dutch trading post and London as the center of the British Empire. As globalization brought formerly isolated cities into the global urban network, their initial linkages were not to other formerly isolated cities, but to NY–LON. In a sense, New York and London started out rich (in network connections) and have gotten richer.[14]

Scale-free networks are more than a statistical curiosity; they are important because they offer a number of advantages over networks with other structures. First, scale-free networks are highly efficient at diffusing information and delivering resources. Recall from Chapter Eight, after the deregulation of the U.S. airline industry in 1978, nearly all major airlines developed a hub-and-spoke route structure, which is an example of a scale-free network. This route structure was appealing to the airlines for its cost effectiveness because they could invest most of their resources in just a few hub airports, and to passengers for its efficiency because it allowed them to fly anywhere usually with just a single connection at one of these hubs. Second, scale-free networks allow the spread of diseases such as influenza and HIV to be closely monitored and prevented. While it may be impossible for public health officials in a large city to vaccinate everyone against the flu or encourage everyone to practice safe sex, they can be just as effective by focusing their preventative efforts on those individuals who occupy the most central positions. For example, even if only the highly connected node in the Figure 10.1 scale-free network received a flu vaccine, the illness might affect one cluster but would not spread to the others.[15]

A final advantage of scale-free networks is their exceptional *resilience* to random breakdowns in the system. In any network, some linkages will fail from time to time. A neighbor who can usually be depended on for the latest gossip may be out of town, or a nonstop flight between two cities may be cancelled owing to weather. However, in scale-free networks, these random failures have very little impact on the entire network because there are alternative paths in the network. The gossip may come second-hand but is still available, and the trip may require an unexpected connection but can still be completed. More generally, the distance between any two nodes in a scale-free network does not increase much when some, or even many, of the nodes or edges are removed. As a result, social networks and transportation networks that have a scale-free structure are surprisingly dependable. Usually. This resilience masks a significant drawback to scale-free networks: if the most central node(s) are removed, they fall apart. That is, while scale-free networks are resilient to random failures, they are vulnerable to targeted attacks. For example, an electrical problem at the New York Stock Exchange or a terrorist attack at London's Heathrow airport can cripple global financial and transportation networks.[16]

Communities Are Everywhere

Small world and scale-free structures can be found in urban networks at the micro, meso, and macro scales. They can even be found in such unlikely places as nematode nervous systems and the power grid. Adopting a network perspective allows us to see some of the universal patterns that underlie not just the modern metropolis, but show up in virtually every corner of the world. This raises some tough questions about how to think about people and cities. Do they really work the same as microscopic worms and high voltage transformers? Surely there is something uniquely human and uniquely urban in the notion of community. Communities, after all, are made up of people.

Perhaps not, or at least, not always. Chapter Two introduced the idea that a community is not a geographic place such as a neighborhood, nor a demographic population such as African Americans, but a repeated pattern of interactions. However, if community is simply a type of network pattern, then communities might be found not only among people, but everywhere that networks are found.[17] There is relatively wide agreement on the type of network pattern that defines a community: a community is a group of nodes that is more connected to other nodes in the same group than to nodes in any other group. Thus, communities are defined by two structural characteristics: internal cohesion and external separation. This idea appeared earlier in the discussion of subculture in Chapter Three, and is illustrated in Figure 3.2. The four subcultural groups, or communities, shown in this figure can be identified not by the characteristics of their members, but by the patterns of relationships among them: most relationships are with others in the same community, while only a few are with members of other communities. By defining community purely in terms of a pattern of relationships, it becomes possible to think about communities in settings quite different from neighborhoods and cities. For example, in a network of biochemical reactions, communities of proteins that serve specific cellular functions have been identified in *Saccharomyces cerevisiae*, the yeast used to brew beer. Similarly, in a network of genetic relationships among common grape cultivars, varietals such as Cabernet Sauvignon and Merlot that yield wines with similar characteristics are found in the same communities.[18]

Of course, communities can be found in the social networks among people living in cities; this is the most conventional notion of community. But, communities can also be found in other types of urban networks at different levels. For example, at the meso-urban level, communities can be found in a network of streets. A community in a street network represents an area of the city within which the streets are well connected and it is easy to reach different locations, but which is difficult to leave because its streets are poorly connected to areas of the city. Returning to Figure

METHOD NOTE 29: COMMUNITIES

Identifying communities in a network is an iterative or trial-and-error search process. First, the nodes are *partitioned* or placed into different groups. Second, a statistic is computed that measures how well this partitioning matches the definition of community: nodes are more connected to other nodes within their partition than to nodes in any other partition. Third, these two steps are repeated to find a partitioning that maximizes the statistic, and thus best matches the definition of community.

There are several different statistics that can be used to measure how well a particular partition matches the definition of community. The E–I Index (see Method Note 6) is a simple one, while a second more sophisticated measure known as Q-modularity has more recently been favored. For even small networks, there are an exceptionally large number of possible ways to partition the nodes, so trying all of them is impractical. However, there are several different methods for selecting partitions to examine. In UCINET: Network → Subgroups → Girvan-Newman, and Network → Subgroups → Factions.

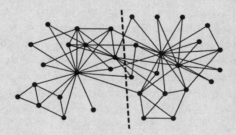

The network above shows the relationship among the students in a karate club that was experiencing a disagreement.[19] Some of the students sided with the club's administrator, while others sided with the karate instructor. The dashed line separates the nodes into two communities that were identified by finding the partition that maximized the value of Q-modularity. More intuitively, the line separates the nodes into two groups so that the majority of relationships are within-group and only a few relationships are between-group. Although these two communities are based solely on the pattern of relationships and not on any characteristics of the students or the conflict, this partition perfectly matches the groups that students actually formed in the disagreement: the students in the community on the left sided with the instructor, while those in the community on the right sided with the administrator.[20]

3.2, if the edges represented streets and the nodes represented intersections, it would clearly be easy to get around *within* one of the four communities, but would be relatively difficult to travel *between* them. This can be a familiar experience in many modern suburban developments where winding loops and cul-de-sacs link houses within the suburb, but where the suburb as a whole is disconnected from the inner city. Thus, communities in street networks can define the boundaries of neighborhoods and other natural areas of the city. This idea appeared earlier in Chapter Five, in the context of T-communities, but the network of canals in Venice offers an even more striking example. There are several communities in the canal network, within which the canals are well connected, but between which there are limited routes. One of these canal network communities—an area known as the Cannaregio—is particularly difficult to reach from other communities in the network. Although this might be merely inconvenient for residents, this structural feature of the canal network served a darker historical function: the Cannaregio is the location of the Venetian Ghetto, where Jews were forced to live from 1516 until 1797. Thus, communities in street (and canal) networks define not only where travel is easy or difficult, but can shape the pattern of segregation in urban areas.[21]

Communities can also be found in the meso-urban networks of collaborative relationships among organizations. This idea first appeared in Chapter Six, as a discussion about the efficiency of modular service delivery networks. Just as with a community of people, a community of organizations exists when a group of organizations interacts more intensely with one another than with other organizations in the city. If the nodes in Figure 3.2 represented organizations and the edges represented collaborations between them, it would be easy for the organizations within each of these four communities to coordinate their services. This can be particularly useful when the organizations with a community perform similar services. For example, providing a city's residents with health care or financial assistance is most efficient when all the hospitals, or all the employment agencies, are 'talking to one another.' In contrast, when service delivery networks do not have such a community structure—when organizations' relationships with one another do not form dense clusters—efficiency and coordination are difficult to achieve because each organization is forced to operate independently and cannot capitalize on the strengths of other similar organizations.

Finally, communities composed of entire cities can be found at the level of macro-urban networks. Indeed, the metropolitan areas and polycentric urban regions introduced in Chapter Seven are examples of communities of cities. The defining feature of the Chicago metropolitan area is that its cities—Chicago, Gary, Waukegan, and others—are more connected to one another through their commuters and interlocal agreements than to cities in other metropolitan areas. Such communities of cities can promote local economic development by keeping resources circulating within the community rather than leaving it, and can insulate urban regions from external dangers such as the spread of disease or economic crisis. Thus, if the nodes in Figure 3.2 represented cities and the edges represented commuting or business partnerships between them, then it is clear that the profits generated by companies within one community would mostly remain in the community, while an illness outbreak in one community would not impact the others. Each of these examples serve to illustrate that while Figure 3.2 was first introduced in Chapter Three as a way of thinking about subcultural groups of people within the city, this same kind of community structure can be found in many different aspects of the modern metropolis.

*   *   *   *   *

The opening chapter described this as a book about urban networks. But, as this final chapter has demonstrated, this description may be a bit misleading because urban networks are not so different from many other kinds of networks. We are all familiar with the experience of discovering that we share a mutual acquaintance with a stranger, but the small world networks that make this so common are not restricted to social relationships among people. They are just as likely to turn up in urban transportation networks as in the nervous systems of microscopic organisms. Similarly, we have all needed to rely on a connecting flight at a busy hub airport to get to our destination, but the scale-free networks that make networks like these so efficient are not restricted to airline routes. We are reminded of this every time a hub node in a scale-free network fails: a closed hub airport means we miss our connection, and a broken router means we miss our email. Even something as seemingly unique to people and cities as the notion of community can be found in many different settings, ranging from communities of streets that define the boundary of a neighborhood to communities of grapes that define how wine should be blended. Thus, while the earliest chapters explored several centuries of claims that community is lost, it is clear that communities are everywhere. One just needs to know where to look, and networks seem to be a good place to start.

Discussion Questions and Activities

1. If you were a participant in Milgram's small world experiment and needed to send a letter to a Boston stockbroker using only a chain of personal acquaintances, could you do it? How would you decide to which of your personal acquaintances you should send the letter?

2 Is the Atlanta reputational influence network in Figure 4.1 a scale-free network or a random network? What might happen to urban politics in Atlanta if person #34 moved away? What if person #27 moved away?

3. Are there communities in either of the networks shown in Figure 10.1? If these were street networks, which one could lead to greater segregation? If these were interorganizational networks, which one could promote the coordination of public services?

4. This chapter has just scratched the surface in terms of the networks that small world, scale-free, and community structures can be found. What other urban networks might have these types of structures? What other non-urban networks might have these types of structures?

5. How could the methods introduced in the previous chapters be used to study the concepts introduced in this chapter? Similarly, how could the methods introduced in this chapter be used to study the concepts introduced in the previous chapters?

NOTES

1 Introduction: Why Cities? Why Networks?

1 For a general discussion of the usefulness of networks for understanding cities, see: Paul Craven and Barry Wellman, "The Network City," *Sociological Inquiry* 43, (1973): 57–88; Charles Tilly and Steve Tilly, "Introduction," in Charles Tilly and Steve Tilly, eds., *An Urban World* (Boston, MA: Brown and Little, 1974), 1–35; Claude S. Fischer, "The Study of Urban Community and Personality," *Annual Review of Sociology* 1, (1975): 67–89.

2 Robert E. Park, "The City: Suggestions for the Investigation of Human Behavior in the City Environment," *American Journal of Sociology* 20, (1915): 608.

3 For a general discussion of the structuralist or relational perspective in the social sciences, see: J. Clyde Mitchell, "The Concept and Use of Social Networks," in J. Clyde Mitchell, ed., *Social Networks in Urban Situations* (Manchester, U.K.: University of Manchester Press, 1969) 1–50; Bruce H. Mayhew, "Structuralism versus Individualism: Part 1, Shadowboxing in the Dark," *Social Forces* 59, (1980): 335–375; Barry Wellman, "Structural Analysis: From Method and Metaphor to Theory and Substance," in Barry Wellman and S. D. Berkowitz, eds., *Social Structures: A Network Approach* (Cambridge: Cambridge University Press, 1988), 19–61; Mustafa Emirbayer, "Manifesto for a Relational Sociology," *American Journal of Sociology* 103, (1997): 281–317.

4 Leonhard Euler, "Solutio Problematis ad Geometriam Situs Pertinentis," *Commentarii Academiae Scientiarum Petropolitanae* 8, (1741): 128–140; John A. Hobson, *The Evolution of Modern Capitalism: A Study of Machine Production*, New Edition (New York: Walter Scott Publishing Company, [1894] 1914); Georg Simmel, *The Sociology of Georg Simmel*, trans. Kurt H. Wolff. (Glencoe, IL: Free Press, [1908] 1950); Jacob Moreno, *Who Shall Survive? A New Approach to the Problem of Human Interrelations* (Washington, DC: Nervous and Mental Disease Publishing Co., 1934); Linton C. Freeman, *The Development of Social Network Analysis: A Study in the Sociology of Science* (Vancouver, BC: Empirical Press, 2004).

5 Karl Marx, *Karl Marx: Selected Writings in Sociology and Social Philosophy*, trans. by T. B. Bottomore (New York: McGraw-Hill, [1857] 1956) 96.

6 Charles Horton Cooley, *Human Nature and the Social Order* (New York: Schocken, [1902] 1964) 148.

7 A. R. Radcliffe-Brown, "On social structure," *Journal of the Royal Anthropological Institute of Great Britain and Ireland* 70, (1940): 2.

8 Roberta Capello, "The City Network Paradigm: Measuring Urban Network Externalities," *Urban Studies* 37 (2000): 1925–1945; Saskia Sassen, "Global Cities and Diasporic Networks: Microsites in Global Civil Society," in *Global Civil Society* (New York: Oxford University Press, 2002) 217–238;

Renaud Payre, "The Importance of Being Connected. City Networks and Urban Government: Lyon and Eurocities (1990–2005)," *International Journal of Urban and Regional Research* 34, (2010): 260–280.

9   Bruno Latour, *Reassembling the Social: An Introduction to Actor–Network Theory* (New York: Oxford University Press, 2005).

10 For examples of Actor Network Theory applied to the study of cities, see: Richard G. Smith, "World City Actor–Networks," *Progress in Human Geography* 27, (2003): 24–44; Gernot Grabher, "Trading Routes, Bypasses, and Risky Intersections: Mapping the Travels of 'Networks' between Economic Sociology and Economic Geography," *Progress in Human Geography* 30, (2006): 163–189; Ignacio Farias and Thomas Bender, eds., *Urban Assemblages: How Actor–Network Theory Changes Urban Studies* (New York: Routledge, 2010); Richard G. Smith and Marcus A. Doel, "Questioning the Theoretical Basis of Current Global-City Research: Structures, Networks, and Actor–Networks," *International Journal of Urban and Regional Research* 35, (2011): 24–39.

11 Stanley Wasserman and Katherine Faust, *Social Network Analysis: Methods and Applications* (Cambridge: Cambridge University Press, 1994); John P. Scott, *Social Network Analysis: A Handbook* (Thousand Oaks, CA: Sage, 2000); Robert A. Hanneman and Mark Riddle, *Introduction to Social Network Methods* (Riverside, CA: University of California, Riverside, 2005), freely available at: www.faculty.ucr.edu/~hanneman/nettext.

12 Barry Wellman, ed., *Networks in the Global Village: Life in Contemporary Communities* (Boulder, CO: Westview Press, 1999); Geraldine Pflieger, Luca Pattaroni, Christophe Jemelin, and Vincent Kaufman, eds., *The Social Fabric of the Networked City* (Lausanne: EPFL Press, 2008); Talja Blokland and Mike Savage, eds., *Networked Urbanism: Social Capital in the City* (Burlington, VT: Ashgate, 2008).

13 For another synthesis of network theory and method, though one not focused on the urban context, see: Charles Kadushin, *Understanding Social Networks: Theories, Concepts, and Findings* (New York: Oxford University Press, 2012).

14 Brian J. L. Berry, "Cities as Systems within Systems of Cities," *Papers of the Regional Science Association* 13, (1964): 147–163. More recently, see: Judith Crews, "Cities as Networks in Networks of Cities: An Interview with Steef C. Buijs," *Flux* 15 (1994): 51–57; "Alternative Explanations of Hierarchical Differentiation in Urban Systems," in Denise Pumain, ed., *Hierarchy in Natural and Social Sciences* (Dordrecht, Netherlands: Springer, 2006) 169–222.

15 For an early attempt at conceptualizing the city as a type of network, see: Christopher Alexander, "A City is Not a Tree," *Architectural Forum* 122, (1965) 58–62; F. Harary and J. Rockey, "A City is Not a Semilattice Either," *Environment and Planning A* 8, (1976): 375–384.

16 Jane Jacobs, *The Death and Life of Great American Cities* (New York: Random House, [1961] 1993) 73.

17 Denise Pumain, "Urban Networks versus Urban Hierarchies?" *Environment and Planning A* 24, (1992): 1377–1380; Roberto P. Camagni, "From City Hierarchy to City Network: Reflections about an Emerging Paradigm," in T. R. Lakshmanan and Peter Nijkamp, eds., *Structure and Change in the Space Economy: Festschrift in Honor of Martin J. Beckman*, (New York: Springer-Verlag, 1993) 66–87; Giuseppe Dematteis, "Global Networks, Local Cities" *Flux* 15, (1994): 17–23.

2 Community: Lost or Found

1   Barry Wellman, "The Community Question: The Intimate Networks of East Yorkers," *American Journal of Sociology* 84, (1979): 1201–1231.

2   Robert Putnam, *Bowling Alone: The Collapse and Revival of American Community* (New York: Simon and Schuster, 2000).

3   For a general discussion of networks and communities in the social sciences, see: Barry Wellman, "The Network Community: An Introduction." in *Networks in a Global Village: Life in Contemporary Communities*, Barry Wellman, ed. (Boulder, CO: Westview Press, 1999) 1–47; Alvin W. Wolfe, "Network Perspectives on Communities," *Structure and Dynamics: eJournal of Anthropological and Related Sciences* 1, (2007).

4   Ferdinand Tönnies, *Community and Civil Society*, Jose Harris, ed. (New York: Cambridge University Press, [1887] 2001).

5   Georg Simmel, "The Metropolis and Mental Life," in *The Sociology of Georg Simmel*, trans. by Kurt H. Wolf (Glencoe, IL: The Free Press, [1903] 1950) 410.

6   Simmel 1950, 415.

7   Louis Wirth, "Urbanism as a Way of Life," *American Journal of Sociology* 44, (1938): 1–24.

8   Much of the recent research on the shrinking of personal social networks continues to focus on those living in cities. However, some evidence for the 'community lost' perspective takes a wider view. For example, see: Miller McPherson, Lynn Smith-Lovin, and Matthew E. Brashears, "Social Isolation in America: Changes in Core Discussion Networks over Two Decades," *American Sociological Review* 71, (2006): 353–375.

9   William H. Key, "Urbanism and Neighboring," *Sociological Quarterly* 6, (1965): 379–385; John Beggs, Valerie A. Haines, and Jeanne S. Hurlbert, "Revisiting the Rural–Urban Contrast: Personal Networks in Nonmetropolitan and Metropolitan Settings," *Rural Sociology* 61, (1996): 306–325.

10 Kenneth T. Jackson, *Crabgrass Frontier: The Suburbanization of the United States* (New York: Oxford University Press, 1985); M. P. Baumgartner, *The Moral Order of a Suburb* (New York: Oxford University Press, 1988); Andres Duany, Elizabeth Plater-Zyberk, and Jeff Speck. *Suburban Nation: The Rise of Sprawl and the Decline of the American Dream* (New York: North Point Press, 2000); Tineke Lupi and Sake Musterd, "The Suburban 'Community Question'," *Urban Studies* 43, (2006): 801–817.

11 R. Kraut, S. Kiesler, B. Boneva, J. Cummings, V. Helgeson, and A. Crawford, "Internet Paradox: A Social Technology that Reduces Social Involvement and Psychological Wellbeing?" *American Psychologist* 59, (1998): 1017–1031; Putnam, 2000; B. Wellman and C. Haythornewaite, eds., *The Internet and Everyday Life* (Oxford: Blackwell, 2002).

12 George A. Hillery, Jr., "Definitions of Community: Areas of Agreement," *Rural Sociology* 20, (1955): 111; also see: Stuart A. Queen, "What is a Community?" *Journal of Social Forces* 1, (1923): 375–382; E. T. Hiller, "The Community as a Social Group," *American Sociological Review* 6, (1941): 189–202; Harold F. Kaufman, "Toward an Interactional Conception of Community," *Social Forces* 38, (1959): 8–17; D. T. Herbert and J. W. Raines, "Defining Communities within Urban Areas: An Analysis of Alternative Approaches," *Town Planning Review* 47, (1976): 325–338.

13 John R. Hipp, Robert W. Faris, and Adam Boessen, "Measuring 'Neighborhood': Constructing Network Neighborhoods," *Social Networks* 34, (2012): 128–140.

14 Moreno 1934, 10.

15 In some fields, notably mathematics, nodes are also called vertices (singular: vertex).

16 Shepard Wolman, "Sociometric Planning of a New Community," *Sociometry* 1, (1937): 221.

17 George A. Lundberg and Margaret Lawsing, "The Sociography of Some Community Relations," *American Sociological Review* 2, (1937): 318–335; George A. Lundberg and Mary Steele, "Social Attraction-Patterns in a Village," *Sociometry* 1, (1938): 375–419.

18 Peter Gutkind, "African Urbanism, Mobility, and the Social Network," *International Journal of Comparative Sociology* 6, (1965): 48–69; Mitchell 1969; Jeremy Boissevain and J. Clyde Mitchell, eds., *Network Analysis Studies in Human Interaction* (Paris: Mouton and Company, 1973); Allen Johnson and George C. Bond, "Kinship, Friendship, and Exchange in Two Communities: A Comparative Analysis of Norms and Behavior," *Journal of Anthropological Research* 30, (1974): 55–66.

19 J. A. Barnes, "Class and Committees in a Norwegian Island Parish," *Human Relations* 7, (1954): 43.

20 A. L. Epstein, "The Network and Urban Social Organization," in J. Clyde Mitchell, ed., *Social Networks in Urban Situations* (Manchester, U.K.: University of Manchester Press, 1969) 77–116.

21 Elizabeth Bott, "Urban Families: Conjugal Roles and Social Networks," *Human Relations* 8, (1955): 345–384.

22 Edward O. Laumann, Peter V. Marsden, and David Prensky, "The Boundary Specification Problem in Network Analysis," in Ronald S. Burt and Michael J. Miner, eds., *Applied Network Analysis: A Methodological Introduction* (Beverly Hills, CA: Sage, 1983).

23 This perspective is known as social exchange theory, which is similar to the network perspective discussed in this book, but is nonetheless somewhat distinct. For a discussion of social exchange from the sociological tradition, see: Richard M. Emerson, "Social Exchange Theory," *Annual Review of Sociology* 2, (1976): 335–362. For a discussion from the anthropological tradition, see: George M. Foster, "The Dyadic Contract: A Model for the Social Strucure of a Mexican Peasant Village," *American Anthropologist*, New Series 63, (1961): 1173–1192. For a comparison of social exchange and social network theories, see: K. S. Cook and J. M. Whitmeyer, "Two Approaches to Social Structure: Exchange Theory and Network Analysis," *Annual Review of Sociology* 18, (1992): 109–127.

24 While most responses to the community lost perspective adopt a social network approach, some take an institutional approach that focuses on the role of community organizations. See, for example: Albert Hunter, "The Loss of Community: An Empirical Test Through Replication," *American Sociological Review* 40, (1975): 537–552; Barrett A. Lee, R. S. Oropesa, Barbara J. Metch, and Avery M. Guest, "Testing the Decline-of-Community Thesis: Neighborhood Organizations in Seattle, 1929 and 1979," *American Journal of Sociology* 89, (1984): 1161–1188.

25 Theodore Caplow and Robert Foreman, "Neighborhood Interaction in a Homogenous Community," *American Sociological Review* 15, (1950): 357–366; Oscar Lewis, "Urbanization without Breakdown: A Case Study," *Scientific Monthly* 75, (1952): 31–41; Wendell Bell and Marion D. Boat, "Urban Neighborhoods and Informal Social Relations," *American Journal of Sociology* 62, (1957): 391–398; Scott Greer, "Urbanism Reconsidered: A Comparative Study of Local Areas in a Metropolis," *American Sociological Review* 21, (1956): 19–25.

26 Leonard Blumberg and Robert R. Bell, "Urban Migration and Kinship Ties," *Social Problems* 6, (1959): 328–333; Albert J. Reiss, "Rural–Urban and Status Differences in Interpersonal Contacts," *American Journal of Sociology* 65, (1959): 182–195.

27 Jacobs, 1993, 13.

28 Herbert J. Gans, *The Urban Villagers: Group and Class in the Life of Italian-Americans* (New York: Free Press, 1962) 74.

29 Wellman, 1999, 1–2; see also: Karen E. Campbell, "Networks Past: A 1939 Bloomington Neighborhood," *Social Forces* 69, (1990): 139–155.

30 Claude S. Fischer, *To Dwell Among Friends: Personal Networks in Town and City* (Chicago: University of Chicago Press, 1982): 81.

31 Barry Wellman, "The Place of Kinfolk in Personal Community Networks," *Marriage and Family Review* 15, (1990): 195–228; Danching Ruan, "Interpersonal Networks and Workplace Controls in Urban China," *Australian Journal of Chinese Affairs* 29, (1993): 89–105.

32 Fischer, 1982 (see chapters 7–10); Katherine J. Curtis White and Avery M. Guest, "Community Lost or Transformed? Urbanization and Social Ties," *City and Community* 2, (2003): 239–259.

33 Lynne McCallister and Claude S. Fischer, "A Procedure for Surveying Personal Networks," *Sociological Methods and Research* 7, (1978): 131–148; Ronald S. Burt, "Network Items and the General Social Survey," *Social Networks* 6, (1984): 293–339; Karen E. Campbell and Barrett A. Lee, "Name Generators in Surveys of Personal Networks," *Social Networks* 13, (1991): 203–221.

34 Paul W. Holland and Samuel Leinhardt, "The Structural Implications of Measurement Error in Sociometry," *Journal of Mathematical Sociology* 3, (1973): 85–111.

35 Claude S. Fischer, *Networks and Places: Social Relations in the Urban Setting* (New York: Free Press, 1977); Fischer, 1982.

36 Paul F. Lazarsfeld and Robert K. Merton, "Friendship as a Social Process: A Substantive and Methodological Analysis," in Morroe Berger, Theodore Abel, and Charles H. Page, eds., *Freedom and Control in Modern Society* (New York: Octagon Books, 1964) 18–66; Miller McPherson, Lynn Smith-Lovin, and James M. Cook, "Birds of Feather: Homophily in Social Networks," *Annual Review of Sociology* 27, (2001): 415–444.

37 Edward O. Laumann, *Bonds of Pluralism: Form and Substance of Urban Social Networks* (New York: John Wiley & Sons, 1973) chapter 5; Fischer, 1982, chapter 14.

38 Claude S. Fischer, "Toward a Subcultural Theory of Urbanism," *American Journal of Sociology* 80, (1975): 1319–1341.

39   Herbert Blumer, "Race Prejudice as a Sense of Group Position," *Pacific Sociological Review* 1, (1958): 3–7; Yehuda Amir, "Contact Hypothesis in Ethnic Relations," *Psychological Bulletin* 71, (1969): 319–342; Fischer, 1982, chapter 18.

40   Lee Siegelman, Timothy Bledsoe, Susan Welch, and Michael W. Combs, "Making Contact? Black–White Social Interaction in an Urban Setting," *American Journal of Sociology* 101, (1996): 1306–1332; Xavier de Souza Briggs, "'Some of My Best Friends Are . . . ': Interracial Friendships, Class, and Segregation in America," *City and Community* 6, (2007): 263–290.

41   Laumann, 1973.

42   Lazarsfeld and Merton (1964, see pg 27) define a similar measure of homophily as: (observed-expected)/expected. Another similar measure is used by Herminia Ibarra, "Homophily and Differential Returns: Sex Differences in Network Structure and Access in an Advertising Firm," *Administrative Science Quarterly* 37, (1992): 422–447. The primary difference in these measures are the range of values they can take. The measure defined here ranges from 0 to positive infinity, and is centered at 1. It can be useful to use the natural logarithm of this measure of unbiased homophily, which yields a more symmetric measure that ranges from negative infinity to positive infinity, and is centered at 0.

43   Laumann, 1973, 118.

44   Mark Baldassare, "Residential Density, Household Crowding, and Social Networks," in Claude S. Fischer, ed., *Networks and Places* (New York: Free Press, 1977) 101–115; Susan D. Greenbaum and Paul E. Greenbaum, "The Ecology of Social Networks in Four Urban Neighborhoods," *Social Networks* 7, (1985): 47–76; John R. Logan and Glenna D. Spitze, "Family Neighbors," *American Journal of Sociology* 100, (1994): 453–476; Briggs, 2007; John R. Hipp and Andrew J. Perrin, "The Simultaneous Effect of Social Distance and Physical Distance on the Formation of Neighborhood Ties," *City and Community* 8, (2009): 5–25.

45   John D. Kasarda and Morris Janowitz, "Community Attachment in Mass Society," *American Sociological Review* 39, (1974): 326–339; Robert J. Sampson, "Local Friendship Ties and Community Attachment in Mass Society: A Multilevel Systemic Model," *American Sociological Review* 53, (1988): 766–779; Hipp and Perrin, 2009.

46   Paul Deutschberger, "Interaction Patterns in Changing Neighborhoods: New York and Pittsburgh," *Sociometry* 9, (1946): 303–315; Robert Max Johnson, "Social Structure and Process in Friendship Choice," in Claude S. Fischer, ed., *Networks and Places* (New York: Free Press, 1977) 59–78; R. Robert Huckfeldt, "Social Contexts, Social Networks, and Urban Neighborhoods: Environmental Constraints on Friendship Choice," *American Journal of Sociology* 89, (1983): 651–669; Hipp and Perrin, 2009.

47   Jacobs, 1993; William A. Fischel, "Why Voters Veto Vouchers: Public Schools and Community-Specific Social Capital," *Economics of Governance* 7, (2006): 109–132; Andreas Varheim, "Social Capital and Public Libraries: The Need for Research," *Library and Information Science Research* 29, (2007): 416–428; Beate Völker and Henk Flap, "Sixteen Million Neighbors: A Multilevel Study of the Role of Neighbors in the Personal Networks of the Dutch," *Urban Affairs Review* 43, (2007): 256–284.

48   Peter McGahan, "The Neighbor Role and Neighboring in a Highly Urban Area," *Sociological Quarterly* 13, (1972): 397–408; Putnam, 2000; Briggs, 2007.

49   Michel Grossetti, "Where Do Social Relations Come From? A Study of Personal Networks in the Toulouse Area of France," *Social Networks* 27, (2005): 289–300.

50   Scott Greer, *The Emerging City: Myth and Reality* (New York: Free Press, 1962) chapter 4; Charles E. Connerly, "The Community Question: An Extension of Wellman and Leighton," *Urban Affairs Review* 20, (1985): 537–556.

51   Jacob Riis, "The Rights of Children," *Charities* 7, (1901): 48.

52   Gary Bridge, "The Neighbourhood and Social Networks," *CNR Paper 4, ESRC Centre for Neighbourhood Research (2002)*; Beate Völker, Henk Flap, and Siegwart Lindenberg, "When are Neighborhoods Communities? Community in Dutch Neighborhoods," *European Sociological Review* 23, (2007): 99–114.

53   Gans, 1962, 23. Also see: Barnes, 1954; Melvin M. Webber, "Order in Diversity: Community without Propinquity," in Lowdon Wingo, ed., *Cities and Space: The Future Use of Urban Land* (Baltimore, MD: Johns Hopkins Press, 1963); Eugene Litwak and Ivan Szelenyi, "Primary Group Structures and Their Functions: Kin, Neighbors, and Friends," *American Sociological Review* 34, (1969): 465–481.

54   Wellman, 1979; Barry Wellman and Barry Leighton, "Networks, Neighborhoods, and Communities: Approaches to the Study of the Community Question," *Urban Affairs Review* 14, (1979): 363–390.

55   Claude S. Fischer and C. Ann Steuve, " 'Authentic Community': The Role of Place in Modern Life," in Claude S. Fischer, ed., *Networks and Places* (New York: Free Press, 1977) 163–186; Andreas Frei, Kay W. Axhausen, and Timo Ohnmacht, "Mobilities and Social Network Geography: Size and Spatial Dispersion-The Zurich Case Study," in Timo Ohnmacht, Hanja Maksim, and Manfred Max, eds., *Mobilities and Inequalities* (Burlington, VT: Ashgate, 2009).

56   Avery M. Guest and Susan K. Wierzbicki, "Social Ties at the Neighborhood Level: Two Decades of GSS Evidence," *Urban Affairs Review* 35, (1999): 92–111.

57   Avery M. Guest, "The Mediate Community: The Nature of Local and Extralocal Ties Within the Metropolis," *Urban Affairs Review* 35, (2000): 603–627; Marina Hennig, "Re-evaluating the Community Question from a German Perspective," *Social Networks* 29, (2007): 375–390.

58   Jacobs, 1993, 72–73.

59   Fischer, 1982, chapter 13.

60   Barry Wellman and Milena Gulia, "Net-Surfers Don't Ride Alone: Virtual Communities as Communities," in Barry Wellman, ed., *Networks in the Global Village: Life in Contemporary Communities* (Boulder, CO: Westview Press, 1999) 331–366; John G. Bruhn, *The Sociology of Community Connections* (New York: Kluwer Academic, 2005) chapter 9; Mary Chayko, *Portable Communities: The Social Dynamics of Online and Mobile Connectedness* (Albany, NY: SUNY Press, 2008).

61   Gustavo S. Mesch and Yael Levanon, "Community Networking and Locally-Based Social Ties in Two Suburban Localities," *City and Community* 2, (2003): 335–351; Keith Hampton and Barry Wellman, "Neighboring in Netville: How the Internet Supports Community and Social Capital in a Wired Suburb," *City and Community* 2, (2004): 277–311; Diana Mok, Barry Wellman, and Juan Carrasco, "Does Distance Matter in the Age of the Internet?" *Urban Studies* 47, (2010): 2747–2783.

62   Stanley Milgram and Paul Hollander, "The Murder They Heard," *The Nation* 198, (1964): 602–604; A. M. Rosenthal, *Thirty-Eight Witnesses: The Kitty Genovese Case* (Berkeley, CA: University of California Press, 1999).

63   Although this chapter has focused primarily on the social network conception of communities in the fields of sociology, geography, and anthropology, many of these ideas have appeared, somewhat independently, in the field of history. Many years after studies advancing the 'community saved' perspective, and about the same time as Wellman's 'community liberated' studies of East York, one historian noted that "most observers agree that the concept [of networks] is a useful one . . . yet no one has really found a way of utilizing the concept properly" (Alan Macfarlane, "History, Anthropology, and the Study of Communities," *Social History* 2, (1977): 638). A few years later, another historian defined community as "made up of relationships among social actors, and relations among these relationships" (C. J. Calhoun, "Community: Toward a Variable Conceptualization for Comparative Research," *Social History* 5, (1980): 116). These comments illustrate how the notion of communities as networks has spread to nearly every social science discipline, and highlights the importance of building on the work of scholars in other fields to avoid 'reinventing the wheel.'

64   Gunnar Myrdal, *An American Dilemma* (New York: McGraw Hill, 1964); William Julius Wilson, *The Truly Disadvantaged: The Inner City, The Underclass, and Public Policy* (Chicago: University of Chicago Press, 1987).

65   Ulf Hannerz, "Gossip, Network, and Culture in a Black American Ghetto," *Ethnos* 32, (1967): 35–60; Joe R. Feagin, "A Note on the Friendship Ties of Black Urbanites," *Social Forces* 49, (1970): 303–308; Carol B. Stack, *All Our Kin* (New York: Harper and Row, 1974); William H. Martineau, "Informal Social Ties Among Urban Black Americans: Some New Data and a Review of the Problem," *Journal of Black Studies* 8, (1977): 84 –104; Melvin L. Oliver, "The Urban Black Community as Network:

Toward a Social Network Perspective," *Sociological Quarterly* 29, (1988): 623–645; Colleen L. Johnson and Barbara M. Barer, "Families and Networks Among Older Inner-city Blacks," *The Gerontologist* 30, (1990): 726–733; Zhong Deng and Philip Bonacich, "Some Effects of Urbanism on Black Social Networks," *Social Networks* 13, (1991): 35–50; Barrett A. Lee and Karen E. Campbell, "Neighbor Networks of Black and White Americans," in Barry Wellman, ed., *Networks in the Global Village: Life in Contemporary Communities* (Boulder, CO: Westview Press, 1999) 119–146.

66   Bruce D. Haynes and Jesus Hernandez, "Place, Space, and Race: Monopolistic Group Closure and the Dark Side of Social Capital," in Talja Blokland and Mike Savage, eds., *Networked Urbanism: Social Capital in the City* (Burlington, VT: Ashgate, 2008) 59–82; Rachel Garshick Kleit, "Neighborhood Segregation, Personal Networks, and Access to Social Resources," in James H. Carr and Nandinee K. Kutty, eds., *Segregation: The Rising Costs for America* (New York: Routledge, 2008).

67   Vincente Espinosa, "Social Networks Among the Urban Poor: Inequality and Integration in a Latin American City," in Barry Wellman, ed., *Networks in the Global Village: Life in Contemporary Communities* (Boulder, CO: Westview Press, 1999) 151.

68   Larissa Adler Lomnitz, *Networks and Marginality: Life in a Mexican Shantytown* (New York: Academic Press, 1977); Stacy Rowe and Jennifer Wolch, "Social Networks in Time and Space: Homeless Women in Skid Row, Los Angeles," *Annals of the Association of American Geographers* 80, (1990): 184–204; Rachel Garshick Kleit, "Neighborhood Relations in Suburban Scattered-Site and Clustered Public Housing," *Journal of Urban Affairs* 23, (2001): 409–430; Sandra L. Barnes, "Determinants of Individual Neighborhood Ties and Social Resources in Poor Urban Neighborhoods," *Sociological Spectrum* 23, (2003): 463–497; Bruhn, 2005, chapter 4; Rachel Garshick Kleit, "HOPE IV New Communities: Neighborhood Relationships in Mixed-Income Housing," *Environment and Planning A* 37, (2005): 1413–1441; Alexandra M. Curley, "A New Place, A New Network? Social Capital Effects of Residential Relocation for Poor Women," in Talja Blokland and Mike Savage, eds., *Networked Urbanism: Social Capital in the City* (Burlington, VT: Ashgate, 2008) 85–103; Talja Blokland and Floris Noordhoff, "The Weakness of Weak Ties: Social Capital to Get Ahead Among the Urban Poor in Rotterdam and Amsterdam," in Talja Blokland and Mike Savage, eds., *Networked Urbanism: Social Capital in the City* (Burlington, VT: Ashgate, 2008) 105–125; Eduardo Marques et al., "Networks and Spatial Segregation in the Production of Urban Poverty in Sao Paulo," *Local Environment* 14, (2009): 809–817.

69   Sylvia Fleis Fava, "Suburbanism as a Way of Life," *American Sociological Review* 21, (1956): 34–37; Aida K. Tomeh, "Informal Group Participation and Residential Patterns," *American Journal of Sociology* 70, (1964): 28–35; Herbert J. Gans, "Planning and Social Life: Friendship and Neighbor Relations in Suburban Communities," *Journal of the American Institute of Planners* 27, (1961): 134–140; Herbert J. Gans, "Urbanism and Suburbanism as Ways of Life: A Re-evaluation of Definitions," in Arnold Rose, ed., *Human Behavior and Social Processes: An Interactionist Approach* (Boston, MA: Houghton Mifflin, 1962); Claude S. Fischer and Robert Max Johnson, "Suburbanism and Localism," in Claude S. Fischer, ed., *Networks and Places* (New York: Free Press, 1977) 117–138.

70   Bruhn, 2005, chapter 6; Lupi Musterd 2006.

71   William T. Liu and Robert W. Duff, "The Strength in Weak Ties," *Public Opinion Quarterly* 36, (1972): 361–366; Mark S. Granovetter, "The Strength of Weak Ties," *American Journal of Sociology* 78, (1973): 1360–1380; James S. Coleman, "Social Capital in the Creation of Human Capital," *American Journal of Sociology* 94, (1988): S95-S120; Alejandro Portes, "Social Capital: Its Origins and Applications in Modern Sociology," *Annual Review of Sociology* 24, (1998): 1–24; Ronald S. Burt, "Structural Holes versus Network Closure as Social Capital," in Nan Lin, Karen Cook, and Ronald S. Burt, eds., *Social Capital Theory and Research* (New Brunswick, NJ: Transaction Publishers, 2001); Ronald S. Burt, *Brokerage and Closure: An Introduction to Social Capital* (New York: Oxford University Press, 2005).

72   Talja Blokland, "Gardening with a Little Help from your (Middle Class) Friends: Bridging Social Capital Across Race and Class in a Mixed Neighborhood," in Talja Blokland and Mike Savage, eds., *Networked Urbanism: Social Capital in the City* (Burlington, VT: Ashgate, 2008) 147–170.

73 Bridging ties are often, but do not need to be, weak ties. For example, a strong relationship between two close friends might also be a bridging tie if these two individuals do not have any other friends in common. Similarly, while bonding ties are often strong, they do not need to be. For example, a neighborhood in which all the residents know one another, but only casually, is an example of a weak and bonding network.

74 Thomas Hobbes, *Leviathan*, edited by A. R. Waller (Cambridge, Cambridge University Press, [1651] 1904) 54.

75 Donald I. Warren, *Helping Networks: How People Cope with Problems in the Urban Community* (Notre Dame, IN: University of Notre Dame Press, 1981); Barry Wellman and Scot Wortley, "Different Strokes for Different Folks: Community Ties and Social Support," *American Journal of Sociology* 96, (1990): 558–588; Barry Wellman and Milena Gulia, "The Network Basis of Social Support: A Network is More than the Sum of Its Ties," in in Barry Wellman, ed., *Networks in the Global Village: Life in Contemporary Communities* (Boulder, CO: Westview Press, 1999) 83–118; Bruhn, 2005, chapter 8; Curley, 2008.

76 Jacobs, 1993, 73.

77 Albert Hunter, "Private, Parochial, and Public Social Orders: The Problem of Crime and Incivility in Urban Communities," in Gerald D. Suttles and Meyer N. Zald, eds., *The Challenge of Social Control: Citizenship and Institution Building in Modern Society* (Norwood, NJ: Ablex Publishing, 1985); Coleman, 1988; Robert J. Sampson and W. Byron Groves, "Community Structure and Crime: Testing Social-Disorganization Theory," *American Journal of Sociology* 94, (1989): 774–802; Robert J. Bursik Jr. and Harold G. Grasmick, "Neighborhood-based networks and the control of crime and delinquency," in High Barlow, ed., *Crime and Public Policy: Putting Theory to Work* (Boulder: Westview, 1995) 107–130; Barbara D. Warner and Pamela Wilcox Roundtree, "Local Social Ties in a Community Crime Model: Questioning the Systemic Nature of Informal Social Control," *Social Problems* 44, (1997): 520–536.

78 Kathleen Gerson, C. Ann Steuve, and Claude S. Fischer, "Attachment to Place," in Claude S. Fischer, ed., *Networks and Places* (New York: Free Press, 1977) 139–160; Stephanie Riger and Paul J. Lavrakas, "Community Ties: Patterns of Attachment and Social Interaction in Urban Neighborhoods," *American Journal of Community Psychology* 9, (1981): 55–66; Charles Kadushin and Delmos J. Jones, "Social Networks and Urban Neighborhoods in New York City," *City and Society* 6, (1992): 58–75; John R. Hipp and Andrew Perrin, "Nested Loyalties: Networks' Effects on Neighborhood and Community Cohesion," *Urban Studies* 43, (2006): 2503–2523; Alberta Andreotti and Patrick Le Gales, "Middle Class Neighborhood Attachment in Paris and Milan: Partial Exit and Profound Rootedness," in Talja Blokland and Mike Savage, eds., *Networked Urbanism: Social Capital in the City* (Burlington, VT: Ashgate, 2008) 127–143.

79 Moreno, 1934; Wolman, 1937.

80 Beate Völker and Henk Flap, "The Comrades' Belief: Intended and Unintended Consequences of Communism for Neighborhood Relations in the Former GDR," *European Sociological Review* 13, (1997): 241–265.

81 Deborah A. Phillips, "Information Diffusion within an Inner City Neighbourhood," *Geografiska Annaler B* 61, (1979): 30–42; Richard Meegan and Alison Mitchell, "'It's Not Community Round Here, It's Neighbourhood': Neighbourhood Change and Cohesion in Urban Regeneration Policies," *Urban Studies* 38, (2001): 2167–2194; Everett M. Rogers, *The Diffusion of Innovations*, 5th Edition (New York: Free Press, 2003); Lai Fong Chiu and Robert M. West, "Health Intervention in Social Context: Understanding Social Networks and Neighborhood," *Social Science & Medicine* 65, (2007): 1915–1927; Brian D. Christens, "Public Relationship Building in Grassroots Community Organizing: Relational Intervention for Individual and Systems Change," *Journal of Community Psychology* 38, (2010): 886–900; Jonathan Rowson, Steve Broome, and Alasdair Jones, *Connected Communities: How Social Networks Power and Sustain the Big Society* (London: Royal Society for the Encouragement of Arts, Manufactures, and Commerce, 2010).

3 Subculture: Finding Your Crowd in a Crowd

1 Park, 1915, 608. This was echoed by Wirth several years later, who similarly described the city as "a mosaic of social worlds" (1938, p. 15).

2 Melena Ryzik, "The Anti-Restaurants," *New York Times*, August 27, 2008, F1.

3 Arnold W. Green, "Sociological Analysis of Horney and Fromm," *American Journal of Sociology* 51, (1946): 534.

4 Milton M. Gordon, "The Concept of the Sub-Culture and Its Application," *Social Forces* 26, (1947): 42.

5 Georg Simmel, "The Web of Group Affiliations," in Reinhard Bendix, trans., *Conflict and the Web of Group Affiliations* (Glencoe, IL: The Free Press, [1922] 1955) 126–195. The literal translation of the title of Simmel's essay *Die Kreuzung Sozialer Kreise* is "The Intersection of Social Circles," but the translator chose to use the alternate title above. Also see: Aiden Southall, "The Density of Role-Relationships as a Universal Index of Urbanization," in Aiden Southall, ed., *Urban Anthropology: Cross-Cultural Studies of Urbanization* (New York: Oxford University Press, 1973) 71–106.

6 Fischer 1975.

7 Thomas C. Wilson, "Community Population Size and Social Heterogeneity: An Empirical Test," *American Journal of Sociology* 91, (1986): 1154–1169; Charles R. Tittle, "Urbanness and Unconventional Behavior: A Partial Test of Claude Fischer's Subcultural Theory," *Criminology* 27, (1989): 273–306; Charles R. Tittle, "Influences on Urbanism: A Test of Predictions from Three Perspectives," *Social Problems* 36, (1989): 270–288; Sung Joon Jang and Richard D. Alba, "Urbanism and Nontraditional Opinion: A Test of Fischer's Subcultural Theory," *Social Science Quarterly* 73, (1992): 596–609.

8 These ideas were introduced from a symbolic interactionist perspective, but drew at least metaphorically on notions of network structure, by Gary Alan Fine and Sherryl Kleinman, "Rethinking Subculture: An Interactionist Approach," *American Journal of Sociology* 85, (1979): 1–20. For two closely related earlier discussions that also hint at the role of networks, see: A. B. Holingshead, "Behavior Systems as a Field for Research," *American Sociological Review* 4, (1939): 816–822; Tamotsu Shibutani, "Reference Groups as Perspectives," *American Journal of Sociology* 60, (1955): 562–569.

9 Jeremy Boissevain, "The Place of Non-Groups in the Social Sciences," *Man* 3, (1968): 542–556; Wellman 1988.

10 Scott L. Feld, "The Focused Organization of Social Ties," *American Journal of Sociology* 86, (1981): 1015–1035. While focus theory views social networks as forming based on characteristics of the social environment, an alternative approach known as balance theory views social networks as forming based on the psychological characteristics of individuals, see method note 22.

11 These social worlds, including social groups, social circles, and other subcultural urban groups, may not interpenetrate, but they do often interact with and influence one another. Indeed, frequently such intergroup interactions are a source of conflict, and can serve to strengthen a group's boundaries and commitment to its own particular subcultural values and practices.

12 Coleman, 1988; Barak D. Richman, "How Community Institutions Create Economic Advantage: Jewish Diamond Merchants in New York," *Law and Social Inquiry* 31, (2006): 383–420.

13 Ruth C. Young and Olaf F. Larson, "A New Approach to Community Structure," *American Sociological Review* 30, (1965): 926–934; Ronald L. Breiger, "The Duality of Persons and Groups," *Social Forces* 53, (1974): 181–190.

14 David Krackhardt and Robert N. Stern, "Informal Networks and Organizational Crises: An Experimental Simulation," *Social Psychology Quarterly* 51, (1988): 123–140.

15 This example is adapted from Breiger, 1974, p. 182.

16 Zachary Neal, "Structural Determinism in the Interlocking World City Network," *Geographical Analysis*.

17 Charles Kadushin, "The Friends and Supporters of Psychotherapy: On Social Circles in Urban Life," *American Sociological Review* 31, (1966): 786–802. Interestingly, this study did not directly apply social network methods because, at the time, "even with modern computers, we do not know how to study the complex chains of interaction that exist in a relatively small social system" (p. 789). Instead,

Kadushin argues that by adopting the proposed latent class approach "we obviate the need for actual sociometric data, which we agreed was too difficult to manage" (p. 793).

18 Fischer, 1982, chapter 17; Abel Valenzuela, Jr., "Day Labor Work," *Annual Review of Sociology* 29, (2003): 307–333.

19 Bruhn, 2005, 162. See also Fischer, 1982, chapter 16.

20 Japonica Brown-Saracino, "Social Preservationists and the Quest for Authentic Community," *City and Community* 3, (2004): 135–156.

21 Oscar Lewis, "The Culture of Poverty," *Society* 1, (1963): 17–19; Norman J. Johnston and Peggy R. Sanday, "Subcultural Variations in an Urban Poor Population," *American Anthropologist* 73, (1971): 128–143.

22 Mary Pattillo, *Black on the Block: The Politics of Race and Class in the City* (Chicago: University of Chicago Press, 2007); Bruce D. Haynes and Jesus Hernandez, "Place, Space, and Race: Monopolistic Group Closure and the Dark Side of Social Capital," in Talja Blokland and Mike Savage, eds., *Networked Urbanism: Social Capital in the City* (Burlington, VT: Ashgate, 2008) 59–82.

23 William Foote Whyte, *Street Corner Society: The Social Structure of an Italian Slum* (Chicago: University of Chicago Press, 1943); Gerald D. Suttles, *The Social Order of the Slum: Ethnicity and Territory in the Inner City* (Chicago: University of Chicago Press, 1968).

24 Bill McCarthy and John Hagan, "Getting Into Street Crime: The Structure and Process of Criminal Embeddedness," *Social Science Research* 24, (1995): 63–95; Jeffrey Scott McIllwain, "Organized Crime: A Social Network Approach," *Crime, Law, and Social Change* 32, (1999): 301–323; Mark S. Fleisher and Jessie L. Krienert, "Life-course Events, Social Networks, and the Emergence of Violence among Female Gang Members," *Journal of Community Psychology* 32, (2004): 607–622; Mark S. Fleisher, "Fieldwork Research and Social Network Analysis: Different Methods Creating Complementary Perspectives," *Journal of Contemporary Criminal Justice* 21, (2005): 120–134; Jean Marie McGloin, "Policy and Intervention Considerations of a Network Analysis of Street Gangs," *Criminology and Public Policy* 4, (2005): 607–636; Mark S. Fleisher, "Youth Gang Social Dynamics and Social Network Analysis: Applying Degree Centrality Measures to Assess the Nature of Gang Boundaries," in James F. Short and Lorine A. Hughes, eds., *Studying Youth Gangs* (New York: Rowman & Littlefield, 2006) 85–98; Andrew V. Papachristos, "Social Network Analysis and Gang Research: Theory and Methods," in James F. Short and Lorine A. Hughes, eds., *Studying Youth Gangs* (New York: Rowman & Littlefield, 2006) 99–116.

25 Alexis de Tocqueville, *Democracy in America*, Gerald Bevan, trans. (New York: Penguin Books, [1838] 2003).

26 Wirth, 1938, 20.

27 Frederick A. Bushee, "Social Organization in a Small City," *American Journal of Sociology* 51, (1945): 217–226; Mirra Komarovsky, "The Voluntary Associations of Urban Dwellers," *American Sociological Review* 11, (1946): 686–698; Floyd Dotson, "Patterns of Voluntary Association Among Urban Working-Class Families," *American Sociological Review* 16, (1951): 687–693; Morris Axelrod, "Urban Structure and Social Participation," *American Sociological Review* 21, (1956): 13–18; Wendell Bell and Maryanne T. Force, "Urban Neighborhood Types and Participation in Formal Associations," *American Sociological Review* 21, (1956): 25–34; Bell and Boat 1957; Walter M. Gerson, "Alienation in Mass Society: Some Causes and Responses," *Sociology and Social Research* 49, (1965): 143–152; Stephen J. Cutler, "Voluntary Association Membership and the Theory of Mass Society," in Edward O. Laumann, ed., *Bonds of Pluralism: Form and Substance of Urban Social Networks* (New York: John Wiley & Sons, 1973) 133–159; Putnam, 2000.

28 Charles Kadushin, "Who Benefits from Network Analysis: Ethics of Social Network Research," *Social Networks* 27, (2005): 139–153; Alden S. Klovdahl, "Social Network Research and Human Subjects Protection: Towards More Effective Infectious Disease Control," *Social Networks* 27, (2005): 119–137; Jenine K. Harris, "Consent and Confidentiality: Exploring Ethical Issues in Public Health Social Network Research," *Connections* 28, (2008): 81–96.

29 Eugene Litwak, "Voluntary Association and Neighborhood Cohesion," *American Sociological Review* 26, (1961): 258–271; Alan Booth and Nicholas Babchuck, "Personal Influence Networks and

Voluntary Association Affiliation," *Sociological Inquiry* 39, (1969): 179–188; Noel J. Chrisman, "Situation and Social Network in Cities," *Canadian Review of Sociology and Anthropology* 7, (1970): 245–257; Richard P. Taub, George P. Surgeon, Sara Lindholm, Phyllis Betts Otti, and Amy Bridges, "Urban Voluntary Associations: Locality Based and Externally Induced," *American Journal of Sociology* 83, (1977): 425–442.

30 The framework is called 'Blau Space' in honor of sociologist Peter Blau. J. Miller McPherson, "An Ecology of Affiliation," *American Sociological Review* 48, (1983): 519–532; J. Miller McPherson and Lynn Smith-Lovin, "Homophily in Voluntary Organizations: Status Distance and the Composition of Face-to-Face Groups," *American Sociological Review* 52, (1987): 370–379; Pamela A. Popielarz and J. Miller McPherson, "On the Edge or In Between: Niche Position, Niche Overlap, and the Duration of Voluntary Association Memberships," *American Journal of Sociology* 101, (1995): 698–720; J. Miller McPherson and Thomas Rotolo, "Testing a Dynamic Model of Social Composition: Diversity and Change in Voluntary Groups," *American Sociological Review* 61, (1996): 179–202; J. Miller McPherson, "A Blau Space Primer: Prolegomenon to An Ecology of Affiliation," *Industrial and Corporate Change* 13, (2004): 263–280.

31 It is important to distinguish *social* space from *physical* space. Social networks may be localized in social space, meaning that interactions and network connections tend to occur among people with similar social characteristics. However, as the community liberated perspective in Chapter Two demonstrated, social networks are often not localized in physical space.

32 This example only scratches the surface of the Blau Space framework, which is a powerful tool for understanding how networks and associations interact with one another. The approach draws heavily on ideas from biological ecology, and can be applied in many of the same ways. For example, if two associations have overlapping niches, because they are drawing on the same pool of potential members, they may compete with one another just as two animals compete over a common food source. Similarly, if an individual is at the edge of an association's niche because they do not fit the profile of a 'typical' member, they may easily be pulled away from the association and into another association, just as a single species of animals can evolve into two species. For an extended discussion of the framework, and its relationship to biology, see: Pamela A. Popielarz and Zachary P. Neal, "The Niche as a Theoretical Tool," *Annual Review of Sociology* 33, (2007): 65–84.

33 Kenneth L. Wilson and Alejandro Portes, "Immigrant Enclaves: An Analysis of the Labor Market Experiences of Cubans in Miami," *American Journal of Sociology* 86, (1980): 295–319.

34 John R. Logan, Wenquan Zhang, and Richard D. Alba, "Immigrant Enclaves and Ethnic Communities in New York and Los Angeles," *American Sociological Review* 67, (2002): 299–322.

35 Alejandro Portes and Leif Jensen, "What's an Ethnic Enclave? The Case for Conceptual Clarity," *American Sociological Review* 52, (1987): 768–771.

36 For an extended discussion of ethnic communities and social networks, see: Katharyne Mitchell, "Networks of Ethnicity," in Eric Sheppard and Trevor J. Barnes, eds., *A Companion to Economic Geography* (Malden, MA: Blackwell, 2000): 329–407; Bruhn, 2005, chapter 3.

37 Paul Frederick Cressey, "Population Succession in Chicago: 1898–1930," *American Journal of Sociology* 44, (1938): 59–69; Milton M. Gordon, *Assimilation in American Life: The Role of Race, Religion, and National Origins* (New York: Oxford University Press, 1964).

38 Laumann, 1973, chapter 3; Fischer, 1975, see p. 1330; Fischer, 1982, chapter 16.

39 Wilbur Zelinsky and Barrett A. Lee, "Heterolocalism: An Alternative Model of the Sociospatial Behaviour of Immigrant Ethnic Communities," *International Journal of Population Geography* 4, (1998): 281–298.

40 Raymond Breton, "Institutional Completeness of Ethnic Communities and the Personal Relations of Immigrants," *American Journal of Sociology* 70, (1964): 193–205; Peter J. Venturelli, "Institutions in an Ethnic District," *Human Organization* 41, (1982): 26–35; Sheldon Goldenberg and Valerie A. Haines, "Social Networks and Institutional Completeness: From Territory to Ties," *Canadian Journal of Sociology* 17, (1992): 301–312.

41 Fredrik Barth, "Introduction," in Fredrik Barth, ed., *Ethnic Groups and Boundaries: The Social Organization of Culture Difference* (Boston: Little, Brown, and Company, 1969) 9–38; J. T. Borhek, "Ethnic-Group Cohesion," *American Journal of Sociology* 76, (1970): 33–46; Leo Dreidger, "Ethnic Boundaries: A Comparison of Two Urban Neighborhoods," *Sociology and Social Research* 62, (1978): 193–211; Leo Dreidger, "Maintenance of Urban Ethnic Boundaries: The French in St. Boniface," *Sociological Quarterly* 20, (1979): 89–108; Leo Dreidger, "Jewish Identity: The Maintenance of Urban Religious and Ethnic Boundaries," *Ethnic and Racial Studies* 3, (1980): 67–88.

42 John S. MacDonald and Leatrice D. MacDonald, "Chain Migration, Ethnic Neighborhood Formation, and Social Networks," *Milbank Memorial Fund Quarterly* 42, (1964): 82–97; Martin T. Katzman, "Opportunity, Subculture, and the Economic Performance of Urban Ethnic Groups," *American Journal of Economics and Sociology* 28, (1969): 351–366; Margaret Greico, "Transported Lives: Urban Social Networks and Labour Circulation," in Alisdair Rogers and Steven Vertovec, eds., *The Urban Context: Ethnicity, Social Networks, and Situational Analysis* (Washington, DC: Berg Publishers, 1995); Siu-lun Wong and Janet W. Salaff, "Network Capital: Emigration from Hong Kong," *British Journal of Sociology* 49, (1998): 358–374; Roger Waldinger, "Network, Bureaucracy, and Exclusion: Recruitment and Selection in an Immigrant Metropolis," in Frank D. Bean and Stephanie Bell-Rose, eds., *Immigration and Opportunity: Race, Ethnicity, and Employment in the United States* (New York: Russell Sage Foundation, 1999) 228–259; Maritsa V. Poros, "The Role of Migrant Networks in Linking Local Labour Markets: The Case of Asian Indian Migration to New York and London," *Global Networks* 1, (2001): 243–259; David L. Brown, "Migration and Community: Social Networks in a Multilevel World," *Rural Sociology* 67, (2002): 1–23; Arent Greve and Janet W. Salaff, "Social Network Approach to Understand the Ethnic Economy: A Theoretical Discourse," *Geojournal* 64, (2005): 7–16; Louise Ryan, Rosemary Sales, Mary Tilki, and Bernadetta Siara, "Social Networks, Social Support, and Social Capital: The Experiences of Recent Polish Migrants in London," *Sociology* 42, (2008): 672–690.

43 For a discussion of the broad range of ethnic communities in the United States, see: Jan Lin, *The Power of Urban Ethnic Places: Cultural Heritage and Community Life* (New York: Routledge, 2010). For discussions of social networks in ethnic communities outside the United States, see: Muhammed Anwar, "Social Networks of Pakastanis in the UK: A Re-evaluation," in Alisdair Rogers and Steven Vertovic, eds., *The Urban Context: Ethnicity, Social Networks, and Situational Analysis* (Washington, DC: Berg Publishers, 1995) 237–257; Eric Fong, ed., *Inside the Mosaic* (Toronto: University of Toronto Press, 2006); Mohammed Qadeer and Sandeep Kumar, "Ethnic Enclaves and Social Cohesion," *Canadian Journal of Urban Research* 15, (2006): 1–17; Maritsa Poros, *Modern Migrations: Gujarati Indian Networks in New York and London* (Palo Alto, CA: Stanford University Press, 2010).

44 Timothy Dunnigan, "Segmentary Kinship in an Urban Society: The Hmong of St. Paul-Minneapolis," *Anthropological Quarterly* 55, (1982): 126–134.

45 Coleman, 1988; Steven J. Gold, "Patterns of Economic Cooperation among Israeli Immigrants in Los Angeles," *International Migration Review* 28, (1994): 114–135; Steven J. Gold, "Gender, Class, and Network: Social Structure and Migration Patterns Among Transnational Isrealis," *Global Networks* 1, (2001): 19–40; Rhonda F. Levine, *Class, Networks, and Identity: Replanting Jewish Lives from Nazi Germany to Rural New York* (Lanham, MD: Rowman and Littlefield Publishers, 2001); Naama Sabar, "Kibbutz, L.A.: A Paradoxical Social Network," *Journal of Contemporary Ethnography* 31, (2002): 68–94.

46 Lomnitz 1977; Susan Wierzbicki, *Beyond the Immigrant Enclave: Network Change and Assimilation* (New York: LFB Scholarly Publishing, 2004).

47 T. S. Eliot, *Notes Towards a Definition of Culture* (London: Faber and Faber, 1948) 50; Eric Fong and Wsevolod W. Isajiw, "Determinants of Friendship Choices in Multiethnic Society," *Sociological Forum* 15, (2000): 249–271; Marilyn Fernandez and Laura Nichols, "Bridging and Bonding Capital: Pluralist Ethnic Relations in Silicon Valley," *International Journal of Sociology and Social Policy* 22, (2002): 104–122; Anthony M. Orum, "Circles of Influence and Chains of Command: The Social Processes Whereby Ethnic Communities Influence Host Societies," *Social Forces* 84, (2005): 921–939.

4 Politics: We Don't Want Nobody Nobody Sent

1   Lincoln Steffens, *The Autobiography of Lincoln Steffens* (New York: Harcourt, Brace, World, 1931) 403.

2   Milton L. Rakove, ed., *We Don't Want Nobody Nobody Sent: An Oral History of the Daley Years* (Bloomington, IN: Indiana University Press, 1979) 318. In 1948, Paul Douglas ran for the U.S. Senate and Adlai Stevenston for Governor of Illinois; both won.

3   For a comprehensive discussion of political networks, see David Knoke, *Political Networks: The Structural Perspective* (New York: Cambridge University Press, 1990).

4   Karl Marx and Friedrich Engels, *The Communist Manifesto* (London: Verso, [1848] 1998) 34.

5   Robert S. Lynd and Helen Merrell Lynd, *Middletown in Transition: A Study in Cultural Conflicts* (New York: Harcourt, Brace and Company, 1937) 74. Middletown was a pseudonym for Muncie, Indiana, and Family X was a pseudonym for the Ball Family, who owned the Ball Glass Works famous for making glass canning jars.

6   C. Wright Mills, *The Power Elite* (New York: Oxford University Press, 1956).

7   John T. Salter, *Boss Rule* (New York: Whittlesay House, 1935); August B. Hollingshead, *Elmtown's Youth* (New York: John Wiley, 1949).

8   Leanne Atwater, Robert Penn, and Linda Rucker, "Personal Qualities of Charismatic Leaders," *Leadership and Organization Development Journal* 12, (1993): 7–10; Michael D. Mumford et al., "Patterns of Leader Characteristics: Implications for Performance and Development," *The Leadership Quarterly* 11, (2000): 115–133; Timothy A. Judge, Joyce E. Bono, Remus Ilies, and Megan W. Gerhardt, "Personality and Leadership: A Qualitative and Quantitative Review," *Journal of Applied Psychology* 87, (2002): 765–780. While power and influence may not be personal traits but rather the result of position in a network, when certain individuals are perceived as having leadership ability, this can affect the structure of the network; see: John M. Bolland, "Perceived Leadership Stability and the Structure of Urban Agenda-Setting Networks," *Social Networks* 7, (1985): 153–172.

9   Frank A. Stewart, "A Sociometric Study of Influence in Southtown," *Sociometry* 10, (1947): 11–31; Frank A. Stewart, "A Study of Influence in Southtown: II," *Sociometry* 10, (1947): 273–286; Robert K. Merton, "Patterns of Influence: A Study of Interpersonal Influence and of Communication Behavior in a Local Community," in Paul F. Lazarsfeld and Frank Stanton, eds., *Communications Research, 1948–49* (New York: Harper and Brothers, 1950); Robert O. Schulze and Leonard U. Blumberg, "The Determination of Local Power Elites," *American Journal of Sociology* 63, (1957): 290–296.

10 Proponents of the reputational approach defended it, arguing that while it did not directly measure individuals' involvement in community decision making, it nonetheless mirrored their level of involvement. For a discussion of the critiques of the reputational approach, see: Herbert Kaufman and Victor Jones, "The Mystery of Power," *Public Administration Review* 14, (1954): 205–212; Robert A. Dahl, "A Critique of the Ruling Elite Model," *American Political Science Review* 52, (1958): 463–469; Nelson W. Polsby, "Three Problems in the Analysis of Community Power," *American Sociological Review* 24, (1959): 796–803. For responses to the critiques, see: William V. D'Antonio and Eugene C. Erickson, "The Reputational Technique as a Measure of Community Power: An Evaluation Based on Comparative and Longitudinal Studies," *American Sociological Review* 27, (1962): 362–376; William A. Gamson, "Reputation and Resources in Community Politics," *American Journal of Sociology* 72, (1966): 121–131.

11 Floyd Hunter, *Community Power Structures: A Study of Decision Makers* (Chapel Hill, NC: University of North Carolina Press, 1953) 68. For similar reputational influence networks, see: Delbert C. Miller, "Decision-Making Cliques in Community Power Structures," *American Journal of Sociology* 64, (1958): 302; Charles M. Bonjean, "Community Leadership: A Case Study and Conceptual Refinement," *American Journal of Sociology* 68, (1963): 677.

12 Richard D. Alba and Gwen Moore, "Elite Social Circles," *Sociological Methods and Research* 7, (1987): 167–188.

13 Nelson W. Polsby, "How To Study Community Power: The Pluralist Alternative," *Journal of Politics* 22, (1960): 474–484; Raymond E. Wolfinger, "Reputation and Reality in the Study of 'Community

Power'," *American Sociological Review* 25, (1960): 636–644; Robert A. Dahl, *Who Governs? Democracy and Power in an American City* (New Haven, CT: Yale University Press, 1961); Terry N. Clark, "Community Structure, Decision-Making, Budget Expenditures, and Urban Renewal in 51 American Communities," *American Sociological Review* 33, (1968): 576–593.

14 Thomas J. Anton, "Power, Pluralism, and Local Politics," *Administrative Science Quarterly* 7, (1963): 425–457; John Walton, "Discipline, Method, and Community Power: A Note on the Sociology of Knowledge," *American Sociological Review* 31, (1966): 684–689; John Walton, "Substance and Artifact: The Current Status of Research on Community Power Structure," *American Journal of Sociology* 71, (1966): 430–438.

15 Peter H. Rossi, "Power and Community Structure," *Midwest Journal of Political Science* 4, (1960): 390–401; Michael Aiken, "The Distribution of Community Power: Structural Bases and Social Consequences," in Michael Aiken and Paul E. Mott, eds., *The Structure of Community Power* (New York: Random House, 1970).

16 Charles Kadushin, "Power, Influence, and Social Circles: A New Methodology for Studying Opinion Makers," *American Sociological Review* 33, (1968): 685–699; G. William Domhoff, "Methodology of Power Structure Research" in G. William Domhoff, *Who Really Rules? New Haven and Community Power Reexamined* (New Brunswick, NJ: Transaction Books, 1978); David Knoke, "Networks of Elite Structure and Decision Making," *Sociological Methods and Research* 22, (1993): 23–45. Some have suggested that even combining these various network-based approaches still misses the role of business groups in urban politics. They recommend focusing not on networks of reputation or decision making, but rather on businesses' economic dominance and their ability to move to another city. See: Harvey Molotch, "The City as a Growth Machine: Toward a Political Economy of Place," *American Journal of Sociology* 82, (1976): 309–332; Roger Friedland and Donald Palmer, "Park Place and Main Street: Business and the Urban Power Structure," *Annual Review of Sociology* 10, (1984): 393–416.

17 Linton C. Freeman, Thomas J. Fararo, Warner Bloomberg, Jr., and Morris H. Sunshine, "Locating Leaders in Local Communities: A Comparison of Some Alternative Approaches," *American Sociological Review* 28, (1963): 791–798.

18 Norton E. Long, "The Local Community as an Ecology of Games," *American Journal of Sociology* 64, (1958): 251–261; Orrin E. Klapp and L. Vincent Padgett, "Power Structure and Decision-Making in a Mexican Border City," *American Journal of Sociology* 65, (1960): 400–406; Benjamin Cornwell, Timothy J Curry, and Kent P. Schwirian, "Revisiting Norton Long's Ecology of Games: A Network Approach," *City and Community* 2, (2003): 121–142.

19 Emerson 1976; Cook and Whitmeyer 1992.

20 Foster 1961.

21 Jeremy Boissevain, "Patronage in Sicily," *Man* 1, (1966): 18–33; Jeremy Boissevain, "Poverty and Politics in a Sicilian Agro-Town," *International Archive of Ethnography* 50, (1966): 198–236; Lomnitz, 1977; Larissa Lomnitz, "Horizontal and Vertical Relations and the Social Structure of Urban Mexico," *Latin American Research Review* 17, (1982): 51–74.

22 William Kornblum, *Blue Collar Community* (Chicago, IL: University of Chicago Press, 1974); Milton L. Rakove, *Don't Make No Waves-Don't Back No Losers* (Bloomington, IN: Indiana University Press, 1976); Thomas Guterbock, *Machine Politics in Transition: Party and Community in Chicago* (Chicago, IL: University of Chicago Press, 1980).

23 The patronage system that drove Chicago politics for much of the twentieth century was prohibited by a series of decrees that followed a federal civil lawsuit, *Michael L. Shakman, et al. v. Democratic Organization of Cook County, et al.* Following allegations that the patronage system continued, in 2005 the court appointed a monitor to ensure compliance. Some have questioned whether Mayor Richard M. Daley (1989–2011), Richard J. Daley's son, benefitted from the same patron–client system. See: Dick Simpson and Tom M. Kelly, "The New Chicago School of Urbanism and the New Daley Machine," *Urban Affairs Review* 44, (2008): 218–238.

24 Edward O. Laumann and Franz U. Pappi, "New Directions in the Study of Community Elites," *American Sociological Review* 38, (1973): 212–230; Edward O. Laumann and Franz U. Pappi, *Networks*

of Collective Action: A Perspective on Community Influence Systems (New York: Academic Press, 1976); Edward O. Laumann, Peter V. Marsden, and Joseph Galaskiewicz, "Community-Elite Influence Structures: Extension of a Network Approach," *American Journal of Sociology* 83, (1977): 594–631; Peter V. Marsden and Edward O. Laumann, "Collective Action in a Community Elite: Exchange, Influence Resources, and Issue Resolution," in Roland J. Liebert and Allen W. Imershein, eds., *Power, Paradigms, and Community Research* (Beverly Hills, CA: Sage Publications, 1977); Edward O. Laumann and Peter V. Marsden, "The Analysis of Oppositional Structures in Political Elites: Identifying Collective Actors," *American Sociological Review* 44, (1979): 713–732; Franz U. Pappi, "Boundary Specification and Structural Models of Elite Systems: Social Circles Revisited," *Social Networks* 6, (1984): 79–95; Knoke, 1990. In these studies, Altneustadt was used as a pseudonym for the town of Jürlich.

25   Robert A. Caro, *The Power Broker: Robert Moses and the Fall of New York* (New York: Knopf, 1974); Ronald S. Burt, "Positions in Multiple Network Systems, Part Two: Stratification and Prestige among Elite Decision-Makers in the Community of Altneustadt," *Social Forces* 56, (1977): 551–575; Manuel L. Carlos and Bo Anderson, "Political Brokerage and Network Politics in Mexico: The Case of a Dominance System," in David Willer and Bo Anderson, eds., *Networks, Exchange, and Coercion* (New York: Elsevier, 1981); Lomnitz, 1982; Roger V. Gould, "Power and Social Structure in Community Elites," *Social Forces* 68, (1989): 531–552; Roger V. Gould and Roberto M. Fernandez, "Structures of Mediation: A Formal Approach to Brokerage in Transaction Networks," *Sociological Methodology* 19, (1989): 89–126; John F. Padgett and Christopher K. Ansell, "Robust Action and the Rise of the Medici, 1400–1434," *American Journal of Sociology* 98, (1993): 1259–1319.

26   Hunter, 1953, 69–70.

27   Robert A. Dahl, "The Concept of Power," *Behavioral Science* 2, (1957): 201–215; John R. P. French, Jr. and Bertram Raven, "The Bases of Social Power," in Dorwin Cartwright, ed., *Studies in Social Power* (Ann Arbor, MI: University of Michigan, 1959); Peter Bachrach and Morton S. Baratz, "Two Faces of Power," *American Political Science Review* 56, (1962): 947–952; Richard M. Emerson, "Power-Dependence Relations," *American Sociological Review* 27, (1962): 31–41; Laumann and Pappi, 1976, chapter 11; Jennifer Watling Neal and Zachary Neal, "Power as a Structural Phenomenon," *American Journal of Community Psychology* 48, (2010): 157–167.

28   Neal and Neal, 2010; Zachary Neal, "Differentiating Centrality and Power in the World City Network," *Urban Studies* 48, (2011): 2733–2748.

29   L. David Brown and Lynda B. Detterman, "Small Interventions for Large Problems: Reshaping Urban Leadership Networks," *Journal of Applied Behavioral Science* 23, (1987): 151–168.

30   Anton Blok, "Coalitions in Sicilian Peasant Society," in Jeremy Boissevain and J. Clyde Mitchell, eds., *Network Analysis: Studies in Human Interaction* (The Hague: Mouton and Co., 1973) 151–166; D. G. Jongmans, "Politics on the Village Level," in Jeremy Boissevain and J. Clyde Mitchell, eds., *Network Analysis: Studies in Human Interaction* (The Hague: Mouton and Co., 1973) 167–218; H. U. E. Thoden van Velzen, "Coalitions and Network Analysis," in Jeremy Boissevain and J. Clyde Mitchell, eds., *Network Analysis: Studies in Human Interaction* (The Hague: Mouton and Co., 1973) 219–250.

31   Whyte, 1943, 115.

32   Dick Simpson and Tom Carsey, "Council Coalition and Mayoral Regimes in Chicago," *Journal of Urban Affairs* 21, (1999): 79–100.

33   Research on urban political regimes is vast, and does not always adopt a network perspective. For a more comprehensive discussion of regimes, see: Clarence N. Stone, *Regime Politics: Governing Atlanta, 1946–1988* (Lawrence, KS: University Press of Kansas, 1989); Keith Dowding, "Explaining Urban Regimes," *International Journal of Urban and Regional Research* 25, (2001): 7–19; Karen Mossberger and Gerry Stoker, "The Evolution of Urban Regime Theory: The Challenge of Conceptualization," *Urban Affairs Review* 36, (2001): 810–835.

34   Molotch, 1976; J. Allen Whitt, "Organizational Ties and Urban Growth," in Robert Perrucci and Harry R. Potter, eds., *Networks of Power: Organizational Actors at the National, Corporate, and Community Levels* (New York: Aldine de Gruyter, 1989) 97–109.

35   J. Allen Whitt, "Mozart in the Metropolis: The Arts Coalition and the Urban Growth Machine,"
      Urban Affairs Review 23, (1987): 15–36; Anne B. Shlay and Robert P. Giloth, "The Social
      Organization of a Land-Based Elite: The Case of the Failed Chicago 1992 World's Fair," *Journal of
      Urban Affairs* 9, (1987): 305–324; J. Allen Whitt and John C. Lammers, "The Art of Growth: Ties
      Between Development Organizations and the Performing Arts," *Urban Affairs Quarterly* 26, (1991):
      376–393.

36   Marion E. Orr and Gerry Stoker, "Urban Regimes and Leadership in Detroit," *Urban Affairs Review*
      30, (1994): 48–73; Clarence N. Stone, "The Atlanta Experience Re-examined: The Link Between
      Agenda and Regime Change," *International Journal of Urban and Regional Research* 25, (2001): 20–34.
      Some have suggested that political coalitions in U.K. cities are different from the regimes found in
      U.S. cities. Because the linkages between their members are more formalized and bureaucratic, the
      coalitions are more stable, but also are less likely to be effective in achieving outcomes; see: Jonathan
      S. Davies, "Partnerships Versus Regimes: Why Regime Theory Cannot Explain Urban Coalitions
      in the UK," *Journal of Urban Affairs* 25, (2003): 253–269.

37   Joseph Galaskiewicz, "Interorganizational Networks Mobilizing Action at the Metropolitan Level,"
      in Robert Perrucci and Harry R. Potter, eds., *Networks of Power: Organizational Actors at the National,
      Corporate, and Community Levels* (New York: Aldine de Gruyter, 1989) 81–96.

38   Robert Perrucci and Marc Pilisuk, "Leaders and Ruling Elite: The Interorganizational Bases of
      Community Power," *American Sociological Review* 35, (1970): 1040–1057; G. William Domhoff, "Social
      Clubs, Policy-Planning Groups, and Corporations: A Network Study of Ruling Class Cohesiveness,"
      Critical Sociology 5, (1975): 173–184; Edmund M. McLaughlin, "The Power Network in Phoenix:
      An Application of Smallest Space Analysis," *Critical Sociology* 5, (1975): 185–195; Agnes Koch and
      Sanford Labovitz, "Interorganizational Power in a Canadian Community: A Replication," *Sociological
      Quarterly* 17, (1976): 3–15; Laumann and Pappi, 1976, chapter 10; Richard E. Ratcliff, Mary Elizabeth
      Gallagher, and Kathryn Strother Ratcliff, "The Civic Involvement of Bankers: An Analysis of the
      Influence of Economic Power and Social Prominence in the Command of Civic Policy Positions,"
      Social Problems 26, (1979): 298–313; Richard E. Ratcliff, "Banks and Corporate Lending: An Analysis
      of the Impact of the Internal Structure of the Capitalist Class on the Lending Behavior of Banks,"
      American Sociological Review 45, (1980): 553–570; Robert Perrucci and Bonnie L. Lewis,
      "Interorganizational Relations and Community Influence Structure: A Replication and Extension,"
      Sociological Quarterly 30, (1989): 205–223.

39   John M. Bolland and Debra Moehle McCallum, "Neighboring and Community Mobilization in
      High-Poverty Inner-City Neighborhoods," *Urban Affairs Review* 38, (2002): 42–69; Scott D.
      McClurg, "Social Networks and Political Participation: The Role of Social Interaction in Explaining
      Political Participation," *Political Research Quarterly* 56, (2003): 449–464; Herman Lilieveldt, "Helping
      Citizens Help Themselves: Neighborhood Improvement Programs and the Impact of Social Networks,
      Trust, and Norms on Neighborhood-Oriented Forms of Participation," *Urban Affairs Review* 39,
      (2004): 531–551.

40   Pamela Oliver, "'If You Don't Do It, Nobody Else Will': Active and Token Contributors to Local
      Collective Action," *American Sociological Review* 49, (1984): 601–610; Avery M. Guest and R. S.
      Oropesa, "Informal Social Ties and Political Activity in the Metropolis," *Urban Affairs Review* 21,
      (1986): 550–574; Mike Savage, Gindo Tampubolon, and Alan Warde, "Political Participation, Social
      Networks, and the City," in Talja Blokland and Mike Savage, eds., *Networked Urbanism: Social Capital
      in the City* (Burlington, VT: Ashgate, 2008) 171–196.

41   Ronald S. Burt, "Cohesion Versus Structural Equivalence as a Basis for Network Subgroups,"
      Sociological Methods and Research 7, (1978): 189–212; Ronald S. Burt, "Social Contagion and
      Innovation: Cohesion Versus Structural Equivalence," *American Journal of Sociology* 92, (1987):
      1287–1335; Jennifer Watling Neal, Zachary Neal, Marc S. Atkins, David B. Henry, and Stacy L.
      Frazier, "Channels of Change: Contrasting Network Mechanisms in the Use of Interventions,"
      American Journal of Community Psychology 47, (2011): 277–286.

42   Matthew A. Crenson, "Social Networks and Political Processes in Urban Neighborhoods," *American
      Journal of Political Science* 22, (1978): 578–594; Guest and Oropesa, 1986.

43 Jacobs, 1993, 176.

44 Liu and Duff, 1972; Granovetter, 1973; Susan D. Greenbaum, "Bridging Ties at the Neighborhood Level," *Social Networks* 4, (1982): 367–384.

45 Simon Batterbury, "Environmental Action and Social Networks: Campaigning for Bicycles and Alternative Transport in West London," *Annals of the American Academy of Political and Social Science* 590, (2003): 150–169; Ronit Shemtov, "Social Networks and Sustained Activism in Local NIMBY Campaigns," *Sociological Forum* 18, (2003): 215–244; Gould, 1995.

46 Although discussions of social capital are nearly a century old, the individual form of social capital is often traced to the work of James Coleman (1988), while the community form is often traced to the work of Robert Putnam (2000). For a discussion of the distinction between these two forms, see: Alejandro Portes, "The Two Meanings of Social Capital," *Sociological Forum* 15, (2000): 1–12; Dietland Stolle and Marc Hooghe, "Conflicting Approaches to the Study of Social Capital: Competing Explanations for Causes and Effects of Social Capital," *Ethical Perspectives* 10, (2003): 22–45; Joonmo Son and Nan Lin, "Social Capital and Civic Action: A Network-Based Approach," *Social Science Research* 37, (2008): 330–349.

47 Jacobs, 1993; Oddvar Skjaeveland and Tommy Garling, "Effects of Interactional Space on Neighboring," *Journal of Environmental Psychology* 17, (1997): 181–198; Frances E. Kuo, William C. Sullivan, Rebekah Levine Coley, and Liesette Brunson, "Fertile Ground for Community: Inner-City Neighborhood Common Spaces," *American Journal of Community Psychology* 26, (1998): 823–851.

48 For several examples of the political forces involved in constructing large-scale technical networks, see: Richard E. Hanley, *Moving People, Goods, and Information in the 21st Century: The Cutting-Edge Infrastructures of Networked Cities* (New York: Routledge, 2004) Part III.

49 Joel A. Tarr, "The Municipal Telegraph Network: Origins of the Fire and Police Alarm Systems in American Cities," *Flux* 9, (1992): 5–18.

50 Lorraine Dominique, "The Regulation of Urban Technical Networks (Theories and Pending Issues)," *Flux* 21, (1995): 47–59; Stephen Graham and Simon Marvin, *Splintering Urbanism: Networked Infrastructures, Technological Mobilities, and the Urban Condition* (New York: Routledge, 2001). It is here that the type of networks considered in this book are most closely connected to 'actor–networks.' A researcher adopting an actor–network approach to study ISPs might seek to understand how human actors such as providers and consumers, as well as non-human actors such as regulatory laws or computers, influence one another and together produce a particular kind of internet network. In contrast, this book is more concerned with patterns in, for example, the actual network of interactions among consumers in cities or the actual network of cables running through the city.

51 Bernard Barraqué, "Not Too Much But Not Too Little: The Sustainability of Urban Water Services in New York, Paris, and Delhi," in Olivier Coutard, Richard E. Hanley, and Rae Zimmerman, eds., *Sustaining Urban Networks: The Social Diffusion of Large Technical Systems* (New York: Routledge, 2005) 188–202; Marie Llorente, "Reforming the Municipal Water Supply Service in Delhi: Institutional and Organizational Issues," in Olivier Coutard, Richard E. Hanley, and Rae Zimmerman, eds., *Sustaining Urban Networks: The Social Diffusion of Large Technical Systems* (New York: Routledge, 2005) 172–188; Graciela Schneier-Madanes, "Conflicts and the Rise of Users' Participation in the Buenos Aires Water Supply Concession, 1993–2003," in Olivier Coutard, Richard E. Hanley, and Rae Zimmerman, eds., *Sustaining Urban Networks: The Social Diffusion of Large Technical Systems* (New York: Routledge, 2005) 151–171; Gabriel Dupuy, *Urban Networks-Network Urbanism* (Amsterdam: Techne Press, 2008) chapter 7.

52 Ana Maria Fernández-Maldonado, "The Diffusion of Information and Communication Technologies in Lower-Income Groups: *Cabinas De Internet* in Lima, Peru," in Olivier Coutard, Richard E. Hanley, and Rae Zimmerman, eds., *Sustaining Urban Networks: The Social Diffusion of Large Technical Systems* (New York: Routledge, 2005) 117–134; Stephen Graham and Simon Guy, "'Internetting' Downtown San Francisco: Digital Space Meets Urban Space," in Olivier Coutard, Richard E. Hanley, and Rae Zimmerman, eds., *Sustaining Urban Networks: The Social Diffusion of Large Technical Systems* (New York: Routledge, 2005) 32–47; Dupuy, 2008, chapters 13 and 14.

53   Lewis Mumford, "The Highway and the City," in Lewis Mumford, ed., *The Urban Prospect* (New York: Harcourt, Brace, & World, 1968) 92–107; Dupuy, 2008, chapter 6; Agnes Sander, "Building Development in the 19th Century: Between Planning Procedures and Local Action," in Géraldine Pflieger, Luca Pattaroni, Chrisophe Jemelin, and Vincent Kaufmann, eds., *The Social Fabric of the Networked City* (Oxford: Routledge, 2008) 109–130.

54   Vincent Kaufmann, Marie-Paule Thomas, Luca Pattaroni, and Jerome Chenal, "Public Space Management and Public Transport Quality-Vectors of Gentrification: Six Parisian Case Studies," in Géraldine Pflieger, Luca Pattaroni, Chrisophe Jemelin, and Vincent Kaufmann, eds., *The Social Fabric of the Networked City* (Oxford: Routledge, 2008) 67–88; Fritz Sager, "Planning, Power, and Policy Change in the Networked City: The Politics of a New Tramway in the City of Bern," in Géraldine Pflieger, Luca Pattaroni, Chrisophe Jemelin, and Vincent Kaufmann, eds., *The Social Fabric of the Networked City* (Oxford: Routledge, 2008) 169–186.

55   Andrew R. Goetz and Christopher J. Sutton, "The Geography of Deregulation in the U.S. Airline Industry," *Annals of the Association of American Geographers* 87, (1997): 238–263; John Bowen, "Network Change, Deregulation, and Access in the Global Airline Industry," *Economic Geography* 78, (2002): 425–439.

5 Form: Getting from Here to There

1   Euler initially presented his findings to the St. Petersburg Academy in 1735, but they were not published until 1741; see: Euler 1741.

2   Joel A. Tarr and Gabriel Dupuy, eds., *Technology and the Rise of the Networked City in Europe and America* (Philadelphia, PA: Temple University Press, 1988); Richard E. Schuler, "Transportation and Telecommunications Networks: Planning Urban Infrastructure for the 21st Century," *Urban Studies* 29, (1992): 297–310; Ricardo Toledo Silva, "The Connectivity of Infrastructure Networks and the Urban Space of São Paulo in the 1990s," *International Journal of Urban and Regional Research* 24, (2000): 139–164; Hanley 2004; Christian Kühnert, Dirk Helbing, and Geoffrey B. West, "Scaling Laws in Urban Supply Networks," *Physica A* 363, (2006): 96–103.

3   Joachim Bering (1613); Euler, 1741.

4   B. Antrim Haldeman, "The Street Layout," *Annals of the American Academy of Political and Social Science* 51, (1914): 182–191; Charles Mulford Robinson, "The Sociology of a Street Layout," *Annals of the American Academy of Political Science* 51, (1914): 192–199.

5   Pierre Bélanger, "Underground Landscape: The Urbanism and Infrastructure of Toronto's Downtown Pedestrian Network," *Tunnelling and Underground Space Technology* 22, (2007): 272–292.

6   Hans Blumenfeld, "Theory of City Form, Past and Present," *Journal of the Society of Architectural Historians* 8, (1949): 7–16; Michael Southworth and Peter M. Owens, "The Evolving Metropolis: Studies of Community, Neighborhood, and Street Form at the Urban Edge," *Journal of the American Planning Association* 59, (1993): 271–287; Yasushi Asami, Asye Sema Kubat, and Cihangir Istek, "Characterization of the Street Networks in the Traditional Turkish Urban Form," *Environment and Planning B* 28, (2001): 777–795; Stephen Marshall, *Streets and Patterns* (New York: Spon Press, 2005) chapter 4.

7   These street networks not only shape urban form and the modern urban experience, but also play a role in artistic depictions of the city: In Charles Dickens' *A Christmas Carol*, Bob Cratchit slides down Cornhill twenty times "in honour of its being Christmas Eve."

8   Georg Braun, *Civitates Orbis Terrarum* (Cologne, 1598) 68; John Rocque, *A Plan of the Cities of London and Westminster, and Borough of Southwark; with Contiguous Buildings* (London, 1746) E2; Pierre Charles L'Enfant, *Plan of the City of Washington* (Philadelphia, PA: Thackara and Vallance, 1792).

9   Kevin Lynch, *The Image of the City* (Cambridge, MA: MIT Press, 1960) 2.

10   Lynch, 1960, chapter 3. It is important to note that Lynch did not use the terms 'node' and 'edge' in exactly the same way as they are used in formal network analysis. For example, in network analysis an edge is a connection between two nodes, while for Lynch it is the boundary of a specific region.

Others have proposed slightly different, but related, lists of elements. For example, adopting a more mathematical approach, Salingaros focuses on three elements: nodes, connections, and hierarchy; see Nikos A. Salingaros, "Theory of the Urban Web," *Journal of Urban Design* 3, (1998): 53–71.

11 Donald Appleyard, "Styles and Methods of Structuring a City," *Environment and Behavior* 2, (1970): 100–117; D. C. D. Pocock, "Some Characteristics of Mental Maps: An Empirical Study," *Transactions of the Institute of British Geographers* 1, (1976): 493–512.

12 Peter Gould and Rodney White, *Mental Maps* (New York: Penguin Books, 1974); D. C. D. Pocock, "City of the Mind: A Review of Mental Maps," *Scottish Geographical Magazine* 88, (1976): 115–124; Robin M Haynes, *Geographical Images and Mental Maps* (London: Macmillan Education, 1980).

13 Marshall, 2005, chapter 5; Sergio Porta, Paolo Crucitti, and Vita Latora, "The Network Analysis of Urban Streets: A Primal Approach," *Environment and Planning B* 33, (2006): 705–725; Sergio Porta, Paolo Crucitti, and Vita Latora, "The Network Analysis of Urban Streets: A Dual Approach," *Physica A* 369, (2006): 853–866. For a more comprehensive, but also more technical, discussion of spatial networks, see: Marc Barthélemy, "Spatial Networks," *arXiv:* 1010.0302v2 [cond-mat.stat-mech].

14 A wide range of methods have been developed for the analysis of street networks, many of which rely on complex mathematical techniques that go beyond the scope of this book. For a detailed discussion, see: Philippe Blanchard and Dimitri Volchenkov, *Mathematical Analysis of Urban Spatial Networks* (Heidelberg: Springer-Verlag, 2009).

15 Space syntax is a well-developed theory and methodology for the analysis of urban space, but it has developed largely independent of the network theories and methods discussed throughout this book. As a result, the discussion of space syntax here is very brief. For extended discussions of this approach, see: Bill Hillier and Julienne Hanson, *The Social Logic of Space* (New York: Cambridge University Press, 1984); Bill Hillier, *Space is the Machine: A Configurational Theory of Architecture* (New York: Cambridge University Press, 1996).

16 B. Jiang and C. Claramunt, "A Structural Approach to the Model Generalization of an Urban Street Network," *GeoInformatica* 8, (2004): 157–171.

17 Bin Jiang and Cristophe Claramunt, "Topological Analysis of Urban Street Networks," *Environment and Planning B* 31, (2004): 151–162; Bin Jiang, "A Topological Pattern of Urban Street Networks: Universality and Peculiarity," *Physica A* 384, (2007): 647–655; Porta, Crucitti, and Latora, 2006.

18 In a valued network where some linkages between pairs of nodes are stronger than others, a similar measure called flow betweenness should be used instead. In UCINET: Network → Centrality → Flow Betweenness.

19 Linton C. Freeman, "Centrality in Social Networks: Conceptual Clarification," *Social Networks* 1, (1978/79): 215–239. Each of these measures of centrality depend on the size of the network. The centrality scores will be higher in large networks, and lower in small networks. Thus, when comparing the centrality of nodes in different size networks, it is necessary to first adjust or normalize the scores based on network size.

20 In practice, such decisions involve a whole range of professionals with different skills, including urban planners but also civil engineers and construction managers.

21 Dan Stanislawski, "The Origin and Spread of the Grid-Pattern Town," *Geographical Review* 36, (1946): 105–120; Blumenfeld, 1949; Spiro Kostof, *The City Shaped: Urban Patterns and Meanings Through History* (London: Thames and Hudson, 1991).

22 Horacio Samaniego and Melanie E. Moses, "Cities as Organisms: Allometric Scaling of Urban Road Networks," *Journal of Transport and Land Use* 1, (2008): 21–39; Mark A. Changizi and Marc Destefano, "Common Scaling Laws for City Highway Systems and the Mammalian Neocortex," *Complexity* 15, (2010): 11–18.

23 Adrian Bejan, "Street Network Theory of Organization in Nature," *Journal of Advanced Transportation* 30, (1996): 85–107; Geoffrey B. West, James H. Brown, and Brian J. Enquist, "A General Model for the Origin of Allometric Scaling Laws in Biology," *Science* 276, (1997): 122–126; Jayanth R. Banavar, Amos Maritan, and Andrea Rinaldo, "Size and Form in Efficient Transportation Networks," *Nature* 399, (1999): 130–132.

24 Serge Thibault, "The Morphology and Growth of Urban Technical Networks: A Fractal Approach," *Flux* 19, (1995): 17–30; J. Buhl et al., "Topological Patterns in Street Networks of Self-Organized Urban Settlements," *European Physical Journal B* 49, (2006): 513–522; Michael Batty, "Polynucleated Urban Landscapes," *Urban Studies* 38, (2001): 635–655; A. P. Masucci, D. Smith, A. Crooks, and M. Batty, "Random Planar Graphs and the London Street Network," *European Physical Journal B* 71, (2009): 259–271.

25 Ravindra K. Ahuja, James B. Orlin, Stefano Pallottino, and Maria Grazia Scutella, "Minimum Time and Minimum Cost-Path Problems in Street Networks with Periodic Traffic Lights," *Transportation Science* 36, (2002): 326–336; Ennio Cascetta, Francesco Russo, Francesco A. Viola, and Antonio Vitetta, "A Model of Route Perception in Urban Road Networks," *Transportation Research Part B* 36, (2002): 577–592; Christophe Claramunt and Stephan Winter, "Structural Salience of Elements of the City," *Environment and Planning B* 34, (2007): 1030–1050; Martin Tomko, Stephen Winter, and Christophe Claramunt, "Experiential Hierarchies of Streets," *Computers, Environment, and Urban Systems* 32, (2008): 41–52.

26 Pierre-Henry Derycke, "Urban Concentration and Road Networks: Two Approaches to Congestion," *Flux* 5, (1991): 35–45 and *Flux* 7, (1992): 41–54; A. J. Nicholson, "Road Network Unreliability: Impact Assessment and Mitigation," *International Journal of Critical Infrastructures* 3, (2007): 346–375; Bin Jiang, "Flow Dimension and Capacity for Structuring Urban Street Networks," *Physica A* 387, (2008): 4440–4452.

27 Kevin M. Curtin, "Network Analysis in Geographic Information Science: Review, Assessment, and Projections," *Geography and Geographic Information Science* 34, (2007): 103–111.

28 Jan Gehl, *Life Between Buildings* (New York: Van Nostrand Reinhold, 1987); Christopher Alexander, Hajo Neis, Artemis Anninou, and Ingrid King, *A New Theory of Urban Design* (New York: Oxford University Press, 1987); Salingaros, 1998.

29 Schuler 1992; Stephen Graham, "Constructing Premium Network Spaces: Reflections on Infrastructure Networks and Contemporary Urban Development," *International Journal of Urban and Regional Research* 24, (2000): 183–200; Silva 2000; Graham and Marvin, 2001; Dupuy, 2008, chapter 19.

30 Michael Leccese and Kathleen McCormick, eds., *Charter of the New Urbanism* (New York: McGraw Hill, 2000); Peter Calthorpe, "The Urban Network: A Radical Proposal," *Planning* 68, (2002): 10–15; Susan Handy, Robert G. Paterson, and Kent Butler, *Planning for Street Connectivity: Getting From Here to There* (Chicago, IL: American Planning Association, 2002).

31 From Digital Orthophoto Quadrangle files O3908201.NWS.940734 (1994) and O4008364.NES. 940719 (1995), *U. S. Geological Survey.*

32 Randall Crane, "On Form Versus Function: Will the New Urbanism Reduce Traffic, or Increase It?" *Journal of Planning Education and Research* 15, (1996): 117–126.

33 Robert Cervero and Carolyn Radisch, "Travel Choices in Pedestrian Versus Automobile Oriented Neighborhoods," *Transport Policy* 3, (1996): 127–141; Todd A. Randall and Brian W. Baetz, "Evaluating Pedestrian Connectivity for Suburban Sustainability," *Journal of Urban Planning and Development* 127, (2001): 1–15; Susan L Handy, Marlon G. Boarnet, Reid Ewing, and Richard E. Killingsworth, "How the Built Environment Affects Physical Activity: Views from Urban Planning," *American Journal of Preventative Medicine* 23, (2002): 64–73; Daniel A. Rodriguez, Asad J. Khattak, and Kelly R. Evenson, "Can New Urbanism Encourage Physical Activity? Comparing a New Urbanist Neighborhood with Conventional Suburbs," *Journal of the American Planning Association* 72, (2006): 43–54; Perver K. Baran, Daniel A. Rodriguez, and Asad J. Khattak, "Space Syntax and Walking in New Urbanist and Suburban Nieghborhoods," *Journal of Urban Design* 13, (2008): 5–28.

34 Emily Talen, "Sense of Community and Neighborhood Form: An Assessment of the Social Doctrine of New Urbanism," *Urban Studies* 36, (1999): 1361–1379; Emily Talen, "The Social Goals of New Urbanism," *Housing Policy Debate* 13, (2002): 165–188.

35 Moreno, 1943; Caplow and Forman, 1950; Leon Festinger, Stanley Schachter, and Kurt Black, *Social Pressures in Informal Groups: A Study of Human Factors in Housing* (New York: Harper and Brothers, 1950); Roger V. Gould, *Insurgent Identities* (Chicago: University of Chicago Press, 1995).

36   Paul M. Hess, "Measures of Connectivity," *Places* 11, (1997): 58–65.

37   Frederick P. Stutz, "Distance and Network Effects on Urban Social Travel Fields," *Economic Geography* 49, (1973): 134–144; Lance Freeman, "The Effects of Sprawl on Neighborhood Social Ties: An Exploratory Analysis," *Journal of the American Planning Association* 67, (2001): 69–77; A. Frei and K. W. Axhausen, "Size and Structure of Social Network Geographies," *Arbeitsberichte Verkehrs- und Raumplanung* 439, (2007); Hipp and Perrin, 2009.

38   Rick Grannis, *From the Ground Up: Translating Geography into Community Through Neighbor Networks* (Princeton, NJ: Princeton University Press, 2009).

39   Rick Grannis, "The Importance of Trivial Streets: Residential Streets and Residential Segregation," *American Journal of Sociology* 103, (1998): 1530–1564; Rick Grannis, "T-Communities: Pedestrian Street Networks and Residential Segregation in Chicago, Los Angeles, and New York," *City and Community* 4, (2005): 295–321.

40   Julia Nutter, Douglas W. Frisbie, and Carol Bevis, "Street Layout and Residential Burglary," presented at the *National Conference on Criminal Justice Evaluation*, Washington, D.C., 1977; Patricia L. Brantingham and Paul J. Brantingham, "Nodes, Paths, and Edges: Considerations on the Complexity of Crime and the Physical Environment," *Journal of Environmental Psychology* 13, (1993): 3–28; Daniel J. K. Beavon, P. L. Brantingham, and P. J. Brantingham, "The Influence of Street Networks on the Patterning of Property Offenses," in Ronald V. Clark, ed., *Crime Prevention Studies* (Monsey, NY: Criminal Justice Press, 1994) 115–148.

41   Ernest Burgess, "The Growth of the City: An Introduction to a Research Project," in Robert E. Park and Ernest W. Burgess, eds., *The City* (Chicago: University of Chicago Press, 1925) 47–62; William Alonso, *Location and Land Use: Toward a General Theory of Land Rent* (Cambridge, MA: Harvard University Press, 1964).

42   Kevin Lynch, "The Pattern of the Metropolis," *Daedalus* 90, (1961): 79–98; P. G. Hartwick and J. M. Hartwick, "An Analysis of an Urban Thoroughfare," *Environment and Planning A* 4, (1972): 193–204; Alex Anas and Leon N. Moses, "Mode Choice, Transport Structure, and Urban Land Use," *Journal of Urban Economics* 6, (1979): 228–246; Harry W. Richardson and Ardeshir Anjomani, "The Diamond City: The Case for Rectangular Grid Models," *Socio-Economic Planning Sciences* 15, (1981): 295–303; John Yinger, "Around the Block: Urban Models with a Street Grid," *Journal of Urban Economics* 33, (1993): 305–330.

43   Michael Dear, "Los Angeles and the Chicago School: Invitation to a Debate," *City and Community* 1, (2002): 5–32.

6 Function: Working Together

1   H. Brinton Milward, "Interorganizational Policy Systems and Research on Public Organizations," *Administration and Society* 13, (1982): 457–478.

2   Keith Dowding, "Model or Metaphor? A Critical Review of the Policy Network Approach," *Political Studies* 43, (1995): 136–158; Laurence J. O'Toole, "Treating Networks Seriously: Practical and Research-Based Agendas in Public Administration," *Public Administration Review* 57, (1997): 45–52; Myrna P. Mandell, "The Impact of Network Structures on Community-Building Efforts," in Myrna P. Mandell, ed., *Getting Results Through Collaboration: Networks and Network Structures for Public Policy and Management* (Westport, CT: Quorum Books, 2001) 129–153. For example, Mandell argues that "Network structures may be organized in a number of different ways . . . but it is not these structural differences that are important. Instead, it is a certain mindset . . . that is needed to operate effectively in a network structure" (p. 140). In contrast to this perspective, formal network analysis insists that structural differences are very important, and that 'mindset' is often a consequence of particular types of network structures.

3   In research on the role of interorganizational networks in generating public policy, the English scholars often adopt a metaphorical conception of networks, while German scholars use a more structural conception. For a comparison of these two approaches, see: Tanja A. Börzel, "Organizing Babylon-On the Different Conceptions of Policy Networks," *Public Administration* 76, (1998): 253–273.

4   H. Brinton Milward and Keith G. Provan, "Measuring Network Structure," *Public Administration* 76, (1998): 387–407.

5   For a more extended and comprehensive discussion of interorganizational networks and community development, see: Mulford 1984.

6   Carl Milofsky, "Neighborhood-Based Organizations: A Market Analogy," in Walter W. Powell, ed., *The Nonprofit Sector: A Research Handbook* (New Haven, CT: Yale University Press, 1987) 277–295.

7   Walter W. Powell, "Neither Market nor Hierarchy: Network Forms of Organization," *Research in Organizational Behavior* 12, (1990): 295–336.

8   Mark Granovetter, "Economic Action and Social Structure: The Problem of Embeddedness," *American Journal of Sociology* 91, (1985): 481–510.

9   Kimberley Roussin Isett and Keith G. Provan, "The Evolution of Dyadic Interorganizational Relationships in a Network of Publicly Funded Nonprofit Agencies," *Journal of Public Administration Research* 15, (2005): 149–165.

10 Joseph A. Raelin, "A Mandated Basis of Interorganizational Relations: The Legal–Political Network," *Human Relations* 33, (1980): 57–68; Ranjay Gulati and Martin Gargiulo, "Where Do Interorganizational Networks Come From?" *American Journal of Sociology* 104, (1999): 1439–1493; Jörg Raab, "Where Do Policy Networks Come From," *Journal of Public Administration Research and Theory* 12, (2002): 581–622.

11 Joseph Galaskiewicz, "The Structure of Community Organizational Networks," *Social Forces* 57, (1979): 1346–1364; Andrew H. Van de Ven, Gordon Walker, and Jennie Liston, "Coordination Patterns Within an Interorganizational Network," *Human Relations* 32, (1979): 19–36.

12 Keith G. Provan and H. Brinton Milward, "Do Networks Really Work? A Framework for Evaluating Public-Sector Organizational Networks," *Public Administration Review* 61, (2001): 414–423; Patrick Kenis and Keith G. Provan, "Towards an Exogenous Theory of Public Network Performance," *Public Administration* 87, (2009): 440–456.

13 Sol Levine and Paul E. White, "Exchange as a Conceptual Framework for the Study of Interorganizational Relationships," *Administrative Science Quarterly* 5, (1961): 583–601; J. Kenneth Benson, "The Interorganizational Network as a Political Economy," *Administrative Science Quarterly* 20, (1975): 229–249; Howard Aldrich, "Resource Dependence and Interorganizational Relations: Local Employment Service Offices and Social Services Sector Organizations," *Administration and Society* 7, (1976): 419–454.

14 Joseph Galaskiewicz, *Exchange Networks and Community Politics* (Beverly Hills, CA: Sage Publications, 1979); Galaskiewicz 1979; David Knoke and James R. Wood, *Organized for Action: Commitment in Voluntary Associations* (New Brunswick, NJ: Rutgers University Press, 1981); David Knoke, "Organization Sponsorship and Influence Reputation of Social Influence Associations," *Social Forces* 61, (1983): 1065–1087; Joseph Galaskiewicz and Karl R. Krohn, "Positions, Roles, and Dependencies in a Community Interorganization System," *Sociological Quarterly* 25, (1984): 527–550. Galaskiewicz used 'Towertown' and 'River city' as pseudonyms for the cities of DeKalb and Aurora, respectively.

15 There is a subtle, but important, distinction between the words 'governance' and 'government.' Governance refers to the process of coordinating the various actions that occur in a setting, while government refers to one particular type of institution that can ensure this coordination. In many cases, a government is responsible for governance, but not always. For example, the governance of the free market in pure capitalism is performed by the laws of supply and demand, not by a government.

16 Harrison C. White, Scott A. Boorman, and Ronald L. Breiger, "Social Structure from Multiple Networks. I. Blockmodels of Roles and Positions," *American Journal of Sociology* 81, (1976): 730–780.

17 H. Brinton Milward, "Symposium on the Hollow State: Capacity, Control, and Performance in Interorganizational Settings," *Journal of Public Administration Research and Theory* 6, (1996): 193–195; R. A. W. Rhodes, "The New Governance: Governing Without Government," *Political Studies* 44, (1996): 652–667; Robert Agranoff and Michael McGuire, "Multinetwork Management: Collaboration

and the Hollow State in Local Economic Policy," *Journal of Public Administration Research and Theory* 8, (1998): 67–91; H. Brinton Milward and Keith G. Provan, "Governing the Hollow State," *Journal of Public Administration Research and Theory* 10, (2000): 359–379.

18   Knoke, 1990, 135.

19   Keith G. Provan and Patrick Kenis, "Modes of Network Governance: Structure, Management, and Effectiveness," *Journal of Public Administration Research and Theory* 18, (2007): 229–252. The subject of Business Improvement Districts, or BIDs, is complex but has not yet been carefully studied from a network perspective. For a discussion of BIDs as a form of urban governance, see: Richard Briffault, "A Government for Our Time? Business Improvement Districts and Urban Governance," *Columbia Law Review* 99, (1999): 365–477.

20   Clark, 1968; Alistair Cole and Peter John, "Local Policy Networks in France and Britain: Policy Coordination in Fragmented Political Sub-systems," *West European Politics* 18, (1995): 89–109; Patrick Le Galès, "Urban Governance and Policy Networks: On the Urban Political Boundedness of Policy Networks. A French Case Study," *Public Administration* 79, (2001): 167–184.

21   Freeman, 1978/79. In this method note, 'centrality' is assumed to mean 'degree centrality.' Although the equation is somewhat more complex, a network's centralization can be computed using other conceptions of centrality as well, including closeness or betweenness.

22   Keith Bassett, "Partnerships, Business Elites, and Urban Politics: New Forms of Governance in an English City," *Urban Studies* 33, (1996): 539–555; P. John, "Urban Economic Policy Networks in Britain and France: A Sociometric Approach," *Environment and Planning C* 16, (1998): 307–322; Vivien Lowndes and Chris Skelcher, "The Dynamics of Multi-organizational Partnerships: An Analysis of Changing Modes of Governance," *Public Administration* 76, (1998): 313–333.

23   Christopher Ansell, "Community Embeddedness and Collaborative Governance in the San Francisco Bay Area Environmental Movement," in Mario Diani and Doug McAdam, eds., *Social Movements and Networks: Relational Approaches to Collective Action* (New York: Oxford University Press, 2003) 233–258; Filip De Rynck and Joris Voets, "Democracy in Area-Based Policy Networks: The Case of Ghent," *American Review of Public Policy* 36, (2006): 58–78; Liisa Häikiö, "Expertise, Representation, and the Common Good: Grounds for Legitimacy in the Urban Governance Network," *Urban Studies* 44, (2007): 2147–2162; Henrik Ernstson, Stephan Barthel, Erik Andersson, and Sara T. Bergström, "Scale-Crossing Borders and Network Governance of Urban Ecosystem Services: The Case of Stockholm," *Ecology and Society* 15, (2010): 28.

24   Peter Bogason and Juliet A. Musso, "The Democratic Prospects of Network Governance," *American Review of Public Administration* 36, (2006): 3–18; Tom Entwistle, Gillian Bristow, Frances Hines, Sophie Donaldson, and Steve Martin, "The Dysfunctions of Markets, Hierarchies, and Networks in the Meta-governance of Partnership," *Urban Studies* 44, (2007): 63–79; Erik-Hans Klijn and Chris Skelcher, "Democracy and Governance Networks: Compatible or Not?" *Public Administration* 85, (2007): 587–608; Gerard van Bortel and David Mullins, "Critical Perspectives on Network Governance in Urban Regeneration, Community Involvement, and Integration," *Journal of Housing and the Built Environment* 24, (2009): 203–219.

25   David M. Kennedy, Anthony A. Braga, and Anne M. Piehl, "The (Un)known Universe: Mapping Gangs and Gang Violence in Boston," in David Weisburd and Tom McEwen, eds., *Crime Mapping and Crime Prevention* (Monsey, NY: Criminal Justice Press, 1997) 219–262; Steven M. Radil, Colin Flint, and George E. Tita, "Spatializing Social Networks: Using Social Network Analysis to Investigate Geographies of Gang Rivalry, Territoriality, and Violence in Los Angeles," *Annals of the Association of American Geographers* 100, (2010): 307–326.

26   Pennie G. Foster-Fishman, Shelby L. Berkowitz, David W. Lounsbury, Stephanie Jacobson, and Nicole A. Allen, "Building Collaborative Capacity in Community Coalitions: A Review and Integrative Framework," *American Journal of Community Psychology* 29, (2001): 241–261.

27   Roland L. Warren, "The Interorganizational Field as a Focus for Investigation," *Administrative Science Quarterly* 12, (1967): 396–419; David L. Rogers, "Sociometric Analysis of Interorganizational Relations: Application of Theory and Measurement," *Rural Sociology* 39, (1974): 487–503; Jeff S.

Sharp, "Locating the Community Field: A Study of Interorganizational Network Structure and Capacity for Community Action," *Rural Sociology* 66, (2001): 403–424.

28   Charles L. Mulford and Mary A. Mulford, "Community and Interorganizational Perspectives on Cooperation and Conflict," *Rural Sociology* 42, (1977): 569–590; Derrick Purdue, Mario Diani, and Isobel Lindsay, "Civic Networks in Bristol and Glasgow," *Community Development Journal* 39, (2004): 277–288; Juliet A. Musso, Christopher Weare, Nail Oztas, and William E. Loges, "Neighborhood Governance Reform and Networks of Community Power in Los Angeles," *American Review of Public Administration* 36, (2006): 79–97; Delia Baldassarri and Mario Diani, "The Integrative Power of Civic Networks," *American Journal of Sociology* 113, (2007): 735–780.

29   Chris Ansell, Sarah Reckhow, and Andrew Kelly, "How to Reform a Reform Coalition: Outreach, Agenda Expansion, and Brokerage in Urban School Reform," *Policy Studies Journal* 37, (2009): 717–743; Karien Dekker, Beate Völker, Herman Lelieveldt, and René Torenvlied, "Civic Engagement in Urban Neighborhoods: Does the Network of Civic Organizations Influence Participation in Neighborhood Projects?" *Journal of Urban Affairs* 32, (2010): 609–632.

30   Elizabeth A. Mulroy, "Community as a Factor in Implementing Interorganizational Partnerships: Issues, Constraints, and Adaptations," *Nonprofit Management and Leadership* 14, (2003): 47–66; Charles Kadushin, Matthew Lindholm, Dan Ryan, Archie Brodsky, and Leonard Saxe, "Why It Is So Difficult to Form Effective Community Coalitions," *City and Community* 4, (2005): 255–275; Keith G. Provan, Mark A. Veazie, Lisa K. Staten, and Nicolette I Teufel-Shone, "The Use of Network Analysis to Strengthen Community Partnerships," *Public Administration Review* 65, (2005): 603–613.

31   Robert J. Chaskin, "Organizational Infrastructure and Community Capacity: The Role of Broker Organizations," *Organizational Response to Social Problems* 8, (2001): 143–166; Pennie G. Foster-Fishman, Deborah A. Salem, Nicole A. Allen, and Kyle Fahrbach, "Facilitating Interorganizational Collaboration: The Contributions of Interorganizational Alliances," *American Journal of Community Psychology* 29, (2001): 875–905.

32   Gueorgi Kossinets, "Effects of Missing Data in Social Networks," *Social Networks* 28, (2006): 247–268. Cognitive social structures are one way to reduce the amount of missing data. This strategy involves asking respondents — whether they are people, or organizations, or cities — not only about their own relationships but also about the relationships between others; see: David Krackhardt, "Cognitive Social Structures," *Social Networks* 9, (1987): 109–134; Jennifer Watling Neal, "Kracking the Missing Data Problem: Applying Krackhardt's Cognitive Social Structures to School-Based Social Networks," *Sociology of Education* 81, (2008): 140–162.

33   Jennafer Kwait, Thomas W. Valente, and David D. Celentano, "Interorganizational Relationships Among HIV/AIDS Service Organizations in Baltimore: A Network Analysis," *Journal of Urban Health* 78, (2001): 468–487.

34   Mark E. Feinberg, Nathaniel R. Riggs, and Mark T. Greenberg, "Social Networks and Community Prevention Coalitions," *Journal of Primary Prevention* 26, (2005): 279–298; Thomas W. Valente, Chich Ping Chou, and Mary Ann Pentz, "Community Coalitions as a System: Effects of Network Change on Adoption of Evidence-based Substance Abuse Prevention," *American Journal of Public Health* 97, (2007): 880–886.

35   John M. Bolland and Jan V. Wilson, "Three Faces of Integrative Coordination: A Model of Interorganizational Relations in Community-Based Health and Human Services," *Health Services Research* 29, (1984): 341–366; Joseph P. Morrissey, Mark Tausig, and Michael L. Lindsey, "Community Mental Health Delivery Systems: A Network Perspective," *American Behavioral Scientist* 28, (1985): 704–720; Keith G. Provan and Juliann G. Sebastian, "Networks within Networks: Service Link Overlap, Organizational Cliques, and Network Effectiveness," *Academy of Management Journal* 41, (1998): 453–463.

36   Mario Luis Small, Erin M. Jacobs, and Rebekah Peeples Massengill, "Why Organizational Ties Matter for Neighborhood Effects: Resource Access through Childcare Centers," *Social Forces* 87, (2008): 387–414; Kate Beatty, Jenine K. Harris, and Priscilla A. Barnes, "The Role of Interorganizational Partnerships in Health Services Provision among Rural, Suburban, and Urban Local Health Departments," *Journal of Rural Health* 26, (2010): 248–258.

37   Mark Tausig, "Detecting 'Cracks' in Mental Health Service Systems: Application of Network Analytic Techniques," *American Journal of Community Psychology* 15, (1987): 337–351; David F. Gillespie and Susan A. Murty, "Cracks in a Postdisaster Service Delivery Network," *American Journal of Community Psychology* 22, (1994): 639–660; Charo Rodríguez, Ann Langley, François Béland, and Jean-Louis Denis, "Governance, Power, and Mandated Collaboration in an Interorganizational Network," *Administration and Society* 39, (2007): 150–193.

38   Provan, Nakama, Veazie, Teufel-Shone, and Huddleston 2003; Keith G. Provan, Kimberley R. Isett, and H. Brinton Milward, "Cooperation and Compromise: A Network Response to Conflicting Institutional Pressures in Community Mental Health," *Nonprofit and Voluntary Sector Quarterly* 33, (2004): 489–514.

39   David L. Rogers, "Towards a Scale of Interorganizational Relations Among Public Agencies," *Sociology and Social Research* 59, (1974): 61–70.

7 Regional: From City to Metropolis

1   Camagni 1993; Richard Child Hill, "Cities and Nested Hierarchies," *International Social Science Journal* 56, (2004): 373–384.

2   378 U.S. 184, 197.

3   In this respect, cities are quite similar to corporations, which are also created by filing incorporation paperwork that gives the corporation certain legal privileges including the right to own property. In fact, in the most technical sense, a city is a type of corporation: a municipal corporation. As judge John Dillon eloquently explained in an 1868 decision, "Municipal corporations owe their origin to, and derive their powers and rights wholly from, the legislature. It breathes into them the breath of life, without which they cannot exist;" see: *Clinton v. Cedar Rapids and the Missouri River Railroad* (24 Iowa 475).

4   See Wirth, 1938. Population density should not be confused with network density, introduced in method note 3. Population density is an indicator of the spatial concentration of people, usually measured in people per square mile. Network density is a measure of the concentration of edges in a network.

5   Roderick D. McKenzie, *The Metropolitan Community* (New York: Russell and Russell, 1933) 69–70, 81.

6   Johann Heinrich von Thünen, *The Isolated State: An English Translation of Der Isolierte Staat*, Carla M. Wartenberg, trans., Peter Hall, ed. (New York: Oxford University Press, 1966).

7   Ernest Burgess, 1925; Alonso, 1964.

8   Peter Hall, *The World Cities* (London: Weidenfeld and Nicolson, 1966); William A. V. Clark and Marianne Kuijpers-Linde, "Commuting in Restructuring Urban Regions," *Urban Studies* 31, (1994): 465–483; David F. Batten, "Network Cities: Creative Urban Agglomerations for the 21st Century," *Urban Studies* 32, (1995): 313–327.

9   Office of Management and Budget, "Standards for Defining Metropolitan and Micropolitan Statistical Areas," *Federal Register* 65, (2000): 82228–82238. A similar but smaller type of geographic unit— an urbanized area—is also defined using patterns of interaction, but is based on infrastructure networks of roads rather than movement networks of commuters; see: Department of Commerce, "Urban Area Criteria for Census 2000," *Federal Register* 67, (2002): 11663–11670. Other countries use similar definitions, many of which are based on the U.S. system; see: Peter Hall, "Delineating Urban Territories: Is This a Relevant Issue?" in Nadine Cattan, ed., *Cities and Networks in Europe: A Critical Approach to Polycentrism* (Esher, Surrey: John Libbey Eurotext, 2007) 3–14.

10   Jean Gottman, *Megalopolis: The Urbanized Northeastern Seaboard of the United States* (Norwood, MA: Plimpton Press, 1961); Delbert C. Miller, *Leadership and Power in the Bos-Wash Megalopolis: Environment, Ecology, and Urban Organization* (New York: John Wiley & Sons, 1975); Richard Florida, Tim Gulden, and Charlotta Mellander, "The Rise of the Mega-region," *Cambridge Journal of Regions, Economy, and Society* 1, (2008): 459–476; Pierre Dessemontet, Vincent Kaufmann, and Christophe Jemelin, "Switzerland as a Single Metropolitan Area? A Study of Its Commuting Network," *Urban Studies* 47, (2010): 2785–2802.

11 Edgar S. Dunn, "A Flow Network Image of Urban Structures," *Urban Studies* 7, (1970): 239–258; Michael D. Irwin and Holly L. Hughes, "Centrality and the Structure of Urban Interaction: Measures, Concepts, and Applications," *Social Forces* 71, (1992): 17–51.

12 Richard B. Andrews, "Mechanics of the Urban Economic Base," *Land Economics* 29, (1953): 161–167, 263–268, 343–350; John W. Alexander, "The Basic–Nonbasic Concept of Urban Economic Function," *Economic Geography* 30, (1954): 246–261; Harold M. Mayer, "Urban Nodality and the Economic Base," *Journal of the American Planning Association* 20, (1954): 117–121.

13 Location quotients are commonly reported and interpreted using this formula, but it is often useful to use the natural logarithm of a location quotient instead. Logged location quotients range from negative infinity to positive infinity, and are centered around zero. This transformation allows negative values to be interpreted as evidence of importing and positive values as evidence of exporting, and allows the magnitude of importing and exporting to be compared.

14 Charles Horton Cooley, *The Theory of Transportation* (Baltimore: American Economic Association, 1894); William Cronon, *Nature's Metropolis: Chicago and the Great West* (New York, W. W. Norton, 1991).

15 Walter Christaller, *Central Places in Southern Germany*, trans. D. W. Baskin (Englewood Cliffs, NJ: Prentice Hall, [1933] 1966); Brian J. L. Berry and Allen Pred, *Central Place Studies: A Bibliography of Theory and Applications* (Philadelphia: Regional Science Research Institute, 1965).

16 B. A. Badcock, "Central Place Evolution and Network Development in South Auckland, 1840–1968: A Systems Analytic Approach," *New Zealand Geographer* 26 (1970): 109–135.

17 Richard E. Preston, "A Comparison of Five Measures of Central Place Importance and of Settlement Size," *Tijdschrift voor Economische en Sociale Geografie* 66, (1975): 178–187; Narisra Limtanakool, Tim Schwanen, and Martin Djist, "Ranking Functional Urban Regions: A Comparison of Interaction and Node Attribute Data," *Cities* 24, (2006): 26–42.

18 Robert C. Kloosterman and Sake Musterd, "The Polycentric Urban Region: Towards a Research Agenda," *Urban Studies* 38, (2001): 623–633.

19 Nick Bailey and Ivan Turok, "Central Scotland as a Polycentric Urban Region: Useful Planning Concept or Chimera," *Urban Studies* 38, (2001): 697–715; John Parr, "The Polycentric Urban Region: A Closer Inspection," *Regional Studies* 38, (2004): 231–240; Peter Hall and Kathy Pain, *The Polycentric Metropolis: Learning from Mega-City Regions in Europe* (London: Earthscan, 2006).

20 European Commission, *European Spatial Development Perspective* (Luxembourg: European Communities, 1999); Simin Davoudi, "Polycentricity in European Spatial Planning: From an Analytical Tool to a Normative Agenda," *European Planning Studies* 11, (2003): 979–999; Evert Meijers, "Measuring Polycentricity and Its Promises," *European Planning Studies* 16, (2008): 1313–1323.

21 Michael Arndt, Thomas Gawron, and Petra Jähnke, "Regional Policy through Co-operation: From Urban Forum to Urban Network," *Urban Studies* 37, (2000): 1903–1923; Kurt Thurmaier and Curtis Wood, "Interlocal Agreements as Overlapping Social Networks: Picket-Fence Regionalism in Metropolitan Kansas City," *Public Administration Review* 62, (2002): 585–598; Neil Marshall, Brian Dollery, and Angus Witherby, "Regional Organisations of Councils (ROCS): The Emergence of Network Governance in Metropolitan and Rural Australia," *Australasian Journal of Regional Studies* 9, (2003): 169–188; Louis Albrechts and Griet Lievois, "The Flemish Diamond: Urban Network in the Making?" *European Planning Studies* 12, (2004): 351–370; Francesca Governa and Carlo Salone, "Italy and European Spatial Policies: Polycentrism, Urban Networks, and Local Innovation Practices," *European Planning Studies* 13, (2005): 265–283.

22 Nadine Cattan, ed., *Cities and Networks in Europe: A Critical Approach of Polycentrism* (Esher, Surrey: John Libbey Eurotext, 2007).

23 This measure is a modification of Green's that uses one minus centralization rather than the standard deviation of degree centrality as an indicator of decentralization; see: Nick Green, "Functional Polycentricity: A Formal Definition in Terms of Social Network Analysis," *Urban Studies* 44, (2007): 2077–2103.

24 Clark and Kuijpers-Linde, 1994.

25 David F. Batten, "Network Cities Versus Central Place Cities: Building a Cosmo-Creative Constellation," in A. E. Andersson, D. F. Batten, K. Kobayashi, and K. Yoshikawa, eds., *The Cosmo-Creative Society: Logistical Networks in a Dynamic Economy* (New York: Springer-Verlag, 1993) 137–150; Capello 2000; Edward J. Malecki, "Hard and Soft Networks for Urban Competitiveness," *Urban Studies* 39, (2002): 929–945; Evert Meijers, "Polycentric Urban Regions and the Quest for Synergy: Is a Network of Cities More than the Sum of the Parts?" *Urban Studies* 42, (2005): 765–781.

26 Christopher Clayton, "Interdependence in Urban Systems and Its Application to Political Reorganization," *Geografiska Annaler* 62, (1980): 11–20; Todd Swanstrom, "What We Argue About When We Argue About Regionalism," *Journal of Urban Affairs* 23, (2001): 479–496; Frank Cörvers, Maud Hensen, and Dion Bongaerts, "Delimitation and Coherence of Functional and Administrative Regions," *Regional Studies* 43, (2009): 19–31.

27 Andrew Church and Peter Reid, "Urban Power, International Networks and Competition: The Example of Cross-Border Cooperation," *Urban Studies* 33, (1996): 1297–1318; Thurmaier and Wood, 2002; Simon A. Andrew, "Regional Integration Through Contracting Networks: An Empirical Analysis of Institutional Collection Action Framework," *Urban Affairs Review* 44, (2009): 378–402; Kelly LeRoux, Paul W. Brandenburger, and Sanjay K. Pandey, "Interlocal Service Cooperation in U.S. Cities: A Social Network Explanation," *Public Administration Review* 70, (2010): 268–278.

28 Juliet F. Gainsborough, "Bridging the City–Suburb Divide: States and the Politics of Regional Cooperation," *Journal of Urban Affairs* 23, (2001): 497–512; Donald F. Norris, "Prospects for Regional Governance Under the New Regionalism: Economic Imperatives Versus Political Impediments," *Journal of Urban Affairs* 23, (2001): 557–571.

29 Bennett Harrison, "Industrial Districts: Old Wine in New Bottles?" *Regional Studies* 26, (1992): 469–483; Roberto Camagni, "Inter-Firm Industrial Networks: The Costs and Benefits of Cooperative Behaviour," *Industry and Innovation* 1, (1993): 1–15; Roberto Camagni and Carlo Salone, "Network Urban Structures in Northern Italy: Elements for a Theoretical Framework," *Urban Studies* 30, (1993): 1053–1064; Ian R. Gordon and Philip McCann, "Industrial Clusters: Complexes, Agglomeration, and/or Social Networks?" *Urban Studies* 37, (2000): 513–532; Peter Cabus and Wim Vanhaverbeke, "The Territoriality of the Network Economy and Urban Networks: Evidence from Flanders," *Entrepreneurship and Regional Development* 18, (2006): 25–53.

30 Alfred Marshall, *Principles of Economics* (London: Macmillan and Company, 1890) see book IV, chapter 10; Giacomo Becattini, "The Economic Development of Tuscany: An Interpretation," *Economic Notes* 2–3, (1978): 107–123; Fabio Sforzi, "The Tuscan Model: An Interpretation in the Light of Recent Trends," in R. Leonardi and R. Y. Nanetti, eds., *Regional Development in a Modern European Economy: The Case of Tuscany* (New York: Pinter, 1994) 86–115.

31 S. Christopherson and M. Storper, "The City as Studio; the World as Back Lot: The Impact of Vertical Disintegration on the Location of the Motion Picture Industry," *Environment and Planning D* 4, (1986): 305–320; Mia Gray, Elyse Golub, and Ann Markusen, "Big Firms, Long Arms, Wide Shoulders: The 'Hub-and-Spoke' Industrial District in the Seattle Region," *Regional Studies* 30, (1996): 651–666; Michael E. Porter, "Clusters and the New Economics of Competition," *Harvard Business Review* 76, (1998): 77–90; Ruth Rama, Deron Ferguson, and Ana Melero, "Subcontracting Networks in Industrial Districts: The Electronics Industries of Madrid," *Regional Studies* 37, (2003): 71–88.

32 AnnaLee Saxenian, "Regional Networks and the Resurgence of Silicon Valley," *California Management Review* 33, (1990): 89–112; Neil Reid, Bruce W. Smith, and Michael C. Carroll, "Cluster Regions: A Social Network Perspective," *Economic Development Quarterly* 22, (2008): 345–352.

33 Adapted from Schwanen, Dieleman, and Dijst, 2004, 313.

34 L. van der Laan, J. Vogelzang, and R. Schalke, "Commuting in Multi-nodal Urban Systems: An Empirical Comparison of Three Alternative Models," *Tijdschrift voor Economische en Sociale Geografie* 89, (1989): 384–400; Irwin and Hughes, 1994; Tim Schwanen, Frans M. Dieleman, and Martin Dijst, "The Impact of Metropolitan Structure on Commute Behavior in the Netherlands: A Multilevel

Approach," *Growth and Change* 35, (2004): 304–333; Stephan J. Goetz, Yicheol Han, Jill L. Findeis, and Katheryn J. Brasier, "U.S. Commuting Networks and Economic Growth: Measurement and Implications for Spatial Policy," *Growth and Change* 41, (2010): 276–302; M. J. Burger, B. de Goei, L van der Laan, and F. J. M. Huisman, "Heterogeneous Development of Metropolitan Spatial Structure: Evidence from Commuting Patterns in English and Welsh City-regions, 1981–2001," *Cities* 28, (2011): 160–170; Camille Roth, Soong Moon Kang, Michael Batty, and Marc Barthélemy, "Structure of Urban Movements: Polycentric Activity and Entangled Hierarchical Flows," *PLoS ONE* 6, (2011): e15923.

8 National: The Action is *In* Cities, but also *Between* Them

1 Cronon, 1991, 64 and 296.

2 This pattern was first observed in 1913 by German geographer Felix Auerbach, but is often known as Zipf's rule, after American linguist George Zipf. There are many different variations and much disagreement about why the pattern exists; see: Felix Auerbach, "Das Gesetz der Bevölkerungskonzentration," *Petermann's Geographische Mitteilungen* 59, (1913): 74–76; George Kingsley Zipf, *Human Behavior and the Principle of Least Effort* (Cambridge, MA: Addison-Wesley Press, 1949); Glenn R. Carroll, "National City-Size Distributions: What Do We Know After 67 Years of Research?" *Progress in Human Geography* 6, (1982): 1–43.

3 Kenneth E. Boulding, "General Systems Theory—The Skeleton of Science," *Management Science* 2, (1956): 197–208.

4 Berry 1964; Edgar S. Dunn, Jr., *The Development of the U.S. Urban System, volume 1* (Baltimore, MD: Johns Hopkins University Press, 1980) chapters 1 and 2.

5 Edward L. Ullman, "The Role of Transportation and the Bases for Interaction," in William L. Thomas, Jr., ed., *Man's Role in Changing the Face of the Earth* (Chicago: University of Chicago Press, 1956) 862–880.

6 There are many variations on this basic gravity model; see: George Kingsley Zipf, "The P_1P_2/D Hypothesis: On the Intercity Movement of Persons," *American Sociological Review* 11, (1946): 677–686; A. T. Philbrick, "A Short History of the Development of the Gravity Model," *Australian Road Research* 5, (1973): 40–54.

7 David Batten and Gunnar Törnqvist, "Multilevel Network Barriers: The Methodological Challenge," *Annals of Regional Science* 24, (1990): 271–287; Nadine Cattan, "Barrier Effects: The Case of Air and Rail Flows," *International Political Science Review* 16, (1995): 237–248.

8 Herman Turk, "Interorganizational Networks in Urban Society: Initial Perspectives and Comparative Research," *American Sociological Review* 35, (1970): 1–19; Carl Abbott, "Regional City and Network City: Portland and Seattle in the Twentieth Century," *Western Historical Quarterly* 23, (1992): 293–322.

9 John D. Nystuen and Michael F. Dacey, "A Graph Theory Interpretation of Nodal Regions," *Papers and Proceedings of the Regional Science Association* 7, (1961): 29–42; Javier Gutiérrez Puebla, "Spatial Structures of Network Flows: A Graph Theoretical Approach," *Transportation Research B* 21, (1987): 489–502; Nathalie van Nuffel, "Determination of the Number of Significant Flows in Origin-Destination Specific Analysis: The Case of Commuting in Flanders," *Regional Studies* 41, (2007): 509–524; Nathalie van Nuffel, Ben Derudder, and Frank Witlox, "Even Important Connections are Not Always Meaningful: On the Use of a Polarisation Measure in a Typology of European Cities in Air Transport Networks," *Tijdschrift voor Economische en Sociale Geografie* 101, (2010): 333–348.

10 Rupert B. Vance and Sara Smith, "Metropolitan Dominance and Integration," in Rupert B. Vance and Nicholas J. Demerath, eds., *The Urban South* (Chapel Hill, NC: University of North Carolina Press, 1954) 114–134; Otis Dudley Duncan, W. Richard Scott, Stanley Lieberson, Beverly Duncan, and Hal H. Winsboroug, *Metropolis and Region* (Baltimore, MD: Johns Hopkins University Press, 1960) chapter 3.

11 Narisra Limtanakool, Martin Dijst, and Tim Schwanen, "A Theoretical Framework and Methodology for Characterising National Urban Systems on the Basis of Flows of People: Empirical Evidence for France and Germany," *Urban Studies* 44, (2007): 2123–2145.

12   Francesca Silvia Rota, "Cities as Nodes of Research Networks in Europe," in Nadine Cattan, ed.,
     Cities and Networks in Europe: A Critical Approach to Polycentrism (Esher, Surrey: John Libbey Eurotext,
     2007) 125–137; Gautier Krings, Francesco Calabrese, Carlo Ratti, and Vincent D. Blondel, "Urban
     Gravity: A Model for Inter-city Telecommunication Flows," *Journal of Statistical Mechanics* (2009):
     L07003.

13   William R. Black, "Interregional Commodity Flows: Some Experiments with the Gravity Model,"
     Journal of Regional Science 12, (1972): 107–118; Issac W. Eberstein, "Intercommunity Trade and the
     Structure of Sustenance Organization," *Social Science Quarterly* 63, (1982): 236–248; Issac W. Eberstein
     and W. Parker Frisbie, "Metropolitan Function and Interdependence in the U.S. Urban System,"
     Social Forces 60, (1982): 676–700; Isaac W. Eberstein and Omer R. Galle, "The Metropolitan System
     in the South: Functional Differentiation and Trade Patterns," *Social Forces* 62, (1984): 926–940.

14   Duncan et al., 1960, chapter 6; David R. Meyer, "Control and Coordination Links in the Metropolitan
     System of Cities: The South as Case Study," *Social Forces* 63, (1984): 349–362; Milford B. Green,
     "A Geography of Institutional Stock Ownership in the United States," *Annals of the Association of
     American Geographers* 83, (1993): 66–89.

15   Robert E. Park, "Urbanization as Measured by Newspaper Circulation," *American Journal of Sociology*
     35, (1929): 60–79; Allan R. Pred, "Urban Systems Development and the Long-Distance Flow of
     Information Through Preelectronic U.S. Newspapers," *Economic Geography* 47, (1971): 498–524;
     Allan R. Pred, *Urban Growth and the Circulation of Information: The United States System of Cities,
     1790–1840* (Cambridge, MA: Harvard University Press, 1973); Tom Standage, *The Victorian Internet*
     (New York: Walker, 1998); Richard R. John, *Network Nation: Inventing American Telecommunications*
     (Cambridge, MA: Harvard University Press, 2010).

16   Pred, 1973, chapter 4.

17   Adapted from Pred, 1973, figures 4.3–4.6 and 4.9–4.10. Row cities are the origins; column cities are
     the destinations.

18   Peter V. Marsden and Karen E. Campbell, "Measuring Tie Strength," *Social Forces* 63, (1984):
     482–501.

19   This book does not deal with signed networks; see: Fritz Heider, "Attitudes and Cognitive
     Organization," *Journal of Psychology* 21, (1946): 107–112; Norman P. Hummon and Patrick Doreian,
     "Some Dynamics of Social Balance Processes: Bringing Heider Back Into Balance Theory," *Social
     Networks* 25, (2003) 17–49.

20   Reserve Bank Organization Committee. 1914. *Decision of the Reserve Bank Organization Committee
     Determining the Federal Reserve Districts and the Location of the Federal Reserve Banks Under Federal
     Reserve Act Approved December 23, 1913*. Washington: Government Printing Office.

21   James E. Vance, Jr., *The Merchant's World: The Geography of Wholesaling* (Englewood Cliffs, NJ:
     Prentice-Hall, 1970); Jean Gottman, "The Central City and the Inadequacy of Population Counts,"
     in Jean Gottman, *The Coming of the Transactional City* (College Park, MD: University of Maryland
     Institute for Urban Studies, 1983) 33–46; Evert Meijers, "From Central Place to Network Model:
     Theory and Evidence of a Paradigm Change," *Tijdschrift voor Economische en Sociale Geografie* 98,
     (2007): 245–259; Anne Bretagnolle and Denise Pumain, "Simulating Urban Networks through
     Multiscaling Space–Time Dynamics: Europe and the United States, 17th–20th Centuries," *Urban
     Studies* 47, (2010): 2819–2839; Peter J. Taylor, Michael Hoyler, and Raf Verbruggen, "External Urban
     Relational Process: Introducing Central Flow Theory to Complement Central Place Theory," *Urban
     Studies* 47, (2010): 2803–2818; Zachary P. Neal, "From Central Places to Network Bases: A Transition
     in the U.S. Urban Hierarchy, 1900–2000," *City and Community* 10, (2011): 49–74.

22   Stanley Lieberson and Kent P. Schwirian, "Banking Functions as an Index of Inter-city Relations,"
     Journal of Regional Science 4, (1962): 69–81; Michael P. Conzen, "Capital Flows and the Developing
     Urban Hierarchy: State Bank Capital in Wisconsin, 1854–1895," *Economic Geography* 51, (1975):
     321–338; Michael P. Conzen, "The Maturing Urban System in the United States," *Annals of the
     Association of American Geographers* 67, (1977): 88–108; David Ralph Meyer, "A Dynamic Model of
     the Integration of Frontier Urban Places into the United States System of Cities," *Economic Geography*
     56, (1980): 120–140.

23   Adapted from Taaffe, Morrill, and Gould, 1963), figure 1.

24   Forrest R. Pitts, "A Graph Theoretic Approach to Historical Geography," *Professional Geographer* 17, (1965): 15–20; John R. Borchert, "American Metropolitan Evolution," *Geographical Review* 57, (1967): 301–332; Pred, 1973, chapter 5; T. R. B. Dicks, "Network Analysis and Historical Geography," *Area* 4, (1972): 4–9; Michael P. Conzen, "A Transport Interpretation of the Growth of Urban Regions: An American Example," *Journal of Historical Geography* 1, (1975): 361–382; Forrest R. Pitts, "The Medieval River Trade Network of Russia Revisited," *Social Networks* 1, (1978): 285–292; David F. Batten and Roland Thord, "Europe's Hierarchical Network Economy," in David Batten, John Casti, and Roland Thord, eds., *Networks in Action: Communication, Economics, and Human Knowledge* (New York: Springer-Verlag, 1995) 251–266; Piet Rietvald and Joost van Nierop, "Urban Growth and the Development of Transport Networks: The Case of the Dutch Railways in the Nineteenth Century," *Flux* 19, (1995): 31–43; Janet L. Abu-Lughod, *New York, Chicago, Los Angeles: America's Global Cities* (Minneapolis, MN: University of Minnesota Press, 1999); Jerome I. Hodos, *Second Cities: Globalization and Local Politics in Manchester and Philadelphia* (Philadelphia: Temple University Press, 2011).

25   Edward J. Taaffe, Richard L. Morrill, and Peter R. Gould, "Transport Expansion in Underdeveloped Countries: A Comparative Analysis," *Geographical Review* 53, (1963): 503–529; Yu V. Medvedkov, "An Application of Topology in Central Place Analysis," *Papers in Regional Science* 20, (1967): 77–84; Donald G. Janelle, "Spatial Reorganization: A Model and Concept," *Annals of the Association of American Geographers* 59, (1969): 348–364.

26   Federal Works Agency, "National System of Interstate and Defense Highways" (1955); Delta Air Lines, "United States Route Map," http://images.delta.com.edgesuite.net/delta/pdfs/U.S._6_11.pdf; Amtrak, "National Route Map," www.amtrak.com/pdf/national.pdf.

27   Dunn 1980, volume 2, chapter 6; Edward J. Taaffe, Howard L. Gauthier, and Morton E. O'Kelly, eds., *Geography of Transportation*, 2nd Edition (Upper Saddle River, NJ: Prentice Hall, 1996).

28   Douglas K. Fleming and Yehuda Hayuth, "Spatial Characteristics of Transportation Hubs: Centrality and Intermediacy," *Journal of Transport Geography* 2, (1994): 3–18; Limtanakool, Dijst, and Schwanen 2007; Narisra Limtanakool, Tim Schwanen, and Martin Dijst, "Developments in the Dutch Urban System on the Basis of Flows," *Regional Studies* 43, (2009): 179–196; Zachary Neal, "Refining the Air Traffic Approach to City Networks," *Urban Studies* 47, (2010): 2195–2215.

29   Donald Patton, "The Traffic Pattern on American Inland Waterways," *Economic Geography* 32, (1956): 29–37; Chris Clark, Kevin E. Henrickson, and Paul Thoma, *An Overview of the U.S. Inland Waterway System* (Alexandria, VA: U.S. Army Corps of Engineers, 2005); U.S. Army Corps of Engineers, *Inland Waterway Navigation: Value to the Nation* (Alexandria, VA: U.S. Army Corps of Engineers, 2009).

30   Edward L. Ullman, "The Railroad Pattern of the United States," *Geographical Review* 39, (1949): 242–256; Javier Gutiérrez, Rafael González, and Gabriel Gómez, "The European High-speed Train Network," *Journal of Transport Geography* 4, (1996): 227–238.

31   Shih-Lung Shaw, "Hub Structures of Major US Passenger Airlines," *Journal of Transport Geography* 1, (1993): 47–58; Goetz Sutton 1997; Neil Bania, Paul W. Bauer, and Thomas J. Zlatoper, "U.S. Air Passenger Service: A Taxonomy of Route Networks, Hub Locations, and Competition," *Transportation Research E* 34, (1998): 53–74; Morton W. O'Kelly, "A Geographer's Analysis of Hub-and-Spoke Networks," *Journal of Transport Geography* 6, (1998): 171–186; Kenneth Button and Somik Lall, "The Economics of Being an Airport Hub City," *Research in Transportation Economics* 5, (1999): 75–105.

32   William L. Garrison, "Connectivity of the Interstate Highway System," *Papers and Proceedings of the Regional Science Association* 6, (1960): 121–137; Gabriel Dupuy and Vaclav Stransky, "Cities and Highway Networks in Europe," *Journal of Transport Geography* 4, (1996): 107–121; Donald W. Buckwalter, "Complex Topology in the Highway Network of Hungary, 1990 and 1998," *Journal of Transport Geography* 9, (2001): 125–135; Dupuy, 2008, chapter 10; Woo-Sung Jung, Fengzhong Wang, and H. Eugene Stanley, "Gravity Model in the Korean Highway," *EPL* 81, (2008): 48005.

33 Wallace E. Reed, "Indirect Connectivity and Hierarchies of Urban Dominance," *Annals of the Association of American Geographers* 60, (1970): 770–785; Frank Bruinsma and Piet Rietvold, "Urban Agglomerations in European Infrastructure Networks," *Urban Studies* 30, (1993): 919–934; Tony H. Grubesic and Matthew A. Zook, "A Ticket to Ride: Evolving Landscapes of Air Travel Accessibility in the United States," *Journal of Transport Geography* 15, (2007): 417–430; Tony H. Grubesic, Timothy C. Matisziw, and Matthew A. Zook, "Global Airline Networks and Nodal Regions," *GeoJournal* 71, (2008): 53–66.

34 Janelle 1969; C. C. Kissling, "Linkage Importance in a Regional Highway Network," *Canadian Geographer* 13, (1969): 113–127.

35 D'Arcy Harvey, "Airline Passenger Traffic Pattern within the United States," *Journal of Air Law and Commerce* 18, (1951): 157–165; Edward J. Taaffe, "Air Transportation and United States Urban Distribution," *Geographical Review* 46, (1956): 219–238; Carl Hammer and Fred Charles Ikle, "Intercity Telephone and Airline Traffic Related to Distance and the Propensity to Interact," *Sociometry* 20, (1957): 306–316; John B. Lansing, Jung-Chao Liu, and Daniel B. Suits, "An Analysis of Interurban Air Travel," *Quarterly Journal of Economics* 75, (1961): 87–95; Edward J. Taaffe, "The Urban Hierarchy: An Air Passenger Definition," *Economic Geography* 38, (1962): 1–14; Neal 2010.

36 Michael D. Irwin and John D. Kasarda, "Air Passenger Linkages and Employment Growth in U.S. Metropolitan Areas," *American Sociological Review* 56, (1991): 524–537; R. L. Ivy, T. J. Fik, and E. J. Malecki, "Changes in Air Service Connectivity and Employment," *Environment and Planning A* 27, (1995): 165–179; Keith G. Debbage and Dawn Delk, "The Geography of Air Passenger Volume and Local Employment Patterns by US Metropolitan Core Area: 1973–1996," *Journal of Air Transport Management* 7, (2001): 159–167; Zachary Neal, "The Causal Relationship Between Employment and Business Networks in U.S. Cities," *Journal of Urban Affairs* 33, (2011): 167–184; Zachary Neal, "Creative Employment and Jet Set Cities: Disentangling Causal Effects," *Urban Studies*.

37 R. F. Grais, J. H. Ellis, A. Kress, and G. E. Glass, "Modeling the Spread of Annual Influenza Epidemics in the U.S.: The Potential Role of Air Travel," *Health Care Management Science* 7, (2004): 127–134; Duygu Balcan, Vittoria Colizza, Bruno Gonçalves, Hao Hu, José J. Ramasco, and Alessandro Vespignani, "Multiscale Mobility Networks and the Spatial Spreading of Infectious Diseases," *Proceedings of the National Academy of Sciences* 106, (2009): 21484–21489.

38 Guiseppe Dematteis, "Globalisation and Regional Integration: The Case of the Italian Urban System," *GeoJournal* 43, (1997): 331–338.

39 Tamara de la Mata and Carlos Llano-Verduras, "Spatial Pattern and Domestic Tourism: An Econometric Analysis using Inter-regional Monetary Flows by Type of Journey," *Papers in Regional Science*.

40 Xiulian Ma and Michael F. Timberlake, "Identifying China's Leading World City: A Network Approach," *GeoJournal* 71, (2008): 19–35.

41 Green, 1993.

42 An interlocking directorate is a special application of two-mode networks introduced in Chapter Three. Individuals are affiliated with corporations when they sit on the board of directors; these affiliations constitute a two-mode affiliation network. This network can then be used to define a one-mode network where people are connected when they are affiliated with the same corporation, but also a one-mode network where corporations are connected when the same person is affiliated with both.

43 Milford B. Green and R. Keith Semple, "The Corporate Interlocking Directorate as an Urban Spatial Information Network," *Urban Geography* 2, (1981): 148–160; Milford B. Green, "The Interurban Corporate Interlocking Directorate Network of Canada and the United States: A Spatial Perspective," *Urban Geography* 4, (1983): 338–354; James O. Wheeler, "Corporate Spatial Links with Financial Institutions: The Role of the Metropolitan Hierarchy," *Annals of the Association of American Geographers* 76, (1986): 262–274; Christopher O. Ross, "Organizational Dimensions of Metropolitan Dominance: Prominence in the Network of Corporate Control, 1955–1975," *American Sociological Review* 52, (1987): 258–267; Christpher O. Ross, *The Urban System and Networks of Corporate Control* (Greenwich,

CT: JAI Press, 1992); Murray D. Rice and R. Keith Semple, "Spatial Interlocking Directorates in the Canadian Urban System, 1971–1989," *Urban Geography* 14, (1993): 375–396; Eliana C. Rossi and Peter J. Taylor, "Banking Networks across Brazilian Cities: Interlocking Cities within and beyond Brazil," *Cities* 22, (2005): 381–393.

44   Adrian X. Esparza and Andrew J. Krmenec, "Large City Interaction in the US Urban System," *Urban Studies* 37, (2000): 691–709.

45   James O. Wheeler and Ronald L. Mitchelson, "Atlanta's Role as an Information Center: Intermetropolitan Spatial Links," *Professional Geographer* 41, (1989): 162–172; James O. Wheeler and Ronald L. Mitchelson, "Information Flows among Major Metropolitan Areas in the United States," *Annals of the Association of American Geographers* 79, (1989): 523–543; Mitchelson and Wheeler, 1994; Peter J. Taylor, "Hierarchical Tendencies Amongst World Cities: A Global Research Proposal," *Cities* 14, (1997): 323–332.

46   Sean P. Gorman and Edward J. Malecki, "The Networks of the Internet: An Analysis of Provider Networks in the USA," *Telecommunications Policy* 24, (2000): 113–134; Edward J. Malecki and Sean P. Gorman, "Maybe the Death of Distance, but Not the End of Geography: The Internet as a Network," in Stanley D. Brunn and Thomas Leinbach, eds., *Worlds of E-Commerce: Economic, Geographic, and Social Dimensions* (New York: John Wiley) 87–105.

47   David C. Wheeler and Morton E. O'Kelly, "Network Topology and City Accessiblity of the Commercial Internet," *Professional Geographer* 51, (1999): 327–339; Mitchell L. Moss and Anthony M. Townsend, "The Internet Backbone and the American Metropolis," *The Information Society* 16, (2000): 35–47; Anthony M. Townsend, "The Internet and the Rise of New Network Cities, 1969–1999," *Environment and Planning B* 28, (2001): 39–58; Tony H. Grubesic and Morton E. O'Kelly, "Using Points of Presence to Measure Accessibility to the Commercial Internet," *Professional Geographer* 54, (2002): 259–278; Verizon, "Verizon First Service Provider to Announce 100G Deployment on U.S. Network," 30 March 2011 News Release.

48   Stephen Graham, "Global Grids of Glass: On Global Cities, Telecommunications, and Planetary Urban Networks," *Urban Studies* 36, (1999): 929–949; Peter J. Taylor and Robert E. Lang, "U.S. Cities in the World City Network," *Brookings Institution Metropolitan Policy Program*, February 2005; Ben Derudder, Frank Witlox, and Peter J. Taylor, "U.S. Cities in the World City Network: Comparing Their Positions Using Global Origins and Destinations of Airline Passengers," *Urban Geography* 28, (2007): 74–91.

49   Ronald L. Mitchelson and James O. Wheeler, "The Flow of Information in a Global Economy: The Role of the American Urban System in 1990," *Annals of the Association of American Geographers* 84, (1994): 87–107; Martin Dodge and Rob Kitchin, *Mapping Cyberspace* (New York: Routledge, 2000); Francisca M. Rojas, Clelia Celdesi Valeri, Kristian Kloeckl, and Carlo Ratti, *New York Talk Exchange: The Book* (SA+P Press, 2008).

9 Global: Nylon Holds the World Together

1   In just the last fifteen years, interest in studying global city networks has exploded. This chapter and the reference section at the end of the book contain references to a number of published studies on this topic. The Globalization and World Cities (GaWC) research network maintains a repository at www.lboro.ac.uk/gawc/publicat.html, where additional published and unpublished papers can be downloaded.

2   Jean Gottman, "The Dynamics of City Networks in an Expanding World," *Ekistics* 58, (1991): 277–281.

3   Christopher K. Chase-Dunn, "The System of World Cities, A.D. 800–1975," in Michael Timberlake, ed., *Urbanization in the World-Economy* (Orlando, FL: Academic Press, 1985) 269–292; Terence K. Hopkins and Immanuel Wallerstein, "Commodity Chains in the World-Economy Prior to 1800," *Review of the Ferdinand Braudel Center* 10, (1986): 157–170.

4   The transatlantic telegraph cables directly linked strategic, but non-urban, locations in Ireland and Newfoundland. However, from their landfall at these sites, the cables extended to major cities such

as Washington and New York in the U.S. and London in the U.K. Thus, through a series of indirect physical linkages in an infrastructure network, information could move directly from New York to London in a flow network.

5 Roderick D. McKenzie, "The Concept of Dominance and World-Organization," *American Journal of Sociology* 33, (1927): 28–42, 28. Some have more recently described this as a transition from a "space of places" to a "space of flows"; see: Manuel Castells, *The Rise of the Network Society*, 2nd edition (Malden, MA: Blackwell, 2000), 453.

6 Telegraph Construction and Maintenance Co. Ltd., "Map Showing Submarine Telegraph Cables the Cores of Which Were Manufactured at The Gutta Percha Works," (London: Maclure & Co., 1903); Shizhao, "Transasia Trade Routes 1st C CE gr2.png," *Wikimedia Commons* (20 April 2006); Lampman, "Late Medieval Trade Routes.jpg," *Wikimedia Commons* (28 March 2008).

7 For a general review of world systems research, see: Christopher Chase-Dunn and Peter Grimes, "World-Systems Analysis," *Annual Review of Sociology* 21, (1995): 387–417. For examples of networks applied to world systems theory, see: David Snyder and Edward L. Kick, "Structural Position in the World System and Economic Growth, 1955–1970: A Multiple-Network Analysis of Transnational Interactions," *American Journal of Sociology* 84, (1979): 1096–1126; Roger J. Nemeth and David A. Smith, "International Trade and World-System Structure: A Multiple Network Analysis," *Review of the Ferdinand Braudel Center* 8, (1985): 517–560; David A. Smith and Douglas R. White, "Structure and Dynamics of the Global Economy: Network Analysis of International Trade 1965–1980," *Social Forces* 70, (1992): 857–893; Edward L. Kick and Byron L. Davis, "World-System Structure and Change: An Analysis of Global Networks and Economic Growth across Two Time Periods," *American Behavioral Scientist* 44, (2001): 1561–1578.

8 David A. Smith and Michael Timberlake, "World Cities: A Political Economy/Global Network Approach," *Research in Urban Sociology* 3, (1993): 181–207; Arthur S. Alderson and Jason Beckfield, "Power and Position in the World City System," *American Journal of Sociology* 109, (2004): 811–851; Matthew C. Mahutga, Xiulian Ma, David A. Smith, and Michael Timberlake, "Economic Globalisation and the Structure of the World City System: The Case of Airline Passenger Data," *Urban Studies* 47, (2010): 1925–1947.

9 Stephen Hymer, "The Multinational Corporation and the Law of Uneven Development," in Jagdish N. Bhagwati, ed., *Economics and World Order: From the 1970s to the 1990s* (London: Macmillan, 1972) 113–140; R. B. Cohen, "The New International Division of Labor, Multinational Corporations and Urban Hierarchy," in Michael Dear and Allen J. Scott, eds., *Urbanization and Urban Planning in Capitalist Society* (New York: Methuen, 1981) 287–315.

10 Jean Gottmann, "Urban Centrality and the Interweaving of Quaternary Activities," *Ekistics* 29, (1970): 322–331; David R. Meyer, "Change in the World System of Metropolises: The Role of Business Intermediaries," *Urban Geography* 12, (1991): 393–416; Saskia Sassen, *The Global City: New York, London, Tokyo* (Princeton, NJ: Princeton University Press, 1991).

11 John Friedmann, "The World City Hypothesis," *Development and Change* 17, (1986): 69–83, 71. The world city hypothesis is in fact a series of seven related statements about cities under conditions of contemporary globalization. This one, the second in the series, most directly touches on the role of global urban networks.

12 A geographic layout is a special type of attribute-based layout. Attribute-based layouts position nodes based on their attributes or characteristics. In a geographic layout, these characteristics are their latitude and longitude. But, an attribute-based layout could also be used to position nodes representing people based on, for example, their age and education.

13 Adapted from David A. Smith and Michael Timberlake, "Cities in Global Matrices: Toward Mapping the World-System's City System," in Paul L. Knox and Peter J. Taylor, eds., *World Cities in a World-System* (New York: Cambridge University Press, 1995) 79–97; David A. Smith and Michael Timberlake, "Conceptualising and Mapping the Structure of the World System's City System," *Urban Studies* 32, (1995): 287–302.

14 Nigel Harris, "The Emerging Global City: Transport," *Cities* 11, (1994): 332–336; Ed Brown, Ben Derudder, Christof Parnreiter, Wim Pelupessy, Peter J. Taylor, and Frank Witlox, "World City

Networks and Global Commodity Chains: Towards a World-Systems' Integration," *Global Networks* 10, (2010): 12–34; Markus Hesse, "Cities, Material Flows, and the Geography of Spatial Interaction: Urban Places in the System of Chains," *Global Networks* 10, (2010): 75–91; Saskia Sassen, "Global Inter-city Networks and Commodity Chains: Any Intersections?" *Global Networks* 10, (2010): 150–163; Ingeborg Vind and Niels Fold, "City Networks and Commodity Chains: Identifying Global Flows and Local Connections in Ho Chi Minh City," *Global Networks* 10, (2010): 54–74.

15   J. V. Beaverstock, M. A. Doel, P. J. Hubbard, and P. J. Taylor, "Attending to the World: Competition, Cooperation, and Connectivity in the World City Network," *Global Networks* 2, (2002): 111–132; Céline Rozenblat, "Opening the Black Box of Agglomeration Economies for Measuring Cities' Competitiveness through International Firm Markets," *Urban Studies* 47, (2010): 2841–2865.

16   J. V. Beaverstock, R. G. Smith, P. J. Taylor, D. R. F. Walker, and H. Lorimer, "Globalization and World Cities: Some Measurement Challenges," *Applied Geography* 20, (2000): 43–63; Ben Derudder, "On Conceptual Confusion in Empirical Analyses of a Transnational Urban Network," *Urban Studies* 43, (2006): 2027–2046.

17   Alderson and Beckfield, 2004.

18   William K. Carroll, "Global Cities in the Global Corporate Network," *Environment and Planning A* 39, (2007): 2297–2323; Jeffrey Kentor, Adam Sobek, and Michael Timberlake, "Interlocking Corporate Directorates and the Global City Hierarchy," *Journal of World-Systems Research* 17, (2011): 498–514.

19   Peter J. Taylor, "Specification of the World City Network," *Geographical Analysis* 33, (2001): 181–194; P. J. Taylor, G. Catalano, and D. R. F. Walker, "Measurement of the World City Network," *Urban Studies* 39, (2002): 2367–2376; Peter J. Taylor, *World City Network: A Global Urban Analysis* (New York: Routledge, 2004). Although the interlocking approach is most commonly used to examine global urban networks where cities are linked by the multiple branch office locations of multinational firms, it can also be used to examine networks where cities are linked by other non-economic institutions, such as United Nations agencies or Non-Governmental Organizations (NGOs); see: Peter J. Taylor, "Leading World Cities: Empirical Evaluations of Urban Nodes in Multiple Networks," *Urban Studies* 42, (2005): 1593–1608. However, this approach also has some significant limitations; see: Carl Nordlund, "A Critical Comment on the Taylor Approach for Measuring World City Interlock Linkages," *Geographical Analysis* 36, (2004): 290–296; Neal, "Differentiating Centrality and Power," 2011.

20   For a comparison of the interlocking and corporate relations approaches, see: Peter J. Taylor, "Comment: Parallel Paths to Understanding Global Intercity Relations," *American Journal of Sociology* 112, (2006): 881–194; Jason Beckfield and Arthur S. Alderson, "Reply: Whither The Parallel Paths? The Future of Scholarship on the World City System," *American Journal of Sociology* 112, (2006): 895–904.

21   David J. Keeling, "Transport and the World City Paradigm," in Paul L. Knox and Peter J. Taylor, eds., *World Cities in a World-System* (New York: Cambridge University Press, 1995) 115–131; Peter J. Rimmer, "Transport and Telecommunications among World Cities," in Fu-Chen Lo and Yue-Man Yeung, eds., *Globalization and the World of Large Cities* (New York: United Nations Press, 1998) 433–470; Ben Derudder and Frank Witlox, "An Appraisal of the Use of Airline Data in Assessing the World City Network: A Research Note on Data," *Urban Studies* 42, (2005): 2371–2388.

22   César Ducruet, Céline Rozenblat, and Faraz Zaidi, "Ports in Multi-level Maritime Networks: Evidence from the Atlantic (1996–2006)," *Journal of Transport Geography* 18, (2010): 508–518; Wouter Jacobs, César Ducruet, and Peter de Langen, "Integrating World Cities into Production Networks: The Case of Port Cities," *Global Networks* 10, (2010): 92–113; César Ducruet and Theo Nooteboom, "The Worldwide Maritime Network of Container Shipping: Spatial Structure and Regional Dynamics," *GaWC Research Bulletin 364*.

23   Anthony M. Townsend, "Network Cities and the Global Structure of the Internet," *American Behavioral Scientist* 44, (2001): 1697–1716; Sean P. Gorman and Edward J. Malecki, "Fixed and Fluid: Stability and Change in the Geography of the Internet," *Telecommunications Policy* 26, (2002):

389–413; Lomme Devriendt, Ben Derudder, and Frank Witlox, "Cyberplace and Cyberspace: Two Approaches to Analyzing Digital Intercity Linkages," *Journal of Urban Technology* 15, (2008): 5–32.

24 Junho H. Choi, George A. Barnett, and Bum-Soo Chon, "Comparing World City Networks: A Network Analysis of Internet Backbone and Air Transport Intercity Linkages," *Global Networks* 6, (2006): 81–99; Peter J. Taylor, Ben Derudder, and Frank Witlox, "Comparing Airline Passenger Destinations with Global Service Connectivities: A Worldwide Empirical Study of 214 Cities," *Urban Geography* 28, (2007): 232–248; César Ducruet, Daniele Ietri, and Céline Rozenblat, "Cities in Worldwide Air and Sea Flows: A Multiple Networks Analysis," *Cybergeo*, article 528 (2011).

25 Nathan Mantel, "The Detection of Disease Clustering and a Generalized Regression Approach," *Cancer Research* 27, (1967): 209–220; L. J. Hubert and J. Schultz, "Quadratic Assignment as a General Data Analysis Strategy," *British Journal of Mathematical and Statistical Psychology* 29, (1976): 190–241; David Krackhardt, "Predicting with Networks: Nonparametric Multiple Regression Analysis of Dyadic Data," *Social Networks* 10, (1988): 359–381. Because network data is not statistically independent, many other traditional statistical techniques are also not appropriate for analyzing network data; alternative methods exist and are continuing to be developed.

26 "Liverpool: Port, Docks, and City," *Illustrated London News*, 15 May 1886; Patrick Geddes, *Cities in Evolution* (London: Williams and Norgate, 1915).

27 Peter Hall, 1966, 7.

28 Friedmann, 1986; Sassen, 1991; J. V. Beaverstock, P. J. Taylor, and R. G. Smith, "A Roster of World Cities," *Cities* 16, (1999): 445–458.

29 J. R. Short, Y. Kim, M. Kuus, and H. Wells, "The Dirty Little Secret of World Cities Research: Data Problems in Comparative Analysis," *International Journal of Urban and Regional Research* 20, (1996): 697–717.

30 John Allen, "Cities of Power and Influence: Settled Formations," in John Allen, Doreen Massey, and Michael Pryke, eds., *Unsettling Cities* (New York: Routledge, 1999) 181–218; Peter J. Taylor, David R. F. Walker, Gilda Catalano, and Michael Hoyler, "Diversity and Power in the World City Network," *Cities* 19, (2002): 231–241; John Allen, "Powerful City Networks: More than Connections, Less than Domination and Control," *Urban Studies* 47, (2010): 2895–2911.

31 Neal, "Differentiating Centrality and Power in the World City Network (2011).

32 Reprinted from Neal (2011).

33 Thomas Friedman, *The World is Flat* (New York: Farrar, Straus, and Giroux, 2005); Richard Florida, "The World is Spiky," *Atlantic Monthly* 10, (2005): 48–51; Zachary Neal, "The Duality of World Cities and Firms: Comparing Networks, Hierarchies, and Inequalities in the Global Economy," *Global Networks* 8, (2008): 94–115. Geddes recognized, even in 1915, that the growth of global connections between cities would not lead cities to become equal or the world to be flat: "Despite decentralisation thus preparing with the awakening and development of secondary cities and regions, the conception of the World-City . . . is not exhausted" (p. 278).

34 Ann Markusen and Vicky Gwiasda, "Multipolarity and the Layering of Functions in World Cities: New York City's Struggle to Stay on Top," *International Journal of Urban and Regional Research* 18, (1993): 167–193; Alderson and Beckfield, 2004; Taylor, 2004; Carroll, 2007.

35 Zachary Neal, "Types of Hub Cities and Their Effects on Urban Creative Economies," in *Hub Cities and the Knowledge Economy* (Burlington, VT: Ashgate, in press).

36 Matthew A. Zook and Stanley D. Brunn, "From Podes to Antipodes: Positionalities and Global Airline Geographies," *Annals of the Association of American Geographers* 96, (2006): 471–490; Ben Derudder, Lomme Devriendt, and Frank Witlox, "Flying Where You Don't Want To Go: An Empirical Analysis of Hubs in the Global Airline Network," *Tijdschrift voor Economische en Sociale Geografie* 98, (2007): 307–324.

37 David A. Smith and Michael F. Timberlake, "World City Networks and Hierarchies, 1977–1997," *American Behavioral Scientist* 44, (2001): 1656–1678; Peter J. Taylor, Ben Derudder, Cándida Gago García, and Frank Witlox, "From North–South to 'Global' South? An Investigation of a Changing 'South' Using Airline Flows between Cities, 1970–2005," *Geography Compass* 3, (2009): 836–855;

Arthur S. Alderson, Jason Beckfield, and Jessica Sprague-Jones, "Intercity Relations and Globalization: The Evolution of the Global Urban Hierarchy, 1981–2007," *Urban Studies* 47, (2010): 1899–1923; Ben Derudder et al., "Pathways of Change: Shifting Connectivities in the World City Network, 2000–08," *Urban Studies* 47, (2010): 1861–1877; Renato A. Orozco-Pereira and Ben Derudder, "Determinants of Dynamics in the World City Network, 2000–2004," *Urban Studies* 47, (2010): 1949–1967.

38   David R. Meyer, "The World System of Cities: Relations Between International Financial Metropolises and South American Cities," *Social Forces* 64, (1986): 553–581; Derudder, Taylor, Witlox, and Catalano 2003; Peter J. Taylor, "Regionality in the World City Network," *International Journal of Social Science* 56, (2004): 361–372; Ben Derudder and Peter Taylor, "The Cliqueishness of World Cities," *Global Networks* 5, (2005): 71–91.

39   Kyoung-Ho Shin and Michael Timberlake, "World Cities in Asia: Cliques, Centrality, and Connectedness," *Urban Studies* 37, (2000): 2257–2285; Ed Brown, Gilda Catalano, and Peter J. Taylor, "Beyond World Cities: Central America in a Global Spaces of Flows," *Area* 34, (2002): 139–148; David Bassens, Ben Derudder, and Frank Witlox, "Searching for the Mecca of Finance: Islamic Financial Services and the World City Network," *Area* 42, (2010): 35–46.

40   John Rennie Short, Carrie Breitbach, Steven Buckman, and Jamey Essex, "From World Cities to Gateway Cities: Extending the Boundaries of Globalization Theory," *City* 4, (2000): 317–340; Richard Grant and Jan Nijman, "Globalization and the Corporate Geography of Cities in the Less-Developed World," *Annals of the Association of American Geographers* 92, (2002): 320–340; Josef Gugler, "World Cities in Poor Countries: Conclusions from Case Studies of the Principal Regional and Global Players," *International Journal of Urban and Regional Research* 27, (2003): 707–712; Jennifer Robinson, "Global and World Cities: A View From Off the Map," *International Journal of Urban and Regional Research* 26, (2002): 531–554; John Rennie Short, "Black Holes and Loose Connections in a Global Urban Network," *Professional Geographer* 56, (2004): 295–302;

41   Michael Samers, "Immigration and the Global City Hypothesis: Towards an Alternative Research Agenda," *International Journal of Urban and Regional Research* 26, (2002): 389–402; Lisa Benton-Short, Marie D. Price, and Samantha Friedman, "Globalization from Below: The Ranking of Global Immigrant Cities," *International Journal of Urban and Regional Research* 29, (2005): 945–959; Richard B. Freeman, "People Flows in Globalization," *Journal of Economic Perspectives* 20, (2006): 145–170.

42   Kamran Khan, et al., "Preparing for Infectious Disease Threats at Mass Gatherings: The Case of the Vancouver 2010 Olympic Winter Games," *Canadian Medical Association Journal* 182, (2010): 579–583.

43   Peter J. Taylor, "New Political Geographies: Global Civil Society and Global Governance Through World City Networks," *Political Geography* 24, (2005): 703–730; Hilda Blanco and Tim Campbell, "Social Capital of Cities: Emerging Networks of Horizontal Assistance," *Technology in Society* 28, (2006): 169–181.

44   Stefan Krätke, "Global Media Cities in a World-Wide Urban Network," *European Planning Studies* 11, (2003): 605–628; Paul L. Knox, "World Cities and the Internationalization of Design Services," in Peter J. Taylor, Ben Derudder, Pieter Saey, and Frank Witlox, eds., *Cities in Globalization: Practices, Policies, and Theories* (New York: Routledge, 2007) 72–86; Xuefei Ren, *Building Globalization: Transnational Architecture Production in Urban China* (Chicago: University of Chicago Press, 2011) chapter 2.

45   Christian Wichmann Matthiessen, Annette Winkel Schwartz, and Søren Find, "The Top-level Global Research System, 1997–99: Centres, Networks, and Nodality. An Analysis Based on Bibliometric Indicators," *Urban Studies* 39, (2002): 903–927; Christian Wichmann Matthiessen, Annette Winkel Schwartz, and Søren Find, "World Cities of Scientific Knowledge: Systems, Networks, and Potential Dynamics. An Analysis Based on Bibliometric Indicators," *Urban Studies* 47, (2010): 1879–1897.

46   Wilbur Zelinsky, "The Twinning of the World: Sister Cities in Geographic and Historical Perspective," *Annals of the Association of American Geographers* 81, (1991): 1–31; Rolf D. Cremer, Anne de Bruin, and Ann Dupuis, "International Sister-Cities: Bridging the Global-Local Divide," *American*

Journal of Economics and Sociology 60, (2001): 377–401; Tüzin Baycan-Levent, Seda Kundak, and Aliye Ahu Gülümser, "City-to-city Linkages in a Mobile Society: The Role of Urban Networks in Eurocities and Sister Cities," *International Journal of Services Technology and Management* 10, (2008): 83–109; Julia Grosspietsch, "More than Food and Folk Music? Geographical Perspectives on European Town Twinning," *Geography Compass* 3, (2009): 1–24.

47   Taylor, 1997.

10 Conclusion: The New Science of Urban Networks

1   As with any area of study, the new science of networks is built upon the work of others stretching back many decades. However, its contemporary origin is often traced to a three-page paper published in 1998: Duncan J. Watts and Steven H. Strogatz, "Collective Dynamics of 'Small-World' Networks," *Nature* 393, (1998): 440–442. Since this time, the field has expanded rapidly and although it has become quite complex, several excellent introductions have been written for a general audience; see: Albert-László Barabási, *Linked: How Everything is Connected to Everything and What It Means for Business, Science, and Everyday Life* (New York: Penguin, 2002); Duncan J. Watts, *Six Degrees: The Science of a Connected Age* (New York: Norton, 2003). For a more comprehensive but technical introduction, see: M. E. J. Newman, *Networks: An Introduction* (New York: Oxford University Press, 2010).

2   For an earlier discussion of these three patterns, applied to the urban context, see: Celine Rozenblat and Guy Melançon, "A Small World Perspective on Urban Systems," in F. Bavaud and C. Mager, eds., *Handbook of Theoretical and Quantitative Geography* (Lausanne, Switzerland: University of Lausanne, 2009) 431–467.

3   Stanley Milgram, "The Small-World Problem," *Psychology Today* 1, (1967): 61–67.

4   Several websites exist that allow users to examine the chains that link different people in small world networks. For the acting network, see: www.oracleofbacon.org. For the baseball network, see: www.baseball-reference.com/oracle. For a mathematics network where researchers are connected when they have co-authored a paper, see: www.ams.org/mathscinet/collaborationdistance.html.

5   Michael Batty, "Cities as Small Worlds," *Environment and Planning B* 28, (2001): 637–638.

6   Watts and Strogatz, 1998; M. E. J. Newman, "Models of the Small World," *Journal of Statistical Physics* 101, (2000): 819–841.

7   Jiang and Claramunt, 2004; Jiang, 2007.

8   W. Li and X. Cai, "Statistical Analysis of Airport Network of China," *Physical Review E* 69, (2004): 046106; W. Li and X. Cai, "Empirical Analysis of a Scale-Free Railway Network in China," *Physica A* 382, (2007): 693–703; Ganesh Bagler, "Analysis of the Airport Network of India as a Complex Weighted Network," *Physica A* 387, (2008): 2972–2980; Zengwang Xu and Robert Harriss, "Exploring the Structure of the U.S. Intercity Passenger Air Transportation Network: A Weighted Complex Network Approach," *GeoJournal* 73, (2008): 87–102; Jiaoe Wang, Huihui Mo, Fahui Wang, and Fengjun Jin, "Exploring the Network Structure and Nodal Centrality of China's Air Transport Network: A Complex Network Approach," *Journal of Transport Geography* 19, (2011): 712–721.

9   R. Guimerà and L. A. N. Amaral, "Modeling the World-Wide Airport Network," *European Physical Journal B* 38, (2004): 381–385; R. Guimerà, S. Mossa, A. Turtschi, and L. A. N. Amaral, "The Worldwide Air Transportation Network: Anomalous Centrality, Community Structure, and Cities' Global Roles," *Proceedings of the National Academy of Sciences* 102, (2005): 7794–7799; Yihong Hu and Daoli Zhu, "Empirical Analysis of the Worldwide Maritime Transportation Network," *Physica A* 388, (2009): 2061–2071; Pablo Kaluza, Andrea Kölzsch, Michael T. Gastner, and Bernd Blasius, "The Complex Network of Global Cargo Ship Movements," *Journal of the Royal Society Interface* 7, (2010): 1093–1103.

10   Watts and Strogatz, 1998.

11   Banavar, Maritan, and Rinaldo, 1999; Changizi and Destefano, 2010.

12   Albert-László Barabási and Eric Bonabeau, "Scale-Free Networks," *Scientific American* 288, (2003): 50–59; Guido Caldarelli, *Scale-Free Networks: Complex Webs in Nature and Technology* (New York: Oxford University Press, 2007).

13   Claes Andersson, Alexander Hellervik, and Kristian Lindgren, "Urban Economy as a Scale-Free
     Network," *Physical Review E* 68, (2003): 036124; Sean P. Gorman and Rajendra Kulkarni, "Spatial
     Small Worlds: New Geographic Patterns for an Information Economy," *Environment and Planning
     B* 31, (2004): 273–296; Guimerà and Amaral, 2004; Guimerà, Mossa, Turtschi, and Amaral, 2005;
     Stefan Lammer, Björn Gehlsen, and Dirk Helbing, "Scaling Laws in the Spatial Structure of Urban
     Road Networks," *Physica A* 363, (2006): 89–95; Jiang, 2007; Li and Cai, 2007; A. P. Masucci and
     G. J. Rodgers, "The Network of Commuters in London," *Physica A* 387, (2008): 3781–3788; Hu
     and Zhu, 2009.

14   Albert-László Barabási and Réka Albert, "Emergence of Scaling in Random Networks," *Science* 286,
     (1999): 509–512; Sandra Vinciguerra, Koen Frenken and Marco Valente, "The Geography of Internet
     Infrastructure: An Evolutionary Simulation Approach Based on Preferential Attachment," *Urban
     Studies* 47, (2010): 1969–1984.

15   Banavar, Maritan, and Rinaldo, 1999; Stephen Eubank, Hasan Guclu, V. S. Anil Kumar, Madhav
     V. Marathe, Aravind Srinivasan, Zoltán Toroczkal, and Nan Wang, "Modeling Disease Outbreaks
     in Realistic Urban Social Networks," *Nature* 429, (2004): 180–184.

16   Réka Albert, Hawoong Jeong, and Albert-László Barabási, "Error and Attack Tolerance of Complex
     Networks," *Nature* 406, (2000): 378–382; Tony H. Grubesic and Alan T. Murray, "Vital Nodes,
     Interconnected Infrastructures, and the Geographies of Network Survivability," *Annals of the Association
     of American Geographers* 96, (2006): 64–83.

17   Frederick L. Bates, "Institutions, Organizations, and Communities: A General Theory of Complex
     Structures," *Pacific Sociological Review* 3, (1960): 59–70; Frederick L. Bates and Lloyd Bacon, "The
     Community as a Social System," *Social Forces* 50, (1972): 371–379; Wolfe, 2007.

18   S. Wuchty, Z. N. Oltvai, and A.-L. Barabási, "Evolutionary Conservation of Motif Constituents in
     the Yeast Protein Interaction Network," *Nature Genetics* 35, (2003): 176–179; Sean Myles et al.,
     "Genetic Structure and Domestication History of the Grape," *Proceedings of the National Academy of
     Sciences* (doi: 10.1073/pnas.1009363108).

19   W. W. Zachary, "An Informational Flow Model for Conflict and Fission in Small Groups," *Journal
     of Anthropological Research* 33, (1977): 452–473.

20   M. Girvan and M. E. J. Newman, "Community Structure in Social and Biological Networks,"
     Proceedings of the National Academy of Sciences 99, (2002): 7821–7826; Filippo Radicchi, Claudio
     Castellano, Federico Cecconi, Vittorio Loreto, and Domenico Parisi, "Defining and Identifying
     Communities in Networks," *Proceedings of the National Academy of Sciences* 101, (2004): 2658–2663;
     M. E. J. Newman, "Modularity and Community Structure in Networks," *Proceedings of the National
     Academy of Sciences* 103, (2006): 8577–8582; Santo Fortunato, "Community Detection in Graphs,"
     Physics Reports 486, (2010): 75–174.

21   D. Volchenkov and Ph. Blanchard, "Ghetto of Venice: Access to the Target Node and the Random
     Target Access Time," *arXiv:* 0710.3021v1 [physics.soc-ph].

REFERENCES AND SUGGESTED READING

Abu-Lughod, Janet L. 1999. *New York, Chicago, Los Angeles: America's Global Cities*. Minneapolis, MN: University of Minnesota Press.

Abbott, Carl. 1992. "Regional City and Network City: Portland and Seattle in the Twentieth Century." *Western Historical Quarterly* 23: 293–322.

Agranoff, Robert and Michael McGuire. 1998. "Multinetwork Management: Collaboration and the Hollow State in Local Economic Policy." *Journal of Public Administration Research and Theory* 8: 67–91.

Ahuja, Ravindra K., James B. Orlin, Sefano Pallottino, and Maria Grazia Scutella. 2002. "Minimum Time and Minimum Cost-Path Problems in Street Networks with Periodic Traffic Lights." *Transportation Science* 36: 326–336.

Aiken, Michael. 1970. "The Distribution of Community Power: Structural Bases and Social Consequences." Pp. 487–519 in *The Structure of Community Power*, edited by Michael Aiken and Paul E. Mott. New York: Random House.

Albert, Reka, Hawoong Jeong, and Albert-Laszlo Barabasi. 2000. "Error and Attack Tolerance of Complex Networks." *Nature* 406: 378–382.

Albrechts, Louis, and Griet Lievois. 2004. "The Flemish Diamond: Urban Network in the Making?" *European Planning Studies* 12: 351–370.

Alderson, Arthur S., and Jason Beckfield. 2004. "Power and Position in the World City System." *American Journal of Sociology* 109: 811–851.

Alderson, Arthur S., Jason Beckfield, and Jessica Sprague-Jones. 2010. "Intercity Relations and Globalisation: The Evolution of the Global Urban Hierarchy, 1981–2007." *Urban Studies* 47: 1899–1923.

Aldrich, Howard. 1976. "Resource Dependence and Interorganizational Relations: Local Employment Service Offices and Social Services Sector Organizations." *Administration and Society* 7: 419–454.

Alexander, Christopher. 1965. "A City is Not a Tree." *Architectural Forum* 122: 58–62.

——, Hajo Neis, Artemis Anninou, and Ingrid King. 1987. *A New Theory of Urban Design*. New York: Oxford University Press.

Alexander, John W. 1954. "The Basic-Nonbasic Concept of Urban Economic Function," *Economic Geography* 30: 246–261.

Allen, John. 1999. "Cities of Power and Influence: Settled Formations." Pp. 181–218 in *Unsettling Cities*, edited by John Allen, Doreen Massey, and Michael Pryke. New York: Routledge.

—— 2010. "Powerful City Networks: More than Connections, Less than Domination and Control." *Urban Studies* 47: 2895–2911.

Alonso, William. 1964. *Location and Land Use: Toward a General Theory of Land Rent*. Cambridge, MA: Harvard University Press.

Anas, Alex and Leon N. Moses. 1979. "Mode Choice, Transport Structure and Urban Land Use." *Journal of Urban Economics* 6: 228–246.

Andersson, Claes, Alexander Hellervik, and Kristian Lindgren. 2003. "Urban Economy as a Scale-Free Network." *Physical Review E* 68: 036124.

Andrew, Simon A. 2009. "Regional Integration Through Contracting Networks: An Empirical Analysis of Institutional Collection Action Framework." *Urban Affairs Review* 44: 378–402.

Andrews, Richard B. 1953. "Mechanics of the Urban Economic Base." *Land Economics* 29: 161–167, 263–268, 343–350.

Ansell, Christopher. 2003. "Community Embeddedness and Collaborative Governance in the San Francisco Bay Area Environmental Movement." Pp. 233–258 in *Social Movements and Networks: Relational Approaches to Collective Action*, edited by Mario Diani and Doug McAdam. New York: Oxford University Press.

———, Sarah Reckhow, and Andrew Kelly. 2009. "How to Reform a Reform Coalition: Outreach, Agenda Expansion, and Brokerage in Urban School Reform." *Policy Studies Journal* 37: 717–743.

Anton, Thomas J. 1963. "Power, Pluralism, and Local Politics." *Administrative Science Quarterly* 7: 425–457.

Appleyard, Donald. 1970. "Styles and Methods of Structuring a City." *Environment and Behavior* 2: 100–117.

Arndt, Michael, Thomas Gawron, and Petry Jahnke. 2000. "Regional Policy through Co-operation: From Urban Form to Urban Network." *Urban Studies* 37: 1903–1923.

Asami, Yasushi, Ayse Sema Kubat, and Cihangir Istek. 2001. "Characterization of the Street Networks in the Traditional Turkish Urban Form." *Environment and Planning B* 28: 777–795.

Atwater, Leanne, Robert Penn, and Linda Rucker. 1993. "Personal Qualities of Charismatic Leaders." *Leadership and Organization Development Journal* 12: 7–10.

Auerbach, Felix. 1913. "Das Gesetz der Bevölkerungskonzentration." *Petermann's Geographische Mitteilungen* 59: 74–76.

Axelrod, Morris. 1956. "Urban Structure and Social Participation." *American Sociological Review* 21: 13–18.

Bachrach, Peter and Morton S. Baratz. 1963. "Decisions and Nondecisions: An Analytical Framework." *American Political Science Review* 57: 632–642.

Badcock, B. A. 1970. "Central Place Evolution and Network Development in South Auckland, 1840–1968: A Systems Analytic Approach." *New Zealand Geographer* 26: 109–135.

Bagler, Ganesh. 2008. "Analysis of the Airport Network of India as a Complex Weighted Network." *Physica A* 387: 2972–2980.

Bailey, Nick and Ivan Turok. 2001. "Central Scotland as a Polycentric Urban Region: Useful Planning Concept or Chimera." *Urban Studies* 38: 697–715.

Balcan, Duygu, Vittoria Colizza, Bruno Goncalves, Hao Hu, Jose J. Ramasco, and Alessandro Vespignani. 2009. "Multiscale Mobility Networks and the Spatial Spreading of Infectious Diseases." *Proceedings of the National Academy of Sciences* 106: 21484–21489.

Baldassari, Delia and Mario Diani. 2007. "The Integrative Power of Civic Networks." *American Journal of Sociology* 113: 735–780.

Banavar, Jayanth R., Amos Maritan, and Andrea Rinaldo. 1999. "Size and Form in Efficient Transportation Networks." *Nature* 399: 130–132.

Bania, Neil, Paul W. Bauer, and Thomas J. Zlatoper. 1998. "U.S. Air Passenger Service: A Taxonomy of Route Networks, Hub Locations, and Competition." *Transportation Research E* 34: 53–74.

Barabási, Albert-László. 2002. *Linked: How Everything is Connected to Everything and What It Means for Business, Science, and Everyday Life.* New York: Penguin.

Barabasi, Albert-Laszlo and Reka Albert. 1999. "Emergence of Scaling in Random Networks." *Science* 286: 509–512.

——— and Eric Bonabeau. 2003. "Scale-Free Networks." *Scientific American* 288: 50–59.

Baran, Perver, Daniel A. Rodriguez, and Asad J. Khattak. 2008. "Space Syntax and Walking in a New Urbanist and Suburban Neighborhoods." *Journal of Urban Design* 13: 5–28.

Barnes, J. A. 1954. "Class and Committees in a Norweigian Island Parish." *Human Relations* 7: 39–58.

Barnes, Sandra L. 2003. "Determinants of Individual Neighborhood Ties and Social Resources in Poor Urban Neighborhoods." *Sociological Spectrum* 23: 463–497.

Barth, Fredrik. 1969. "Introduction." Pp. 9–38 in *Ethnic Groups and Boundaries: The Social Organization of Culture Difference*, edited by Fredrik Barth. Boston, MA: Little, Brown, and Company.

Barthélemy, Marc. 2010. "Spatial Networks." *arXiv*: 1010.0302v2 [cond-mat.stat-mech].

Bassens, David, Ben Derudder, and Frank Witlox. 2010. "Searching for the Mecca of Finance: Islamic Financial Services and the World City Network." *Area* 42: 35–46.

Bassett, Keith. 1996. "Partnerships, Business Elites, and Urban Politics: New Forms of Governance in an English City?" *Urban Studies* 33: 539–555.

Bastiaan, Goei de, Martijn J. Burger, Frank G. van Oort, and Michael Kitson. 2010. "Functional Polycentrism and Urban Network Development in the Greater South East United Kingdom: Evidence from Commuting Patterns, 1981–2001." *Regional Studies* 44: 1149–1170.

Bates, Frederick L. 1960. "Institutions, Organizations, and Communities: A General Theory of Complex Structures." *Pacific Sociological Review* 3: 59–70.

Bates, Frederick L. and Lloyd Bacon. 1972. "The Community as a Social System." *Social Forces* 50: 371–379.

Batten, David F. 1993. "Network Cities Versus Central Place Cities: Building as Cosmo-Creative Constellation." Pp. 137–150 in *The Cosmo-Creative Society: Logistical Networks in a Dynamic Economy*, edited by A. E. Andersson, D. F. Batten, K. Kobayashi, and K. Yoshikawa. New York: Springer-Verlag.

—— 1995. "Network Cities: Creative Urban Agglomerations for the 21st Century." *Urban Studies* 32: 313–327.

——and Gunnar Tornqvist. 1990. "Multilevel Network Barriers: The Methodological Challenge." *Annals of the Regional Science Association* 24: 271–287.

—— and Roland Thord. 1995. "Europe's Hierarchical Network Economy." Pp. 251–266 in *Networks in Action: Communication, Economics, and Human Knowledge*, edited by David Batten, John Casti, and Roland Thord. New York: Springer-Verlag.

Batterbury, Simon. 2003. "Environmental Activism and Social Networks: Campaigning for Bicycles and Alternative Transport in West London." *Annals of the American Academy of Political and Social Science* 590: 150–169.

Batty, Michael. 2001. "Polynucleated Urban Landscapes." *Urban Studies* 38: 635–655.

—— 2001. "Cities as Small Worlds." *Environment and Planning A* 28: 637–638.

Baumgartner, M. P. 1988. *The Moral Order of a Suburb*. New York: Oxford University Press.

Baycan-Levent, Tuzun, Seda Kundak, and Aliye Ahu Gulumser. 2008. "City-to-city Linkages in a Mobile Society: The Role of Urban Networks in Eurocities and Sister Cities." *International Journal of Services Technology and Management* 10: 83–109.

Beatty, Kate, Jenine K. Harris, and Priscilla A. Barnes. 2010. "The Role of Interorganizational Partnerships in Health Services Provision Among Rural, Suburban, and Urban Local Health Departments." *Journal of Rural Health* 26: 248–258.

Beaverstock, J. V., M. A. Doel, P. J. Hubbard, and P. J. Taylor. 2002. "Attending to the World: Competition, Cooperation, and Connectivity in the World City Network." *Global Networks* 2: 111–132.

——, R. G. Smith, P. J. Taylor, D. R. F. Walker, and H. Lorimer. 2000. "Globalization and World Cities: Some Measurement Methodologies." *Applied Geography* 20: 43–63.

——, P. J. Taylor, and R. G. Smith. 1999. "A Roster of World Cities." *Cities* 16: 445–458.

Beavon, Daniel J. K., P. L. Brantingham, and P. J. Brantingham. 1994. "The Influence of Street Networks on the Patterning of Property Offenses." Pp. 115–148 in *Crime Prevention Studies, vol. 2*, edited by Ronald V. Clark. Monsey, NY: Criminal Justice Press.

Becattini, Giacomo. 1978. "The Economic Development of Tuscany: An Interpretation." *Economic Notes* 2–3: 107–123.

Beckfield, Jason, and Arthur S. Alderson. 2006. "Whither the Parallel Paths? The Future of Scholarship on the World City System." *American Journal of Sociology* 112: 895–904.

Beggs, John J., Valerie A. Haines, and Jeanne S. Hurlburt. 1996. "Revisiting the Rural–Urban Contrast: Personal Networks in Nonmetropolitan and Metropolitan Settings." *Rural Sociology* 61: 306–325.

Bejan, Adrian. 1996. "Street Network Theory of Organization in Nature." *Journal of Advanced Transportation* 30: 85–107.

Belanger, Pierre. 2007. "Underground Landscape: The Urbanism and Infrastructure of Toronto's Downtown Pedestrian Network." *Tunnelling and Underground Space Technology* 22: 272–292.

Bell, Wendell, and Marion D. Boat. 1957. "Urban Neighborhoods and Informal Social Relations." *American Journal of Sociology* 62: 391–398.

——and Maryanne T. Force. 1956. "Urban Neighborhood Types and Participation in Formal Associations." *American Sociological Review* 21: 25–34;

Benson, J. Kenneth. 1975. "The Interorganizational Network as a Political Economy." *Administrative Science Quarterly* 20: 229–249.

Benton-Short, Lisa, Marie D. Price, and Samantha Friedman. 2005. "Globalization from Below: The Ranking of Global Immigrant Cities." *International Journal of Urban and Regional Research* 29: 945–959.

Berry, Brian J. L. 1964. "Cities as Systems Within Systems of Cities." *Papers of the Regional Science Association* 13: 147–163.

—— and Allen Pred. 1965. *Central Place Studies: A Bibliography of Theory and Applications.* Philadelphia: Regional Science Research Institute.

Black, William R. 1972. "Interregional Commodity Flows: Some Experiments with the Gravity Model." *Journal of Regional Science* 12: 107–118.

Blanchard, Philippe and Dimitri Volchenkov. 2009. *Mathematical Analysis of Urban Spatial Networks.* Berlin: Springer-Verlag.

Blanco, Hilda and Tim Campbell. 2006. "Social Capital of Cities: Emerging Networks of Horizontal Assistance." *Technology in Society* 28: 169–181.

Blokland, Talja, and Mike Savage. 2008. *Networked Urbanism: Social Capital in the City.* Burlington, VT: Ashgate.

Blumberg, Leonard, and Robert R. Bell. 1959. "Urban Migration and Kinship Ties." *Social Problems* 6: 328–333.

Blumenfeld, Hans. 1949. "Theory of City Forms, Past and Present." *Journal of the Society of Architectural Historians* 8: 7–16.

Blumer, Herbert. 1958. "Race Prejudice as a Sense of Group Position." *Pacific Sociological Review* 1: 3–7.

Bogason, Peter and Juliet A. Musso. 2006. "The Democratic Prospects of Network Governance." *American Review of Public Administration* 36: 3–18.

Boissevain, Jeremy. 1966. "Poverty and Politics in a Sicilian Agro-Town." *International Archive of Ethnography* 50: 198–236.

—— 1966. "Patronage in Sicily." *Man, New Series* 1: 18–33.

—— 1968. "The Place of Non-Groups in the Social Sciences." *Man, New Series* 3: 542–556.

Boissevain, Jeremy, and J. Clyde Mitchell (eds.). 1973. *Network Analysis: Studies in Human Interaction.* The Hague: Mouton and Company.

Bolland, John M. 1985. "Perceived Leadership Stability and the Structure of Urban Agenda-Setting Networks." *Social Networks* 7: 153–172.

—— and Debra Moehle McCallum. 2002. "Neighboring and Community Mobilization in High-Poverty Inner-City Neighborhoods." *Urban Affairs Review* 38: 42–69.

—— and Jan V. Wilson. 1994. "Three Faces of Integrative Coordination: A Model of Interorganizational Relations in Community-Based Health and Human Services." *Heath Services Research* 29: 341–366.

Bonjean, Charles M. 1963. "Community Leadership: A Case Study and Conceptual Refinement." *American Journal of Sociology* 68: 672–681.

Booth, Alan and Nicholas Babchuk. 1969. "Personal Influence Networks and Voluntary Association Affiliation." *Sociological Inquiry* 39: 179–188.

Borchert, John R. 1967. "American Metropolitan Evolution." *Geographical Review* 57: 301–332.

Borhek, J. T. 1970. "Ethnic-Group Cohesion." *American Journal of Sociology* 76: 33–46.

Bortel, Gerard van and David Mullins. 2009. "Critical Perspectives on Network Governance in Urban Regeneration, Community Involvement, and Integration." *Journal of Housing and the Built Environment* 24: 203–219.

Börzel, Tanja A. 1998. "Organizing Babylon—On the Different Conceptions of Policy Networks." *Public Administration* 76: 253–273.

Bott, Elizabeth. 1955. "Urban Families: Conjugal Roles and Social Networks." *Human Relations* 8: 345–384.

Boulding, Kenneth E. 1956. "General Systems Theory—The Skeleton of Science." *Management Science* 2: 197–208.

Bowen, John. 2002. "Network Change, Deregulation, and Access in the Global Airline Industry." *Economic Geography* 78: 425–439.

Brantingham, Patricia L. and Paul J. Brantingham. 1993. "Nodes, Paths, and Edges: Considerations on the Complexity of Crime and the Physical Environment." *Journal of Environmental Psychology* 13: 3–28.

Breiger, Ronald L. 1974. "The Duality of Persons and Groups." *Social Forces* 53: 181–190.

Bretagnolle, Anne and Denise Pumain. 2010. "Simulating Urban Networks through Multiscalar Space-Time Dynamics: Europe and the United States, 17th–20th Centuries." *Urban Studies* 47: 2819–2839.

Breton, Raymond. 1964. "Institutional Completeness of Ethnic Communities and the Personal Relations of Immigrants." *American Journal of Sociology* 70: 193–205.

Bridge, Gary. 2002. "The Neighbourhood and Social Networks." *CNR Paper 4, ESRC Centre for Neighbourhood Research.*

Briffault, Richard. 1999. "A Government for Our Time? Business Improvement Districts and Urban Governance." *Columbia Law Review* 99: 365–477.

Briggs, Xavier de Souza. 2007. "'Some of my Best Friends Are . . . ': Interracial Friendships, Class, and Segregation in America." *City and Community* 6: 263–290.

Brown, David L. 2002. "Migration and Community: Social Networks in a Multilevel World." *Rural Sociology* 67: 1–23.

Brown, Ed, Gilda Catalano, and Peter J. Taylor. 2002. "Beyond World Cities: Central America in a Global Space of Flows." *Area* 34: 139–148.

——, Ben Derudder, Christof Parnreiter, Wim Pelupessy, Peter J. Taylor, and Frank Witlox. 2010. "World City Networks and Global Commodity Chains: Towards a World-Systems Integration." *Global Networks* 10: 12–34.

Brown, L. David and Lynda B. Detterman. 1987. "Small Interventions for Large Problems: Reshaping Urban Leadership Networks." *Journal of Applied Behavioral Science* 23: 151–168.

Brown-Saracino, Japonica. 2004. "Social Preservationists and the Quest for Authentic Community." *City and Community* 3: 135–156.

Bruhn, John G. 2005. *The Sociology of Community Connections.* New York: Kluwer.

Bruinsma, Frank and Piet Rietveld. 1993. "Urban Agglomerations in European Infrastructure Networks." *Urban Studies* 30: 919–934.

Buckwalter, Donald W. 2001. "Complex Topology in the Highway Network of Hungary, 1990 and 1998." *Journal of Transport Geography* 9: 125–135.

Buhl, J., J. Gautrais, N. Reeves, R. V. Sole, S. Valverde, P. Kuntz, and G. Theraulaz. 2006. "Topological Patterns in Street Networks of Self-Organized Urban Settlements." *European Physics Journal B* 49: 513–522.

Bulmer, Martin. 1985. "The Rejuvenation of Community Studies? Neighbors, Networks, and Policy." *Sociological Review* 33: 430–448.

Burger, M. J., B. de Goei, B., L. van der Laan, and F. J. M. Huisman. 2011. "Heterogeneous Development of Metropolitan Spatial Structure: Evidence from Commuting Patterns in English and Welsh City-regions, 1981–2001." *Cities* 28: 160–170.

Burgess, Ernest. 1925. "The Growth of the City: An Introduction to a Research Project." Pp. 47–62 in *The City*, edited by Robert E. Park and Ernest W. Burgess. Chicago: University of Chicago Press.

Burns, Malcolm C., Josep Roca Cladera, and Montserrat Moix Bergada. 2008. "The Spatial Implications of the Functional Proximity Deriving from Air Passenger Flows between European Metropolitan Urban Regions." *Geojournal* 71: 37–52.

Bursik, Robert, J., Jr. and Harold G. Grasmick. 1995. "Neighborhood-based Networks and the Control of Crime and Delinquency." Pp. 107–130 in *Crime and Public Policy: Putting Theory to Work*, edited by High Barlow. Boulder: Westview.

Burt, Ronald S. 1977. "Positions in Multiple Network Systems, Part Two: Stratification and Prestige among Elite Decision-Makers in the Community of Altneustadt." *Social Forces* 56: 551–575.

—— 1978. "Cohesion versus Structural Equivalence as a Basis for Network Subgroups." *Sociological Methods and Research* 7: 189–212.

—— 1984. "Network Items and the General Social Survey." *Social Networks* 6: 293–339.

—— 1987. "Social Contagion and Innovation: Cohesion Versus Structural Equivalence." *American Journal of Sociology* 92: 1287–1335.

—— 2001. "Structural Holes versus Network Closure as Social Capital." Pp. 31–56 in *Social Capital: Theory and Research*, edited by Nan Lin, Karen S. Cook, and Ron S. Burt. New York: Aldine de Gruyter.

—— 2005. *Brokerage and Closure: An Introduction to Social Capital*. New York: Oxford University Press.

Bushee, Frederick A. 1945. "Social Organization in a Small City." *American Journal of Sociology* 51: 217–226.

Button, Kenneth and Somik Lall. 1999. "The Economics of Being an Airport Hub City." *Research in Transportation Economics* 5: 75–105.

Cabus, Peter and Wim Vanhaverbeke. 2006. "The Territoriality of the Network Economy and Urban Networks: Evidence from Flanders." *Entrepreneurship and Regional Development* 18: 25–53.

Caldarelli, Guido. 2007. *Scale-Free Networks: Complex Webs in Nature and Technology*. New York: Oxford University Press.

Calhoun, C. J. 1980. "Community: Toward a Variable Conceptualization for Comparative Research." *Social History* 5: 105–129.

Calthorpe, Peter. 2002. "The Urban Network: A Radical Proposal." *Planning* 68: 10–15.

Camagni, Roberto P. 1993. "From City Hierarchy to City Network: Reflections About an Emerging Paradigm." Pp. 66–87 in *Structure and Change in the Space Economy: A Festschrift in Honor of Martin J. Beckmann*, edited by T. R. Lakshmanan and Peter Nijkamp. New York: Springer-Verlag.

—— 1993. "Inter-Firm Industrial Networks: The Costs and Benefits of Cooperative Behaviour." *Industry and Innovation* 1: 1–15.

—— and Carlo Salone. 1993. "Network Urban Structures in Northern Italy: Elements for a Theoretical Framework." *Urban Studies* 30: 1053–1064.

——, Stefano Stabilini, and Lidia Diappi. 1994. "City Networks in the Lombardy Region: An Analysis in Terms of Communication Flows." *Flux* 15: 37–50.

Campbell, Karen E. 1990. "Networks Past: A 1939 Bloomington Neighborhood." *Social Forces* 69: 139–155.

——and Barrett A. Lee. 1991. "Name Generators in Surveys of Personal Networks." *Social Networks* 13: 203–221.

—— and Barrett A. Lee. 1992. "Sources of Personal Neighbor Networks: Social Integration, Need, or Time." *Social Forces* 70: 1077–1100.

Capello, Roberta. 2000. "The City Network Paradigm: Measuring Urban Network Externalities." *Urban Studies* 37: 1925–1945.

Caplow, Theodore and Robert Forman. 1950. "Neighborhood Interaction in a Homogeneous Community." *American Sociological Review* 15: 357–366.

Carlos, Manual L. and Bo Anderson. 1981. "Political Brokerage and Network Politics in Mexico: The Case of a Dominance System." Pp. 169–187 in *Networks, Exchange, and Coercion*, edited by David Willer and Bo Anderson. New York: Elsevier.

Caro, Robert A. 1974. *The Power Broker: Robert Moses and the Fall of New York*. New York: Knopf.

Carroll, Glenn R. 1982. "National City-Size Distributions: What Do We Know After 67 Years of Research." *Progress in Human Geography* 6: 1–43.

Carroll, William K. 2007. "Global Cities in the Global Corporate Network." *Environment and Planning A* 39: 2297–2323.

Cascetta, Ennio, Francesco Russo, Francesco A. Viola, and Antonino Vitetta. 2002. "A Model of Route Perception in Urban Road Networks." *Transportation Research B* 36: 577–592.

Castells, Manuel. 2000. *The Rise of the Network Society*, 2nd edition. Malden, MA: Blackwell.

Cattan, Nadine. 1995. "Barrier Effects: The Case of Air and Rail Flows." *International Political Science Review* 16: 237–248.

—— (ed.). 2007. *Cities and Networks in Europe: A Critical Approach of Polycentrism*. Montrouge, France: John Libbey Eurotext.

Cattell, Vicky. 2001. "Poor People, Poor Places, and Poor Health: The Mediating Role of Social Networks and Social Capital." *Social Science and Medicine* 52: 1501–1516.

Cervero, Robert and Carolyn Radisch. 1996. "Travel Choices in Pedestrian Versus Automobile Oriented Neighborhoods." *Transport Policy* 3: 127–141.

Changizi, Mark A. and Marc Destefano. 2010. "Common Scaling Laws for City Highway Systems and the Mammalian Neocortex." *Complexity* 15: 11–18.

Chase-Dunn, Christopher K. 1985. "The System of World Cities: A.D. 800–1975." Pp. 269–292 in *Urbanization in the World Economy*, edited by Michael Timberlake. Orlando: Academic Press.

—— and Peter Grimes. 1995. "World-Systems Analysis." *Annual Review of Sociology* 21: 387–417.

Chaskin, Robert J. 2001. "Organizational Infrastructure and Community Capacity: The Role of Broker Organizations." *The Organizational Response to Social Problems* 8: 143–166.

Chayko, Mary. 2008. *Portable Communities: The Social Dynamics of Online and Mobile Communities*. Albany, NY: SUNY Press.

Chiu, Lai Fong, and Robert M. West. 2007. "Health Intervention in Social Context: Understanding Social Networks and Neighborhood." *Social Science and Medicine* 65: 1915–1927.

Choi, Junho H., George A. Barnett, and Bum-Soo Chon. 2006. "Comparing World City Networks: A Network Analysis of Internet Backbone and Air Transport Intercity Linkages." *Global Networks* 6: 81–99.

Chrisman, Noel J. 1970. "Situation and Social Network in Cities." *Canadian Review of Sociology and Anthropology* 7: 245–257.

Christaller, Walter. [1933] 1966. *Central Places in Southern Germany*, translated by D. W. Baskin. Englewood Cliffs, NJ: Prentice Hall.

Christens, Brian D. 2010. "Public Relationship Building in Grassroots Community Organizing: Relational Intervention for Individual and Systems Change." *American Journal of Community Psychology* 38: 886–900.

Christopherson, S. and M. Storper. 1986. "The City as Studio; the World as Back Lot: The Impact of Vertical Disintegration on the Location of the Motion Picture Industry." *Environment and Planning D* 4: 305–320.

Church, Andrew and Peter Reid. 1996. "Urban Power, International Networks, and Competition: The Example of Cross-Border Cooperation." *Urban Studies* 33: 1297–1318.

Claramunt, Christophe, and Stephan Winter. 2007. "Structural Salience of Elements of the City." *Environment and Planning B* 34: 1030–1050.

Clark, Chris, Kevin E. Henrickson, and Paul Thoma. 2005. *An Overview of the U.S. Inland Waterway System*. Alexandria, VA: U.S. Army Corps of Engineers.

Clark, Terry N. 1968. "Community Structure, Decision-Making, Budget Expenditures, and Urban Renewal in 51 American Communities." *American Sociological Review* 33: 576–593.

Clark, William A. V., and Marianne Kuijpers-Linde. 1994. "Commuting in Restructuring Urban Regions." *Urban Studies* 31: 465–483.

Clayton, Christopher. 1980. "Interdependence in Urban Systems and Its Application to Political Reorganization." *Geografiska Annaler: Series B* 62: 11–20.

Cohen, R. B. 1981. "The New International Division of Labor, Multinational Corporations, and Urban Hierarchy." Pp. 287–315 in *Urbanization and Urban Planning in Capitalist Society*, edited by Michael Dear and Allan J. Scott. New York: Methuen.

Cole, Alistair and Peter John. 1995. "Local Policy Networks in France and Britain: Policy Co-ordination in Fragmented Political Subsystems." *West European Politics* 18: 89–109.

Coleman, James S. 1988. "Social Capital in the Creation of Human Capital." *American Journal of Sociology* 94: S95-S120.

Connerly, Charles E. 1985. "The Community Question: An Extension of Wellman and Leighton." *Urban Affairs Quarterly* 20: 537–556.

Conzen, Michael P. 1975. "Capital Flows and the Developing Urban Hierarchy: State Bank Capital in Wisconsin, 1854–1895." *Economic Geography* 51: 321–338.

—— 1975. "A Transport Interpretation of the Growth of Urban Regions: An American Example." *Journal of Historical Geography* 1: 361–382.

—— 1977. "The Maturing Urban System in the United States, 1840–1910." *Annals of the Association of American Geographers* 67: 88–108.

Cook, Karen S. and J. M. Whitmeyer. 1992. "Two Approaches to Social Structure: Exchange Theory and Network Analysis." *Annual Review of Sociology* 18: 109–127.

Cooley, Charles H. 1894. *The Theory of Transportation*. Baltimore: American Economic Association.

—— [1902] 1964. *Human Nature and the Social Order*. New York: Schocken.

Cornwell, Benjamin, Timothy J. Curry, and Kent P. Schwirian. 2003. "Revisiting Norton Long's Ecology of Games: A Network Approach." *City and Community* 2: 121–142.

Corvers, Frank, Maud Hensen, and Dion Bongaerts. 2009. "Delimitation and Coherence of Functional and Administrative Regions." *Regional Studies* 43: 19–31.

Coutard, Olivier, Richard E. Hanley, and Rae Zimmerman. 2005. *Sustaining Urban Networks: The Social Diffusion of Large Technical Systems*. New York: Routledge.

Crane, Randall. 1996. "On Form Versus Function: Will the New Urbanism Reduce Traffic, or Increase It." *Journal of Planning Education and Research* 15: 117–126.

Craven, Paul, and Barry Wellman. 1973. "The Network City." *Sociological Inquiry* 43: 57–88.

Cremer, Rolf D., Anne de Bruin, and Ann Dupuis. 2001. "International Sister-Cities: Bridging the Global–Local Divide." *American Journal of Economics and Sociology* 60: 377–401.

Crenson, Matthew A. 1978. "Social Networks and Political Processes in Urban Neighborhoods." *American Journal of Political Science* 22: 578–594.

Cressey, Paul Frederick. 1938. "Population Succession in Chicago: 1898–1930." *American Journal of Sociology* 44: 59–69.

Crews, Judith. 1994. "Cities as Networks in Networks of Cities: An Interview with Steef C. Buijs." *Flux* 15: 51–57.

Cronon, William. 1991. *Nature's Metropolis: Chicago and the Great West*. New York, W. W. Norton.

Crucitti, Paolo, Vito Latora, and Sergio Porta. 2006. "Centrality in Networks of Urban Streets." *Chaos* 16: 015113.

Curtin, Kevin M. 2007. "Network Analysis in Geographic Information Systems: Review, Assessment, and Projections." *Cartography and Geographic Information Science* 34: 103–111.

D'Antonio, William V. and Eugene C. Erickson. 1962. "The Reputational Technique as a Measure of Community Power: An Evaluation Based on Comparative and Longitudinal Studies." *American Sociological Review* 27: 362–376.

Dahl, Robert A. 1957. "The Concept of Power." *Behavioral Science* 2: 201–215.

—— 1958. "A Critique of the Ruling Elite Model." *American Political Science Review* 52: 463–469.

—— 1961. *Who Governs? Democracy and Power in an American City*. New Haven, CT: Yale University Press.

Davies, Jonathan S. 2003. "Partnerships Versus Regimes: Why Regime Theory Cannot Explain Urban Coalitions in the UK." *Journal of Urban Affairs* 25: 253–269.

Davies, Wayne K. D. and David T. Herbert. 1993. "Interactions, Social Networks, and Communites." Pp. 63–84 in *Communities within Cities: An Urban Social Geography*, edited by Wayne K. D. Davies and David T. Herbert. New York: John Wiley & Sons.

Davoudi, Simin. 2003. "Polycentricity in European Spatial Planning: From an Analytical Tool to a Normative Agenda." *European Planning Studies* 11: 979–999.

De Montis, Andrea, Marc Barthelemy, Alessandro Chessa, and Alessandro Vespignani. 2007. "The Structure of Interurban Traffic: A Weighted Network Analysis." *Environment and Planning B* 34: 905–924.

——, Alessandro Chessa, Simone Caschili, Michele Campagna, and Giancarlo Deplano. 2010. "Modeling Commuting Systems Through a Complex Network Analysis: A Study of the Italian Islands of Sardinia and Sicily." *Journal of Transport and Land Use* 2: 39–55.

De Rynck, Filip and Joris Voets. 2006. "Democracy in Area-Based Policy Networks: The Case of Ghent." *American Review of Public Administration* 36: 58–78.

De Tocqueville, Alexis. [1838] 2003. *Democracy in America*, translated by Gerald Bevan. New York: Penguin Books.

Dear, Michael. 2002. "Los Angeles and the Chicago School: Invitation to a Debate." *City and Community* 1: 5–32.

Debbage, Keith G., and Dawn Delk. 2001. "The Geography of Air Passenger Volume and Local Employment Patterns by US Metropolitan Core Area: 1973–1996." *Journal of Air Transport Management* 7: 159–167.

Dekker, Karien, Beate Volker, Herman Lelieveldt, and Rene Torenvlied. 2010. "Civic Engagement in Urban Neighborhoods: Does the Network of Civic Organizations Influence Participation in Neighborhood Projects?" *Journal of Urban Affairs* 32: 609–632.

Dematteis, Giuseppe. 1994. "Global Networks, Local Cities." *Flux* 15: 17–23.

—— 1997. "Globalization and Regional Integration: The Case of the Italian Urban System." *Geojournal* 43: 331–338.

Deng, Zhong, and Phillip Bonacich. 1991. "Some Effects of Urbanism on Black Social Networks." *Social Networks* 13: 35–50.

Department of Commerce. 2002. "Urban Area Criteria for Census 2000." *Federal Register* 67: 11663–11670.

Derudder, Ben. 2006. "On Conceptual Confusion in Empirical Analyses of a Transnational Urban Network." *Urban Studies* 43: 2027–2046.

—— 2008. "Mapping Global Urban Networks: A Decade of Empirical World Cities Research." *Geography Compass* 2: 559–574.

—— and Peter Taylor. 2005. "The Cliqueishness of World Cities." *Global Networks* 5: 71–91.

—— and Frank Witlox. 2005. "An Appraisal of the Use of Airline Data in Assessing the World City Network: A Research Note on Data." *Urban Studies* 42: 2371–2388.

——, Lomme Devriendt, and Frank Witlox. 2007. "Flying Where You Don't Want to Go: An Empirical Analysis of Hubs in the Global Airline Network." *Tijdschrift voor Economische en Sociale Geographie* 98: 307–324.

——, Frank Witlox, and Peter J. Taylor. 2007. "U.S. Cities in the World City Network: Comparing Their Positions Using Global Origins and Destinations of Airline Passengers." *Urban Geography* 28: 74–91.

——, P. J. Taylor, F. Witlox, and G. Catalano. 2003. "Hierarchical Tendencies and Regional Patterns in the World City Network: A Global Urban Analysis of 234 Cities." *Regional Studies* 37: 875–886.

——, Peter Taylor, Pengfei Ni, Anneleen De Vos, Michael Hoyler, et al. 2010. "Pathways of Change: Shifting Connectivities in the World City Network, 2000–2008." *Urban Studies* 47: 1861–1877.

Derycke, Pierre-Henri. 1991. "Urban Concentration and Road Networks: Two Approaches to Congestion, Part I." *Flux* 5: 35–45.

—— 1992. "Urban Concentration and Road Networks: Two Approaches to Congestion, Part II." *Flux* 7: 41–54.

Dessemontet, Pierre, Vincent Kaufmann, and Christophe Jemelin. 2010. "Switzerland as a Single Metropolitan Area? A Study of Its Commuting Network." *Urban Studies* 47: 2785–2802.

Deutschberger, Paul. 1946. "Interaction Patterns in Changing Neighborhoods: New York and Pittsburg." *Sociometry* 9: 303–315.

Devriendt, Lomme, Ben Derudder, and Frank Witlox. 2008. "Cyberplace and Cyberspace: Two Approaches to Analysing Digital Intercity Linkages." *Journal of Urban Technology* 15: 5–32.

Dicks, T. R. B. 1972. "Network Analysis and Historical Geography." *Area* 4: 4–9.

Dodge, Martin and Rob Kitchin. 2000. *Mapping Cyberspace*. New York: Routledge.

Domhoff, G. William. 1975. "Social Clubs, Policy-Planning Groups, and Corporations: A Network Study of Ruling-Class Cohesiveness." *Critical Sociology* 5: 171–184.

—— 1978. *Who Really Rules? New Haven and Community Power Reexamined*. New Brunswick, NJ: Transaction Books.

Dotson, Floyd. 1951. "Patterns of Voluntary Association among Urban Working-Class Families." *American Sociological Review* 16: 687–693.

Dowding, Keith. 1995. "Model or Metaphor? A Critical Review of the Policy Network Approach." *Political Studies* 43: 136–158.

—— 2001. "Explaining Urban Regimes." *International Journal of Urban and Regional Research* 25: 7–19.

Driedger, Leo. 1978. "Ethnic Boundaries: A Comparison of Two Urban Neighborhoods." *Sociology and Social Research* 62: 193–211.

—— 1979. "Maintenance of Urban Ethnic Boundaries: The French in St. Boniface." *Sociological Quarterly* 20: 89–108.

—— 1980. "Jewish Identity: The Maintenance of Urban Religious and Ethnic Boundaries." *Ethnic and Religious Studies* 3: 67–88.

Duany, Andres, Elizabeth Plater-Zyberk, and Jeff Speck. 2000. *Suburban Nation: The Rise of Sprawl and the Decline of the American Dream*. New York: North Point Press.

Ducruet, Cesar and Theo Nooteboom. 2010. "The Worldwide Maritime Network of Container Shipping: Spatial Structure and Regional Dynamics." *GaWC Research Bulletin 364*.

——, Daniele Ietri, and Celine Rozenblat. 2011. "Cities in Worldwide Air and Sea Flows: A Multiple Networks Analysis." *Cybergeo*: 528.

——, Celine Rozenblat, and Faraz Zaidi. 2010. "Ports in Multi-level Maritime Networks: Evidence from the Atlantic (1996–2006)." *Journal of Transport Geography* 18: 508–518.

Duncan, Otis Dudley, W. Richard Scott, Stanley Lieberson, Beverly Duncan, and Hal H. Winsborough. 1960. *Metropolis and Region*. Baltimore, MD: Johns Hopkins University Press.

Dunn, Edgar S. Jr. 1970. "A Flow Network Image of Urban Structures." *Urban Studies* 7: 239–258.

—— 1980. *The Development of the US Urban System*. Baltimore, MD: Johns Hopkins University Press.

Dunnigan, Timothy. 1982. "Segmentary Kinship in an Urban Society: The Hmong of St. Paul-Minneapolis." *Anthropological Quarterly* 55: 126–134.

Dupuy, Gabriel. 2008. *Urban Networks—Network Urbanism*. Amsterdam: Techne Press.

—— and Vaclav Stransky. 1996. "Cities and Highway Networks in Europe." *Journal of Transport Geography* 4: 107–121.

Eberstein, Isaac W. 1982. "Intercommunity Trade and the Structure of Sustenance Organization." *Social Science Quarterly* 63: 236–248.

—— and W. Parker Frisbie. 1982. "Metropolitan Function and Interdependence in the U.S. Urban System." *Social Forces* 60: 676–700.

——and Omer R. Galle. 1984. "The Metropolitan System in the South: Functional Differentiation and Trade Patterns." *Social Forces* 62: 926–940.

Elliott, James R. 1999. "Social Isolation and Labor Market Insulation: Network and Neighborhood Effects on Less-Educated Urban Workers." *Sociological Quarterly* 40: 199–216.

Eliot, T. S. *Notes Towards a Definition of Culture*. London: Faber and Faber.

Emerson, Richard M. 1962. "Power-Dependence Relations." *American Sociological Review* 27: 31–41.

—— 1976. "Social Exchange Theory." *Annual Review of Sociology* 2: 335–362.

Emirbayer, Mustafa. 1997. "Manifesto for a Relational Sociology." *American Journal of Sociology* 103: 281–317.

Entwistle, Tom, Gillian Bristow, Frances Hines, Sophie Donaldson, and Steve Martin. 2007. "The Dysfunctions of Markets, Hierarchies, and Networks in the Meta-governance of Partnership." *Urban Studies* 44: 63–79.

Ernstson, Henrik, Stephan Barthel, Erik Andersson, and Sara T. Borgström. 2010. "Scale-Crossing Brokers and Network Governance of Urban Ecosystem Services: The Case of Stockholm." *Ecology and Society* 15(4): article 28.

Esparza, Adrian X., and Andrew J. Krmenec. 2000. "Large City Interaction in the US Urban System." *Urban Studies* 37: 691–709.

Eubank, Stephen, Hasan Guclu, V. S. Anil Kumar, Madhav V. Marathe, Aravind Srinivasan, Zoltan Toroczkal, and Nan Wang. 2004. "Modeling Disease Outbreaks in Realistic Urban Social Networks." *Nature* 429: 180–184.

Euler, Leonhard. 1741. "Solutio Problematis ad Geometriam Situs Pertinentis." *Commentarii Academiae Scientiarum Petropolitanae* 8: 128–140.

European Commission. 1999. *European Spatial Development Perspective*. Office for Official Publications of the European Communities: Luxembourg.

Fanelli, A. Alexander. 1956. "A Typology of Community Leadership Based on Influence and Interaction within the Leader Subsystem." *Social Forces* 34: 332–338.

Farias, Ignacio and Thomas Bender. 2010. *Urban Assemblages: How Actor–Network Theory Changes Urban Studies*. New York: Routledge.

Fava, Sylvia Fleis. 1956. "Suburbanism as a Way of Life." *American Sociological Review* 21: 34–37.

Feagin, Joe R. 1970. "A Note on the Friendship Ties of Black Urbanites." *Social Forces* 49: 303–308.

Feinberg, Mark E., Nathaniel R. Riggs, and Mark T. Greenberg. 2005. "Social Networks and Community Prevention Coalitions." *Journal of Primary Prevention* 26: 279–298.

Feld, Scott L. 1981. "The Focused Organization of Social Ties." *American Journal of Sociology* 86: 1015–1035.

Fernandez, Marilyn and Laura Nichols. 2002. "Bridging and Bonding Social Capital: Pluralist Ethnic Relations in Silicon Valley." *International Journal of Sociology and Social Policy* 22: 104–122.

Festinger, Leon, Stanley Schachter, and Kurt Back. 1950. *Social Pressures in Informal Groups: A Study of Human Factors in Housing*. New York: Harper and Brothers.

Fine, Gary Alan, and Sherryl Kleinman. 1979. "Rethinking Subculture: An Interactionist Analysis." *American Journal of Sociology* 85: 1–20.

Fischel, William A. 2006. "Why Voters Veto Vouchers: Public Schools and Community-Specific Social Capital," *Economics of Governance* 7: 109–132.

Fischer, Claude S. 1975. "Toward a Subcultural Theory of Urbanism." *American Journal of Sociology* 80: 1319–1341.

—— 1975. "The Study of Urban Community and Personality." *Annual Review of Sociology* 1: 67–89.

—— 1977. *Networks and Places: Social Relations in the Urban Setting*. New York: Free Press.

—— 1982. *To Dwell Among Friends: Personal Networks in the City*. Chicago: University of Chicago Press.

Fleisher, Mark. 2005. "Fieldwork Research and Social Network Analysis: Different Methods Creating Complementary Perspectives." *Journal of Contemporary Criminal Justice* 21: 120–134.

—— and Jessie L. Krienert. 2004. "Life-Course Events, Social Networks, and the Emergence of Violence Among Female Gang Members." *Journal of Community Psychology* 32: 607–622.

Fleming, Douglas K., and Yehuda Hayuth. 1994. "Spatial Characteristics of Transportation Hubs: Centrality and Intermediacy." *Journal of Transport Geography* 2: 3–18.

Florida, Richard. 2005. "The World is Spiky." *Atlantic Monthly* 2005: 48–51.

——, Tim Gulden, and Charlotta Mellander. 2008. "The Rise of the Mega-Region." *Cambridge Journal of Regions, Economy, and Society* 1: 459–476.

Foley, Donald. 1952. *Neighbors or Urbanites: A Study of a Rochester Residential District*. Rochester, NY: University of Rochester.

Fong, Eric and Wsevolod W. Isajiw. 2000. "Determinants of Friendship Choices in Multiethnic Society." *Sociological Forum* 15: 249–271.

Form, William H. and William V. D'Antonio. 1959. "Integration and Cleavage Among Community Influentials in Two Border Cities." *American Sociological Review* 24: 804–814.

Forrest, Ray and Ade Kearns. 2001. "Social Cohesion, Social Capital, and the Neighborhood." *Urban Studies* 38: 2125–2143.

Fortunato, Santo. 2010. "Community Detection in Graphs." *Physics Reports* 486: 75–174.

Foster-Fishman, Pennie G., Shelby L. Berkowitz, David W. Lounsbury, Stephanie Jacobson, and Nicole A. Allen. 2001. "Building Collaborative Capacity in Community Coalitions: A Review and Integrative Framework." *American Journal of Community Psychology* 29: 241–261.

——, Deborah A. Salem, Nicole A. Allen, and Kyle Fahrbach. 2001. "Facilitating Interorganizational Collaboration: The Contributions of Interorganizational Alliances." *American Journal of Community Psychology* 29: 875–905.

Foster, George M. 1961. "The Dyadic Contract: A Model for the Social Structure of a Mexican Peasant Village." *American Anthropologist* 63: 1173–1192.

Freeman, Lance. 2001. "The Effects of Sprawl on Neighborhood Social Ties." *Journal of the American Planning Association* 67: 69–77.

Freeman, Linton C. 1978/79. "Centrality in Social Networks: Conceptual Clarification." *Social Networks* 1: 215–239.

——. 2004. *The Development of Social Network Analysis: A Study in the Sociology of Science*. Vancouver, BC: Empirical Press.

——, Thomas J. Fararo, Warner Bloomberg Jr., and Morris H. Sunshine. 1963. "Locating Leaders in Local Communities: A Comparison of some Alternative Approaches." *American Sociological Review* 28: 791–798.

Freeman, Richard B. 2006. "People Flows in Globalization." *Journal of Economic Perspectives* 20: 145–170.

Frei, A. and K. W. Axhausen. 2007. "Size and Structure of Social Network Geographies." *Arbeitsberichte Verkehrs- und Raumplanung* 439.

——, ——, and Timo Ohnmacht. 2009. "Mobilities and Social Network Geography: Size and Spatial Dispersion—The Zurich Case Study." Pp. 99–120 in *Mobilities and Inequality*, edited by Timo Ohnmacht, Hanja Maksim, and Manfred Max Bergman. Burlington, VT: Ashgate.

French, John R. P. Jr. and Bertram Raven. 1959. "The Bases of Social Power." Pp. 150–167 in *Studies in Social Power*, edited by Dorwin Cartwright. Ann Arbor, MI: University of Michigan.

Freudenburg, William R. 1986. "The Density of Acquaintanceship: An Overlooked Variable in Community Research." *American Journal of Sociology* 92: 27–63.

Friedland, Roger and Donald Palmer. 1984. "Park Place and Main Street: Business and the Urban Power Structure." *Annual Review of Sociology* 10: 393–416.

Friedmann, John. 1986. "The World City Hypothesis." *Development and Change* 17: 69–83.

Friedman, Thomas. 2005. *The World is Flat*. New York: Farrar, Straus, and Giroux.

Gainsborough, Juliet F. 2001. "Bridging the City–Suburb Divide: States and the Politics of Regional Cooperation." *Journal of Urban Affairs* 23: 497–512.

Galaskiewicz, Joseph. 1979. *Exchange Networks and Community Politics*. Beverly Hills, CA: Sage Publications.

—— 1979. "The Structure of Community Organizational Networks." *Social Forces* 57: 1346–1364.

—— and Karl R. Krohn. 1984. "Positions, Roles, and Dependencies in a Community Interorganization System." *Sociological Quarterly* 25: 527–550.

Gamson, William A. 1966. "Reputation and Resources in Community Politics." *American Journal of Sociology* 72: 121–131.

Gans, Herbert J. 1961. "Planning and Social Life: Friendship and Neighbor Relations in Suburban Communities." *Journal of the American Institute of Planners* 27: 134–140.

—— 1962. *The Urban Villagers: Group and Class in the Life of Italian-Americans*. New York: Free Press.

—— 1962. "Urbanism and Suburbanism as Ways of Life: A Re-evaluation of Definitions." Pp. 625–648 in *Human Behavior and Social Processes: An Interactionist Approach*, edited by Arnold Rose. Boston, MA: Houghton Mifflin Company.

Garrison, William L. 1960. "Connectivity of the Interstate Highway System." *Papers and Proceedings of the Regional Science Association* 6: 121–137.

Geddes, Patrick. 1915. *Cities in Evolution*. London: Williams and Norgate.

Gehl, Jan. 1987. *Life Between Buildings*. New York: Van Nostrand Reinhold.

Gerson, Walter M. 1965. "Alienation in Mass Society: Some Causes and Responses." *Sociology and Social Research* 49: 143–152.

Gillespie, David F. and Susan A. Murty. 1994. "Cracks in a Postdisaster Service Delivery Network." *American Journal of Community Psychology* 22: 639–660.

Girvan, M. and M. E. J. Newman. 2002. "Community Structure in Social and Biological Networks." *Proceedings of the National Academy of Sciences* 99: 7821–7826.

Goetz, Andrew R., and Christopher J. Sutton. 1997. "The Geography of Deregulation in the U.S. Airline Industry." *Annals of the Association of American Geographers* 87: 238–263.

Goetz, Stephan J., Yicheol Han, Jill L. Findeis, and Kathryn J. Brasier. 2010. "U.S. Commuting Networks and Economic Growth: Measurement and Implications for Spatial Policy." *Growth and Change* 41: 276–302.

Gold, Steven J. 1994. "Patterns of Economic Cooperation among Israeli Immigrants in Los Angeles." *International Migration Review* 28: 114–135.

—— 2001. "Gender, Class, and Network: Social Structure and Migration Patterns Among Transnational Israelis." *Global Networks* 1: 19–40.

Goldenberg, Sheldon and Valerie A. Haines. 1992. "Social Networks and Institutional Completeness: From Territory to Ties." *Canadian Journal of Sociology* 17: 301–312.

Gordon, Ian R. and Philip McCann. 2000. "Industrial Clusters: Complexes, Agglomerations, and/or Social Networks." *Urban Studies* 37: 513–532.

Gordon, Milton M. 1947. "The Concept of the Sub-Culture and Its Application." *Social Forces* 26: 40–42.

—— 1964. *Assimilation in American Life: The Role of Race, Religion, and National Origins.* New York: Oxford University Press.

Gorman, Sean P. and Rajendra Kulkarni. 2004. "Spatial Small Worlds: New Geographic Patterns for an Information Economy." *Environment and Planning B* 31: 273–296.

Gorman, Sean P. and Edward J. Malecki. 2000. "The Networks of the Internet: An Analysis of Provider Networks in the USA." *Telecommunications Policy* 24: 113–134.

——, —— 2002. "Fixed and Fluid: Stability and Change in the Geography of the Internet." *Telecommunications Policy* 26: 389–413.

Gottman, Jean. 1961. *Megalopolis: The Urbanized Northeastern Seaboard of the United States.* New York: Twentieth Century Fund.

—— 1970. "Urban Centrality and the Interweaving of Quaternary Activities." *Ekistics* 29: 322–331.

—— 1983. *The Coming of the Transactional City.* College Park, MD: University of Maryland Institute for Urban Studies.

—— 1991. "The Dynamics of City Networks in an Expanding World." *Ekistics* 58: 277–281.

Gould, Peter and Rodney White. 1974. *Mental Maps.* New York: Penguin.

Gould, Roger V. 1989. "Power and Social Structure in Community Elites." *American Sociological Review* 68: 531–552.

—— 1995. *Insurgent Identities.* Chicago: University of Chicago Press.

—— and Roberto M. Fernandez. 1989. "Structures of Mediation: A Formal Approach to Brokerage in Transaction Networks." *Sociological Methodology* 19: 89–126.

Governa, Francesca and Carlo Salone. 2005. "Italy and European Spatial Policies: Polycentrism, Urban Networks, and Local Innovation Practices." *European Planning Studies* 13: 265–283.

Grabher, Gernot. 2006. "Trading Routes, Bypasses, and Risky Intersections: Mapping the Travels of 'Networks' Between Economic Sociology and Economic Geography." *Progress in Human Geography* 30: 163–189.

Graham, Stephen. 1999. "Global Grids of Glass: On Global Cities, Telecommunications, and Planetary Urban Networks." *Urban Studies* 36: 929–949.

—— 2000. "Constructing Premium Network Spaces: Reflections on Infrastructure Networks and Contemporary Urban Development." *International Journal of Urban and Regional Research* 24: 183–200.

Graham, Stephen and Simon Marvin. 2001. *Splintering Urbanism: Networked Infrastructures, Technological Mobilities, and the Urban Condition.* New York: Routledge.

Grais, R. F., J. H. Ellis, A. Kress, and G. E. Glass. 2004. "Modeling the Spread of Annual Influenza Epidemics in the U.S.: The Potential Role of Air Travel." *Health Care Management Science* 7: 127–134.

Grannis, Rick. 1998. "The Importance of Trivial Streets: Residential Streets and Residential Segregation." *American Journal of Sociology* 103: 1530–1564.

—— 2005. "T-Communities: Pedestrian Street Networks and Residential Segregation in Chicago, Los Angeles, and New York." *City and Community* 4: 295–321.

—— 2009. *From the Ground Up: Translating Geography into Community through Neighbor Networks.* Princeton, NJ: Princeton University Press.

Granovetter, Mark S. 1973. "The Strength of Weak Ties." *American Journal of Sociology* 78: 1360–1380.

—— 1985. "Economic Action and Social Structure: The Problem of Embeddedness." *American Journal of Sociology* 91: 481–510.

Grant, Richard and Jan Nijman. 2002. "Globalization and the Corporate Geography of Cities in the Less-Developed World." *Annals of the Association of American Geographers* 92: 320–340.

Gray, Mia, Elyse Golub and Ann Markusen. 1996. "Big Firms, Long Arms, Wide Shoulders: The 'Hub-and-Spoke' Industrial District in the Seattle Region." *Regional Studies* 30: 651–666.

Green, Arnold W. 1946. "Sociological Analysis of Horney and Fromm." *American Journal of Sociology* 51: 533–540.

Green, Milford B. 1983. "The Interurban Corporate Interlocking Directorate Network of Canada and the United States: A Spatial Perspective." *Urban Geography* 4: 338–354.

—— 1993. "A Geography of Institutional Stock Ownership in the United States." *Annals of the Association of American Geographers* 83: 66–89.

—— and R. Keith Semple. 1981. "The Corporate Interlocking Directorate as an Urban Spatial Information Network." *Urban Geography* 2: 148–160.

Green, Nick. 2007. "Functional Polycentricity: A Formal Definition in Terms of Social Network Analysis." *Urban Studies* 44: 2077–2103.

Greenbaum, Susan D. 1982. "Bridging Ties at the Neighborhood Level." *Social Networks* 4: 367–384.

—— and Paul E. Greenbaum. 1985. "The Ecology of Social Networks in Four Urban Neighborhoods." *Social Networks* 7: 47–76.

Greer, Scott. 1956. "Urbanism Reconsidered: A Comparative Study of Local Areas in a Metropolis." *American Sociological Review* 21: 19–25.

—— 1962. *The Emerging City: Myth and Reality.* New York: Free Press.

Greve, Arent, and Janet W. Salaff. 2005. "Social Network Approach to Understand the Ethnic Economy: A Theoretical Discourse." *Geojournal* 64: 7–16.

Grossetti, Michel. 2005. "Where do Social Relations Come From? A Study of Personal Networks in the Toulouse Area of France." *Social Networks* 27: 289–300.

Grosspietsch, Julia. 2009. "More than Food and Folk Music? Geographical Perspectives on European Town Twinning." *Geography Compass* 3: 1–24.

Grubesic, Tony H., and Alan T. Murray. 2006. "Vital Nodes, Interconnected Infrastructures, and the Geographies of Network Survivability." *Annals of the Association of American Geographers* 96: 64–83.

Grubesic, Tony H. and Morton E. O'Kelly. 2002. "Using Points of Presence to Measure Accessibility to the Commercial Internet." *Professional Geographer* 54: 259–278.

—— and Matthew Zook. 2007. "A Ticket to Ride: Evolving Landscapes of Air Travel Accessibility in the United States." *Journal of Transport Geography* 15: 417–430.

——, Timothy C. Matisziw, and Matthew A. Zook. 2008. "Global Airline Networks and Nodal Regions." *GeoJournal* 71: 53–66.

Guest, Avery M. 2000. "The Mediate Community: The Nature of Local and Extralocal Ties within the Metropolis." *Urban Affairs Review* 35: 603–627.

—— and R. S. Oropesa. 1986. "Informal Social Ties and Political Activity in the Metropolis." *Urban Affairs Review* 21: 550–574.

—— and Susan K. Wierzbicki. 1999. "Social Ties at the Neighborhood Level: Two Decades of GSS Evidence." *Urban Affairs Review* 35: 92–111.

——, Jane K. Cover, Ross L. Matsueda, and Charis E. Kubrin. 2006. "Neighborhood Context and Neighboring Ties." *City and Community* 5: 363–385.

Gugler, Josef. 2003. "World Cities in Poor Countries: Conclusions from Case Studies of the Principal Regional and Global Players." *International Journal of Urban and Regional Research* 27: 707–712.

Guimera, B. and L. A. N. Amaral. 2004. "Modeling the World-Wide Airport Network." *European Physical Journal B* 38: 381–385.

Guimera, R., S. Mossa, A. Turtschi, and L. A. N. Amarai. 2005. "The Worldwide Air Transportation Network: Anomolous Centrality, Community Structure, and Cities' Global Roles." *Proceedings of the National Academy of Sciences* 102: 7794–7799.

Gulati, Ranjay and Martin Gargiulo. 1999. "Where do Interorganizational Networks Come From?" *American Journal of Sociology* 104: 1439–1493.

Guterbock, Thomas. 1980. *Machine Politics in Transition: Party and Community in Chicago*. Chicago: University of Chicago Press.

Gutierrez, Javier, Rafael Gonzalez, and Gabriel Gomez. 1996. "The European High-Speed Train Network." *Journal of Transport Geography* 4: 227–238.

Gutkind, Peter C. W. 1965. "African Urbanism, Mobility, and the Social Network." *Journal of Comparative Sociology* 6: 48–60.

—— 1965. "Network Analysis and Urbanism in Africa: The Use of Micro and Macro Analysis." *Canadian Review of Sociology and Anthropology* 2: 123–131.

Häikiö, Liisa. 2007. "Expertise, Representation, and the Common Good: Grounds for Legitimacy in the Urban Governance Network." *Urban Studies* 44: 2147–2162.

Haldeman, B. Antrim. 1914. "The Street Layout." *Annals of the American Academy of Political and Social Science* 51: 182–191.

Hall, Peter. 1966. *The World Cities*. London: Wiedenfeld and Nicolson.

Hall, Peter and Kathy Pain. 2006. *The Polycentric Metropolis: Learning from Mega-City Regions in Europe*. London: Earthscan.

Hammer, Carl and Fred Charles Ikle. 1957. "Telephone and Airline Traffic Related to Distance and the 'Propensity to Interact'." *Sociometry* 20: 306–316.

Hampton, Keith and Barry Wellman. 2003. "Neighboring in Netville: How the Internet Supports Community and Social Capital in a Wired Suburb." *City and Community* 2: 277–311.

Handy, Susan L., Marlon G. Boarnet, Reid Ewing, and Richard E. Killingsworth. 2002. "How the Built Environment Affects Physical Activity: Views from Urban Planning." *American Journal of Preventative Medicine* 23: 64–73.

——, Robert G. Paterson, and Kent Butler. 2003. *Planning for Street Connectivity: Getting from Here to There*. Chicago, IL: American Planning Association.

Hanley, Richard T. (ed.). 2004. *Moving People, Goods and Information into the 21st Century: The Cutting-Edge Infrastructures of Networked Cities*. New York: Routledge.

Hanneman, Robert A. and Mark Riddle. 2005. *Introduction to Social Network Methods*. Riverside, CA: University of California, Riverside.

Hannerz, Ulf. 1967. "Gossip, Network, and Culture in a Black American Ghetto." *Ethnos* 32: 35–60.

Harary, F. and J. Rockey. 1976. "A City is Not a Semilattice Either." *Environment and Planning A* 8: 375–384.

Harris, Jenine K. 2008. "Consent and Confidentiality: Exploring Ethical Issues in Public Health Social Network Research." *Connections* 28: 81–96.

Harris, Nigel. 1994. "The Emerging Global City: Transport." *Cities* 11: 332–336.

Harrison, Bennett. 1992. "Industrial Districts: Old Wine in New Bottles?" *Regional Studies* 26: 469–483.

Hartwick, P. G. and J. M. Hartwick. 1972. "An Analysis of an Urban Thoroughfare." *Environment and Planning A* 4: 193–204.

Harvey, D'Arcy. 1951. "Airline Passenger Traffic Pattern Within the United States." *Journal of Air Law and Commerce* 18: 157–165.

Haynes, Robin M. 1980. *Geographical Images and Mental Maps*. New York: Macmillan Education Ltd.

Heider, Fritz. 1946. "Attitudes and Cognitive Organization." *Journal of Psychology* 21: 107–112.

Helbing, Dirk, Christian Kuhnert, Stefan Lammer, Anders Johansson, Bjorn Gehlsen, Hendrik Ammoser, and Geoffrey B. West. 2009. "Power Laws in Urban Supply Networks, Social Systems, and Dense

Pedestrian Crowds." Pp. 433–450 in *Complexity Perspectives in Innovation and Social Change,* edited by D. Lane, et al. New York: Springer.

Hennig, Marina. 2007. "Re-evaluating the Community Question from a German Perspective." *Social Networks* 29: 375–390.

Henning, Cecilia and Mats Liesberg. 1996. "Strong Ties or Weak Ties? Neighborhood Networks in a New Perspective." *Scandanavian Housing & Planning Research* 13: 3–26.

Herbert, D. T. and J. W. Raine. 1976. "Defining Communities within Urban Areas: An Analysis of Comparative Approaches." *Town Planning Review* 47: 325–338.

Hess, Paul M. 1997. "Measures of Connectivity." *Places* 11: 58–65.

Hesse, Markus. 2010. "Cities, Material Flows, and the Geography of Spatial Interaction: Urban Places in the System of Cities." *Global Networks* 10: 75–91.

Hill, Gretchen J. 1987. "Close Personal Relationships at Work and With Kin: Testing an Urban Subculture Theory Model." *Mid-American Review of Sociology* 12: 51–70.

Hill, Richard Child. 2004. "Cities and Nested Hierarchies." *International Social Science Journal* 56: 373–384.

Hiller, E. T. 1941. "The Community as a Social Group." *American Sociological Review* 6: 189–202.

Hillery, George Jr. 1955. "Definitions of Community: Areas of Agreement." *Rural Sociology* 20: 111–123.

Hillier, Bill. 1996. *Space is the Machine: A Configurational Theory of Architecture.* New York: Cambridge University Press.

—— and Julienne Hanson. 1984. *The Social Logic of Space.* New York: Cambridge University Press.

—— and Shinichi Iida. 2005. "Network and Psychological Effects in Urban Movement." Pp. 475–490 in *Conference on Spatial Information Theory,* edited by A. G. Cohn and D. M. Mark. Berlin: Springer-Verlag.

Hipp, John R. and Andrew Perrin. 2006. "Nested Loyalties: Local Networks' Effects on Neighborhood and Community Cohesion." *Urban Studies* 43: 2503–2523.

——, —— 2009. "The Simultaneous Effect of Social Distance and Physical Distance on the Formation of Neighborhood Ties." *City and Community* 8: 5–25.

——, Robert W. Faris, and Adam Boessen. 2012. "Measuring 'Neighborhood': Constructing Network Neighborhoods." *Social Networks* 34: 128–140.

Hobbes, Thomas. [1651] 1904. *Leviathan,* edited by A. R. Waller. Cambridge, Cambridge University Press.

Hobson, John A. [1894] 1914. *The Evolution of Modern Capitalism: A Study of Machine Production.* New York: Walter Scott Publishing Company.

Hodos, Jerome I. 2011. *Second Cities: Globalization and Local Politics in Manchester and Philadelphia.* Philadelphia: Temple University Press.

Holland, Paul W. and Samuel Leinhardt. 1973. "The Structural Implications of Measurement Error in Sociometry." *Journal of Mathematical Sociology* 3: 85–111.

Hollingshead, August B. 1939. "Behavior Systems as a Field for Research." *American Sociological Review* 4: 816–822.

—— 1949. *Elmtown's Youth.* New York: John Wiley.

Hopkins, Terence K. and Immanuel Wallerstein. 1986. "Commodity Chains in the World-Economy Prior to 1800." *Review (Ferdinand Braudel Center)* 10: 157–170.

Hove, Erik van. 2001. *Networking Neighborhoods.* Columbia, SC: University of South Carolina Press.

Hu, Yihong and Daoli Zhu. 2009. "Empirical Analysis of the Worldwide Maritime Transportation Network." *Physica A* 388: 2061–2071.

Hubert, Lawrence and James Schultz. 1976. "Quadratic Assignment as a General Data Analysis Strategy." *British Journal of Mathematical and Statistical Psychology* 29: 190–241.

Huckfeldt, R. Robert. 1983. "Social Contexts, Social Networks, and Urban Neighborhoods: Environmental Constraints on Friendship Choice." *American Journal of Sociology* 89: 651–669.

Hummon, Norman P. and Patrick Doreian. 2003. "Some Dynamics of Social Balance Processes: Bringing Heider Back Into Balance Theory." *Social Networks* 25: 17–49.

Hunter, Albert. 1975. "The Loss of Community: An Empirical Test Through Replication." *American Sociological Review* 40: 537–552.

—— 1985. "Private, Parochial and Public Social Orders: The Problem of Crime and Incivility in Urban Communities." Pp. 230–242 in *The Challenge of Social Control: Citizenship and Institution Building in Modern Society: Essays in Honor of Morris Janowitz*, edited by Gerald D. Suttles and Mayer N. Zald. Norwood, NJ: Ablex Publishing.

Hunter, Floyd. 1953. *Community Power Structure: A Study of Decision Makers*. Chapel Hill, NC: University of North Carolina Press.

Hymer, Stephen. 1972. "The Multinational Corporation and the Law of Uneven Development." Pp. 113–140 in *Economics and World Order: From the 1970s to the 1990s*, edited by Jagdish N. Bhagwati. London: Macmillan.

Ibarra, Herminia. 1992. "Homophily and Differential Returns: Sex Differences in Network Structure and Access in an Advertising Firm." *Administrative Science Quarterly* 37: 422–447.

Irwin, Michael D. and Holly L. Hughes. 1992. "Centrality and the Structure of Urban Interaction: Measures, Concepts, and Applications." *Social Forces* 71: 17–51.

—— and John D. Kasarda. 1991. "Air Passenger Linkages and Employment Growth in U.S. Metropolitan Areas." *American Sociological Review* 56: 524–537.

Isett, Kimberley Roussin and Keith G. Provan. 2005. "The Evolution of Dyadic Interorganizational Relationships in a Network of Publicly Funded Nonprofit Agencies." *Journal of Public Administration Research and Theory* 15: 149–165.

Ivy, R. L., T. J. Fik, and E. J. Malecki. 1995. "Changes in Air Service Connectivity and Employment." *Environment and Planning A* 27: 165–179.

Jackson, Kenneth T. 1985. *Crabgrass Frontier: The Suburbanization of the United States*. New York: Oxford University Press.

Jacobs, Jane. [1961] 1993. *The Death and Life of Great American Cities*. New York: Random House.

Jacobs, Wouter, Cesar Ducruet, and Peter de Langen. 2010. "Integrating World Cities into Production Networks: The Case of Port Cities." *Global Networks* 10: 92–113.

Janelle, Donald G. 1969. "Spatial Reorganization: A Model and Concept." *Annals of the Association of American Geographers* 59: 348–364.

Jang, Sung Joon and Richard D. Alba. 1992. "Urbanism and Nontraditional Opinion: A Test of Fischer's Subcultural Theory." *Social Science Quarterly* 73: 596–609.

Jiang, Bin. 2007. "A Topological Pattern of Urban Street Networks: Universality and Peculiarity." *Physica A* 384: 647–655.

—— 2008. "Flow Dimension and Capacity for Structuring Urban Street Networks." *Physica A* 387: 4440–4452.

—— and Christophe Claramunt. 2004. "A Structural Approach to the Model Generalization of an Urban Street Network." *GeoInformatica* 8: 157–171.

——,—— 2004. "Topological Analysis of Urban Street Networks." *Environment and Planning B* 31: 151–162.

John, P. 1998. "Urban Economic Policy Networks in Britain and France: A Sociometric Approach." *Environment and Planning C* 16: 307–322.

John, Richard R. 2010. *Network Nation: Inventing American Telecommunications*. Cambridge, MA: Harvard University Press.

Johnson, Allen and George C. Bond. 1974. "Kinship, Friendship, and Exchange in Two Communities: A Comparative Analysis of Norms and Behaviors." *Journal of Anthropological Research* 30: 55–68.

Johnson, Colleen L. and Barbara M. Barer. 1990. "Families and Networks Among Older Inner-City Blacks." *The Gerontologist* 30: 726–733.

Johnson, Norman J. and Peggy R. Sanday. 1971. "Subcultural Variations in an Urban Poor Population." *American Anthropologist* 73: 128–143.

Judge, Timothy A., Joyce E. Bono, Remus Ilies, and Megan W. Gerhardt. 2002. "Personality and Leadership: A Qualitative and Quantitative Review." *Journal of Applied Psychology* 87: 765–780.

Jung, Woo-Sung, Fengzhong Wang, and H. Eugene Stanley. 2008. "Gravity Model in the Korean Highway." *EPL* 81: 48005.

Kadushin, Charles. 1966. "The Friends and Supporters of Psychotherapy: On Social Circles in Urban Life." *American Sociological Review* 31: 786–802.

—— 1968. "Power, Influence, and Social Circles: A New Methodology for Studying Opinion Makers." *American Sociological Review* 33: 685–699.

—— 2005. "Who Benefits from Network Analysis: Ethics of Social Network Research." *Social Networks* 27: 139–153.

—— 2012. *Understanding Social Networks: Theories, Concepts, and Findings.* New York: Oxford University Press.

Kadushin, Charles, and Delmos J. Jones. 1992. "Social Networks and Urban Neighborhoods in New York City." *City and Society* 6: 58–75.

——, Matthew Lindholm, Dan Ryan, Archie Brodsky, and Leonard Saxe. 2005. "Why Is It So Difficult to Form Effective Community Coalitions." *City and Community* 4: 255–275.

Kaluza, Pablo, Andrea Kölzsch, Michael T. Gastner, and Bernd Blasius. 2010. "The Complex Network of Global Cargo Ship Movements." *Journal of the Royal Society* 7: 1093–1103.

Kasarda, John D. and Morris Janowitz. 1974. "Community Attachment in Mass Society." *American Sociological Review* 39: 328–339.

Katzman, Martin T. 1969. "Opportunity, Subculture, and the Economic Performance of Urban Ethnic Groups." *American Journal of Economics and Sociology* 28: 351–366.

Kaufman, Harold F. 1959. "Toward an Interactional Conception of Community." *Social Forces* 38: 8–17.

Kaufman, Herbert and Victor Jones. 1954. "The Mystery of Power." *Public Administration Review* 14: 205–212.

Kenis, Patrick and Keith G. Provan. 2009. "Towards an Exogenous Theory of Public Network Performance." *Public Administration* 87: 440–456.

Kennedy, David M., Anthony A. Braga and Anne M. Piehl. 1997. "The (Un)known Universe: Mapping Gangs and Violence in Boston." Pp. 219–262 in *Crime Mapping and Crime Prevention*, edited by David Weisburd and Tom McEwen. Monsey, NY: Criminal Justice Press.

Kentor, Jeffrey, Adam Sobek, and Michael Timberlake. 2011. "Interlocking Corporate Directorates and the Global City Hierarchy." *Journal of World-Systems Research* 17: 498–514.

Key, William H. 1965. "Urbanism and Neighboring." *Sociological Quarterly* 6: 379–385.

Khan, Kamran, Clark C. Freifeld, Jun Wang, Sumiko R. Mekaru, David Kossowsky, et al. 2010. "Preparing for Infectious Disease Threats at Mass Gatherings: The Case of the Vancouver 2010 Olympic Winter Games." *Canadian Medical Association Journal* 182: 579–583.

Kick, Edward L., and Byron L. Davis. 2001. "World-System Structure and Change: An Analysis of Global Networks and Economic Growth Across Two Time Periods." *American Behavioral Scientist* 44: 1561–1578.

Kissling, C. C. 1969. "Linkage Importance in a Regional Highway Network." *Canadan Geographer* 13: 113–127.

Klapp, Orrin E. and L. Vincent Padgett. 1960. "Power Structure and Decision-Making in a Mexican Border City." *American Journal of Sociology* 65: 400–406.

Kleit, Rachel Garschick. 2001. "Neighborhood Relations in Suburban Scattered-Site and Clustered Public Housing." *Journal of Urban Affairs* 23: 409–430.

—— 2005. "HOPE VI New Communities: Neighborhood Relationships in Mixed-Income Housing." *Environment and Planning A* 37: 1413–1441.

—— 2008. "Neighborhood Segregation, Personal Networks, and Access to Social Resources." Pp. 237–260 in *Segregation: The Rising Costs for America*, edited by James H. Carr and Nandinee K. Kutty. New York: Routledge.

Klijn, Erik-Hans and Chris Skelcher. 2007. "Democracy and Governance Networks: Compatible or Not?" *Public Administration* 85: 587–608.

Kloosterman, Robert C. and Sako Musterd. 2001. "The Polycentric Urban Region: Towards a Research Agenda." *Urban Studies* 38: 623–633.

Klovdahl, Alden S. 1989. "Urban Social Networks: Some Methodological Problems and Possibilities." Pp. 176–210 in *The Small World*, edited by Manfred Kochen. Norwood, NJ: Ablex Publishing Corp.

——— 2005. "Social Network Research and Human Subjects Protection: Towards More Effective Infectious Disease Control." *Social Networks* 27: 119–137.

Knoke, David. 1983. "Organization Sponsorship and Influence Reputation of Social Influence Associations." *Social Forces* 61: 1065–1087.

——— 1990. *Political Networks: The Structural Perspective.* New York: Cambridge University Press.

——— 1993. "Networks of Elite Structure and Decision Making." *Sociological Methods and Research* 22: 23–45.

———and James R. Wood. 1981. *Organized for Action: Commitment in Voluntary Associations.* New Brunswick, NJ: Rutgers University Press.

Knox, Paul L. and Peter J. Taylor, eds. 1995. *World Cities in a World System.* New York: Cambridge University Press.

Koch, Agnes and Sanford Labovitz. 1976. "Interorganizational Power in a Canadian Community: A Replication." *Sociological Quarterly* 17: 3–15.

Komarovsky, Mirra. 1946. "The Voluntary Associations of Urban Dwellers." *American Sociological Review* 11: 686–698.

Kornblum, William. 1974. *Blue Collar Community.* Chicago, IL: University of Chicago Press.

Kossinets, Gueorgi. 2006. "Effects of Missing Data in Social Networks." *Social Networks* 28: 247–268.

Kostof, Spiro. 1991. *The City Shaped: Urban Patterns and Meanings Through History.* London: Thames and Hudson.

Krackhardt, David. 1987. "Cognitive Social Structures." *Social Networks* 9: 109–134.

——— 1988. "Predicting with Networks: Nonparametric Multiple Regression Analysis of Dyadic Data." *Social Networks* 10: 359–381.

——— and Robert N. Stern. 1988. "Informal Networks and Organizational Crises: An Experimental Simulation." *Social Psychology Quarterly* 51: 123–140.

Krätke, Stefan. 2003. "Global Media Cities in a World-wide Urban Network." *European Planning Studies* 11: 605–628.

Kraut, R., S. Kiesler, B. Boneva, J. Cummings, V. Helgeson, and A. Crawford. 1998. "Internet Paradox: A Social Technology that Reduces Social Involvement and Psychological Wellbeing?" *American Psychologist* 59: 1017–1031.

Krings, Gautier, Francesco Calabrese, Carlo Ritti, and Vincent D. Blondel. 2009. "Urban Gravity: A Model for Inter-city Telecommunications Flows." *Journal of Statistical Mechanics* L07003.

Kühnert, Christian, Dirk Helbing, and Geoffrey B. West. 2006. "Scaling Laws in Urban Supply Networks." *Physica A* 363: 96–103.

Kuo, Frances E., William C. Sullivan, Rebekah Levine Coley, and Liesette Brunson. 1998. "Fertile Ground for Community: Inner-City Neighborhood Common Spaces." *American Journal of Community Psychology* 26: 823–851.

Kwait, Jennafer, Thomas W. Valente, and David D. Celentano. 2001. "Interorganizational Relationships Among HIV/AIDS Service Organizations in Baltimore: A Network Analysis." *Journal of Urban Health* 78: 468–487.

Laan, L. van der, J. Vogelzang, and R. Schalke. 1998. "Commuting in Multi-Nodal Urban Systems: An Empirical Comparison of Three Alternative Models." *Tijdschrift voor Economische en Sociale Geografie* 89: 384–400.

Lai, Gina. 2001. "Social Support Networks in Urban Shanghai." *Social Networks* 23: 73–85.

Lammer, Stefan, Bjorn Gehlsen, and Dirk Helbing. 2006. "Scaling Laws in the Spatial Structure of Urban Road Networks." *Physica A* 363: 89–95.

Lansing, John B., Jung-Cho Liu, and Daniel B. Suits. 1961. "An Analysis of Interurban Travel." *Quarterly Journal of Economics* 75: 87–95.

Latour, Bruno. 2005. *Reassembling the Social: An Introduction to Actor-Network Theory.* New York: Oxford University Press.

Laumann, Edward O. 1973. *Bonds of Pluralism: The Form and Substance of Urban Social Networks.* New York: John Wiley & Sons.

——and Peter V. Marsden. 1979. "The Analysis of Oppositional Structures in Political Elites: Identifying Collective Actors." *American Sociological Review* 44: 713–732.

—— and Franz Urban Pappi. 1973. "New Directions in the Study of Community Elites." *American Sociological Review* 38: 212–230.

——, —— 1976. *Networks of Collective Action: A Perspective on Community Influence Systems*. New York: Academic Press.

——, Peter V. Marsden, and Joseph Galaskiewicz. 1977. "Community-Elite Influence Structures: Extension of a Network Approach." *American Journal of Sociology* 83: 594–631.

——, ——, and David Prensky. 1983. "The Boundary Specification Problem in Network Analysis." Pp. 18–34 in *Applied Network Analysis: A Methodological Introduction*, edited by Ronald S. Burt and Michael J. Miner. Beverly Hills, CA: Sage.

Lazarsfeld, Paul F. and Robert K. Merton. 1964. "Friendship as a Social Process: A Substantive and Methodological Analysis." Pp. 18–66 in *Freedom and Control in Modern Society*, edited by Morroe Berger, Theodore Abel, and Charles H. Page. New York: Octagon Books.

Leccese, Michael and Kathleen McCormick, eds. 2000. *Charter of the New Urbanism*. New York: McGraw Hill.

Lee, Barrett A., R. S. Oropesa, Barbara J. Metch, and Avery M. Guest. 1984. "Testing the Decline-of-Community Thesis: Neighborhood Organizations in Seattle, 1929 and 1979." *American Journal of Sociology* 89: 1161–1188.

Lee, Ho-Sang. 2009. "The Networkability of Cities in the International Air Passenger Flows 1992–2004." *Journal of Transport Geography* 17: 166–175.

Leffler, Ann, Richard S. Krannich, and Dair L. Gillespie. 1986. "Contact, Support, and Friction: Three Faces of Networks in Community Life." *Sociological Perspectives* 29: 337–355.

LeGalès, Patrick. 2001. "Urban Governance and Policy Networks: On the Urban Political Boundedness of Policy Networks. A French Case Study." *Public Administration* 79: 167–184.

Leitner, Helga, Claire Pavlik, and Eric Sheppard. 2002. "Networks, Governance, and the Politics of Scale: Inter-urban Networks and the European Union." Pp. 274–303 in *Geographies of Power*, edited by Andrew Herrod and Melissa W. Wright. Malden, MA: Blackwell.

Lelieveldt, Herman. 2004. "Helping Citizens Help Themselves: Neighborhood Improvement Programs and the Impact of Social Networks, Trust, and Norms on Neighborhood-Oriented Forms of Participation." *Urban Affairs Review* 39: 531–551.

LeRoux, Kelly, Paul W. Brandenburger, and Sanjay K. Pandey. 2010. "Interlocal Service Cooperation in U.S. Cities: A Social Network Explanation." *Public Administration Review* 70: 268–278.

Levine, Rhonda F. *Class, Networks, and Identity: Replanting Jewish Lives from Nazi Germany to Rural New York*. Lanham, MD: Rowman and Littlefield Publishers.

Levine, Sol, and Paul E. White. 1961. "Exchange as a Conceptual Framework for the Study of Interorganizational Relationships." *Administrative Science Quarterly* 5: 583–601.

Lewis, Oscar. 1952. "Urbanization without Breakdown: A Case Study." *Scientific Monthly* 75: 31–41.

—— 1963. "The Culture of Poverty." *Society* 1: 17–19.

Li, W. and X. Cai. 2004. "Statistical Analysis of Airport Network of China." *Physical Review E* 69: 046106.

Li, W. and X. Cai. 2007. "Empirical Analysis of a Scale-Free Railway Network in China." *Physica A* 382: 693–703.

Lieberson, Stanley, and Kent P. Schwirian. 1962. "Banking Functions as an Index of Inter-city Relations." *Journal of Regional Science* 4: 69–81.

Liebert, Roland J. and Allen W. Imershein (eds.). 1977. *Power, Paradigms, and Community Research*. Beverly Hills, CA: Sage Publications.

Limtanakool, Narisra, Martin Dijst, and Tim Schwanen. 2007. "A Theoretical Framework and Methodology for Characterising National Urban Systems on the Basis of Flows of People: Empirical Evidence for France and Germany." *Urban Studies* 44: 2123–2145.

——, Tim Schwanen, and Martin Dijst. 2007. "Ranking Functional Urban Regions: A Comparison of Interaction and Node Attribute Data." *Cities* 24: 26–42.

——, ——, —— 2009. "Developments in the Dutch Urban System on the Basis of Flows." *Regional Studies* 43: 179–196.

Lin, Jan. 2010. *The Power of Urban Ethnic Places: Cultural Heritage and Community Life.* New York: Routledge.

Litwak, Eugene. 1961. "Voluntary Associations and Neighborhood Cohesion." *American Sociological Review* 26: 258–271.

—— and Ivan Szelenyi. 1969. "Primary Group Structures and Their Functions: Kin, Neighbors, and Friends." *American Sociological Review* 34: 465–481.

Liu, William T. and Robert W. Duff. 1972. "The Strength in Weak Ties." *Public Opinion Quarterly* 36: 361–366.

Logan, John R. and Glenna D. Spitze. 1994. "Family Neighbors." *American Journal of Sociology* 100: 453–476.

——, Wenquan Zhang, and Richard D. Alba. 2002. "Immigrant Enclaves and Ethnic Communities in New York and Los Angeles." *American Sociological Review* 67: 299–322.

Lomnitz, Larissa Adler. 1977. *Networks and Marginality: Life in a Mexican Shantytown.* New York: Academic Press.

—— 1982. "Horizontal and Vertical Relations and the Social Structure of Urban Mexico." *Latin American Research Review* 17: 51–74.

Long, Norton E. 1958. "The Local Community as an Ecology of Games." *American Journal of Sociology* 64: 251–261.

Lorrain, Dominique. 1995. "The Regulation of Urban Technical Networks (Theories and Pending Issues)." *Flux* 21: 47–59.

Lowndes, Vivien and Chris Skelcher. 1998. "The Dynamics of Multi-Organizational Partnerships: An Analysis of Changing Modes of Governance." *Public Administration* 76: 313–333.

Lundberg, George A. and Margaret Lawsing. 1937. "The Sociography of Some Community Relations." *American Sociological Review* 2: 318–335.

—— and Mary Steele. 1938. "Social Attraction-Patterns in a Village." *Sociometry* 1: 375–419.

Lupi, Tineke and Sake Musterd. 2006. "The Suburban 'Community Question'." *Urban Studies* 43: 801–817.

Lynch, Kevin. 1960. *The Image of the City.* Cambridge, MA: MIT Press.

—— 1961. "The Pattern of the Metropolis." *Daedalus* 90: 78–98.

Lynd, Robert S. and Helen Merrell Lynd. 1937. *Middletown in Transition: A Study in Cultural Conflicts.* New York: Harcourt, Brace and Company.

Ma, Xiulian, and Michael Timberlake. 2008. "Identifying China's Leading World City: A Network Approach." *Geojournal* 71: 19–35.

McCallister, Lynne and Claude S. Fischer. 1978. "A Procedure for Surveying Personal Networks." *Sociological Methods and Research* 7: 131–148.

McCarthy, Bill and John Hagan. 1995. "Getting Into Street Crime: The Structure and Process of Criminal Embeddedness." *Social Science Research* 24: 63–95.

McClurg, Scott D. 2003. "Social Networks and Political Participation: The Role of Social Interaction in Explaining Political Participation." *Political Research Quarterly* 56: 449–464.

MacDonald, John S., Leatrice D. MacDonald. 1964. "Chain Migration, Ethnic Neighborhood Formation, and Social Networks." *Milbank Memorial Fund Quarterly* 42: 82–97.

Macfarlane, Alan. 1977. "History, Anthropology, and the Study of Community." *Social History* 2: 631–652.

McGahan, Peter. 1972. "The Neighbor Role and Neighboring in a Highly Urban Area." *Sociological Quarterly* 13: 397–408.

McGloin, Jean Marie. 2005. "Policy and Intervention Considerations of a Network Analysis of Street Gangs." *Criminology and Public Policy* 4: 607–636.

McIllwain, Jeffrey Scott. 1999. "Organized Crime: A Social Network Approach." *Crime, Law, and Social Change* 32: 301–323.

McKenzie, Roderick D. 1927. "The Concept of Dominance and World-Organization." *American Journal of Sociology* 33: 28–42.

—— 1933. *The Metropolitan Community.* New York: McGraw-Hill.

McLaughlin, Edmund M. 1975. "The Power Network in Phoenix: An Application of Smallest Space Analysis." *Critical Sociology* 5: 185–195.

McPherson, J. Miller. 1983. "An Ecology of Affiliation." *American Sociological Review* 48: 519–532.

—— 2004. "A Blau Space Primer: Prolegomenon to An Ecology of Affiliation" *Industrial and Corporate Change* 13: 263–280.

—— and Thomas Rotolo. 1996. "Testing a Dynamic Model of Social Composition: Diversity and Change in Voluntary Groups." *American Sociological Review* 61: 179–202.

—— and Lynn Smith-Lovin. 1987. "Homophily in Voluntary Organizations: Status Distance and the Composition of Face-to-Face Groups." *American Sociological Review* 52: 370–379.

——, Lynn Smith-Lovin, and James M. Cook. 2001. "Birds of a Feather: Homophily in Social Networks." *Annual Review of Sociology* 27: 415–444.

——, Lynn Smith-Lovin, and Matthew E. Brashears. 2006. "Social Isolation in America: Changes in Core Discussion Networks over Two Decades." *American Sociological Review* 71: 353–375.

Mahutga, Matthew C., Xiulian Ma, David A. Smith, and Michael Timberlake. 2010. "Economic Globalization and the Structure of the World City System: The Case of Airline Passenger Data." *Urban Studies* 47: 1925–1947.

Malecki, Edward J. 2002. "Hard and Soft Networks for Urban Competitiveness." *Urban Studies* 39: 929–945.

—— and Sean P. Gorman. 2001. "Maybe the Death of Distance, but not the End of Geography: The Internet as a Network." Pp. 87–105 in *Worlds of E-Commerce: Economic, Geographic, and Social Dimensions*, edited by Stanley D. Brunn and Thomas Leinbach. New York: John Wiley.

Mandell, Myrna P. 2001. "The Impact of Network Structures on Community-Building Efforts: The Los Angeles Roundtable for Children Community Studies." Pp. 129–153 in *Getting Results Through Collaboration: Networks and Network Structures for Public Policy and Management*, edited by Myrna P. Mandell. Westport, CT: Quorum Books.

Mantel, Nathan. 1967. "The Detection of Disease Clustering and a Generalized Regression Approach." *Cancer Research* 27: 209–220.

Markusen, Ann and Vicky Gwiasda. 1993. "Multipolarity and the Layering of Functions in World Cities: New York City's Struggle to Stay on Top." *International Journal of Urban and Regional Research* 18: 167–193.

Marques, Eduardo, Renata Bichir, Thais Pavez, Miranda Zoppi, Encarnacion Moya, and Igor Pantoja. 2009. "Networks and Spatial Segregation in the Production of Urban Poverty in Sao Paulo." *Local Environment* 14: 809–817.

Marsden, Peter V. and Karen E. Campbell. 1984. "Measuring Tie Strength." *Social Forces* 63: 482–501.

Marshall, Alfred. 1890. *Principles of Economics*. London: Macmillan and Company.

Marshall, Neil, Brian Dollery, and Angus Witherby. 2003. "Regional Organizations of Councils (ROCs): The Emergence of Network Governance in Metropolitan and Rural Australia." *Australian Journal of Regional Studies* 9: 169–188.

Marshall, Stephen. 2005. *Streets and Patterns*. New York: Spon Press.

Martineau, William H. 1977. "Informal Social Ties among Urban Black Americans: Some New Data and a Review of the Problem." *Journal of Black Studies* 8: 83–104.

Masucci, A. P. and G. J. Rodgers. 2008. "The Network of Commuters in London." *Physica A* 387: 3781–3788.

——, D. Smith, A. Crooks, and M. Batty. 2009. "Random Planar Graphs and the London Street Network." *European Physical Journal B* 71: 259–271.

Mata, Tamara de la and Carlos Llano-Verduras. 2011. "Spatial Pattern and Domestic Tourism: An Econometric Analysis Using Inter-regional Monetary Flows by Type of Journey." *Papers in Regional Science*.

Matsumoto, Hidenobu. 2004. "International Urban Systems and Air Passenger and Cargo Flows: Some Calculations." *Journal of Air Transport Management* 10: 241–249.

Matthiessen, Christian Wichmann, Annette Winkel Schwartz, and Soren Find. 2002. "The Top-level Global Research System, 1997–99: Centres, Networks, and Nodality. An Analysis Based on Bibliometric Indicators." *Urban Studies* 39: 903–927.

——, ——, —— 2010. "World Cities of Scientific Knowledge: Systems, Networks, and Potential Dynamics. An Analysis Based on Bibliometric Indicators." *Urban Studies* 47: 1879–1897.

Marx, Karl. [1857] 1956. *Karl Marx: Selected Writings in Sociology and Social Philosophy*, translated by T. B. Bottomore. New York: McGraw-Hill.

Marx, Karl and Friedrich Engels. [1848] 1998. *The Communist Manifesto*. London: Verso.

Mayer, Harold M. 1954. "Urban Nodality and the Economic Base." *Journal of the American Planning Association* 20: 117–121.

Mayhew, Bruce H. 1980. "Structuralism versus Individualism: Part 1, Shadowboxing in the Dark." *Social Forces* 59: 335–375.

Medvedkov, Yu V. 1967. "An Application of Topology in Central Place Analysis." *Papers in Regional Science* 20: 77–84.

Meegan, Richard and Alison Mitchell. 2001. "'It's Not Community Round Here, It's Neighborhood': Neighborhood Change and Cohesion in Urban Regeneration Policies." *Urban Studies* 38: 2167–2194.

Meijers, Evert. 2005. "Polycentric Urban Regions and the Quest for Synergy: Is a Network of Cities More than the Sum of its Parts." *Urban Studies* 42: 765–781.

—— 2007. "From Central Place to Network Model: Theory and Evidence of a Paradigm Change." *Tijdschrift voor Economische en Sociale Geographie* 98: 245–259.

—— 2008. "Measuring Polycentricity and Its Promises." *European Planning Studies* 16: 1313–1323.

Merton, Robert K. 1950. "Patterns of Influence: A Study of Interpersonal Influence and of Communications Behavior in a Local Community." Pp. 180–219 in *Communications Research, 1948–49*, edited by Paul F. Lazarsfeld and Frank Stanton. New York: Harper & Brothers.

Mesch, Gustavo S. and Yael Levanon. 2003. "Community Networking and Locally-Based Social Ties in Two Suburban Localities." *City and Community* 2: 335–351.

Meyer, David R. 1980. "A Dynamic Model of the Integration of Frontier Urban Places into the United States System of Cities." *Economic Geography* 56: 120–140.

—— 1984. "Control and Coordination Links in the Metropolitan System of Cities: The South as Case Study." *Social Forces* 63: 349–362.

—— 1986. "The World System of Cities: Relations between International Financial Metropolises and South American Cities." *Social Forces* 64: 553–581.

—— 1991. "Change in the World System of Metropolises: The Role of Business Intermediaries." *Urban Geography* 12: 393–416.

Meyer, David R. 2003. "The Challenges of Research on the Global Network of Cities." *Urban Geography* 24: 301–313.

Milgram, Stanley. 1967. "The Small-World Problem." *Psychology Today* 1: 61–67.

Milgram, Stanley and Paul Hollander. 1964. "The Murder They Heard." *The Nation* 198: 602–604.

Miller, Delbert C. 1958. "Decision-making Cliques in Community Power Structures: A Comparative Study of an American and English City." *American Journal of Sociology* 64: 299–310.

—— 1970. *International Community Power Structures: Comparative Studies of Four World Cities*. Bloomington, IN: Indiana University Press.

—— 1975. *Leadership and Power in the Bos-Wash Megalopolis: Environment, Ecology, and Urban Organization*. New York: John Wiley & Sons.

Miller, Katherine, Craig R. Scott, Christina Stage, and Marty Birkholt. 1995. "Communication and Coordination in an Interorganizational System: Service Provision for the Urban Homeless." *Communication Research* 22: 679–699.

Mills, C. Wright. 1956. *The Power Elite*. New York: Oxford University Press.

Milofsky, Carl. 1987. "Neighborhood-Based Organizations: A Market Analogy." Pp. 277–295 in *The Nonprofit Sector: A Research Handbook*, edited by Walter W. Powell. New Haven, CT: Yale University Press.

Milward, H. Brinton. 1982. "Interorganizational Policy Systems and Research on Public Organizations." *Administration and Society* 13: 457–478.

—— 1996. "Symposium on the Hollow State: Capacity, Control, and Performance in Interorganizational Settings." *Journal of Public Administration Research and Theory* 6: 193–195.

Milward, H. Brinton and Keith G. Provan. 1998. "Measuring Network Structure." *Public Administration* 76: 387–407.

——, —— 2000. "Governing the Hollow State." *Journal of Public Administration Research and Theory* 10: 359–379.

Mitchell, Katharyne. 2000. "Networks of Ethnicity." Pp. 329–407 in *A Companion to Economic Geography*, edited by Eric Sheppard and Trevor J. Barnes. Malden, MA: Blackwell.

Mitchell, J. Clyde. 1969. *Social Networks in Urban Situtations: Analysis of Personal Relationships in Central African Towns.* Manchester: Manchester University Press.

Mitchelson, Ronald L., and James O. Wheeler. 1994. "The Flow of Information in a Global Economy: The Role of the American Urban System in 1990." *Annals of the Association of American Geographers* 84: 87–107.

Mok, Diana, Barry Wellman, and Juan Carrasco. 2010. "Does Distance Matter in the Age of the Internet?" *Urban Studies* 47: 2747–2783.

Molotch, Harvey. 1976. "The City as a Growth Machine: Toward a Political Economy of Place." *American Journal of Sociology* 82: 309–332.

Moreno, Jacob L. 1934. *Who Shall Survive? A New Approach to the Problem of Human Relations.* Washington, DC: Nervous and Mental Disease Publishing Co.

Morrill, Rochard, John Cromartie, and Gary Hart. 1999. "Metropolitan, Urban, and Rural Commuting Areas: Toward a Better Depiction of the United States Settlement System." *Urban Geography* 20: 727–748.

Morrissey, Joseph P., Mark Tausig, and Michael L. Lindsey. 1985. "Community Mental Health Delivery Systems." *American Behavioral Scientist* 28: 704–720.

——, ——, —— 1985. "Network Analysis Methods for Mental Health Service System Research: A Comparison of Two Community Support Systems." *National Institute of Mental Health, Series BN* 6.

Moss, Mitchell L., and Anthony M. Townsend. 2000. "The Internet Backbone and the American Metropolis." *The Information Society* 16: 35–47.

Mossberger, Karen and Gerry Stoker. 2001. "The Evolution of Urban Regime Theory: The Challenge of Conceptualization." *Urban Affairs Review* 36: 810–835.

Mulford, Charles L. 1984. *Interorganizational Relations: Implications for Community Development.* New York: Human Sciences Press.

——and Mary A. Mulford. 1977. "Community and Interorganizational Perspectives on Cooperation and Conflict." *Rural Sociology* 42: 569–590.

Mulroy, Elizabeth A. 2003. "Community as a Factor in Implementing Interorganizational Partnerships: Issues, Constraints, and Adaptations." *Nonprofit Management and Leadership* 14: 47–66.

Mumford, Lewis. 1968. "The Highway and the City." Pp. 92–107 in *The Urban Prospect*, edited by Lewis Mumford. New York: Harcourt, Brace, & World.

Mumford, Michael D., Stephen J. Zaccaro, Julie F. Johnson, Marisa Diana, Janelle A. Gilbert, and K. Victoria Threlfall. 2000. "Patterns of Leader Characteristics: Implications for Performance and Development." *The Leadership Quarterly* 11: 115–133.

Musso, Juliet A., Christopher Weare, Nail Ozfas, and William E. Loges. 2006. "Neighborhood Governance Reform and Networks of Community Power in Los Angeles." *American Review of Public Administration* 36: 79–97.

Myles, Sean, Adam R. Boyko, Christopher L. Owens, Patrick J. Brown, Fabrizio Grassi, et al. in press. "Genetic Structure and Domestication History of the Grape." *Proceedings of the National Academy of Sciences* (doi: 10.1073/pnas.1009363108).

Myrdal, Gunnar. 1964. *An American Dilemma.* New York: McGraw Hill.

Neal, Jennifer Watling. 2008. "'Kracking' the Missing Data Problem: Applying Krackhardt's Cognitive Social Structures to School-Based Social Networks." *Sociology of Education* 81: 140–162.

—— and Zachary Neal. 2010. "Power as a Structural Phenomenon." *American Journal of Community Psychology* 48: 157–167.

——, ——, Marc S. Atkins, David B. Henry, and Stacy L. Frazier. 2011. "Channels of Change: Contrasting Network Mechanisms in the Use of Interventions." *American Journal of Community Psychology* 47: 277–286.

Neal, Zachary. 2008. "The Duality of World Cities and Firms: Comparing Networks, Hierarchies and Inequalities in the Global Economy." *Global Networks* 8: 94–115.

—— 2010. "Refining the Air Traffic Approach to City Networks." *Urban Studies* 47: 2195–2215.

—— 2011. "The Causal Relationship Between Employment and Business Networks in U.S. Cities." *Journal of Urban Affairs* 33: 167–184.

—— 2011. "From Central Places to Network Bases: A Transition in the U.S. Urban Hierarchy, 1900–2000." *City and Community* 10: 49–74.

—— 2011. "Differentiating Centrality and Power in the World City Network." *Urban Studies* 48: 2733–2748.

—— 2012. "Structural Determinism in the Interlocking World City Network." *Geographical Analysis* 44: 162–170.

—— In press. "Types of Hub Cities and Their Effects on Urban Creative Economies." In *Hub Cities and the Knowledge Economy*. Burlington, VT: Ashgate.

—— In press. "Creative Employment and Jet Set Cities: Disentangling Causal Effects." *Urban Studies* (doi: 10.1177/0042098011431282).

Nemeth, Roger J. and David A. Smith. 1985. "International Trade and World-Systems Structure: A Multiple Network Analysis." *Review (Ferdinand Braudel Center)* 8: 517–560.

Newman, M. E. J. 2000. "Models of the Small World." *Journal of Statistical Physics* 101: 819–841.

—— 2006. "Modularity and Community Structure in Networks." *Proceedings of the National Academy of Sciences* 103: 8577–8582.

—— 2010. *Networks: An Introduction*. New York: Oxford University Press.

Nicholson, A. J. 2007. "Road Network Unreliability: Impact Assessment and Mitigation." *International Journal of Critical Infrastructures* 3: 346–375.

Nordlund, Carl. 2004. "A Critical Comment on the Taylor Approach for Measuring World City Interlock Linkages." *Geographical Analysis* 36: 290–296.

Norris, Donald F. 2001. "Prospects for Regional Governance under the New Regionalism: Economic Imperatives Versus Political Impediments." *Journal of Urban Affairs* 23: 557–571.

Nuffel, Nathalie van. 2007. "Determination of the Number of Significant Flows in Origin–Destination Specific Analysis: The Case of Commuting in Flanders." *Regional Studies* 41: 509–524.

Nuffel, Nathalie van, Ben Derudder, and Frank Witlox. 2010. "Even Important Connections Are Not Always Meaningful: On the Use of a Polarisation Measure in a Typology of European Cities in Air Transport Networks." *Tijdschrift voor Economische en Sociale Geografie* 101: 333–348.

Nutter, Julia, Douglas W. Frisbie, and Carol Bevis. 1977. "Street Layout and Residential Burglary." *National Conference on Criminal Justice Evaluation (Washington, DC)*.

Nystuen, John D., and Michael F. Dacey. 1961. "A Graph Theory Interpretation of Nodal Regions." *Papers in Regional Science* 7: 29–42.

Office of Management and Budget. 2000. "Standards for Defining Metropolitan and Micropolitan Statistical Areas." *Federal Register* 65: 82228–82238.

O'Kelly, Morton E. 1998. "A Geographer's Analysis of Hub-and-Spoke Networks." *Journal of Transport Geography* 6: 171–186.

Oliver, Melvin L. 1988. "The Urban Black Community as Network: Toward a Social Network Perspective." *Sociological Quarterly* 29: 623–645.

Oliver, Pamela. 1984. "'If You Don't Do It, Nobody Else Will': Active and Token Contributors to Local Collective Action." *American Sociological Review* 49: 601–610.

Oort, Frank van, Martijn Burger, and Otto Raspe. 2010. "On the Economic Foundation of the Urban Network Paradigm: Spatial Integration, Functional Integration, and Economic Complementarities within the Dutch Randstad." *Urban Studies* 47: 725–748.

Orr, Marion E. and Gerry Stoker. 1994. "Urban Regimes and Leadership in Detroit." *Urban Affairs Review* 30: 48–75.

Orum, Anthony M. 2005. "Circles of Influence and Chains of Command: The Social Processes Whereby Ethnic Communities Influence Host Societies." *Social Forces* 84: 921–939.

O'Toole, Laurence J. 1997. "Treating Networks Seriously: Practical and Research-Based Agendas in Public Administration." *Public Administration Review* 57: 45–52.

Padgett, John F., and Christopher K. Ansell. 1993. "Robust Action and the Rise of the Medici, 1400–1434." *American Journal of Sociology* 98: 1259–1319.

Pappi, Franz Urban. 1984. "Boundary Specification and Stuctural Models of Elite Systems: Social Circles Revisited." *Social Networks* 6: 79–95.

Park, Robert E. 1915. "The City: Suggestions for the Investigation of Human Behavior in the City Environment." *American Journal of Sociology* 20: 577–612.

—— 1929. "Urbanization as Measured by Newspaper Circulation." *American Journal of Sociology* 35: 60–79.

Parr, John B. 1987. "Interaction in an Urban System: Aspects of Trade and Commuting." *Economic Geography* 63: 223–240.

—— 2004. "The Polycentric Urban Region: A Closer Inspection." *Regional Studies* 38: 231–240.

Pattillo, Mary. 2007. *Black on the Block: The Politics of Race and Class in the City*. Chicago: University of Chicago Press.

Patton, Donald. 1956. "The Traffic Pattern of American Inland Waterways." *Economic Geography* 32: 29–37.

Patuelli, Roberto, Aura Reggiani, Peter Nijkamp, and Franz-Josef Bade. 2009. "Spatial and Commuting Networks: A Unifying Perspective." Pp. 257–271 in *Complexity and Spatial Networks: In Search of Simplicity*, edited by Aura Reggiani and Peter Nijkamp. Berlin: Springer-Verlag.

Payre, Renaud. 2010. "The Importance of Being Connected. City Networks and Urban Government: Lyon and Eurocities (1990–2005)." *International Journal of Urban and Regional Research* 34: 260–280.

Peponis, John, Sonit Bafna, and Zongyu Zhang. 2008. "The Connectivity of Streets: Reach and Directional Distance." *Environment and Planning B* 35: 881–901.

Pereira, Renato A. Orozco and Ben Derudder. 2010. "Determinants of Dynamics in the World City Network, 2000–2004." *Urban Studies* 47: 1949–1967.

Perrucci, Robert, and Bonnie I. Lewis. 1989. "Interorganizational Relations and Community Influence Structure: A Replication and Extension." *Sociological Quarterly* 30: 205–223.

—— and Marc Pilisuk. 1970. "Leaders and Ruling Elites: The Interorganizational Bases of Community Power." *American Sociological Review* 35: 1040–1057.

—— and Harry R. Potter (eds.). 1989. *Networks of Power: Organizational Actors at the National, Corporate, and Community Levels*. New York: Aldine de Gruyter.

Pfleiger, Geraldine and Celine Rozenblat. 2010. "Urban Networks and Network Theory: The City as a Connector of Multiple Networks." *Urban Studies* 47: 2723–2735.

——, Luca Pattaroni, Christophe Jemelin, and Vincent Kaufmann. 2008. *The Social Fabric of the Networked City*. Lausanne, Switzerland: EPFL Press.

Philbrick, A. T. 1973. "A Short History of the Development of the Gravity Model." *Australian Road Research* 5: 40–54.

Phillips, Deborah A. 1979. "Information Diffusion within an Inner City Neighborhood." *Geografiska Annaler: Series B, Human Geography* 61: 30–42.

Pitts, Forrest R. 1965. "A Graph Theoretic Approach to Historical Geography." *Professional Geographer* 17: 15–20.

—— 1978. "The Medieval River Trade Network of Russia Revisited." *Social Networks* 1: 285–292.

Pocock, D. C. D. 1972. "City of the Mind: A Review of Mental Maps of Urban Areas." *Scottish Geographical Magazine* 2: 115–124.

—— 1976. "Some Characteristics of Mental Maps: An Empirical Study." *Transactions of the Institute of British Geographers* 1: 493–512.

Polsby, Nelson W. 1959. "Three Problems in The Analysis of Community Power." *American Sociological Review* 24: 796–803.

—— 1960. "How to Study Community Power: The Pluralist Alternative." *Journal of Politics* 22: 474–484.

Ponzini, Davide and Ugo Rossi. 2010. "Becoming a Creative City: The Entreprenuerial Mayor, Network Politics, and the Promise of an Urban Renaissance." *Urban Studies* 47: 1037–1057.

Popielarz, Pamela and J. Miller McPherson. 1995. "On the Edge or In Between: Niche Position, Niche Overlap, and the Duration of Voluntary Association Memberships." *American Journal of Sociology* 101: 698–720.

——and Zachary Neal. 2007. "The Niche as a Theoretical Tool." *Annual Review of Sociology* 33: 65–84.

Poros, Maritsa V. 2001. "The Role of Migrant Networks in Linking Local Labor Markets: The Case of Asian Indian Migration to New York and London." *Global Networks* 1: 243–259.

—— 2008. "A Social Networks Approach to Migrant Mobilization in Southern Europe." *American Behavioral Scientist* 51: 1611–1626.

—— 2010. *Modern Migrations: Gujarati Indian Networks in New York and London*. Palo Alto, CA: Stanford University Press.

Porta, Sergio, Paolo Crucitti, and Vito Latore. 2006. "The Network Analysis of Urban Streets: A Primal Approach." *Environment and Planning B* 33: 705–725.

——, ——, —— 2006. "The Network Analysis of Urban Streets: A Dual Approach." *Physica A* 369: 853–866.

Porter, Michael E. 1998. "Clusters and the New Economics of Competition." *Harvard Business Review* 1998: 77–90.

Portes, Alejandro. 1998. "Social Capital: Its Origins and Applications in Modern Sociology." *Annual Review of Sociology* 24: 1–24.

—— 2000. "The Two Meanings of Social Capital." *Sociological Forum* 15: 1–12.

—— and Leif Jensen. 1987. "What's an Ethnic Enclave? The Case for Conceptual Clarity." *American Sociological Review* 52: 768–771.

Powell, Walter W. 1990. "Neither Market nor Hierarchy: Network Forms of Organization." *Research in Organizational Behavior* 12: 295–336.

Pred, Allan R. 1971. "Urban Systems Development and the Long-Distance Flow of Information Through Preelectronic U.S. Newspapers." *Economic Geography* 47: 498–524.

—— 1973. *Urban Growth and the Circulation of Information: The United States System of Cities, 1790–1840*. Cambridge, MA: Harvard University Press.

Preston, Richard E. 1975. "A Comparison of Five Measures of Central Place Importance and of Settlement Size." *Tijdschrift voor Economische en Sociale Geographie* 66: 178–187.

Provan, Keith G. and Patrick Kenis. 2007. "Modes of Network Governance: Structure, Management, and Effectiveness." *Journal of Public Administration Research and Theory* 18: 229–252.

—— and H. Brinton Milward. 1995. "A Preliminary Theory of Interorganizational Network Effectiveness: A Comparative Study of Four Community Mental Health Systems." *Administrative Science Quarterly* 40: 1–33.

——, —— 2001. "Do Networks Really Work? A Framework for Evaluating Public-Sector Organizational Networks." *Public Administration Review* 61: 414–423.

—— and Juliann G. Sebastian. 1998. "Networks within Network: Service Link Overlap, Organizational Cliques, and Network Effectiveness." *Academy of Management Journal* 41: 453–463.

——, Kimberley R. Isett, and H. Brinton Milward. 2004. "Cooperation and Compromise: A Network Response to Conflicting Institutional Pressures in Community Mental Health." *Nonprofit and Voluntary Sector Quarterly* 33: 489–514.

——, Leigh Nakama, Mark A. Veazie, Nicolette I. Teufel-Shone, and Carol Huddleston. 2003. "Building Community Capacity Around Chronic Disease Services through a Collaborative Interorganizational Network." *Health Education and Behavior* 30: 646–662.

——, Mark A. Veazie, Lisa K. Staten, and Nicolette I. Teufel-Shone. 2005. "The Use of Network Analysis to Strengthen Community Partnerships." *Public Administration Review* 65: 603–613.

Puebla, Javier Gutierrez. 1987. "Spatial Structures of Network Flows: A Graph Theoretial Approach." *Transportation Research B* 21: 489–502.

Pumain, Denise. 1992. "Urban Networks versus Urban Hierarchies." *Environment and Planning A* 24: 1377–1380.

—— 2006. "Alternative Explanations of Hierarchical Differentiation in Urban Systems." Pp. 169–222 in *Hierarchy in Natural and Social Sciences*, edited by Denise Pumain. Dordrecht: Springer.

Purdue, Derrick, Mario Diani, and Isobel Lindsay. 2004. "Civic Networks in Bristol and Glasgow." *Community Development Journal* 39: 277–288.

Putnam, Robert D. 2000. *Bowling Alone: The Collapse and Revival of American Community*. New York: Simon and Schuster.

Qadeer, Mohammed and Sandeep Kumar. 2006. "Ethnic Enclaves and Social Cohesion." *Canadian Journal of Urban Research* 15: 1–17.

Queen, Stuart A. 1923. "What is a Community?" *Journal of Social Forces* 1: 375–382.

Raab, Jorg. 2002. "Where Do Policy Networks Come From?" *Journal of Public Administration Research and Theory* 12: 581–622.

Radcliffe-Brown, A. R. 1940. "On Social Structure." *Journal of the Royal Anthropological Institute of Great Britain and Ireland* 70: 1–12.

Radicchi, Filippo, Claudio Castellano, Federico Cecconi, Vittorio Loreto, and Domenico Parisi. 2004. "Defining and Identifying Communities in Networks." *Proceedings of the National Academy of Sciences* 101: 2658–2663.

Radil, Steven M., Colin Flint, and George E. Tita. 2010. "Spatializing Social Networks: Using Social Network Analysis to Investigate Geographies of Gang Rivalry, Territoriality, and Violence in Los Angeles." *Annals of the Association of American Geographers* 100: 307–326.

Raelin, Joseph A. 1980. "A Mandated Basis of Interorganizational Relations: The Legal–Political Network." *Human Relations* 33: 57–68.

Rain, David R. 1999. "Commuting Directionality, a Functional Measure for Metropolitan and Nonmetropolitan Area Standards." *Urban Geography* 20: 749–767.

Rakove, Milton L. 1976. *Don't Make No Waves—Don't Back No Losers*. Bloomington, IN: Indiana University Press.

—— 1979. *We Don't Want Nobody Nobody Sent: An Oral History of the Daley Years*. Bloomington, IN: Indiana University Press.

Rama, Ruth, Deron Ferguson, and Ana Melero. 2003. "Subcontracting Networks in Industrial Districts: The Electronics Industries of Madrid." *Regional Studies* 37: 71–88.

Randall, Todd A. and Brian W. Baetz. 2001. "Evaluating Pedestrian Connectivity for Suburban Sustainability." *Journal of Urban Planning and Development* 127: 1–15.

Ratcliff, Richard E. 1980. "Banks and Corporate Lending: An Analysis of the Impact of the Internal Structure of the Capitalist Class on the Lending Behavior of Banks." *American Sociological Review* 45: 553–570.

——, Mary Elizabeth Gallagher, and Kathryn Strother Ratcliff. 1979. "The Civic Involvement of Bankers: An Analysis of the Influences of Economic Power and Social Prominence in the Command of Civic Policy Positions." *Social Problems* 26: 298–313.

Reed, Wallace E. 1970. "Indirect Connectivity and Hierarchies of Urban Dominance." *Annals of the Association of American Geographers* 60: 770–785.

Reid, Neil, Bruce W. Smith, and Michael C. Carroll. 2008. "Cluster Regions: A Social Network Perspective." *Economic Development Quarterly* 22: 345–352.

Reiss, Albert J. 1959. "Rural–Urban and Status Differences in Interpersonal Contacts." *American Journal of Sociology* 65: 182–195.

Ren, Xuefei. 2011. *Building Globalization: Transnational Architecture Production in Urban China*. Chicago: University of Chicago Press.

Reserve Bank Organization Committee. 1914. *Decision of the Reserve Bank Organization Committee Determining the Federal Reserve Districts and the Location of the Federal Reserve Banks Under Federal Reserve Act Approved December 23, 1913*. Washington: Government Printing Office.

Rhodes, R. A. W. 1996. "The New Governance: Governing without Government." *Political Studies* 44: 652–667.

Rice, Murray D. and R. Keith Semple. 1993. "Spatial Interlocking Directorates in the Canadian Urban System, 1971–1989." *Urban Geography* 14: 375–396.

Richard D. Alba and Gwen Moore. 1978. "Elite Social Circles." *Sociological Methods and Research* 7: 167–188.

Richardson, Harry W. and Ardeshir Anjomani. 1981. "The Diamond City: The Case for Rectangular Grid Models." *Socio-Economic Planning Science* 15: 295–303.

Richman, Barak D. 2006. "How Community Institutions Create Economic Advantage: Jewish Diamond Merchants in New York." *Law and Social Inquiry* 31: 383–420.

Rietveld, Piet, and Joost van Nierop. 1995. "Urban Growth and the Development of Transport Networks: The Case of the Dutch Railways in the Nineteenth Century." *Flux* 19: 31–43.

Riger, Stephanie, and Paul L. Lavrakas. 1981. "Community Ties: Patterns of Attachment and Social Interaction in Urban Neighborhoods." *American Journal of Community Psychology* 9: 55–66.

Riis, Jacob. 1901. "The Rights of Children." *Charities* 7: 47–49.

Rimmer, Peter J. 1998. "Transport and Telecommunications Among World Cities." Pp. 433–480 *in Globalization and the World of Large Cities*, edited by Fu-Chen Lo and Yue-Man Yeung. New York: United Nations Press.

Robinson, Charles Mulford. 1914. "The Sociology of a Street Layout." *Annals of the American Academy of Political and Social Science* 51: 192–199.

Robinson, Jennifer. 2002. "Global and World Cities: A View from Off the Map." *International Journal of Urban and Regional Research* 26: 531–554.

Rogers, Alisdair and Steven Vertovec (eds.). 1995. *The Urban Context: Ethnicity, Social Networks, and Situational Analysis*. Washington, DC: Berg Publishers.

Rogers, Everett A. 2003. *The Diffusion of Innovations*, 5th Edition. New York: Free Press.

Rodriguez, Charo, Ann Langley, Francois Beland, and Jean-Louis Denis. 2007. "Governance, Power, and Mandated Collaboration in an Interorganizational Network." *Administration and Society* 39: 150–193.

Rodriguez, Daniel A., Asad J. Khattak, and Kelly R. Evenson. 2006. "Can New Urbanism Encourage Physical Activity? Comparing a New Urbanist Neighborhood with Conventional Suburbs." *Journal of the American Planning Association* 72: 43–54.

Rogers, David L. 1974. "Sociometric Analysis of Interorganizational Relations: Application of Theory and Measurement." *Rural Sociology* 39: 487–503.

—— 1974. "Towards a Scale of Interorganizational Relations Among Public Agencies." *Sociology and Social Research* 59: 61–70.

Rojas, Francisca M., Clelia Celdesi Valeri, Kristian Kloeckl, and Carlo Ratti. 2008. *New York Talk Exchange: The Book*. SA+P Press.

Rosenthal, A. M. 1999. *Thirty-Eight Witnesses: The Kitty Genovese Case*. Berkeley, CA: University of California Press.

Ross, Christopher O. 1987. "Organizational Dimensions of Metropolitan Dominance: Prominance in the Network of Corporate Control, 1955–1975." *American Sociological Review* 52: 258–267.

—— 1992. *The Urban System and Networks of Corporate Control*. Greenwich, CT: JAI Press.

Rossi, Eliana C. and Peter J. Taylor. 2005. "Banking Networks Across Brazilian Cities: Interlocking Cities Within and Beyond Brazil." *Cities* 22: 381–393.

Rossi, Peter H. 1960. "Power and Community Structure." *Midwest Journal of Political Science* 4: 390–401.

Roth, Camille, Soong Moon Kang, Michael Batty, and Marc Barthelemy. 2011. "Structure of Urban Movements: Polycentric Activity and Entangled Hierarchical Flows." *PLoS ONE* 6: e15923.

Rowe, Stacy, and Jennifer Wolch. 1990. "Social Networks in Time and Space: Homeless Women in Skid Row, Los Angeles." *Annals of the Association of American Geographers* 80: 184–204.

Rowson, Jonathan, Steve Broome, and Alasdair Jones. 2010. "Connected Communities: How Social Networks Power and Sustain the Big Society." *Royal Society for the Encouragement of Arts, Manufactures, and Commerce*.

Rozenblat, Celine. 2010. "Opening the Black Box of Agglomeration Economies for Measuring Cities' Competitiveness through International Firm Networks." *Urban Studies* 47: 2841–2865.

—— and Guy Melançon. 2009. "A Small World Perspective on Urban Systems." Pp. 431–467 in *Handbook of Theoretical and Quantitative Geography*, edited by F. Bavaud and C. Mager. Lausanne: University of Lausanne.

Ruan, Danching. 1993. "Interpersonal Networks and Workplace Controls in Urban China." *Australian Journal of Chinese Affairs* 29: 89–105.

——, Linton C. Freeman, Xinyuan Dai, Yunkang Pan, and Wenhong Zhang. 1997. "On the Changing Structure of Social Networks in Urban China." *Social Networks* 19: 75–89.

Ryan, Louise, Rosemary Sales, Mary Tilki, and Bernadetta Siara. 2008. "Social Networks, Social Support, and Social Capital: The Experiences of Recent Polish Migrants in London." *Sociology* 42: 672–690.

Ryan, S. and M. G. McNally. 1995. "Accessibility of Neotraditional Neighborhoods: A Review of Design Concepts, Policies, and Recent Literature." *Transportation Research A* 29A: 87–105.

Sabar, Naama. 2002. "Kibbutz, LA: A Paradoxical Social Network." *Journal of Contemporary Ethnography* 31: 68–94.

Sacchetti, Silvia. 2009. "Why, Where, and With Whom Do You Link? The Nature and Motivations of Linkages Within and Outside an Italian Local System." *Regional Studies* 43: 197–209.

Salingaros, Nikos A. 1998. "Theory of the Urban Web." *Journal of Urban Design* 3: 53–71.

Salter, John T. 1935. *Boss Rule*. New York: Whittlesay House.

Samaniego, Horacio, and Melanie E. Moses. 2008. "Cities as Organisms: Allometric Scaling of Urban Road Networks." *Journal of Transport and Land Use* 1: 21–39.

Samers, Michael. 2002. "Immigration and the Global City Hypothesis: Towards an Alternative Research Agenda." *International Journal of Urban and Regional Research* 26: 389–402.

Sampson, Robert J. 1988. "Local Friendship Ties and Community Attachment in Mass Society: A Multilevel Systemic Model." *American Sociological Review* 53: 766–779.

—— 1991. "Linking the Micro- and Macrolevel Dimensions of Community Social Organization." *Social Forces* 70: 43–64.

—— and W. Byron Groves. 1989. "Community Structure and Crime: Testing Social-Disorganization Theory." *American Journal of Sociology* 94: 774–802.

Sanders, Jimy M. and Victor Nee. 1987. "Limits of Ethnic Solidarity in the Enclave Economy." *American Sociological Review* 52: 745–773.

—— 1996. "Immigrant Self-Employment: The Family as Social Capital and the Value of Human Capital." *American Sociological Review* 61: 231–249.

——, Victor Nee, and Scott Sernau. 2002. "Asian Immigrants' Reliance on Social Ties in a Multiethnic Labor Market." *Social Forces* 81: 281–314.

Sanjek, Roger. 1978. "A Network Method and Its Uses in Urban Ethnography." *Human Organization* 37: 257–268.

Sassen, Saskia. 1991. *The Global City: New York, London, Tokyo*. Princeton, NJ: Princeton University Press.

—— 2002. "Global Cities and Diasporic Networks: Microsites in Global Civil Society." Pp. 217–238 in *Global Civil Society*, edited by Helmut Anheler, Marlies Glasius, Mary Kaldor, Diana Osgood, et al. New York: Oxford University Press.

—— 2010. "Global Inter-city Networks and Commodity Chains: Any Intersections?" *Global Networks* 10: 150–163.

Saxenian, AnnaLee. 1990. "Regional Networks and the Resurgence of Silicon Valley." *California Management Review* 33: 89–112.

Schneider, Simon and Daniel Schultz. 2007. "Specifying Essential Features of Street Networks." *Lecture Notes in Computer Science* 4736: 169–185.

Schuler, Richard E. 1992. "Transportation and Telecommunications Networks: Planning Urban Infrastructure for the 21st Century." *Urban Studies* 29: 297–310.

Schultze, Robert O., and Leonard U. Blumberg. 1957. "The Determination of Local Power Elites." *American Journal of Sociology* 63: 290–296.

Schwanen, Tim, Frans M. Dieleman, and Martin Dijst. 2004. "The Impact of Metropolitan Structure on Commute Behavior in the Netherlands: A Multilevel Approach." *Growth and Change* 35: 304–333.

Schweitzer, Thomas, Michael Schnegg, and Susanne Berzborn. 1998. "Personal Networks and Social Support in a Multiethnic Community of Southern California." *Social Networks* 20: 1–21.

Scott, John P. 2000. *Social Network Analysis: A Handbook*. Thousand Oaks, CA: Sage.

Sforzi, Fabio. 1994. "The Tuscan Model: An Interpretation in the Light of Recent Trends." Pp. 86–115 in *Regional Development in a Modern European Economy: The Case of Tuscany*, edited by R. Leonardi and R. Y. Nanetti. New York: Pinter.

Sharp, Jeff S. 2001. "Locating the Community Field: A Study of Interorganizational Network Structure and Capacity for Community Action." *Rural Sociology* 66: 403–424.

Shaw, Shih-Lung. 1993. "Hub Structures of Major US Passenger Airlines." *Journal of Transport Geography* 1: 47–58.

Shemtov, Ronit. 2003. "Social Networks and Sustained Activism in Local NIMBY Campaigns." *Sociological Forum* 18: 215–244.

Sheppard, Eric. 2002. "The Spaces and Times of Globalization: Place, Scale, Networks, and Positionality." *Economic Geography* 78: 307–330.

Shibutani, Tamotsu. 1955. "Reference Groups as Perspectives." *American Journal of Sociology* 60: 562–569.

Shin, Kyoung-Ho, and Michael Timberlake. 2000. "World Cities in Asia: Cliques, Centrality, and Connectedness." *Urban Studies* 37: 2257–2285.

Shlay, Anne B. and Robert P. Giloth. 1987. "The Social Organization of a Land-Based Elite: The Case of the Failed Chicago 1992 World's Fair." *Journal of Urban Affairs* 9: 305–324.

Short, James F. Jr. and Lorine A. Hughes (eds.) 2006. *Studying Youth Gangs.* New York: Rowman and Littlefield.

Short, John Rennie. 2004. "Black Holes and Loose Connections in a Global Urban Network." *Professional Geographer* 56: 295–302.

——, Carrie Breitbach, Steven Buckman, and Jamey Essex. 2000. "From World Cities to Gateway Cities: Extending the Boundaries of Globalization Theory." *City* 4: 317–340.

——, Y. Kim, M. Kuus, and H. Wells. 1996. "The Dirty Little Secret of World Cities Research: Data Problems in Comparative Analysis." *International Journal of Urban and Regional Research* 20: 697–717.

Sigelman, Lee, Timothy Bledsoe, Susal Welch, and Michael W. Combs. 1996. "Making Contact? Black–White Social Interaction in an Urban Setting." *American Journal of Sociology* 101: 1306–1332.

Silva, Ricardo Toledo. 2000. "The Connectivity of Infrastructure Networks and the Urban Space of Sao Paulo in the 1990s." *International Journal of Urban and Regional Research* 24: 139–164.

Simmel, Georg. [1908] 1950. *The Sociology of Georg Simmel,* translated by Kurt H. Wolff. Glencoe, IL: Free Press.

—— [1922] 1955. "The Web of Group Affiliations" Pp. 126–195 in *Conflict and the Web of Group Affiliations,* translated by Reinhard Bendix. Glencoe, IL: The Free Press.

Simpson, Dick, and Tom Carsey. 1999. "Council Coalitions and Mayoral Regimes in Chicago." *Journal of Urban Affairs* 21: 79–100.

—— and Tom M. Kelly. 2008. "The New Chicago School of Urbanism and the New Daley Machine." *Urban Affairs Review* 44: 218–238.

Skelcher, Chris, Angus McCabe, and Vivien Lowndes. 1996. *Community Networks in Urban Regeneration: It All Depends on Who You Know.* Bristol, U.K.: Policy Press.

Skjaeveland, Oddvar and Tommy Garling. 1997. "Effects of Interactional Space on Neighboring." *Journal of Environmental Psychology* 17: 181–198.

Small, Mario Luis, Erin M. Jacobs, and Rebekah Peeples Massengill. 2008. "Why Organizational Ties Matter for Neighborhood Effects: Resource Access through Childcare Centers." *Social Forces* 87: 387–414.

Smith, David A. and Douglas R. White. 1992. "Structure and Dynamics of the Global Economy: Network Analysis of International Trade 1965–1980." *Social Forces* 70: 857–893.

—— and Michael F. Timberlake. 1993. "World Cities: A Political Economy/Global Network Approach." *Research In Urban Sociology* 3: 181–207.

——, —— 1995. "Cities in Global Matrices: Toward Mapping the World-System's City System." Pp. 79–97 in *World Cities in a World-System,* edited by Paul L. Knox and Peter J. Taylor. New York: Cambridge University Press.

——, —— 1995. "Conceptualizing and Mapping the Structure of the World System's City System." *Urban Studies* 32: 287–302.

——, —— 2001. "World City Networks and Hierarchies, 1977–1997." *American Behavioral Scientist* 44: 1656–1678.

Smith, Richard G. 2003. "World City Actor Networks." *Progress in Human Geography* 27: 25–44.

—— and Marcus A. Doel. 2011. "Questioning the Theoretical Basis of Current Global-City Research: Structures, Networks, and Actor-Networks." *International Journal of Urban and Regional Research* 35: 24–39.

Snyder, David and Edward L. Kick. 1979. "Structural Position in the World System and Economic Growth, 1955–1970: A Multiple-Network Analysis of Transnational Interactions." *American Journal of Sociology* 84: 1096–1126.

Son, Joonmo and Nan Lin. 2008. "Social Capital and Civic Action: A Network-based Approach." *Social Science Research* 37: 330–349.

Sorensen, Eva and Jacob Torfing. 2003. "Network Politics, Political Capital, and Democracy." *International Journal of Public Administration* 26: 609–634.

Southall, Aidan. 1973. "The Density of Role-Relationships as a Universal Index of Urbanization." Pp. 71–106 in *Urban Anthropology: Cross-Cultural Studies of Urbanization*, edited by Aidan Southall. New York: Oxford University Press.

Southworth, Michael and Peter M. Owens. 1993. "The Evolving Metropolis: Studies of Community, Neighborhood, and Street Form at the Urban Edge." *Journal of the American Planning Association* 59: 271–287.

Spence, Nigel and Brian Linneker. 1994. "Evolution of the Motorway Network and Changing Levels of Accessibility in Great Britain." *Journal of Transport Geography* 2: 247–264.

Stack, Carol B. 1974. *All Our Kin*. New York: Harper and Row.

Standage, Tom. 1998. *The Victorian Internet*. New York: Walker.

Stanislawski, Dan. 1946. "The Origin and Spread of the Grid-Pattern Town." *Geographical Review* 36: 105–120.

Stanley, Bruce. 2005. "Middle East City Networks and the 'New Urbanism'." *Cities* 22: 189–199.

Steffens, Lincoln. 1931. *The Autobiography of Lincoln Steffens*. New York: Harcourt, Brace, World.

Stewart, Frank A. 1947. "A Sociometric Study of Influence in Southtown." *Sociometry* 10: 11–31.

—— 1947. "A Sociometric Study of Influence in Southtown: II." *Sociometry* 10: 273–286.

Stolle, Dietlind and Marc Hooghe. 2003. "Conflicting Approaches to the Study of Social Capital: Competing Explanations for Causes and Effects of Social Capital." *Ethical Perspectives* 10: 22–45.

Stone, Clarence N. 1989. *Regime Politics: Governing Atlanta, 1946–1988*. Lawrence, KS: University Press of Kansas.

—— 2001. "The Atlanta Experience Re-visited: The Link Between Agenda and Regime Change." *International Journal of Urban and Regional Research* 25: 20–34.

Stutz, Frederick P. 1973. "Distance and Network Effects on Urban Social Travel Fields." *Economic Geography* 49: 134–144.

Sutcliffe, Anthony R. 1995. "A Tale of Two Cities: Urban Networks in Paris and London—An Interview with Anthony R. Sutcliffe." *Flux* 19: 56–58.

Suttles, Gerald D. 1968. *The Social Order of the Slum: Ethnicity and Territory in the Inner City*. Chicago, IL: University of Chicago Press.

Swanstrom, Todd. 2001. "What We Argue About When We Argue About Regionalism." *Journal of Urban Affairs* 23: 479–496.

Taaffe, Edward J. 1956. "Air Transportation and United States Urban Distribution." *Geographical Review* 46: 219–238.

—— 1962. "The Urban Hierarchy: An Air Passenger Definition." *Economic Geography* 38: 1–14.

——, Howard L. Gauthier, and Morton E. O'Kelly. 1996. *Geography of Transportation*, 2nd Edition. Upper Saddle River, NJ: Prentice Hall.

——, Richard L. Morrill, and Peter R. Gould. 1963. "Transport Expansion in Underdeveloped Countries: A Comparative Analysis." *Geographical Review* 53: 503–529.

Talen, Emily. 1999. "Sense of Community and Neighborhood Form: An Assessment of the Social Doctrine of New Urbanism." *Urban Studies* 36: 1361–1379.

—— 2002. "The Social Goals of New Urbanism." *Housing Policy Debate* 13: 165–188.

Tarr, Joel A. 1992. "The Municipal Telegraph Network: Origins of the Fire and Police Alarm Systems in American Cities." *Flux* 9: 5–18.

——and Gabriel Dupuy. 1988. *Technology and the Rise of the Networked City in Europe and America*. Philadelphia: Temple University Press.

——, Joseph W. Konvit, and Mark Rose. 1990. "Technological Networks and the American City: Some Historiographical Notes." *Flux* 1: 85–91.

Taub, Richard P., George P. Surgeon, Sara Lindholm, Phyllis Betts Otti, and Amy Bridges. 1977. "Urban Voluntary Associations: Locality Based and Externally Induced." *American Journal of Sociology* 83: 425–442.

Tausig, Mark. 1987. "Detecting 'Cracks' in Mental Health Service Systems: Application of Network Analytic Techniques." *American Journal of Community Psychology* 15: 337–351.

Taylor, Peter J. 2001. "Specification of the World City Network." *Geographical Analysis* 33: 181–194.

—— 2004. "Regionality and the World City Network." *International Social Science Journal* 56: 361–372.

—— 2004. *World City Network: A Global Urban Analysis*. New York: Routledge.

—— 2005. "New Political Geographies: Global Civil Society and Global Governance Through World City Networks." *Political Geography* 24: 703–730.

—— 2005. "Leading World Cities: Empirical Evaluations of Urban Nodes in Multiple Networks." *Urban Studies* 42: 1593–1608.

—— 2006. "Parallel Paths to Understanding Global Inter-City Relations." *American Journal of Sociology* 112: 881–894.

—— and Robert E. Lang. 2005. "U.S. Cities in the 'World City Network'." *Brookings Institution, Survey Series*.

——, G. Catalano, and D. R. F. Walker. 2002. "Measurement of the World City Network." *Urban Studies* 39: 2367–2376.

——, Ben Derudder, and Frank Witlox. 2007. "Comparing Airline Passenger Destinations With Global Service Connectivities: A Worldwide Empirical Study of 214 Cities." *Urban Geography* 28: 232–248.

——, D. M. Evans, and K. Pain. 2008. "Application of the Interlocking Network Model to Mega-City-Regions: Measuring Polycentricity Within and Beyond City-Regions." *Regional Studies* 42: 1079–1093.

——, Michael Hoyler, and Raf Verburggen. 2010. "External Urban Relational Process: Introducing Central Flow Theory to Complement Central Place Theory." *Urban Studies* 47: 2803–2818.

——, Ben Derudder, Candida Gago Garcia, and Frank Witlox. 2009. "From North–South to 'Global' South? An Investigation of a Changing 'South' Using Airline Flows between Cities, 1970–2005." *Geography Compass* 3: 836–855.

——, ——, Pieter Saey, and Frank Witlox. 2007. *Cities in Globalization: Practices, Policies, and Theories*. New York: Routledge.

——, D. R. F. Walker, G. Catalano, and M. Hoyler. 2002. "Diversity and Power in the World City Network." *Cities* 19: 231–241.

Thibault, Serge. 1995. "The Morphology and Growth of Urban Technical Networks: A Fractal Approach." *Flux* 19: 17–30.

Thünen, Johann Heinrich von. 1966. *The Isolated State: An English Translation of Der Isolierte Staat*, translated by Carla M. Wartenberg, edited by Peter Hall. New York: Oxford University Press.

Thurmaier, Kurt, and Curtis Wood. 2002. "Interlocal Agreements as Overlapping Social Networks: Picket-Fence Regionalism in Metropolitan Kansas City." *Public Administration Review* 62: 585–598.

Tilly, Charles and Steve Tilly. 1974. "Introduction." Pp. 1–35 in *An Urban World*, edited by Charles Tilly and Steve Tilly. Boston, MA: Brown and Little.

Tittle, Charles R. 1989. "Influences on Urbanism: A Test of Predictions from Three Perspectives." *Social Problems* 36: 270–288.

—— 1989. "Urbanness and Unconventional Behavior: A Partial Test of Claude Fischer's Subcultural Theory." *Criminology* 27: 273–306.

Tomeh, Aida K. 1964. "Informal Group Participation and Residential Patterns." *American Journal of Sociology* 70: 28–35.

Tomko, Martin, Stephan Winter, and Christophe Claramunt. 2008. "Experiential Hierarchies of Streets." *Computers, Environments, and Urban Systems* 32: 41–52.

Tonnies, Ferdinand. 2001. *Community and Civil Society*, edited by Jose Harris. New York: Cambridge University Press.

Townsend, Anthony M. 2001. "The Internet and the Rise of the New Network Cities, 1969–1999." *Environment and Planning B* 28: 39–58.

—— 2001. "Network Cities and the Global Structure of the Internet." *American Behavioral Scientist* 44: 1697–1716.

Tranos, Emmanouil and Andy Gillespie. 2009. "The Spatial Distribution of Internet Backbone Networks in Europe: A Metropolitan Knowledge Economy Perspective." *European Urban and Regional Studies* 16: 423–437.

Turk, Herman. 1970. "Interorganizational Networks in Urban Society: Initial Perspectives and Comparative Research." *American Sociological Review* 35: 1–19.

—— 1973. *Interorganizational Activation in Urban Communities: Deductions from the Concept of System*. Washington, DC: American Sociological Association.

—— 1973. "Comparative Urban Structure from an Interorganizational Perspective." *Administrative Science Quarterly* 16: 37–55.

—— 1977. *Organizations in Modern Life: Cities and Other Large Networks*. San Francisco, CA: Jossey-Bass.

Ullman, Edward L. 1949. "The Railroad Patterns of the United States." *Geographical Review* 39: 242–256.

—— 1956. "The Role of Transportation and the Bases for Interaction." Pp. 862–880 in *Man's Role in Changing the Face of the Earth*, edited by William L. Thomas, Jr. Chicago, IL: University of Chicago Press.

U.S. Army Corps of Engineers. 2009. *Inland Waterway Navigation: Value to the Nation*. Alexandria, VA: U.S. Army Corps of Engineers.

Valente, Thomas W., Chich Ping Chou, and Mary Ann Pentz. 2007. "Community Coalitions as a System: Effects of Network Change on Adoption of Evidence-Based Substance Abuse Prevention." *American Journal of Public Health* 97: 880–886.

Valenzuela, Abel. 2003. "Day Labor Work." *Annual Review of Sociology* 29: 307–333.

Van de Ven, Andrew H, Gordon Walker, and Jennie Liston. 1979. "Coordination Patterns Within an Interorganizational Network." *Human Relations* 32: 19–36.

Vance, James E. 1970. *The Merchant's World: The Geography of Wholesaling*. Englewood Cliffs, NJ: Prentice Hall.

Vance, Rupert B. and Sara Smith. 1954. "Metropolitan Dominance and Integration." Pp. 114–134 in *The Urban South*, edited by Rupert B. Vance and Nicholas J. Demerath. Chapel Hill, NC: University of North Carolina Press.

Varheim, Andreas. 2007. "Social Capital and Public Libraries: The Need for Research." *Library and Information Science Research* 29: 416–428.

Veneri, Paolo. 2010. "Urban Polycentricity and the Costs of Commuting: Evidence from Italian Metropolitan Areas." *Growth and Change* 41: 403–429.

Venturelli, Peter J. 1982. "Institutions in an Ethnic District." *Human Organizations* 41: 26–35.

Vinciguerra, Sandra, Koen Frenken, and Marco Valente. 2010. "The Geography of Internet Infrastructure: An Evolutionary Simulation Approach Based on Preferential Attachment." *Urban Studies* 47: 1969–1984.

Vind, Ingeborg and Niels Fold. 2010. "City Networks and Commodity Chains: Identifying Global Flows and Local Connections in Ho Chi Minh City." *Global Networks* 10: 54–74.

Volchenkov, C. and Ph. Blanchard. 2008. "Ghetto of Venice: Access to the Target Node and the Random Target Access Time." *arXiv*: 0710.3021v1 [physics.soc-ph].

Volker, Beate and Henk Flap. 1997. "The Comrade's Belief: Intended and Unintended Consequences of Communism for Neighborhood Relations in the Former GDR." *European Sociological Review* 13: 241–265.

——, —— 2007. "Sixteen Million Neighbors: A Multilevel Study of the Role of Neighbors in the Personal Networks of the Dutch." *Urban Affairs Review* 43: 256–284.

——, ——, and Siegwart Lindenberg. 2007. "When are Neighborhoods Communities? Community in Dutch Neighborhoods." *European Sociological Review* 23: 99–114.

Waldinger, Roger. 1999. "Network, Bureaucracy, and Exclusion: Recruitment and Selection in an Immigrant Metropolis." Pp. 228–259 in *Immigration and Opportunity: Race, Ethnicity, and Employment in the United States*, edited by Frank D. Bean and Stephanie Bell-Rose. New York: Russell Sage Foundation.

Walker, Gerald. 1977. "Social Networks and Territory in a Commuter Village, Bond Head, Ontario." *Canadian Geographer* 21: 329–350.

Walton, John. 1966. "Discipline, Method, and Community Power: A Note on the Sociology of Knowledge." *American Sociological Review* 31: 684–689.

—— 1966. "Substance and Artifact: The Current Status of Research on Community Power Structure." *American Journal of Sociology* 71: 430–438.

Wang, Jiaoe, Huihui Mo, Fahui Wang, and Fengjun Jin. 2011. "Exploring the Network Structure and Nodal Centrality of China's Air Transport Network: A Complex Network Approach." *Journal of Transport Geography* 19: 712–721.

Warner, Barbara D. and Pamela Wilcox Roundtree. 1997. "Local Social Ties in a Community and Crime Model: Questioning the Systemic Nature of Informal Social Control." *Social Problems* 44: 520–536.

Warren, Donald I. 1981. *Helping Networks: How People Cope with Problems in the Urban Community*. Notre Dame, IN: University of Notre Dame Press.

Warren, Roland L. 1967. "The Interaction of Community Decision Organizations: Some Basic Concepts and Needed Research." *Social Service Review* 41: 261–270.

—— 1967. "The Interorganizational Field as a Focus for Investigation." *Administrative Science Quarterly* 12: 396–419.

Wasserman, Stanley and Katherine Faust. 1994. *Social Network Analysis: Methods and Applications*. Cambridge: Cambridge University Press.

Watts, Duncan J. 2002. *Six Degrees: The Science of a Connected Age*. New York: Norton.

—— and Stephen H. Strogatz. 1998. "Collective Dynamics of 'Small-World' Networks." *Nature* 393: 440–442.

Webber, Melvin M. 1963. "Order in Diversity: Community without Propinquity." Pp. 23–54 in *Cities and Space: The Future Use of Urban Land*, edited by Lowdon Wingo. Baltimore: Johns Hopkins Press.

Wellman, Barry. 1979. "The Community Question: The Intimate Networks of East Yorkers." *American Journal of Sociology* 84: 1201–1231.

—— 1988. "Structural Analysis: From Method and Metaphor to Theory and Substance." Pp. 19–61 in *Social Structure: A Network Approach*, edited by Barry Wellman and S. D. Berkowitz. Cambridge: Cambridge University Press.

—— 1990. "The Place of Kinfolk in Personal Community Networks." *Marriage and Family Review* 5: 195–228.

—— 1996. "Are Personal Communities Local? A Dumptarian Reconsideration." *Social Networks* 18: 347–354.

—— 1999. *Networks in the Global Village: Life in Contemporary Communities*. Boulder, CO: Westview Press.

Wellman, Barry and C. Haythornewaite (eds.). 2002. *The Internet and Everyday Life*. Oxford: Blackwell.

—— and Barry Leighton. 1979. "Networks, Neighborhoods, and Communities: Approached to the Study of the Community Question." *Urban Affairs Review* 14: 363–390.

—— and Scot Wortley. 1990. "Different Strokes from Different Folks: Community Ties and Social Support." *American Journal of Sociology* 96: 558–588.

West, Geoffrey B., James H. Brown, and Brian J. Enquist. 1997. "A General Model for the Origin of Allometric Scaling Laws in Biology." *Science* 276: 122–126.

Wheeler, David C. and Morton E. O'Kelly. 1999. "Network Topology and City Accessibility of the Commercial Internet." *Professional Geographer* 51: 327–339.

Wheeler, James O. 1986. "Corporate Spatial Links with Financial Institutions: The Role of the Metropolitan Hierarchy." *Annals of the Association of American Geographers* 76: 262–274.

—— and Ronald L. Mitchelson. 1989. "Atlanta's Role as an Information Center: Intermetropolitan Spatial Links." *Professional Geographer* 41: 162–172.

——, —— 1989. "Information Flows among Major Metropolitan Areas in the United States." *Annals of the Association of American Geographers* 79: 523–543.

White, Harrison C., Scott A. Boorman, and Ronald L. Breiger. 1976. "Social Structure from Multiple Networks. I. Blockmodels of Roles and Positions." *American Journal of Sociology* 81: 730–780.

White, Katherine J. Curtis, and Avery M. Guest. 2003. "Community Lost or Transformed? Urbanization and Social Ties." *City and Community* 2: 239–259.

Whitt, J. Allen. 1987. "Mozart in the Metropolis: The Arts Coalition and the Urban Growth Machine." *Urban Affairs Review* 23: 15–36.

—— and John C. Lammers. 1991. "The Art of Growth: Ties Between Development Organizations and the Performing Arts." *Urban Affairs Quarterly* 26: 376–393.

Whyte, William F. 1943. *Street Corner Society: The Social Structure of an Italian Slum*. Chicago, IL: University of Chicago Press.

Wierzbicki, Susan. 2004. *Beyond the Immigrant Enclave: Network Change and Assimilation*. New York: LFB Scholarly Publishing.

Wilson, Kenneth L. and Alejandro Portes. 1980. "Immigrant Enclaves: An Analysis of the Labor Market Experiences of Cubans in Miami." *American Journal of Sociology* 86: 295–319.

Wilson, Thomas C. 1986. "Community Population Size and Social Heterogeneity: An Empirical Test." *American Journal of Sociology* 91: 1154–1169.

Wilson, William Julius. 1987. *The Truly Disadvantaged: The Inner City, The Underclass, and Public Policy*. Chicago, IL: University of Chicago Press.

Wireman, Peggy. 1984. *Urban Neighborhoods, Networks, and Families*. Lexington, MA: Lexington Books.

Wirth, Louis. 1938. "Urbanism as a Way of Life." *American Journal of Sociology* 44: 1–24.

Wolfe, Alvin W. 2007. "Network Perspectives on Communities." *Structure and Dynamics: eJournal of Anthropological and Related Sciences* 1.

Wolfinger, Raymond E. 1960. "Reputation and Reality in the Study of "Community Power"." *American Sociological Review* 25: 636–644.

Wolman, Shepard. 1937. "Sociometric Planning of a New Community." *Sociometry* 1: 220–254.

Wong, Siu-lun and Janet W. Salaff. 1998. "Network Capital: Emigration from Hong Kong." *British Journal of Sociology* 49: 358–374.

Wuchty, S., Z. N. Oltvai, and A-L Barabasi. 2003. "Evolutionary Conservation of Motif Constituents in the Yeast Protein Interaction Network." *Nature Genetics* 35: 176–179.

Xu, Zengwang, and Robert Harriss. 2008. "Exploring the Structure of the U.S. Intercity Passenger Air Transportation Network: A Weighted Complex Network Approach." *Geojournal* 73: 87–102.

Yehuda, Amir. 1969. "Contact Hypothesis in Ethnic Relations." *Psychological Bulletin* 71: 319–342.

Yinger, John. 1993. "Around the Block: Urban Models with a Street Grid." *Journal of Urban Economics* 33: 305–330.

Young, Carl E., Dwight E. Giles, and Margaret C. Plantz. 1982. "Natural Networks: Help-Giving and Help-Seeking in Two Rural Communities." *American Journal of Community Psychology* 10: 457–469.

Young, Ruth C. and Olaf F. Larson. 1965. "A New Approach to Community Structure." *American Sociological Review* 30: 926–934.

Zachary, W. W. 1977. "An Informational Flow Model for Conflict and Fission in Small Groups." *Journal of Anthropological Research* 33: 452–473.

Zelinsky, Wilbur. 1991. "The Twinning of the World: Sister Cities in Geographic and Historical Perspective." *Annals of the Association of American Geographers* 81: 1–31.

—— and Barrett A. Lee. 1998. "Heterolocalism: An Alternative Model of the Sociospatial Behavior of Immigrant Ethnic Communities." *International Journal of Population Geography* 4: 281–298.

Zipf, George Kingsley. 1946. "The $(P_1 \times P_2)/D$ Hypothesis: On the Intercity Movement of Persons." *American Sociological Review* 11: 677–686.

—— 1949. *Human Behavior and the Principle of Least Effort*. Cambridge, MA: Addison-Wesley Press.

Zook, Matthew A. and Stanley D. Brunn. 2006. "From Podes to Antipodes: Positionalities and Global Airline Geographies." *Annals of the Association of American Geographers* 96: 471–490.

INDEX